Full Throttle

Full Throttle

The Life and Fast Times of NASCAR Legend Curtis Turner

Robert Edelstein

The Overlook Press
Woodstock & New York

First published in paperback in the United States in 2006 by
The Overlook Press, Peter Mayer Publishers, Inc.
Woodstock & New York

WOODSTOCK:
One Overlook Drive
Woodstock, NY 12498
www.overlookpress.com
[for individual orders, bulk and special sales, contact our Woodstock office]

NEW YORK:
141 Wooster Street
New York, NY 10012

Library of Congress Cataloging-in-Publication Data

Edelstein, Robert.
Full throttle : the life and fast times of NASCAR legend
Curtis Turner / Robert Edelstein.
p. cm.
1. Turner, Curtis, 1924-1970. 2. Stock car drivers—
United States—Biography. I. Title
GV1032.T83 E34 2005 796.72/092 B 22 2004066260

Type formatting by Bernard Schleifer Company
Manufactured in the United States of America
ISBN 1-58567-751-5
1 2 3 4 5 6 7 8 9 10

For Rachel, Nellie and Jake Bailey,
from your loving, grateful Daddy

and for Loren, always

"I go from this to that, and why be ashamed of it? It seems to me this is the human experience."

—LARRY RIVERS, artist

So, seize the day! hold holiday!
Be unwearied, unceasing, alive
you and your own true love;
Let not your heart be troubled during your sojourn on earth,
but seize the day as it passes!…

Let your heart be drunk on the gift of Day
until that day comes when you anchor.
From "The Harper's Song for Inherkhawy"

I was raised in the country, I been workin' in the town
I been in trouble ever since I set my suitcase down
—BOB DYLAN, from "Mississippi"

CONTENTS

PROLOGUE
July 23, 1967
"I don't really think I'd be happy if I wasn't in some sort of trouble."

Easley, South Carolina, about ten miles west of Greenville as the crow flies, is a town where everyone knows everybody else. On this hot July Sunday in 1967, with the mercury having hit ninety for the second day in a row, folks are greeting neighbors while giving thanks for each bit of breeze as they head into church for the evening service. There are 5,000 people living in Easley's eleven square miles, and about a hundred area churches serve the faithful. Nearly half of these are Baptist churches. G. B. Nalley has just built Town and Country Plaza, the first mall in the area. It's doing a good bit of business.

There is an old saying in town: "You can easily do better in Easley."

One thing Easley *doesn't* have is an airport, but it doesn't need one. Greenville-Spartanburg Airport is only twenty-five miles to the east.

This fact of geography is relatively inconsequential on most days. On July 23, however, it matters a lot.

At first, the few folks walking at dusk near the Southern Railroad tracks—which run right behind where Main Street turns into Highway 123—hear only an odd, insistent buzz. But the volume reaches that of a swarm very quickly as a large, loud twin-engine Aero Commander grows in view in the near distance. There is nothing strained about its approach; the pilot seems to be holding the craft's line steadily without wavering in the orange-gray sky, and his path continues with confidence. The only problem is, if the plane keeps this course, it will touch down in the heart of Easley.

Inside the Glenwood Baptist Church and the Faith Missionary Baptist

Church, which both sit along the same stretch of Saco Lowell Road—a stone's throw from the railroad tracks—it is getting harder to hear the organ. Parishioners have given up trying to sing over the din of the plane. Many are wide-eyed with fear that they may be under attack.

None of this concerns the pilot of the Aero Commander, who's busily searching for the right place to put his plane down. He is Curtis Turner, a handsome, self-assured, baritone-voiced forty-three-year-old business-man; he is also an entrepreneur, legendary party animal and arguably the most popular and daring stock car racer of his day. If NASCAR is the only other religion followed as rabidly in the region, Turner may be its most worshipped, beloved and bedeviling practitioner. He quietly smokes a Camel and adjusts his aviator shades and trusty Stetson. The open seat-belt dangles off his lap.

For Turner, this will be an emergency landing: he and his three pas-sengers are dangerously low on whiskey, and the Easley resident on board—Mr. Nalley of the Town and Country Plaza—has suggested they land in town and maneuver through the streets to his house so he can jump out and "refuel."

For most people, such a suggestion will inspire little more than an appreciative chuckle. But the time it usually takes Curtis Turner to con-sider all the drawbacks of such a startlingly odd idea is equal only to the few seconds that a sly little grin forms on his face. Yes, he thinks, we're goin' in.

Turner has landed in rougher spots than this—small grassy fields, backstretches of raceways, parking lots, tiny single-engine landing strips on chicken farms, icy banks near the edges of cliffs, places no one would even consider touching down for reasons he can't quite understand. He'd once gotten into trouble trying to land his plane at an airport socked in by terrible weather. The tower commander told him to turn around and land elsewhere. Turner made one last pass and radioed the tower, saying, "Pop, I think I can make it." Then he switched off the radio and came on in any-way. Man's gotta land his plane, after all. Much like he is behind the wheel of a race car, Turner, when up in the sky, is a master of control who always understands his limitations. There aren't many.

But a man can go only so long without a "shooter" of Canadian Club and Coke, especially with a close friend and two women in your plane on a lazy, dusky Sunday evening.

Turner has his gaze fixed: his "runway" will be a field adjoining the Faith Missionary Church, right across from the new Stayon Products Inc. plant on Saco Lowell Road. By now, both churches have begun to empty as the noise grows to an alarming volume. For Turner, the landing presents its challenges: trees, telephone lines and cars being highest on the list. The Aero Commander swoops in as nearby churchgoers scatter for cover, and the plane makes several low passes, buzzing the crowd from one hundred feet in the air, before coming in for a bumpy landing, cradled finally in the grass. Turner whips the craft around and points it toward Saco Lowell Road with tiny tree branches rattling in the wings.

He moves up to the road; cars careen out of the way, vexed by the sudden sight of a twin-engine plane in the rearview mirror. Turner is stuck behind a young woman driving a sedan. Trying to obey logical traffic laws, the woman nervously puts on her right directional—but then turns left. Turner, already moving left to get around her, has to pour on the gas to arc around the car, and still cannot avoid clipping the woman's radio antenna with his wing.

With some damage already done, Turner senses the need to quicken his pace. In order to get to Nalley's, he heads back for the gap between the two Baptist churches. Congregants are racing off, jumping for cover. Looking through the windshield of the Aero Commander, Turner catches sight of a preacher in collar and black robe, moving toward him slowly, as if preparing to take on a vampire. With his flock shouting behind him, the preacher points a menacing finger at the pilot.

"It was then," Turner will later recall, "that we got to decidin' we'd made a mistake."

He steers back around toward Saco Lowell Road, now accepting the idea that no liquor will be had this Sunday in Easley. Watching the scene unfold, Nalley is insistent that, given his standing in the community, he can't possibly be caught in such a situation. "Pop, I got this thing *in* here," Turner tells his good friend and frequent business partner, "but I can't get it out the same way." Heading for the highway, he impulsively gives the craft a bit of gas, getting up to flying speed and taking the wheels off the ground; that way, he can jerk the plane all the way into the air at the next convenient location.

Cars continue to surrender the right of way but Turner is forced to hedgehop the ones that don't. Up ahead, a deputy sheriff for the Easley Police Department has moved onto the road. Turner bounds over the lawman who, later on, will tell federal aviation officials, "I was driving along, minding my own business, and I looked up and here comes a goddamned *airplane!*"

But for Turner, the real problem lies ahead. There is an intersection in the distance—as major an intersection as you'll find in Easley—with one of the town's few stoplights suspended from heavy wires. Turner's dilemma is the design of his craft. The Aero Commander's third wheel sits out in front; its tail is raised tall above the body of the plane.

So he raises his wheels up a touch more. At this angle, the tail drops down—just enough to let him below the wire, as if he's playing some odd game of aviation limbo. He clears it by inches, the traffic light swaying in his wake.

And, as Turner's close friend Charlie Williamson will later relate, "I'm pretty sure he didn't run that red light."

Turner senses he's home free—except for the big oak tree now in his path. He pulls up as quickly as possible, yet not fast enough to avoid clipping the upper branches. He also inadvertently cuts two telephone cable "drop lines," pulling a section of them with him as he climbs clear of Easley air space. It'll be a day before phone service is fully restored, and Easley gets the chance to return to some semblance of normalcy, and gossip.

Aboard the Aero Commander, normalcy and gossip return much quicker, after some whooping, and even applause. There is, however, one final challenge: getting away with this.

Turner puts the plane down momentarily at Greenville-Spartanburg Airport, hoping to drop off some passengers, but has to take off again quickly to avoid curiosity. He decides on a clever strategy: he'll keep the plane down low, under the radar, in order to sneak into another airport. He will fly this way the entire route back home to Charlotte, North Carolina, some 90 miles to the east-northeast.

What he doesn't realize is, he's already caught. As soon as he gets within earshot of the other airport, the call will come in over the radio: "Ain't gonna do you no good, Curtis. They're looking for you everywhere." The FAA officials will eventually come calling with some questions, followed by a two-year suspension of his flying license.

But none of that matters now, as Turner begins his low flight home. Yes, he thinks, with bits of wire and branch still wedged in his wings, maybe I can go in unnoticed.

In the brief, outrageous life of Curtis Turner, this is not what you would call an "isolated incident."

Like everything else about the man, the story is now steeped in legend, with countless variations on what really happened in Easley. Ask those who knew Turner, loved him, were in awe of him or were at odds with him—and people sometimes fit into all categories at once—and some will say he *really* landed in a parking lot in the center of town. Or that he made it to Nalley's house and had a relaxing night of drink. Anything was possible with Curtis Turner, so what's the harm in exaggerating? Nearly forty years later, it helps make his life seem even larger than it was.

But Turner needs no help. He embodied a quality that only a handful of sports stars—or human beings for that matter—ever truly possess: audacity. He did things because he believed unreservedly that he could, as part of the sheer momentum of living the life of Curtis Turner.

Behind the wheel of a stock car, Turner won more than 350 races, driving on any surface he could find: asphalt, concrete, rickety single-lane bridges, off-roads, swamps, gravel on dangerous cliffsides, or on the highway during his days as Virginia's most elusive moonshine runner. But no thrill could match the sight of him racing on the sands of Daytona Beach, where he literally threw his car sideways and slid it past competitors the length of two football fields—a show that made him the original superstar of NASCAR. He drove in the sport's first race in 1949; and at the start of its modern era in the late 1960s, when speeds had more than doubled, Turner was still among the guys to beat. By then, he had become the first driver ever put on the cover of *Sports Illustrated* after having had his license revoked in two states. Trying to explain himself to writer Kim Chapin in the story, Turner said, "I don't really think I'd be happy if I wasn't in some sort of trouble." He was, as newspapers, magazines and thousands of screaming fans called him, "The Babe Ruth of Stock Car Racing."

That might have been enough for some, but Turner was also "the millionaire lumberman," who bought and sold the whopping equivalent of more than six percent of the state of North Carolina in his career as a timber broker. With the commissions, he ran parties that were legend, several-day affairs where hundreds made a habit of excess. No driver exuded such charm and intimidation at the track, and incredible business savvy away from it. As Hall of Fame engine builder Smokey Yunick put it, "There never would have been a Dale Earnhardt without Curtis Turner."

And then, at the height of Turner's fame, fortune and popularity, he sank every ounce of all three into the most glorious and disastrous dream of his life: cobuilding the 1.5-mile oval racing mecca known as the Charlotte Motor Speedway. The effort required, at various times, Job-like fortitude, wily bookkeeping and several loaded guns.

No accomplishment meant more to him. And the threat of losing it brought Turner to his most audacious gamble: he broke ranks with the sport, taking on one of his closest friends, NASCAR founder Bill France, when he led the battle to form a union among the drivers. Their clash planted the seed for the biggest scandal in the sport's history, and it led to Turner's undoing: He became the first driver ever banned from the sport for life.

But what truly amazes about Turner is his resolve: At this low ebb, he remained convinced the only way to go was up. He struggled for years. Enduring at one point the worst personal loss of his life, and a sadness that consumed him, he refused to break.

Perhaps he saw the future, as he seemed to do in several other business ventures. Thanks to the rabid pressure of fans, Turner was given one more chance to race. Now past his prime, some believed that, competing against a new generation of NASCAR stars, Turner would be left in the dust. The only thing he wanted was an opportunity to prove them wrong, a chance to engineer one of the great comebacks in the sport's history— and to party afterwards.

Friends can still picture him, holding court behind the bar at his sprawling house in Charlotte. He stood six-foot-two, just shy of 200 pounds, with a shock of dark curly hair, blue-gray eyes and the mischievous smile of a naughty schoolboy. His hands seemed about as big as paddleball rackets. Striding into a room, exuding confidence, with a long, easy gait, frequently wearing a $600 suit and wing tip shoes—an outfit he sometimes raced in—he spoke with a voice that befitted his size, a warm, relaxing baritone with an easy Virginia drawl. "The man was a lion," says Turner's friend, the writer Marshall Spiegel.

Turner hated sleep, considering the need for it almost an injustice. He would take cat naps; after an all-night party leading up to a race, he'd sleep for an hour laying on the hood of his race car. "And he could eat faster than any human on earth," adds his brother-in-law Danny Vance. "He could finish an entire New York strip in the time it'd take you to eat two bites of yours." He took life in gulps. And women were perenially drawn to him, perhaps because, as he liked to say, he'd never met an ugly one.

And then, at the very end, he met the one for him. He'd been married all his life, and restless for just as long, someone for whom settling down seemed as inconceivable as slowing down. But the time was finally right to try this kind of comeback as well—as short-lived as it would ultimately be.

Turner's death—the sudden, mysterious loss of someone who loomed so large—seemed inconceivable. There are as many theories about how it happened as there are about his landing in Easley.

But as with Easley, there is only one real explanation.

So there is no sense in exaggerating about Turner, to make his life seem larger than it was. One only needs to remember it all, to sit in the backyard with a Canadian Club and Coke and spin yarns about slaloming telephone poles on the highway for fun, driving rental cars into motel swimming pools or trying to become the first private citizen to send communication satellites into space.

"What made Curtis Turner a legend?" says his friend, the actor James Garner. "He *knew* he was a legend and, therefore, he lived it."

"You see a person, when they open the bottle, they throw the cap away? Well that's Curtis Turner's life, right there," adds racing hall of famer Buddy Baker. "When he turned in his chips, he'd played the game."

Chapter One
1924-1946
"Rough roads make things more interesting."

As he rolls toward the gate leading out of the U.S. Naval Base in Little Creek, Virginia, Curtis Turner can see trouble. He slows to a crawl, scanning the view through the windshield. Two officers he's never seen before are standing guard, trying to appear nonchalant as they glance in his direction. A couple of Turner's buddies are usually stationed at this gate, smiling and winking while they wave him on. Turner has long paid good money—not to mention plenty of homemade liquor—to make sure of that. But these new officers: they look mighty thorough.

Turner rests an elbow out the window as a light breeze picks up. It is July 2, 1946, and Turner should have every reason to be cheerful. It's been a few weeks since the twenty-two-year-old ex-Chief Bosons Mate received his honorable discharge from the Navy after spending two years patrolling the Virginia coastline during and after the war. Things are getting more serious with his longtime girlfriend, Ann Ross. And he's back to making good money full time, doing things he loves, and keeping trouble behind him. But now he's got five hundred pounds of government sugar in the trunk of his 1941 black Ford Coupe, and if he's stopped here, his unblemished record as one of the region's most elusive moonshine runners will suffer a great blow. Lots of guys would be mighty happy to cart him off to jail.

The deal had worked out so sweetly for years now: haul liquor into the base and exchange it for sugar cobbled together by the mess staff. Sugar, a vital ingredient in white lightning, had been in such short supply during the war years; Turner's practical plan made everybody happy, especially the folks at the officer's club. This was America's free enterprise system at work, with nobody worse off because of it—the kind of move his dad might have tried years earlier and his mom would have said an angry prayer about on Sunday. But someone must have found it all out.

Nobody has closed in on Turner; they're waiting for him to make a move. While he inches slowly forward, his expression doesn't shift; he remains calm, steely blue-gray eyes unblinking, slender lips turned down, one hand on the wheel as if he's out on the town.

In a burst, he slams on the gas and charges toward the gatekeepers. At first, the two guards make a heroic, instinctive move to cover, but then think better of it and scatter. Turner crashes through the barricade as a slew of other officers race in his direction, shouting him down. The Ford's rear swerves, and Turner catches the glint of firearms in the rearview mirror. With ease he regains control and is off, but the pop of gunfire fills the night. Turner hears a low thump as a shell burrows into the soft sugar in the trunk and stops there. He ducks for a second, but he is free.

It will take a minute before anybody picks up the chase and Turner settles in for what he knows will be a long ride. Inevitably, the screech of sirens becomes vaguely audible, then grows in volume. Turner speeds straight west at better than one hundred miles per hour, toward Nansemond County, where he can pick up 460 and head for the hills.

The sirens fill the night and it's hard to figure where they're all coming from. Given the fact that they'd tried to ambush him at the base, chances are patrolmen from several different counties have been alerted. After making the turn onto 460, he arrows straight up northwest, toward Petersburg. Cresting a hill a few miles up the highway, Turner can see police lights in the distance. They're in front of him and behind him.

In a mile, Turner is right on the tail of a couple of state troopers. At this speed, there are no strategies, no quick movements to slow him down. Besides, he clearly has the best car of the night. Without lifting off the gas, and offering only a blank stare, Turner powers past the two cars, who radio ahead, attempting to set up a distant checkpoint. Some patrolmen have long gone to the same garages as the moonshine runners, to get their engines charged as powerfully. But ask the mechanics and they might say that when the fixing is done, some cars end up being slightly more equal than others.

And Turner is the kind of guy you want showing up at your garage: a soft-spoken, deep-voiced kid given to telling the kind of tale that will leave you wide-eyed. At Sweeney's Garage out near his home in Floyd, Virginia, they love the one about the time two patrol cars chased him through the backwoods of the Blue Ridge Mountains, with Turner carrying a load of whiskey in the trunk. Turner had some distance on the law and a creaky single-lane bridge lay ahead. Entering the bridge at sixty miles per hour, he pulled out his signature move, slamming on the brakes and whipping the car around, deftly screeching through a 180-degree turn with inches to spare on either side and the bridge bopping momentarily from the shock. Now facing the lawmen coming his way, Turner reached over, calmly stuck his own makeshift siren on the roof and flipped the switch. He bounded back toward the patrol cars, which gave way for what seemed like one of their own. Turner had escaped another fix.

Normally, he has nothing against the police. He'd even shown a few how the bridge spin is done, like a magician who spills only as many secrets as he needs to.

Turner leads his chase posse heading north to Blackstone, but all is not well. He is low on gas. It will now be less a question of outrunning as outlasting.

Past Blackstone, he dips over onto the much more rural highway 40. Through Eureka and Henry, and past Fears Corner he goes, whipping through the towns that dot the dirt landscape west through Virginia. The ride back home from the base to Roanoke will be more than 250 miles and there won't be enough gas to go the whole way.

But he is back in the Blue Ridge Mountains, where every bump is familiar. At another intersection, still more patrol cars give chase.

The engine knocks on an incline and when Turner rolls back down-hill, all is momentarily black and somewhat still, the sirens now muted by the earth between him and the law. Once level again, he spots a familiar hidden turn-off and slams on the brakes, sliding nearly sideways, turns off his headlights and ducks left into the anonymous backwoods. Through the moonlit brush he goes, snapping the scrub pines as he cuts his way in for a moment before putting on the brakes. Turner breathes quietly, craning his neck and looking behind him. The sirens, out of sync, noisy, are getting closer and then come upon his exit from the road; and then they pass, leaving a Doppler wave that makes the cars sound harmless, like toys.

Now out of sight, he flips on his headlights, but the bulbs have been knocked out by the knotty pines in the hasty exit. He rolls forward slowly, finding himself on the edge of a farmyard. He can barely make out the sight of an awning in the darkness where he parks and shuts down the overtaxed motor. It will take some time, even a close call or two, but the sirens will eventually grow softer, leaving Curtis Turner with only his car, a pack of cigarettes and the calm serenity of a safe night in the woods. That's when the tall, slender Turner grows restless. Bring in some friends and let the liquor flow; that would be a good time.

And yet, walking through the low grass, there's something extraordinarily calming about this terrain: another place where Turner feels very much at home. For five years he'd been hauling as much liquor as he could, working at first with his dad who had been, at one time, one of the more successful home brewers and transporters in Floyd County. But Turner's introduction to the timber business went back even further, to the days eight years earlier when his father began teaching him all about tree varieties, beginning when he was fourteen. A wonderful stillness pervades the night, or maybe it's just that all the effort has brought on a certain fatigue.

Turner climbs back in the car, smokes a Camel and stares out at the night. Thoughts swirl in his head, beginning with his father's recent prescient words: stop running liquor. Morton Turner has been making this request of his oldest son, like a retired gunslinger with a long memory and a regret or two. Curtis' eyes grow heavy, and he can see his father's point, but only to a degree.

He was nine, living with his parents, sister Ruby and younger brother Darnell in Maryland while his oldest sister, Dove, stayed in school, boarding with friends in Virginia. The police came charging up the walk one evening with some questions for Morton Turner about illegal liquor and Curtis ran and ran, hunting for his father until he was out of breath. Eventually his dad told him, 'That's all right son, we haven't been doing right and we've got to pay for it," and Curtis stood and watched his father being led away. The penalty would turn out to be only a stiff fine, but as Curtis' mother pulled him into the house, the sound of the patrol car doors closing, the tires spinning on the gravel—the moment did nothing but stiffen some resolve inside of him.

"I'll never get caught," the younger Turner says out loud, in his car, on that farm in the dark.

It had always been less a decision than a simple fact of life, a lesson to prepare for any eventuality. Even if it means taking the occasional bullet in the trunk.

His father had been starting to tell him that any money he made running liquor would never do him any good. But for as long as Curtis could remember, he had every reason to believe this couldn't be any further from the truth.

As a bootlegger in the 1920s in Floyd, Virginia, Morton Turner had been a man among men. He'd buy Oldsmobiles by the truckload, have all the necessary speed adjustments made, set the springs mighty tight in the back and run the cars in a row, creating a powerful convoy, each car heavy with hundreds of pounds of liquor packed snug in the trunk. They were like wolves, running in turbocharged packs.

On any ride through the backwoods, there might be at least one or two lawmen taking up chase, leaving everybody to scatter in the dirt-flying mess and find their way back home. Some of the local police could be bought off by the more successful moonshine runners but there'd be no guarantees. Turner and a partner had once come upon two officers stopping their path on a trail. The policemen forced them to pay an additional $100 "toll" before allowing further passage. Turner's partner kept fuming as they continued the run.

"Let's go back and get that hundred," he finally said.

They did, and then tied the two cops under a bridge with their own handcuffs.

"It wasn't a game, where everybody was real nice to everybody else," Curtis would say years later. "They were shootin' real bullets."

In the 1920s, Floyd County, with 13,000 residents, had only one state policeman, one sheriff and one deputy representing the entire county. However, revenue hunters and federal agents eagerly joined the party. Liquor hauling had long been a serious business, not to mention a popular and profitable one.

"At that time," says lifelong Floyd resident and Turner family friend Bruce Sweeney, "we only had one little factory in the county, a shirt factory; women worked there. That's all, except farmers and bootleggers."

Bootlegging had been deemed illegal by the U.S. government. The sale and distribution of liquor had long been a hot button issue in the United States, with prohibition groups working to get the eighteenth amendment passed in 1920, and the government not permitting traffic of home-sold—and therefore untaxed—alcohol. But to Morton Turner, a government edict outlawing the sale of liquor went counter to his inalienable rights guaranteed by the constitution. Brew your own concoction on a stove or in a still, let the grains ferment, strain it, drain it, in time you're drinking the spirit of the south, and then making a profit from it. For many, it was a way of life and a livelihood. And there seemed to be no reason to stop doing it, especially in Floyd County and neighboring Franklin County, Virginia, where the liquor trade ran rampant in a well-satisfied system of supply and demand. Folks would say that no water runs into Floyd; it only runs out of it. Turner, like many people living in the hill country, grew indignant that the government would be so stupid as to try to control alcohol. So he did whatever he knew was right. And he was capable and willing to spread the wealth. "If somebody wanted to start their own operation, and didn't have any money, they would come to Curtis' Daddy," recalls Sweeney. "He'd get them set up."

But he'd never been content doing only one thing. Dairy farming, sawmilling and used car sales also kept him good and busy, since by then he had a growing family to support.

He had married Minnie O. Thomas on October 27, 1916 when they were both twenty-one years old, settling briefly near his family in Smartview Park, Virginia. Their first daughter, Dove, was born a year later, inside her Granddaddy Turner's store. She was only a few years old when her father and some of his workers built the two-story house on a dairy farm out on Route 4 in Floyd—a town within the same-named county— that would be the family's home for years. "They used lumber boards, about twelve inches wide for planks for the inside of the rooms," Dove remembers. "They took those boards over from the old house where they lived. We did not have paved roads, electricity, running water in the bathroom—we had a pipe from a spring that ran into a cistern on the porch."

Minnie Turner was humble and kind, generous to her neighbors and devout. At five-foot-five with thick dark hair, she was considered to be quite lovely. Inside the household, however, ironing, cleaning and other chores always needed doing and to her children, Minnie could be a stern taskmaster.

She and her husband made a handsome couple. Morton Turner stood six-foot-three, with broad shoulders, dark hair and a calm and confident demeanor. He put people at ease with his quiet manner, earning their respect as a levelheaded businessman.

"My mother was very conservative, very firm, strict, she loved her family and her church," remembers Dove. "She was the disciplinarian of my parents: 'You do this and you do that, period.' My father—everybody wanted to please him. He didn't ever raise his voice to anybody. He didn't spank the kids; my mother did that. My father would look at you, and you'd know what he meant. But everybody loved him. He was successful, and true to his word. Whatever his word was was good."

That code defined Floyd, a small mountain town of about five hundred close-knit people for whom family, respect and honor were the measure of a man; it was not unlike a rural Mafia mentality. In Floyd, as in many stops along the southern hill country, you minded your own business, helped your neighbors, settled many a deal with a handshake and then, above all, kept your word. As Curtis once told his friend, motorsports writer Brock Yates, "Where I come from, if you needed something, they would give you the shirt off their back, but if you took something, they would kill you without remorse."

Adds Sweeney, "In a county with only 13,000 people, most people knew everybody. And everybody was pretty proud."

Into this mix of speed and pride, with the sounds of hard farm work punctuated by the roar of engines, Curtis Morton Turner, blue-eyed and sandy-haired, arrived on April 12, 1924.

He was the first son in the Turner family after three girls (Morton and Minnie's second daughter died weeks after childbirth).

Almost immediately, the Turner family faced a series of transitions, shifting locations and long journeys. Morton Turner tried expanding his moonshining business into Maryland, following a migration along with many other Virginians. Sawmilling too had become more than a sideline, and he moved into lumbering to a much greater degree, finding fresh tracts of land to harvest both in Maryland and then down in northern Virginia, on the Potomac River. He moved up north, commuting frequently, and then brought his family with him to a spot outside of Baltimore in 1927, keeping the home in Virginia occupied by trusted friends Tas and Kate Janney, and boarding Dove with a local family so she could complete high school. The 250-mile rides back and forth from Maryland to Virginia were scenic and serene, except for the fuss made by the baby. Sitting in the backseat as a toddler, Curtis would get car sick.

"You're going too fast," Minnie would shout to her husband who'd grip the wheel and suppress his instincts for speed.

Morton Turner shrewdly decided to shift his balance from bootlegging to timber in the early 1930s, a business with great profit potential in the area, even during the Depression. He didn't, however, give up running moonshine.

Both professions intrigued his young son. As a small boy, Curtis trailed along with his father on many timber trips. He got past his motion sickness, frequently imploring his father to pass other cars on the road. It became a little game for the pair, a point of pride, with Morton Turner smiling sheepishly and putting on the gas. Just a little innocent fun—nothing that Mrs. Turner ever needed to find out about.

At age nine, with the family having moved back to Virginia permanently, Curtis finally got his father to agree to let him take the wheel on his own. The incident forever amused Curtis—once he got older.

He took a car to the warehouse where the moonshining operation kept surplus, and left with 110 gallons of liquor in the trunk. Driving back along a nice dirt road, he enjoyed the command of the car, feeling very good about himself. But coming up a road leading to the farm house, young Curtis, glancing over the considerable dashboard, spotted a familiar obstacle: the mailman's car. He had a moment of classic indecision: Which side was he supposed to pass on again?

"I passed him on the wrong side, he kept nudging me the wrong way and I wound up against a fence," Curtis said.

He had inherited his father's quiet manner, and it was also clear from boyhood that he'd grown enamored of the world Morton Turner traveled in. Father and son could be trudging through endless acreage of forest and Morton Turner felt at home, schooling his boy on the clues to recognizing all the different tree varieties they saw. At the family sawmills, enormous harvested trees were carted in for slicing and cutting. Curtis watched his dad striking deals to buy or sell land and wood, and then it was off to arrange more moonshining runs, with snarling, land-beaten cars collecting jugs of liquor for the night's travels. Learning quickly after his first run,

Curtis became a skilled asset behind the wheel of a car years before his teens, practicing dirt-road moves with the enthusiasm some boys use when playing with G.I. Joe's. In Curtis, Morton Turner found a young and willing charge.

At times he even seemed too willing. As he headed toward his teens, school made Curtis more and more restless, much to his mother's consternation. Dove and Ruby continued to apply themselves to their studies. Girls traditionally did all their chores inside the house: cooking, cleaning, ironing. Boys worked outside on the farms. But Curtis was not so predictable.

By 1938, Morton Turner was paying his fourteen-year-old son ten cents an hour to be a waterboy and general helper in his timber business, while also spending hours teaching him how best to estimate board feet of lumber in a tract of land. Making money, Curtis came to understand, required having the ability to handle yourself with confidence, to exude knowledge and the right kind of principles. It was about doing whatever needed to be done to get that handshake.

By comparison, book smarts seemed worthless. Curtis left school at age fifteen to start working a crosscut saw for his father in the woods at fifteen cents an hour. Watching his dad make deals, feeling money in his pocket, Curtis began to get a sensation unfamiliar to many of his peers. To him, Floyd grew smaller by the day. Within a year, even though his father's moonshining business was ebbing, Curtis started running liquor for him and on his own, bringing down $50 a keg for the deliveries. Success brought validation. He could read the dirt roads he'd constantly traveled over in the years before getting his license at fourteen, and the local lands around home became familiar allies. Each groove in a hidden path offered a fresh challenge to hit a curve that much faster than the time before. As he drove these roads, the notion of escape was never far from his mind. And he played hard, drank and fought, and had a hell of a good time. He'd occasionally visit Dove, who by now had moved out on her own and found work in a nearby town. "I think our friendship really started around then," she says of the brother seven years her junior whom she'd hardly known as a boy, other than some recollections of taking rifle practice in Maryland with Curtis and their dad when Curtis was all of seven years old. Even at that point, she was well aware of a division in the family. "My mother and Ruby didn't approve of Curtis' ways of life. They didn't like some of the guys he ran around with. They didn't disown him but it embarrassed them; that's what it amounted to. They embarrassed very easily with everything that wasn't on the up and up. My dad and I were the only members of our family—neither one approved of it either, but we didn't condemn him."

By age eighteen, in 1942, Curtis Turner was tall, slender, well-liked and successful, the owner of three sawmills, and thousands of dollars of logging equipment, bulldozers, lumber haulers and tractors and trailers. He could have a good time in the evening, haul liquor at night and run his businesses by day. He was burning the candle at as many ends as he could find.

Officers would get a run on him, but he always managed to stay ahead of them. Dashing through a liquor run, leaving a sheriff literally in the dust, was a beautiful thing: a defiant challenge much as it had once been for his father. And he, too, had businesses to run, and payrolls to keep. Other sawmillers needed to cut their wood and sell it immediately. Turner waited for the best price before selling. "Everybody wondered how I could cut so much without sellin' and still meet the payroll," he told *Sports Illustrated* years later. "Well, I had to make runs every night to make the payroll but I did."

He was, in a sense, an anomaly, an overgrown kid with bills to pay trying not to miss out on any fun.

"In the mountains you grow up in a hurry," Turner's longtime friend John Griffin would recall years later. "Eighteen's an old man."

Morton Turner recognized his son's skill behind the wheel, and understood the inherent risks—and the rush—of running liquor better than most. But it was time to stop, he warned Curtis. He could see the innate feel his son had for the land, picturing a rich future for Curtis in timbering. The safe and easier way befitted Morton Turner, a man now in his late forties. But Curtis still had plenty of runs left in him.

The runs made for colorful tales, filled with swift moves and great escapes that he'd tell the crowd at El Tenador's and other local spots. In those days, there were gentleman's agreements about running liquor: If you didn't get caught on the road, you were safe once you got off it. Turner talked to the troopers frequently, even befriended them.

"There's this one guy who had been with the state troopers for years and he'd been stationed up in Floyd," says Turner's friend Henry Mason.

"When he was a rookie on the force, they'd given him his new police car and life was good. But he said the rumor was, if you could catch Curtis Turner running liquor, you could make rank in a heartbeat. So he says one night here comes old Curtis. He says, 'I know this is my man, I got him.' And he said he started pulling up behind him; Curtis starts to run, he's got a load of liquor in the car. The trooper says, 'Hell I'll catch him; I just know I'm going to be sergeant in no time.' But all of a sudden, Curtis Turner turned that sonofabitch around in the middle of the road and came head on at him. Trooper says, 'I panicked and ran my brand new police car right into a ditch!' He said, 'The sonofabitch turned back around, pulled up, leaned out the window and wanted to know if I was okay. And then he drove off.'"

One particular trooper always found all the talk unnerving. He had run Turner 39 times without coming close to catching him. Turner saw him at a local lunch spot every once in awhile; the man would just shake his head and say, "I'm gonna catch you if it's the last thing I do."

"Later on, that ol' boy committed suicide," Turner recalled years after he'd stopped running. "So the last thing he did was die."

The kids at El Tenador's would eat up all the stories. Sometimes he'd take a passel of younger ones on rides, work up some speed and twirl them through a quick 180. They'd holler and shout his name. Says Bruce Sweeney, "He was all the boys' hero around here."

Curtis Turner wakes up from a short, rejuvenating nap and adjusts his eyes to the moonlight. The farmhouse near where he's parked is dark, tucked in for the night, and he can barely make out a path leading back to the road where, a few hours before, he'd made a spirited run with his sugar.

Yes, the sugar. Turner gets out of the car and runs his hands over the trunk, discovering at least three bullet holes. There's no way to assess the damage in the darkness. He'll get a better look in the morning, provided he can make it home in the middle of the night with almost no gas and no headlights.

Turner steers his car back onto the local road, scouting around for a creative solution. There's a school bus parked on the side of the road and he pulls over, siphons a few gallons into his tank and gets to work on the headlights. One will do, and he removes it from the bus and wires it to replace one of his busted lamps. Feeling suddenly guilty, he opens the school bus door and tosses a couple of dollars on the seat.

Given how organized the chase from the naval base seemed, there's no telling if anyone is still patrolling the roads, looking for him. But he'll need to get home as soon as possible. His sister Dove is getting married at the Floyd Baptist Church in the morning, and he'll have to pick up Ann on the way there. Things with Ann have gotten more serious as of late. Chances are they'd have already gotten married by now, if Ann's family didn't utterly object to her going out with a moonshining, fast-living boyfriend.

Curtis had met Lilian Ann Ross three years earlier, just before his induction into the Navy. Ann was fifteen at the time, and it would be the only blind date she'd ever go on. Her family owned one of the largest farms in Franklin County, where they raised chickens, had three large gardens and a fishing lake.

Ann went to high school in the town of Ferrum, where her friend Nolan Stafford had gone on and on about Curtis, wanting to introduce them. "He's real exciting," Stafford said. "You don't just go to the movies on Saturday nights, you go somewhere; you *do* something!"

All the buildup colored Ann's judgment at their first meeting. "Well, I liked him, but I was thinking he might be a little boring, in the very beginning," she remembers.

Early on, Curtis *did* take Ann somewhere: to meet his parents and family. Clearly, the slight, pretty teenager with wavy dark hair, brown eyes and bright wit stood out in Turner's mind. She was young and respectable: since she was still too young to go out alone, the pair always dated with one or more couples. She might appear vulnerable at times but an underlying feisty strength made her even more attractive. During a date, watching Ann's tender smile, Curtis informed her that one day she was going to be his wife.

"I'll get married," she told him with a playful grin, "when I'm good and ready."

To Ann, Curtis' family felt especially welcoming. The only thing her family really knew about Curtis was his reputation. But everybody seemed more at ease in the Turner home. "Mrs. Turner was a good cook," Ann remembers, "but she'd never let you compliment her food." Compared to

Ann's home situation, the Turner house seemed as normal as a scene from a picture postcard.

Twenty years earlier, Ann's father had brought his new bride home to the family farm in Franklin County from Ohio. Ann's mother was Catholic; her father Protestant. The extended Ross family was filled with strong-willed folks who didn't approve of the union. The pressure they exerted helped drive the couple apart, and Ann and her sister Margaret and brother Johnny were toddlers when they returned to Ohio with their mother.

Ann was a six-year-old when, during a visit to her father's family, her entire life was turned upside down.

A new arrangement had been made between Ann's parents, and she was now to live with her father's extended family on the farm in Virginia.

Ann's Aunt Emma and her sisters had decided they would not let her brother's ex-wife "ruin" the children, and exerted pressure on their brother, who had by now remarried. Ann's mother returned to Ohio, now living a life less pressured by the responsibilities of children. But Ann's father remained at his new home with his second wife, who did not relish the idea of suddenly raising three small children. Ann and her sister and brother were now left primarily in their aunt's hands. Aunt Emma more or less became Ann's mother. Years later, when Ann's brother Johnny was a teenager, he fled from the farm and made his way back to his mother in Ohio, but the events had left the family emotionally fractured.

As Ann grew, a part of her remained hidden, suppressed and alone. To meet a vital young man, with an exciting life and a protective nature, seemed the most treasured thing imaginable. And yet there was nothing she could count on. Who knew if Curtis Turner was someone whose life she could crawl into? Not much was certain—except that Turner had met a person who desired a fast escape even more than he did.

The United States might have been in the middle of World War II in early 1943 but the conflict felt distant to Turner, who didn't have a world of respect for the government's vicissitudes. Visiting Ruby's apartment with Ann, he picked up a newspaper and pretended to read the headlines. "I see where the Japs have killed 5,000 Germans," he said with a laugh. "He was working and living and doing as he pleased," says Ann. "He didn't want to be bothered."

All that changed when he received his induction papers, and a notice to report to the naval base in Norfolk on June 16, 1943 to begin serving. It wasn't so much a question of being unpatriotic; Turner's youthful enthusiasm had already been channeled into business and pleasure. After reading the notice, he stormed out of the house angrily and joined his friends on a drunken tear through the center of town. "Floyd has just one stoplight," Ann recalls of the town's main intersection right in front of the Floyd Courthouse. "And they just shot out that stoplight."

For the remainder of the war, Turner was stationed in Virginia, helping to guard the coastline from Norfolk to Virginia Beach. Much of his sawmilling and moonshining work fell by the wayside, but he made up for it a bit by running tires from the naval base up to friends in the hills, making a nice profit. His budding relationship with Ann was also curtailed, due to their long separations. In time they fell out of touch.

Turner and Ann Ross met again by chance in the Spring of 1946, after his April honorable discharge from the Navy. By now, Curtis had resumed his runs, with the added element of Navy sugar in the mix. "He had sort of a triangular trade going," says Brock Yates. "He'd run booze into the Naval station in Norfolk and trade it for sugar and money and then bring the sugar back to the mountains to brew more white liquor." Meanwhile, Ann had begun attending a teachers' college. She was an independent-minded eighteen-year-old with an appreciation for adventure. As fast as Turner might be driving, it was impossible not to feel safe with him. He would weave his way through "Dead Man's Curve" in Floyd, all the while instructing Ann on the best way to take the turns, and cautioning her to always drive carefully. Together they'd take long trips and talk for hours as he thundered through what was known as "Shootin' Creek" Road, heading up through the rugged mountain terrain.

"Why don't you take the paved roads?" Ann asked him one night.

"Long, straight roads put me to sleep," he told her. "I think it's more fun to travel the rough roads. Makes things more interesting."

Preparations are under way at the Floyd Baptist Church, and the hour is approaching when the Turner family will leave for the wedding of their oldest daughter. Curtis Turner makes his swift trip through the local roads that July morning as dawn continues its patient ascent in the mountains.

It is a brilliant morning: a hint of wind, a cloudless sky, the open road. Turner cannot believe his sweet fortune.

He parks at his parents' house and gets out to inspect the damage to the car. With the trunk open, he notices that one of the bullets went clean through the trunk and busted into the coupe's cab, settling finally in the back of the driver's seat. With a little more speed, it would have kept its path right through his back. Turner smiles: through the long ride, straight into morning, he has dodged one bullet after another.

That's when the policeman makes his way swiftly around the back of the barn, his gun poised. He'd been posted there through the night, waiting for Turner to make an appearance.

It had been easy enough to get Turner's license plate number both when he left the naval base and during the long chase west through Virginia. It will now be hard to explain a trunk full of government sugar and a mess of bullet holes in his trunk. It also won't be easy to convey why he's the only member of the family not at the church.

"I didn't have any idea why Curtis wasn't at my wedding," Dove remembers with a laugh. "I didn't know he was picked up by the law that day. I didn't know a thing about it at the time."

Days later, when it is time for Curtis to stand before the judge, he is, for perhaps the first time in his life, genuinely frightened. He rides the ferry down to Portsmouth with his father and a lawyer in tow, pondering the consequences.

"Son," the lawyer says, "we're riding over here together and I hate to tell you, but I don't think you'll be coming back with me."

His father is reassuring, but he can see his worst nightmare fulfilled. Great opportunities are about to be squandered for a simple thrill, and Morton Turner feels the tug of his own responsibility.

Curtis is dumfounded. "I don't want to go to jail," he tells them. "I just got out of the service."

Says Turner's friend Charlie Williamson, "He was worried to death."

The judge in the trial has a good poker face, as if there isn't a tale he hasn't heard, and he asks the young man if he has anything to say. As the buzz in the court grows dim, something impulsive comes into Turner's head, and he nods quietly to himself, suddenly as calm as he's been since his moonshine run. He looks around the room at an audience filled with court personnel and curiosity seekers, and then he glances over at his father, who wears the weight of concern on his face, and he feels the great need to remove that weight. Turner waves off his lawyer.

And then he begins to speak about his hill country. It is poor country, he reminds the judge, ravaged by the Depression and the war years, with people doing without the simple means of sustaining themselves. And here he is, a Navy man, a local boy with an honorable discharge, helping to protect the coastline of his country and yet feeling the tug of responsibility for his people. So yes, he took that sugar—and he was proud to do it, he says.

His plan all along was to bring the sugar back home to his neighbors and family. That, he admits to the judge, is the only way they could use it to concoct a delightful, even necessary, local specialty.

"Apple butter," Turner says.

Morton Turner's brows wrinkle and he turns slowly to look at his son.

It takes so little to provide this to the locals, and they could use that apple butter now and then store some for the winter months—an effort that might even keep some people alive. It was all the more necessary with sugar is such short supply.

Yes, what he did was wrong, but in this case, given the result, Turner had no choice, he says. Isn't this, after all, what the war had been fought for?

It is hard not to be moved. "He was so convincing, they were crying in there," Williamson says with a laugh.

But the judge fully understands what's going on. He offers a strong warning to Turner: give up such activity immediately. He fines Turner $1,000 and hands down a two-year suspended sentence. Turner is free to go. "I'll be making sure my boy keeps to your advice," Morton Turner tells the judge, moving to pay the fine.

On the ferry back from Portsmouth, Turner is gleeful. His lawyer stands there, scratching his head. "I don't know how you did it," he says. "I never thought you were going to get out of that."

Morton Turner stares at his son with awe, and a hint of dread. C'mon, his son says, trying to draw his dad into this celebration. Morton Turner had secretly wondered if there might be a lesson learned in all this. His oldest son had never really had to struggle, had always been given every opportunity and perhaps too much leeway.

Every once in awhile, especially when doing so well, a man needs to know what it feels like to be humbled.

Days after returning from Portsmouth, Turner presents Ann with an engagement ring; in their giddiness, they decide to wait only a few months before getting married. "I was afraid my aunt would see the ring," remembers Ann. "So I didn't wear it."

They also don't share the news with many people. Among the handful they confide in are Ann's sister Margaret and her husband Earl. On July 12, Ann has the ring and impulsively shows it to her sister while the two couples drive toward the Tanglewood Mall near Margaret and Earl's Roanoke home. A shocked and overjoyed Margaret rejoices with her sister, who busily chats about the future plans.

"Well, why not get married tonight?" Earl says suddenly.

Everybody looks over at Curtis, who sits behind the wheel of his car, shaking his head, with a smile growing into a deep growl of a laugh. "That suits me," he shouts.

Curtis turns around and the couples head west. About a hundred miles away, there is a discreet justice of the peace in the town where Bristol, Virginia, shares a border with Bristol, Tennessee.

Soon after getting married, the twenty-two-year-old Turner presents his father with a gift he's long been asking for. On tight ovals cut into cornfields throughout Virginia and the Carolinas, countless little dirt tracks, most barely a quarter-mile around, have served as proving grounds for local 'shine runners. Turner has made his way to a number of these events: impulsive, makeshift affairs where folks take up a collection, and the guy with the best car and the greatest nerves usually takes the pot. Or the course heads down some long mountain road, with Turner frequently in front.

By now the races are starting to get somewhat more organized, with local promoters dangling prize money to lure drivers and fans. The rosters at these races feature some of most legendary names in the liquor hauling fraternity. There isn't a great deal of money to be made, but it's safer than a high-speed chase. And there's an appreciative crowd.

Curtis agrees to give it a shot, and one week after eloping, Curtis and Ann Turner drive to a half-mile dirt track in Mt. Airy, North Carolina, with

Curtis hoping to make his debut behind the wheel in a real race. Their hopes are dashed, however—the race has been called off till the following weekend due to rain that has recently soaked the area. Dejected fans are milling out when Turner drops Ann off and drives cautiously onto the track. He's here and this is a new experience for him; he might as well get a feel for the place.

Turner's tires alternately grip and slip on the dirt oval but after a lap or two, he's starting to find the right groove. By now, patrons have turned back to check out the show.

Over the same ground he goes, again and again, picking up speed in the straightaways and seeing no reason to really slow down much in the curves. For years he's done this quietly, stealthily in the backwoods; now Turner, like a scientist with a prized discovery, shows off some impeccable fishtail turns. He powers into each curve and slides sideways, sending long shots of mud and dirt flying into the distance, and somehow managing to keep the car on at least two wheels at a time. Then he swiftly recovers and is back on the straightaway. Each fishtail grows longer and bolder and more fans return as the cheering gets louder. The display goes on and the appreciation feels endless. Careening down the track, he slams on the brakes and twists into a 180-degree spin; then he whips back around and continues on.

When Turner finally parks the car, applause showers down. The shouting quiets him, and after a few waves and some congratulations, he moves toward Ann, intending to leave. But he is suddenly stopped by one patron: A hat had been passed during his several-lap exhibition, and money raised; in all $22 has been collected from the fans cheering his dirty, brilliant dance in the wet red clay.

The money is wonderful, but it feels like suitable icing on an exceptional cake. It is all about being there, showing up and making a show of it all. It's speed and the fleeting muse of traction, the joy of the slide, and driving through that moment, with the fans, the dirt and the payoff. The racing—*this* is everything, Curtis Turner thinks. This, he realizes, is living.

Chapter Two
1946-1950
"I guess I'll be in the sport until I die. That's how much I like it."

In the light of day, with the sun warming every dirt groove and cut notch in each fence post, the half-mile dirt track in Mt. Airy, North Carolina, looks impressive but makeshift, like a cleared patch of land waiting for a traveling circus. There are no frills about the place, just a length of oval cut into the ground with an earth grater, and now glistening with a sheen of water and oil. A cornfield adjoins the track, and kids screech and laugh as they race around near the stalks. Minding the kids are racing wives and spectator wives, trading gossip, stories and road tips, and perhaps rummaging through bags for a sandwich or a piece of fruit. A few hundred people have congregated to watch the action, mostly men craning their necks in search of their favorites, or settling in for a better view. Ann Turner joins the group this Sunday afternoon in July, 1946, seeing some of the people she'd met a week earlier, when her new husband had put on a little rained-out show for the benefit of the faithful, and for himself.

None of the racers in the infield, now tinkering with their cars, had hung around to watch Curtis Turner's little display, and if they had, chances are that few would have been impressed. But most of them seem cordial enough as Turner drives up in his regular street car, parks and noses around a little. Red Byron, a slender but solidly built driver in a short-sleeve racing suit, nods in passing; he walks with a limp, the result of a bad leg wound during the war, yet there is something especially sturdy about him nonetheless. Bob Flock, with piercing blue eyes intent on the view under the hood, barely looks up in greeting. It's been said that if a stranger places even a friendly hand on Bob's shoulder, he is apt to reel around and punch him. It is therefore hardly surprising that when Bob gets behind the wheel of a car, he reputedly becomes possessed.

Everybody appears matter-of-fact and calm, while Turner can hear his heart thumping in his ears.

These turn out to be the last pleasant moments of the day for him.

Turner lines up for the afternoon's feature race near the rear of the pack, and when it starts, he quickly discovers the limitations of his car. With each lap, he falls further off pace and finishes dead last. Even his slides are little; it's embarrassing when each one only pushes you further back.

No one says anything to him about it afterwards and they don't have to. Every other car in the place is meant for racing or hauling, with better engines and more efficient gears.

During the next week, he and some friends at the local Sweeney's Garage rip apart and retool one of his moonshine-hauling cars into something with an affinity for short bursts of speed. This is a question of pride, after all.

He tests his work the following Sunday at another half-mile dirt track, in Marion, Virginia. Lined up next to last among the nineteen cars, he takes off at the wave of the starter's flag and begins an impatient climb through the field. His first turn is impressive, a half-spin deep into the curve that he controls perfectly. Given the increase in his horsepower, he picks up speed on the straight and bears down on turn two, which comes upon him all too quickly. He crosses up the wheels again in another half turn, and manages to keep them on the ground through the curve and again finds himself pointed straight up the track.

Dirt is flying everywhere. Turner vaguely hears the smack of pebbles against his windshield over the roar of the engine. He keeps squinting, trying to keep a clear view ahead of him.

The further he moves through the field, the more skilled are the blocks thrown his way. Going into one turn, Buddy Shuman, an innovative engine builder from Charlotte, North Carolina, who'd once done time on a chain gang for liquor running, begins his own spin to the inside of Turner's Ford. As the drivers head around the curve, the force of Shuman's momentum—helped along by a sufficient jerk on his steering wheel—sends him smacking into the side of Turner, nearly spinning the rookie around. Turner loses ground a moment, watching Shuman's trunk pull away up the track. After several laps—because nobody is too eager to let him by—he is reeling Shuman in on the straightaway. Shuman crowds him and offers up another little tap, but Turner keeps his line steady, and by the time he goes through another swerve, he is around Shuman and nearing the lead.

Seventeen cars had separated Turner from the lead, and he jockeys past them all, many delivering a rub or a tap in the process. Now with the lead, he throws his coupe even deeper into turns, getting his bearings on how far he can push it. The car feels like an extension of his own body, each muscle along his arms and legs calmly bending the Ford to his will.

He gets only a few serious challenges for the rest of the race, and when he takes the checkered flag, there is a smattering of applause from the Marion crowd for the newcomer.

Most everybody, however, is angry. No other driver likes to lose, and several have had scrapes that their unsatisfying shares of the purse won't fully pay for. No one among the few hundred in the stands enjoys seeing the guy he roots for on the losing end either, especially when that fan has lost some side-bet money as a result. And the promoter isn't interested in the new guy besting the regulars. But for Turner, the moment is thrilling and warm. He climbs from his car and accepts a $500 check for the winner's share. Turner will have a good time that night.

Meanwhile, his competitors survey their damage, settle a few arguments, grab much smaller checks and get the cars ready for the ride home. Some drivers need to tie a fender on to keep it from scraping on the road all the way back home, and a few have to hammer the metal away from a tire. The only good news in all this, win or lose, is that there are plenty of these tracks everywhere. Go one hundred miles in any direction from the Christiansburg, Virginia, home where Curtis and Ann Turner have temporarily settled and you can hit half a dozen tracks easily, with races during the week, and certainly on the weekends. These are quarter-mile tracks, or half-mile, or three-eights.

A ragtag assembly of drivers always competes, and there is no real sense of organization. Competition is spirited and raucous, and since amateurs are as welcome as regulars, and handling the terrain requires a great deal of skill, there is a fresh risk to your livelihood every few days. All the tracks are ovals, and when there are thirty or forty drivers slamming their way around the course, the dust, dirt and mud fly into the trees, the windshields and frequently the stands.

But at these races, a driver can shine for an afternoon or an evening, and bring home enough money to live on for a few weeks, and a good enough story to tell for longer than that. So he keeps working on the one car that will take him to the next track, for another shot at finishing the day in front.

In the late 1940s, the South is car country. Tall oaks and vast farmlands are set back along the main roads, which course through the steady curves and steep climbs of Virginia and North Carolina. Every few miles, the landscape shifts and the odd building or general store pops up, followed by the local filling station, usually with a couple of beat-up cars out front, in various states of being shaped into something fast. Then it's back to the roadways, the mountains and the horizon.

To drive these roads is a serene pleasure or a squirrelly challenge, depending on the read of your speedometer. And there lies the rub for many residents of the southern states. The ever-present distant sounds of high speed are the almost exclusive issue of the young: teens and twenty-year-olds challenging each other in drag races, or moonshiners making runs. And now comes stock car racing.

When Curtis and Ann Turner move to Roanoke, Virginia, in early 1947, there are races taking place in Mt. Airy, Winston-Salem, Charlotte, Shelby and Concord, North Carolina, to name a few; and in Covington Virginia, in Norfolk and Richmond, and in Roanoke's own Victory Stadium. The City of Roanoke officials would prefer the races didn't run but they can't shut them down. That doesn't mean, however, that they approve. Racing is not for decent people. It doesn't matter that people pay their hard-earned money—a buck and a half—to see the races, with crowds growing larger all the time and kids under twelve getting in for free. It might *seem* fun, they say, but it's *not*. City fathers eventually take it so far as to have the police pull flyers that announce the Victory Stadium schedule off telephone poles. It doesn't matter—the fans show up in increasing numbers each week, from several hundred to several thousand over time. "They put some good races on there," says Paul Cawley, then the co-owner of the town filling station on Grandon Road, "and in time, there was nothing that would make the city the money that that stadium made for them."

The scene at the various tracks is always combustible and outrageously dirty, thrilling and extraordinarily loud. Cawley fondly recalls the practice of opening up the engine to pump up a car's volume before a race. "The fans," he says, "like a little extra racket from the exhaust."

The filling stations are the hub of the local racing scenes. Former moonshiners, kids with fast cars and anyone else with high-speed dreams come to trade stories and brag, compare notes on local tracks and brag some more.

The drivers who hang around have long excelled at the practice of pulling auto bodies and parts out of junk heaps and crafting them into "Modifieds": cars that resemble anything from a pre-war Ford to a post-war Buick on the outside, with a potpourri of cam shafts, gears and engines inside. Cars that are thick, hulky and formidable. Sometimes the cars have windshields; other times, they have thick wire mesh covers for better visibility. The metal mesh keeps rock and the larger pieces of dirt from getting through. If it gets too thick with dirt, just slam the mesh once and off you go. To drive and maintain one of these modifieds means embracing futility, but to win is a wondrous exercise in pride and accomplishment. These modifieds are ugly beautiful.

According to the saying, auto racing has been around since the building of the second car. But the racing that has long gone on in Europe, and at Indianapolis since 1909, is for the leisure of the rich. In the Carolinas, it is an escape route for the poor. The difference between the two pursuits is obvious with a single, startling glance. The cars racing around the chicanes of Le Mans, with their long noses, sleek bodies and open-wheel design, are the stuff of dreams. In the post-war South, the Ford Coupes and other rebuilt racing cars, with their fenders, windshields and conventional design, are the stuff of possibility. They're the promise that anything can happen, beginning with them.

In early 1947, Turner becomes a regular at Paul Cawley's filling station. Among the boasters and businessmen, weekend competitors and newcomers, Turner instantly impresses Cawley. He is quick with a good tale and fun to run around with. But there is also a quiet confidence about him, and the energy of a room shifts a little whenever Turner enters it.

"Of all the guys I've known in racing, he's about the smartest," Cawley says. "And he had nerves of steel.

"He was friendly with everybody. He was just a likable guy. He'd come down to the filling station and meet a lot of guys over there. Some of those guys ran the local races and some who came by indulged in the [moonshining] 'recipe business.' Sometimes a guy would say one car was better than another, and Curtis would say, 'We'll see.'"

On Saturday nights, the drag races begin on the road in front of Cawley's station and turn sharply onto a two-mile highway stretch, followed by a hairpin turn back to a parallel highway. The route is like one lap on some imaginary two-lane superspeedway. Some guys will frequently spin before they even come to the highway. Others wipe out at the first turn. For Turner, winning the $100 to $150 pot—the winner-take-all collection from everybody's ante—quickly becomes a given. And it hurts the competition less when everybody can share a drink afterwards, courtesy of the winner.

Turner is impulsive and engaging, the kind of person who's quick with a good idea that you know will cause a bit of trouble. Whenever he gets restless on the local roads, he leaves his particular mark on car country by smacking into a series of wooden mailbox posts and then watching in the rearview mirror as each now-detached box sails clear over his car. The twenty-one-year-old Cawley, two years Turner's junior, takes to him immediately. One Sunday morning, while the pair are having breakfast at the Coffee Pot in Roanoke after a long night, Turner suggests a race, heading the five miles over to Floyd County and then back.

The contest turns into a Sunday morning ritual, the pair running side by side out on Crooked Road. Their throttles open, they trade leads at better than a hundred miles per hour, and screech around the curves in their '40 Coupes. "It was thrilling," Cawley says. "There wasn't any traffic. The only thing is, sometimes we'd get to racing when church is going on and the church is out through there and the sheriff would call down to the filling station and say, 'For Christ sakes, y'all please quit that racing; it's Sunday morning. I'm trying to keep the telephone on the hook.' He was nice so we wiped that out."

At the filling station, Cawley begins working on Turner's race cars, joining Turner's childhood friend Acey Janey in constructing something dominant. Turner is as restless to race as anybody but he is unlike the vast majority of his competitors in one vital way: he doesn't have a pressing need to worry about money. The successful Morton Turner takes so much pride in his son's early promise on the race track that at one point, he gives him access to his bank account to support the racing. Cawley accompanies Curtis to a Buick dealer where he hands over a Morton Turner check and leaves with two shiny new Buicks. A little later on, it is a Ford Coupe. Morton eventually studies his checkbook and decides enough is enough, but he never tires of the excitement his son generates, continuously bragging about it to his friends and inspiring the admonishments of his wife.

"Turner, some folks don't approve of racing," Minnie tells him.

"Of *course* we don't approve of it," Morton Turner tells her, "but he did win the race!"

Without his father's funds, Curtis can always rely on his aunt, Bess Weitzel, Minnie Turner's sister, who'd married into the family that owned Coca-Cola, and never minded pointing that out to folks. Whenever Curtis pays her a visit, he acts as if the weight of the automobile racing world is on his shoulders. He can't possibly succeed without her help.

"How much do you need?" she asks and, with a smile at her charming, enthusiastic nephew, heads into the house for a check. There is a skill in knowing how to convince someone to give you money, and then making them feel they're all the richer for having done so, and Turner is gaining valuable, practical experience at it.

"We'd be at the garage, wondering what we were gonna do, and he'd come up [to Bess] and put an act on and all," Cawley says. "I'd get tickled just watching him. Then we'd cash the check and off to the races we'd go."

Ann Turner lies comfortably in her hospital bed with a lazy smile on her face. Curtis Turner leans over to get a closer look at his fragile-looking newborn daughter resting comfortably in her mother's arms.

"You can pick her up," Ann tells him. Curtis cautiously raises Margaret Sue Turner to his chest, and her head rolls contentedly against his jaw.

"Do you think she hurt herself?" he asks wide-eyed. Ann laughs and Curtis smiles as he gingerly moves his daughter's head till it rests against his shoulder. He stands awkwardly for a moment, hands the baby back and stares at his young family as a first-time father at age twenty-three.

Curtis Turner owns sawmills and is starting to harvest some lumber to sell. He has bought a local movie theatre in Roanoke and owns a fine house. If he spends more of his time in sawmilling and timber, like his father, there is every reason to believe he can make an extremely good living and sit back frequently enough to enjoy it. But there are drag races on Saturday nights, and the adrenalin rush of the moonshine run has been replaced by as many stock car races as he can get himself into.

He leaves the hospital later that morning, accepting congratulations all around, and heads over to the track in Covington, Virginia, where he bests the field in the feature race and captures the winner's trophy. Turner lugs the hardware with him back to the hospital and presents it to his wife and new baby. And he smiles at them with the fresh pride of a kid.

In the summer of 1947, Turner wins five straight races at one of the area tracks, and the large golden trophy he earns for one of them remains in his street car for months. At every stop for business or pleasure, the trophy's bright glint becomes his calling card, like a fine pistol carried by the local gunslinger.

Turner is establishing a reputation as a winner, and is a bright new favorite in a sport that wears its growing pains like ugly bruises after a brawl. Stock car races are raucous affairs. Drivers learn quickly that safety comes first—not in the form of a seatbelt, which is optional, but in terms of weaponry. A moonshiner-turned-racer will frequently come to the track with a gun handy, as a matter of principle; it would seem strange to travel without one, even if you're not going to use it. And every driver has a stick somewhere in the car, to fight the angry rabble who might be dissatisfied with the outcome of a race. It is not uncommon for the day to end with a riot, as drivers and fans engage in a free-for-all, with Coke bottles flying. All it takes is for some also-ran to swerve into the favorite with a few laps to go, and you've got the makings of a nice Sunday afternoon meleé. "It was different back then," says Buck Baker, one of the most successful racers of the era. "You'd drive 30 minutes and fight 30 minutes."

An associate of Turner's, Billy Triplett, recalls a prerace spectacle put on by racing brothers Bobby and Billy Myers: "The Myers brothers got up on the hoods of their cars and pulled out knives, saying, 'We'll whip everybody's ass in the place.'" It does not feel like an especially casual threat. Says Buck Baker's racing son Buddy, "I don't think anybody'd want to jump out of the car and grab hold of Bobby, unless he had a death wish.

"The Myers Brothers, Buddy Shuman, my dad—you had to be insane to want to mess with any of those people," he says. "They made their living with their wit. You knock somebody in the fence, you better be able to either outrun him or whip his fanny 'cause those guys went to it. There weren't any regulations back then. You had to be able to survive till the next week and those guys made sure that it wasn't pleasant if you [hit] him."

Among the racers, Turner is an anomaly. His success in business and the bankrolling of his family sets him apart. But to top that off, he is not a fighter. He is vigilant in his desire to avoid conflict, even after his frequent metal-crunching movements through the field in any given race. "There wasn't anything physical about him," says H.A. "Humpy" Wheeler, the famed auto racing promoter. "He couldn't lick a postage stamp. 'Discretion is the better part of valor' was his whole motto. He'd knock somebody off the race track, and after the race he was up there saying, 'Ahh pal, you did a great job, you just happened to be there when I got there. I'm really sorry, what can I do for you? Just don't ask me to replace your car.'"

While Turner often drives the auto Janey and Cawley construct for him, there are local car owners who might show up with faster cars, or ones promoted by larger local businesses, looking for the driver who can handle the ride and the publicity, and Turner is their guy. With his charisma, he brings things to the table many drivers lack.

But it is what Turner does on the race track that everybody starts talking about by the fall of 1947. His driving style is already putting hundreds more people into seats at races, then forcing them to jump up out of them all day long.

Given the size and shape of the average dirt track, there is very little margin for error when it comes to making a turn at high speed. Every time Turner goes into a corner, he not only exceeds the margin, he flaunts it.

And he batters cars, and he wins; when he loses, he makes the kind of noisy, impactful exit that forces local car owners to wonder why they chose him for their rides in the first place—until he wins again. And no fan ever leaves a track disappointed after viewing Curtis Turner in the midst of the most thrilling maneuver in motor sports: the dirt track power slide. Plenty of drivers can do it; no one can do it like he can.

To most drivers, the instructions for a power slide seem understandable enough on paper: Cock the wheels of your car as you head into a turn, and keep the throttle open with the back wheels spinning. But do this at high speed on dirt and your car gets nearly perpendicular. Keep turning your angle, or head into the curve faster, and you're pushing an envelope beyond fear: now your car is completely sideways. But how early do you start the slide? How long can you hold it like that? And *how* do you get out of it without crashing?

Some drivers are tentative and clunky; they get the timing off, bounce and bop over the dirt and barely manage to keep all their wheels on the track once the straightaway comes. Others try to overcorrect; the force of being sideways shocks them into an instinctive movement, and they might easily slam the back of their car into a fence.

Turner doesn't so much slide as glide through a turn, starting earlier than anybody else, holding it longer than physics allows and then recovering with a level of flair and ease that is at once outrageous and remarkable.

"When Curtis Turner was on dirt—that was the greatest thrill. Oh *man*, could that cat drive on dirt. Good grief!" says Hal Hambrick, a racing announcer who also managed five speedways in the 1950s. "It was poetry in motion."

Bob Moore, a frequent spectator with his dad at the races in the 1940s long before his stellar career in motorsports journalism, recalls, "Curtis just had an ability to start the slide almost before anyone else. So as everyone else was turning the wheel, he was going underneath them or even on the outside of them and you think there's no way he'll get through this corner. He's either going to hit the guy or hit the wall. But he was one of these velvet-smooth race drivers.

"The first time you see him do it, you say, 'Oh this guy's nuts, no one can get through this corner that way.' You go to this race and that race and about the third or fourth time you see him do it at different race tracks, you think this guy's as good as everyone says he is. Maybe even better."

The spectacle of Turner awakens something not only in fans, but in the promoters watching the tickets fly whenever Turner and his chief rivals make an appearance. Years before he will become the sport's premier promotion man, Wheeler is mesmerized by the sight.

"Back in the days of the power slide, red-clay tracks were prepared very very wet, because nobody wanted any dust. So the tracks, when prepared right, would get this sheen on them that looked like 40 coats of clear lacquer and were slick, just like [skating rinks], and that's the way you wanted them because you were trying to excite the fans," he says. "So a lot of these tracks that Turner drove on, you couldn't get the car totally straight; you were always turning right a little bit to go left. And it really required a tremendous seat-of-the-pants driver to be able to run fast on that because that was very much like driving on hard packed snow. You felt like you were in control but you knew that you were right on the edge all the time and if you did anything really hairy you were probably going to crash; and if you let up a little bit, the whole field was gonna pass you. So you're sitting on that ragged edge all the time. But Curtis Turner knew how to do that power slide, and throw the dirt up in the air and rooster tail it as well as anybody I ever saw."

To the faithful, and to the local newspapers who are starting to give the sport occasional coverage, Turner becomes Virginia's own "Blond Blizzard," a sandy-haired menace to his fellow racers and a tall, slender, twinkle-eyed favorite son to fans. To Turner, it doesn't matter if he emerges victorious; what matters is emerging, period, after the hardest run imaginable. "I've seen him in the early days going into a curve so fast, and if the car wasn't running fast enough to keep up, he'd run it through the wall to get out of [the race]," says Cawley of Turner's desire to always put on a show for fans, no matter what. "He'd wreck it or do something. Then he'd get out and walk away from it." Win or lose, Turner exits the car with the red clay glistening in his hair, and the sound of the crowd in his head. Guys like Speedy Thompson, the Myers brothers, Buck Baker, Bob Flock, Buddy Shuman, they don't exactly appreciate being tapped by Turner, and they'll slam back just as hard. But this only makes him knock them again, and with Turner driving a car he doesn't *have* to care about, what is his incentive to hold back? There is no winning the battle for anybody whose personal assets are poured into his race car. Besides, it's hard to hate a guy when he offers you the first drink after the race ends.

Turner is not the average stock car racer, but his name and grinning face are showing up on posters drawing several thousands more in to see the sport run. And a guy can get used to that. "I guess I'll be in the sport until I die," he tells one reporter after a race. "That's how much I like it."

By the middle of 1947, Turner is an electric force in the reckless circuit overload that is southern stock car racing. He is also about to become a lightening rod for the one man struggling to bring the sport the vital element it lacks: a tempered plan for legitimacy and organization. This man, Bill France, is starting to gather the disparate track owners, promoters and drivers together to create a sense of order out of a mass of chaos. And for a successful, if fleeting time, he will find the ideal friend and ally in Turner.

Chapter Three
1947-1950
"He could talk anybody out of their breakfast."

William Henry Getty France has a gift for getting folks to see things exactly his way. It doesn't matter if those other people have vastly conflicting interests and are dead set against agreeing with anybody. By the end of a speech, a cajole, a pressing point of debate, it becomes clear that everybody is miraculously on the same page.

He is gregarious, friendly, stern and commanding: a classic model CEO in the decades before the term is popular. As a racing promoter—and American history will arguably find none better—he's the kind of guy who can settle an argument with a very firm handshake while also offering a warm pat on the back for everybody else to see. And though he is six-foot-four, it is for these other reasons that everybody calls him "Big Bill."

"Bill was a very likeable person but he could talk anybody out of their breakfast," says longtime car owner Ray Fox. "If something was gonna hurt him, he had a way around it."

In 1947, France is trying to find his way around a distressing dilemma. Stock car races are increasing in popularity, yet they are still run in a haphazard way, not far removed from the ones he himself drove in as far back as 1929. In one such race, a promoter announced a $500 winners' purse, and afterwards, when France questioned his $10 third-place share, he was told the money had all been a ruse to increase spectator interest. It is a typical scenario. In the infant stock car racing world, drivers sometimes find after a race that a promoter has skipped town with the entire purse. Or, recalls Buck Baker, "You might win a race and all you'd get is a bottle of wine and a damn ham meat."

In 1934, France leaves Washington D.C., settles with his wife and young son Billy in Daytona Beach and begins racing and working at a local gas station. By 1936, the biggest racing event in town, and one of the most popular on the eastern seaboard, takes place on the Daytona beach-and-road course, a 3.2-mile circuit where drivers run along both a stretch of highway and a parallel patch of tightly packed sand that has been the site of many land-speed records. Joining both straightaways are north and south turns that, once the races begin, become nearly impassable, as car after car digs ripples into the loose dirt surface, creating what feels like an ever-changing pattern of deep-pile carpeting. Pileups become plentiful and fans rejoice in the banging action.

The races are big draws but do not make money, since many of the thousands in attendance sneak into the surrounding field without paying. When France starts copromoting at the course in 1938, his wife Anne devises a simple solution. At various points throughout the brush, signs are placed that read, "Warning: Rattlesnakes."

In the years after World War II, and the Great Depression that preceded it, America returns to a state of normalcy and the tentative sense of relief that comes from having some pocket money. After spending years helping to support the war effort, Detroit begins manufacturing new cars again in 1946. The renewed public confidence helps to firm up a grand dream in Bill France's head. To him, stock car racing is a diamond in the rough, with a growing fan base. What better way to lure more spectators than to hold races for cars that are "strictly stock," so that they match the models coming out of factories in Detroit? This way, a man can buy a new car and run it to glory himself on any given Sunday. Isn't this the American way? And if a Ford wins Sunday's race, won't that help sway Monday's prospective consumer to buy Ford?

But France doesn't count on one thing: At the races in the mid-1940s, cars are likely to be roughed up in frequent crashes. A battle-weary America is not yet ready to plunk down newly minted bills to watch brand new cars that might end up looking like junk.

France devises and promotes the National Championship Stock Car Circuit (NCSCC), which, in 1947, runs some forty modified events, mostly in the deep south. Bob Flock's younger brother Fonty starts twenty-four of the races, wins seven and walks away with the NCSCC title. Fonty is Bob's polar opposite with his jutting chin, pencil mustache, bright smile and endless mass of teeth. He also forgoes the standard overall racing suit, and frequently drives in wild print shirts and Bermuda shorts. Fonty's championship is a popular feat, considering he had spent the war years recovering from a crushed chest, broken pelvis and head and back injuries suffered in a 1941 track crash.

The Flocks, Buddy Shuman, and the couple hundred other drivers in the region's stellar home-grown talent pool help keep France wedded to another long-range idea—a racing body to govern the uncontrolled sport, with growth spurred on by star drivers. But he has a big hurdle. Stock car racing track owners, promoters, drivers and mechanics—there is no end to the level of self-interest in these groups. To ask them to join together in one organization under the same set of rules and expect everybody to follow them seems preposterous.

And yet on December 14, 1947, France invites representatives of each group to the Ebony Room at Daytona's Streamline Hotel and offers them his plan for the future.

"We are all interested in one thing: improving present conditions. The answer lies in our group here today to do it," he tells the 35 people assembled in the smoke-filled cocktail lounge. "Nothing stands still in this world; things get better or worse, bigger or smaller. Stock car racing has distinct possibilities for Sunday races. This would allow race-minded boys who work all week, and who don't have enough money to afford a regular racing car, to be in competition with the rich guy. They can show their stuff and maybe win something.

"We don't know how big this can all be if it's handled properly, and neither does anybody else here."

France's message is clear: the potential for the sport is enormous if it's handled properly, and that necessitates working together—and following his lead. In his hour-long welcoming speech, he is, by turns, both benevolent host and stern prophet.

His speech, and his reputation for fair play, are enough to galvanize the group. Through three days of rule-making and guideline-writing, a charter is set. Guaranteed purses are agreed upon, along with basic benefits and the beginning of a plan to deal with "after-race arguments." Organization names are tossed around until renowned mechanic Red Vogt suggests the National Association for Stock Car Auto Racing, or NASCAR. A set of governing officers is voted on, and it doesn't take long to elect the president.

On March 7, 1935, Sir Malcolm Campbell strapped himself into his sleek Rolls Royce-powered Bluebird Streamliner, which looked like an elongated version of what would one day be known as the Batmobile. He had come to the hard-packed sands of Daytona Beach attempting to become the first man to drive the measured mile at over 300 miles per hour. But wind resistance would be his undoing that day and he failed, able to get only as high as 276.82 mph. It was a fascinating run for all those in attendance, including a young Bill France.

Almost thirteen years later, on February 15, 1948, France is back at Daytona, where he witnesses a different kind of spectacle. At the first official points race in NASCAR's 1948 Championship Stock Car Racing season, the coupes are making their spirited runs around the fabled course, trying to carve a way through the turns and back onto the straightaways. The fastest anybody can travel is about half of the brave Sir Malcolm's time, so nobody poses a threat to the beach speed record.

But then, all Campbell ever did was go straight. He never tested how far the Streamliner could slide going sideways.

Curtis Turner's sideways-sliding, sand-tossing, wheel-crossing glide down the beach is like an ice dance that lasts an astonishing quarter of a mile or more. At times his car's movements are so smooth, he appears to be airborne, until his tires make a couple of quick chops on the sand that for many drivers would lead to an endless set of spins and barrel rolls. Turner, however, keeps his tires on the ground, making the recovery look so easy, it's more like a part of the show, the way a daredevil will give a false slip and then go on with impeccable, validating showmanship. And Turner continues his slide right into the turn, sometimes passing a driver or two struggling through the looser sand, and shoots on to the adjoining road where he marches down the straightaway.

"It was art," says Hank Schoolfield, a longtime promoter and journalist, of the Turner beach-course powerslide. Adds Leonard Wood who, with his brother Glen, will form the legendary Wood Brothers racing team and begin to field their first cars in 1950, "As far as controlling the car in the slide, keeping it from spinning out, holding onto it, of all the drivers I've ever known, ever heard of, ever worked with, nobody was better than him."

"There's this story of Curtis," continues Leonard Wood, "and about this guy who kept talking to Glen. This guy kept running off the end of the road and he couldn't ever make the turn back onto the beach! On the first lap of the race, he'd always run right off. He said 'Glen, what do you think I'm doing wrong?' Glen asks what he's doing and the guy says, 'Well, I follow Curtis in there, and when he lets off I hold it a little bit longer.' And Glen says, 'That's your mistake right there!'"

If Turner's slide is art, it doesn't lack for method to go along with his creative instinct. Paul Cawley remembers walking with Turner on the beach the day before a race, discussing high and low tides and the hard-packed sand. "We got out there on the sand and where the water would come up and get that sand, it was more solid than where the dry sand was," Cawley says. "So we walked the track and found out if you get over on the edge, where that water comes up and get that wet sand, you could get more speed and not get bogged down. Some of the others figured that too, but some of them would get too close to the water and hit where the water would come in. They'd hit that and go airborne into the water. But Curtis knew that and he'd get up there perfectly and he'd throw it sideways into a slide and he'd throw the sand as high as a telephone pole."

There were also practical considerations involved in the slide. "That's how Curtis slowed the car down," says famed car owner Bud Moore. "Going into the north turn, he'd start sideways way before he ever got there because back then, the brakes weren't all that good for running as fast as they'd run."

"We used to go watch him race before I started running and he was our hero back then," says Glen Wood. "He was one of the most exciting race drivers who ever lived—especially at Daytona on the sand. Anybody that ever saw him driving there remembers that."

It is particularly memorable for France, even on a day filled with stellar moments, from the first lap led by local favorite Marshall Teague, to the victory by popular star Red Byron after 150 miles of racing. But among the competitors, Turner lures the crowd with flash and expertise.

There are fifty-one more races to run in this first year, which will continue through the middle of November, and travel to tracks in Florida, Georgia, North Carolina, Virginia and Alabama, with one special expansion stop each in Dover, New Jersey and the incredible circular track in Langhorne, Pennsylvania. It is a well-organized, manageable season with guaranteed purses (and a few hundred dollars going to each winner), appearance fees and a check for $1,250 waiting at season's end for the champion.

Competing for the NASCAR racing prize are the most talented local southern stars. All three racing Flock brothers are now in competition, with youngest brother Tim having finally joined up. The boys' late father had once been a tightrope walker, oldest brother Carl a champion outboard speedboat racer, older sister Reo (named for a car make) had been a professional airplane wing walker and middle sister Ethel a stock car racer as well; any dull career choice for Tim seemed not in the cards. Along with the Flocks, Teague, Byron and Buddy Shuman, Buck Baker, Cotton Owens and Speedy Thompson are among the regulars; and a nineteen-year-old rookie named Glenn Roberts—whose nickname "Fireball" comes from the baseball heat he throws at home on the pitchers' mound—makes his first appearance. All comers going for the title are forbidden, by league rules, to run for any other series, except to race at tracks sanctioned by the league. Several other promoters have also embraced the idea of starting a stock car league and France, who flies around the south in his single-engine plane to promote the sport, has his hands full keeping his league filled with the most visible, bankable racers. He tries a number of methods to bring fans in: races with inverted starts where the winner of one race starts last in the next feature, and so forth; three races running in three different cities on the same day; and a "Southeastern Championship," where the top driver in one 10-race stretch of North Carolina tracks wins a separate title.

Turner does his sawmilling and lumbering during the week and heads out to the tracks on the weekends, occasionally taking Ann along. On the drives, the baby lays peacefully on a pillow on the ledge beneath the back window, and the race car is towed behind them.

The first half of the season is frustrating for Turner, who blows several engines and finishes out of the top tier in the majority of races. Meanwhile, a Flock brother wins fourteen of the first twenty-six races, with Fonty getting eight checkered flags on his own (including an early win at Jacksonville where, after his steering wheel breaks, he has to drive a bulk of the race turning the spokes). Turner's anger comes to a head on July 4 at Martinsville Speedway in Virginia. For several laps, Turner and Speedy Thompson engage in a spirited battle over a couple of spots in the running order, cutting each other off from one turn to the next. Finally, the two slam together and the force of the collision sends both cars flying toward the outside guardrail.

From where Ann is sitting in the stands, it is impossible to make out whether Curtis pushes Thompson or if it's the other way around. All she can see is her husband's ugly, metal-bending vault over an embankment and down a hill, with Thompson's car following.

Ann charges out of her seat, gets down the grandstand steps and breaks into a run. She is within a hundred feet when the sight of a helmet pops up over the ridge; a hand grabs hold of the ground and Curtis hoists himself up. When he is on level ground again, he circles and lets Thompson pull himself up over the embankment so the two can begin pushing each other again, swinging wildly.

Officials and a couple of fans come over to separate the pair, but even after they're seemingly calm, Turner and Thompson seek each other out and go at it again, in a battle that will go on even after the cars are towed back from beyond the embankment. "They had to get into their cars and roll up the windows to keep each other from fighting over what really happened," Ann says.

It is a rare blow-up for Turner, but it leads to a more determined, successful set of runs. He wins two weeks later at North Wilkesboro, which he quickly tells reporters is "the best among dirt tracks." The next week, at Greensboro, North Carolina, Turner wins again, but the day is marked by tragedy. Young North Carolina driver W.R. "Slick" Davis gets killed in a crash at the track. Meanwhile, France has promoted a second race that same day in Columbus, Georgia, to try to bring in more fans, but there, Red Byron blows a tire, pounds through a wooden retaining wall and slices into the crowd. Sixteen fans are injured and a seven-year-old boy is killed.

It is a horrific blow for France, and leads to greater safety discussions, but the tour continues, and Turner wins the next week in Lexington, North Carolina. After a two-week pause due to a polio outbreak, France's title-within-a-title Southestern Championship run begins. The timing is perfect for Turner, and the tracks are especially good to him; he wins four of the ten races (including two more at North Wilkesboro) on the way to the championship. Afterwards, thinking back to July 4 and Thompson, he credits his trophy win to keeping the car upright and on track.

"I haven't been through a fence in awhile," he tells a gathering of local writers with a smile, at a little party afterwards. "In fact, the last wreck I had was when I went over a bank at [a sanctioned Modified race] at Hendersonville Raceway a few weeks ago."

Get Turner one on one with a microphone in front of him, and ask him about the day's race, and most of the time you'll get a few sentences and very little meat on the bone. But Turner is clearly at ease with the few newspaper writers and radio reporters who, responding to France's promotional legwork, begin covering the sport, and don't mind sitting back with a drink to hear a story or two when the running is over. In a race car, he is fully at ease with himself and his talent and abilities. But in the infield, he is sometimes at pains to describe it, especially among people he doesn't know very well.

"He did not enjoy the media part of it in a formal atmosphere," says Bob Moore. "His whole personality would revert to this shy individual, which no one believes: 'This can't be Curtis Turner because Curtis Turner is not a shy individual.' But under those conditions, that's what he became."

Recalls Ann, "He didn't say anything unless he had something to say."

And that usually happens when he's given a chance, in much more relaxed situations, to wax about what can sometimes happen behind the wheel. Articles rarely go beyond a brief summary of the action, but when the occasional longer piece gives him a chance to weigh in on something more vital, he frequently does so with disarming humor. Asked about the relative level of safety in stock car racing, Turner tells a newspaperman, "I've never turned a car over on a racetrack in my years of driving. But I have turned over about fifteen cars on the highways."

By year's end, Turner has posted seven victories on the way to a fourth-place NASCAR Modified title finish behind champion Red Byron, Fonty Flock and Tim Flock.

By all accounts—starting, literally, with gate receipts, and the crowds at races that have grown from an average of several hundred to several thousand—France's first NASCAR year is a major hit. At the same time, business is booming; Americans are embracing a much rosier outlook in the wake of fifteen years of economic and international uncertainty. Regardless of overseas concerns, domestic recovery is in full swing. And new cars are being purchased faster than they're manufactured. In 1946, the first full year after the war, U.S. auto factories sold 2.1 million units, less than half the all-time high of 4.6 million in 1929, on the eve of the Depression. Only two years later, in 1948, consumers bought nearly 4 million units; in 1950, the annual number will beat five million for the first time, topping off at 5.1.

Bill France is convinced that Americans are now ready to see what some of those new cars will look like coursing around dirt tracks.

On April 11, 1949, Bill France, standing at a microphone in the late-day sun, has brought the few thousand faithful at the Greensboro Fairgrounds track to their feet. They've just seen a fine Modified race with a popular, dominating performance, but as France pops open a bottle of champagne, there's more to celebrate.

"I'd like you to join me in wishing a happy twenty-fifth birthday to today's winner, Virginia's own Curtis Turner," he shouts.

Turner removes his arm from around the shoulder of a local beauty queen, puts his trophy down and accepts the drink France has just poured for his young friend. As the pair shake hands, and lift their arms in the air like a ref and a tired ring champion, the crowd breaks into a disjointed, laugh-filled "Happy Birthday." For France, it is a perfect day, a celebration of all that is rugged and appealing about stock car racing. Turner, knowing the bubbly would taste better in victory circle—and look better for the fans—has put on a show. France had gone to the trouble of making this nice little party, and Turner hadn't planned on letting him down.

France is fifteen years older than Turner, but you wouldn't think so to look at the ease with which they regard the other. At well over six feet, with a tendency to enjoy a hearty laugh when they're together, the pair might even pass for close siblings.

They've been spending a great deal of time together since their meeting the season before. Turner knows enough about business to have a keen understanding of France's master plan, and can see the advantage of being a big part of it. And the fan reaction to Turner's dazzling slides is hardly lost on France.

But there is also a friendly competition between France, the former racer, and Turner, himself a successsful businessman. There is a part of each that yearns to do what the other does, and do it better, but it is not in either's DNA to switch. Instead, they get vicarious thrills out of watching the other ply his trade. By hanging around with Turner, the freewheeling, freespirited racer, France can let down his guard, and enjoy the camaraderie he once reveled in before promotion and marketing became his prime concerns. And there's something about being with France, who flies around the country in a single-engine plane to promote races, and has his way with track owners, that gives Turner an idea of how big his own dreams can get. The pair begin promoting races together at some Virginia tracks, and the Frances and Turners become frequent dinner companions.

"Bill France would come to Roanoke and stay at our house," remembers Ann Turner. "Maybe they'd have a race at Victory Stadium, or at Starkey. Bill France loved to cook. He'd get in the pots and pans and start cooking—and this is after we got home at one o'clock in the morning.

"My job during the race was to go around to where they were selling tickets and bring the money in to Anne France. She counted the tickets and the money. Both families were promoting the races together. The city police started, voluntarily, taking care of me, because I was riding around with all these bags of money to take them to the office. And then the next day, Curtis and Bill would count the money and take it to the bank.

"Bill France liked Curtis—he kinda took him under his wing."

With their friendship and partnership, Turner becomes one of France's main attractions luring fans to the Charlotte Speedway on June 19, 1949 for NASCAR's first-ever Strictly Stock race. France plans to use all the resources and drivers available to him, since the competition for stock car supremacy isn't only taking place on the red clay. There are at least four other sanctioning bodies running races at local tracks, with each planning to crown the official national champion. Chief among the leagues is the National Stock Car Racing Association (NSCRA), run by a stocky, energetic young promoter named Olin Bruton Smith. France needs his "Strictly Stock" brainstorm to separate him from Smith and all other comers.

The field for the Charlotte race is filled with fan favorites. All three Flock brothers make the field; Sara Christian, called "the leading woman Stock Car Driver in the country" in early NASCAR press releases, is the only woman to run. Byron, Baker and Olivia, North Carolina tobacco farmer-turned-racer Herb Thomas are in. Lee Petty, a delivery driver for a bakery, steers his new Buick Roadmaster over from Randleman, North Carolina. Jim Roper shows up after reading about the race in his local newspaper, although not in an ad or an article. A mention had appeared in the comic strip "Smilin' Jack," written by cartoonist and racing fan Zack Mosley.

But the real stars will be the cars, new and gleaming models, from the 1946 Buick Roadmaster Turner uses to qualify sixth, to the Novelty '49 Olds

88 Byron rides for master car owner Raymond Parks, which starts third. "Guys just showed up in the same cars their families went grocery shopping in," says Bob Moore, whose father, a Dayton Ohio racer, saw an ad for the race in *National Speed Sport News* and, along with his two brothers, got into a car and drove nonstop to Charlotte to witness the event. France has taken no chances on this one, buying lots of ads, flying his plane, and drumming up support for what will either be the start of something huge, or a bust.

France gets his answer when spectators begin to show up at around six A.M. on the morning of the nineteenth. The single-lane road leading to the Speedway has never known gridlock before, and the police, not expecting a crowd of more than a few thousand, have no real game plan. Some fans, tired of the wait on the road, will park four miles away and make the long trek on this bright Sunday, looking forward with great curiosity to the sight of brand new cars slamming into each other. Crowd estimates will range as high as 22,500. France will later lay claim to a healthy paying attendance of 13,000.

The day is like a carnival. Car numbers are crudely painted on the doors of the smart, pristine models. There are no elaborate paint schemes or sponsorship logos—most cars are simply black. Masking tape covers the headlights, the bumpers, front ends—all meant to protect the cars from sustaining too much damage. But given the bumps the autos will navigate through, the elaborate taping is like putting on boxing gloves and thinking your punches won't draw blood.

Seat belts are exercises in creativity. Some drivers use their regular leather waist belts to tie them to the doors. Others use those belts around the front and rear doors on the drivers' side, to keep them from spilling out in a wreck. One driver uses a popular method of sitting in a rubber inner tube, which he then ties by his belt to the door.

Turner's huge, blocky "41" takes up the entire side door of his Roadmaster. For pit crew, he brings only Cawley along. "We took the car down and all we did was tape up the headlights, take the rear seat, spare tire and jack out of it and brought all the tires we could get. He wore all the tires out that day, and I haven't wanted to change a tire since."

The cars represent a cross-section of U.S. auto manufacturing: Lincoln, Hudson, Ford, Olds, Cadillac, Buick, Chrysler, Kaiser and Mercury are all among the field of thirty-three cars on the three-quarter-mile dirt track, with the winning driver taking home $2,000 of the $5,000 purse. Rounding the track for the last of three pace laps, with the crowd's buzz growing louder by the second, Turner can hear the snarling engines, and the tires crunching over the gravel and the dusty red earth. The starter is poised to wave the green flag in the near distance, and Turner and the field prepare to take off, with no inkling that they are at the official start of a new American sport. To Turner, it is just another Sunday afternoon, and a chance to drive around, over, through or past whoever gets in his way.

The cars roar out from the start and the field is immediately enveloped by huge clouds of dirt rustled up from below, like a western posse leaving a dust trail in its wake. Turner quickly chokes out a cough as the brown air flies through his open side window while he slides into the first turn. Pole-sitter Bob Flock, taking advantage of the rare visibility, runs up front.

New cars, not quite used to this punishment, bop and vault over the unpredictable, rut-filled track. When the fans, soon covered in dust and dirt, don't see the action, they hear it, as tires screech, radiators explode in geysers of steaming water and fenders tap in rather ungentlemanly displays of competition. Getting the worst of it all is Petty, the day's only real casualty, who loses control in turn three near the middle of the race, and begins a tumbling barrel roll that seems to go on forever. The startled deliveryman grips the wheel and is again shocked when the car stops its rolls by ending up back on its four wheels. The car is in shambles, and Petty leaves his cockpit, sits down with a sigh and wonders how he'll tell his unsuspecting wife about what happened to the family car.

For Turner, the day is an exercise in survival. He remains near the front of the field without a strong enough car to lead. Bob Flock leaves the race early on with an oil leak, and before long, he is joined by more than a third of the field, many of whom are nursing overheated engines. Flock takes over driving duties from Christian, who has retired early from the punishing run.

The field decreases every few laps with another blown engine until Glenn Dunnaway inherits the lead with fifty laps to go. Dunnaway, piloting moonshiner Hubert Westmoreland's 1947 Ford, continues making his turns and shows no signs of letting go, and after two hundred laps, he takes the checkered flag, running a full three laps ahead of runner-up Jim Roper. Turner finishes the day ninth.

The success of the run and the goodwill of even the most dust-soiled fans makes the day a winner for France. And the use of the new cars lends a bit of camaraderie to the procedings. Seeing Lee Petty's dilemma, several drivers join in to help fix the car after the race; fans even offer to lend parts of their own home autos for the repair.

But as monumental a triumph as the race is, it can never match the victory Bill France gains in the days that follow.

NASCAR officials, curious about the ease with which Dunnaway's car navigated the track's bumpier sections, inspect the Ford after the race and discover that the rear springs have been altered. It is actually a moonshining car, with a wedge placed in the springs meant to balance the huge loads of whiskey normally packed in the trunk. The wedge is a modification not permitted in the new NASCAR strictly stock rulebook.

Dunnaway is immediately disqualified and Jim Roper earns $2,000 for being both a fine driver and a faithful reader of "Smilin' Jack." But Westmoreland, Dunnaway's car owner, will not let the matter stand. He angrily sues NASCAR for $10,000 in damages.

The evidence is presented to the Greensboro, North Carolina, court, and France offers a compelling argument. Here he is, trying to bring some legitimacy to stock car racing. Rules are rules, and the premier league he hopes to create is no place for cars used in illegal activities, he tells Judge John J. Hayes. To believe otherwise seems, frankly, unAmerican.

Judge Hayes tosses Westmoreland's case out of court, and by doing so, sends an incontrovertible message: Bill France has the power to legislate what is right and wrong in the world of NASCAR. After one race of France's grand experiment, he has drawn a thick line between racing's past and future. Getting around that line will be a never-ending creative challenge for mechanics and engineers in the years to come, and many racers will challenge France's edicts, but it is made clear from day one who runs the show. According to the courts, Bill France is the law.

Paul Cawley leans against his car and takes a terse glance at his watch. Dusk settles over Virginia, and he kicks the gravel at his feet. A door opens in the near distance and Cawley hears some giggles and a low voice talking. He looks down as the door closes and the shuffle of someone walking with an easy gate over the dirt driveway gets louder. When Cawley looks up, Curtis Turner has already emerged from beyond the outside of another house of another woman, rubbing the side of his nose to hide the smile on his face. The friends enter the car together without a word and head for home.

In mid-1949, the NASCAR Strictly Stock division is underway. Throughout the south, Modified races go on weekly. Different tracks sponsor annual championships for local drivers as well. Traveling from track to track, Turner is an attraction, guaranteeing a good time for all during a race and after, and reveling in the attention. The scene quickly becomes difficult for Ann Turner to keep up with, given her young child and the late hours. She frequently elects to stay home for the races, leaving Turner to bask in the spotlight on his own, where he is quite comfortable.

"For a year or two after he moved down here, Curtis was pretty much a family man, but as he got involved in the racing and got popular, why, the ladies and girls—I guess it just overpowered him," says Cawley. "In those days Curtis was kinda like somebody from outer space. He was so popular, he could race, drive, do anything, and was just unusual from anybody else. He was such a good driver, and his personality—anything he went after he was successful at it. He was really confident. He was friendly with everybody, he got to be known and people would come from far and near to see him and talk with him.

"Ann was one wonderful woman. You can't imagine marrying a better lady, I don't guess. But she didn't have a chance, given how popular he was and all the ladies wanting to get him in trouble. It was every week, and everywhere. He got popular with all the woman—married, single, all of that. Ann didn't hardly go to these races and it was Curtis running wild. And Ann was at home tending to that one daughter. She had a car and that little girl. That was their life."

Turner feeds off the attention and admiration, and his increasing savvy and nerves on the track frequently leave fans amazed. "I boggled at what he could do with a car," says Ned Jarrett, the future champion driver, who attended the first strictly stock race and was nearly speared by a flying fender for his troubles. "His talent as a race driver and the fact that he could drive so hard and still maintain control was something I had personally not seen a lot of, although there were some great drivers back in that era. But he set himself apart."

Fans at Winston-Salem's Bowman Gray Stadium and on the beach at Daytona wait for Turner's power slides at the turns. In one particular run on the beach, he weaves his car between two competitors while still sideways, and passes two more cars the instant he begins racing forward again.

"He loved to put on a show," recalls Glen Wood. "I guarantee you, if he was running twenty laps down, and he could figure a way to gain two feet on his last lap, he'd do it. That's how competitive he was. He wanted to go as fast as he could go no matter what."

This makes Turner a pre-race favorite in every contest of the 1949 Strictly Stock season. It also earns him the wrath of competitors who've seen what happens when they get in his way. At a Modified race at Virginia's Martinsville Speedway, Turner and Fonty Flock enter a turn going for the same patch of dirt, and are soon slamming and pressed side by side. With their wheels locked, neither man can stop the momentum that carries them in a screaming slide toward the planks of the track's board fence. Through the wood they go and finally tumble over a bank. Turner, steamed at the result, gets out of his car and heads back toward the pits, with the chin strap hanging off his helmet. Talking to some friends about the crash, he suddenly notices their eyes grow wide, but he never notices the normally unflappable Flock coming toward him with a tire iron.

"Back in the early races, they didn't have racing helmets; they had football helmets," remembers Paul Cawley. "Curtis is standing there with his helmet on and Fonty came down there and all at once, 'Bam!'—he hit Curtis over the head with the tire iron, and busted up his football helmet. And Curtis just shook his head—and that Fonty could *run*. Curtis turned around and I could see Fonty Flock going up through the track. He was gonna knock him out but he just made him mad. Curtis didn't get hurt, he just lit out after Fonty but Fonty got a running start. I'm telling you, that was the life."

Winners' shares during the first Strictly Stock season average out to $2,000; a tenth-place finisher might get $50 or $100. It is often less at the Modifieds. Pride remains the only thing of value at stake from one race day to the next. In the eight-race season of Bill France's biggest attraction, he starts six times and wins once. His victory comes at Pennsylvania's Langhorne Speedway, a perilous track considered by many to be the most challenging in the sport because, being nearly circular, it forces drivers to spend the majority of the race in a long, dizzying turn. In front of 20,000 spectators, the largest crowd to see a 1949 NASCAR race, Turner tops the field of forty-nine drivers. He is joined in victory lane by Sara Christian. The sport's leading female driver finishes sixth in a stellar performance on the brutal track, and the pair are given the royal treatment for the day by the fans.

Engine trouble sidelines Turner in a couple of strictly stock events and he ends the year in sixth place, earning $2,675; series winner Red Byron takes home $5,800.

During the 1950 season, France, acknowledging that "strictly stock" is too dry and technical a phrase, makes a change. From now on, the new cars will compete in NASCAR's Grand National Division, a designation with much more pizzazz.

The racing, however, is still unpredictable and, at times, brutal. And attendance at the larger events is starting to hit 20,000 routinely. Some two or three years after a promoter might be able to count on only a couple of hundred fans. France and Turner continue to promote races at Victory Stadium and discuss plans for the sport's future.

But there is a one month break in the Grand National schedule between Langhorne and the next race at Martinsville. And France and Turner have a good idea for a little racing diversion.

Curtis Turner stands with his hands at his waist, watching Bill France change yet another tire. The Mexican sun seems to pierce him right through the back of his white button-down shirt, which is lined with a pattern of beads one might find on a sombrero. The two friends are silent, huffing quietly. Turner looks over the five-passenger, six-cylinder Nash sedan the pair are driving through the rough, mountainous terrain from El Paso, Texas, to Guatemala. The car is long and broad with an elongated nose and an odd, lengthy slope from the roof to the back fender. It looks like an enormous upside-down bathtub. Inside the car are loads of provisions: cans of franks and beans, bottles of water, a 25-gallon jug with extra gasoline and tires and more tires, with still more tires in the trunk. France and Turner have recently departed Mexico City, where they had the honor of meeting the president of Mexico. When they returned to the Nash, Turner is not especially surprised to find he has been relieved of his wallet.

The Carrera Pan Americana, also known as the Mexican Road Race, is run for the first time in May, 1950. It is organized as part of a celebration: The Mexicali section of the Pan American Highway has just been completed, and the race is to coincide with Cinco de Mayo. But while the handfuls of Mexicans who line streets in the more populated areas drink and cheer for the cars, the Road Race is, for the most part, a grueling event, winding its way on a 2,178-mile course filled with twisting gravel turns and sudden cliffs. The altitude shifts range from sea level to 11,000 feet above, and the heights send competitors onto the craggiest of mountain roads. It is a road racer's great dream and worst nightmare. The competitors who come to the six-day event with experience at the 24 Hours of Le Mans agree that in terms of toughness, that classic course cannot touch the madness of the Mexican route.

The Nash can't exactly be called the pride of the field. Italian stars Piero Taruffi and Felice Bonetto are in much sleeker, more powerful, better handling Alfa Romeos, and there are Cadillacs, Olds 88s and a Delahaye. The foreign cars, with their big brakes and design more suitable to richer pursuits such as the Monte Carlo Rally, are heavily favored. But the Nash came cheap: a dealer lent it to France for use in the race in exchange for some publicity. Among the 132 cars that start, there are millionaire playboys, journeymen, all-women teams, and even a lady from Texas whose sponsor for the race—"Hi-A Brassieres by Marja"—has its logo written in huge letters on both sides of the car. In the event's rules, two racers share each car and switch off driving duties on a daily basis. France and Turner have spent months looking forward to the challenges of the course, and the enjoyment of a week together alone and away from family and NASCAR distractions. Though they had done some practice runs north of El Paso after flying in on France's plane, they started the race having never once set foot on the actual course. But a first-place pot of $6,000 makes one overlook such details.

In ensuing years, the Carrera Pan Americana will be a much more organized, highly attended event. In this first year, the kinks have yet to be worked out. In the first three days of stages, France and Turner grapple with some hard facts. There is almost nowhere to stop and get gas, and no service vehicles to help out if you need to. As the days go on, the course, which winds its way through mountains, desert and coastline, eats up competitors. If the rough roads don't get you, sometimes Montezuma's Revenge will.

But Turner and France set a blistering pace, all things considered, going better than 95 miles per hour through 712 miles in the first two days, which includes time spent fixing the engine. By the halfway point, the pair are in third place.

France finishes fixing the tire midway through the fourth day and they

resume the trek, with Turner driving. The arrangement is sometimes prob-
lematic for France. It is hard enough being the passenger in a racing car;
all he can do is sit, pray and keep his feet pressed to the imaginary pedals
on the floor. With Turner driving, passenger fears take on another dimen-
sion. Huge bumps in the road are ordinary to him; hairpin turns do not
cause the slightest shift in his impassive, mildly sour-looking expression.

The night before, the pair took apart the engine to make sure it was in
good running order. But here, on these hot mountain roads, the friends are
facing a familiar dilemma. When the car hits 100, even 120 mph, the tires
heat up and the brakes give out. The Nash is screaming down the mountain once again with no traditional way to stop.

France tenses his arms, going over scenarios in his mind. There are no
shoulder harnesses in the car, only seat belts. France had devised a plan
in the early going: If either of them started to lose control of the car and
it began to roll, they would immediately try to grab one another's arms in
a pretzel grip to keep both of them from falling out through the windows.
It must have seemed like a good idea at the time.

Turner downshifts, going as low as second gear. The Nash jerks madly
but there are only so many ways to slow things down.

Back on level road for a moment, Turner sees a Mexican boy from a
nearby mountain village waving in their direction, and he downshifts further to stop. In broken English, the boy tells them that right past the next
turn, the road comes to a series of esses, and on one of them, two men just
drove their car straight off the road and into a canyon some five hundred
feet below. Turner thanks the boy and promises to be careful. France
stares wide-eyed into the distance saying nothing. It will be at least a day
before authorities will get to the tangled, fatal wreck using the only
method possible: a helicopter.

France tries to make small talk, when what he really wants to do is
remind Turner about the arm grip plan. Turner, his gaze fixed on the road,
remains quiet. The Nash is back on the descent, picking up speed, going
better than seventy miles per hour again, rolling through different stages
of esses. Turner taps his brakes to make sure they haven't overheated
again. He downshifts again anyway, trying to keep his grip.

But the one turn Turner and France come upon suddenly is a killer:
it's nearly ninety degrees with no room to spare beyond the sheer dropoff
in the distance.

Turner slams on the brakes and throws the car into a broadside, heading to the right. The Nash spins around, treading backwards, with the passenger side heading toward the precipice.

The tires rub against the rocky edge and when one falls and hangs over the cliff, Turner slams the brakes again and turns the wheel, trying to hug the car against the cliffside. The tires spin and dirt flies but in a moment, the Nash comes to a quick halt, with three tires still on level ground.

Turner, a menacing, determined look on his face, surveys the predicament, but France takes one glance out the window at what might have been his destiny and has seen enough. Gripping hard, he yanks onto his friend, pulls his six-foot-plus frame up and claws past Turner and out of the car, rolling with a thud on the dirt road.

With the sudden drop in weight on that side, Turner gingerly puts on the gas and drives the car back onto the road. He shakes his head a moment, trying to rub the sting of fear out of his arms. France stares at him, looking angry enough to dismantle the Nash, and Turner in it, with his bare hands.

"I have a wife and kids at home," he yells. "And I'd like to *see* them again!"

France paces around the narrow patch of road as Turner tries to calm him down, wondering aloud what else he could have done. France looks down the road, which curves along the mountain like swirls on a barber shop pole, and considers which might be the safer route back to civilization. Turner is promising to be more careful, even if he's not sure there's a way to take any more care. At least, he points out, they didn't get killed.

France stands, looking skyward. He wishes Turner would just be quiet while he collects himself. In a moment, he spins and climbs back into the passenger seat. Turner shifts into gear and starts a somewhat slower descent as France stares off into some far distance. "You can go off these mountain roads," he says, "and nobody would *ever* find you."

It is hard to gain any kind of momentum on a long road race when your tires keep blowing or going flat. Turner, trying to be useful, hands jack tools to France like a nurse in an operating room. At first, they'd look up when yet another car passed them, putting them further back in the standings on this fifth, and second-to-last day. Now, with their route mercifully almost over, they don't even take their eyes off the bolts when a Lincoln blows air and fumes as it whips past them.

The pair has already fallen from third place to somewhere outside the top ten, and the ill-handling Nash is smarting from the 2,000 or so miles of effort, from an overheating engine and brake failure.

But France is behind the wheel, and he's frustrated. To be the pilot on so abysmal a day is galling, and he's doing anything he can think of to make up the time as the competitors stampede toward Tuxtla Gutierrez.

And at one turn, he decides, without warning, to keep the car straight and hop a shortcut over a stretch of grass. Turner, looking tired and impassive in the front seat, turns his head slowly to look over at France, as the car bumps and bops both men in the Nash's cab.

France begins wondering if this maneuver is even worth it, when his left front wheel slips into an unseen bump, jerking the car swiftly. France hears an ominous "ping," and steam makes a slender but mad passage through a hole in the radiator.

The Nash limps the rest of the way into town, and when the final tally is listed, France and Turner find they've dropped all the way down to twentieth place.

The radiator adds insult to injury but, as Turner will later tell the Roanoke *World-News*, "We wore out fourteen tires and had three blowouts on the trip," and much of this damage occurs on day five.

Turner is restless the night before the final leg of the race, until he and France meet up with a fellow Nash driver, the Corsicana, Texas, auto dealer Roy Pat Connor. Connor's car is in sixth place, thirty-three minutes behind the leader. He's had no trouble to speak of during the event, but no real enjoyment from the ride either. He makes a great complaint about everything he's been through, from the heat to the desolation, and he tells the pair that he's ready to hang it up. Turner lends a sympathetic ear, and while he does so, listening to Connor vent, he glances over at France. His friend looks tired, and hearing Connor's points is making things worse. But there is an oddly playful look in Turner's eyes. It takes France a moment, but when he does finally catch on, he nods once and a look of relief comes over his face. For the first time in days, France permits himself a laugh.

France and Turner; and Connor, his co-owner Robert Green and co-driver Robert Owens spend the night preparing Connor's Nash, checking the engine and storing all the remaining good tires for the final day's run. Turner will drive and Owens will go along for the ride. And hopefully nobody will catch on to the deception.

The final run is a 160-mile trek through desert and twisting dirt and gravel mountain roads from Tuxtla Gutierrez to El Ocotal, a jungle town on the Guatemalan border. The final day promises to be particularly challenging. Cars will start once every four minutes, since road conditions are not suitable for side-by-side driving.

Turner bids France goodbye, and whatever bitterness there has been due to their circumstances disappears. Both men have gotten what they wanted out of this. For France, it has been an experience, one he survived, and now he can make lots of hay out of it with the folks at Nash. For Turner, there is a chance at one last thrill. He's been given a gift of sorts, a fine working car and a possibility—wildly improbable though it may be—to compete for a win.

What Turner does with his opportunity will be the stuff of dreams. It is a performance upon which reputations are built and legends are fed. But first, it will turn him into Robert Owens' worst nightmare.

After points and times are reviewed, Turner and Owens start the final stretch in eighth place, beginning their run twenty-eight minutes after the leader on the last day of the first Carrera Pan Americana, and head toward the mountains. Owens has become used to his and Connor's pace, and their careful navigating through the course that has kept them in the running. He looks over at Turner, who is mashing the gas without pause and staring ahead with a somewhat unpleasant look on his face.

The expression hardly changes when a flying rock zings against the wheel, snapping a brake line. A bolt has also broken in the clutch. No brakes, and a poorly working clutch, and they are in the mountains, climbing and then swerving around curves.

They are doing ninety down a long road and another curve lays ahead. Turner has learned his lesson from his and France's big near miss: He hugs the road to the right and lets his two right wheels drop off the road, and as the chassis drags along the ground, slowing the Nash down, he powers through the turn and regains his speed.

Up ahead, the seventh-place car is sneaking and disappearing around turns in the distance. Owens rises up in his seat, gripping the door and pressing his feet hard to the floor.

"You're going fast," he observes, the words barely audible from his throat.

There is a straight, flat stretch and Turner stares out at the car ahead of him, getting the Nash up over a hundred miles per hour, concentrating so hard on reeling the car in that he doesn't notice the bump in the road until he's practically upon it.

Turner and Owens are instantly thrown airborne. The Nash comes down hard on its front wheels but when the bumper slams against the ground, the impact tosses the car back onto all four tires, and it rolls for a moment as Turner listens to the sound of the engine over the odd, guttural noises coming from Owens. He had been quiet during the broad jump; it is only when Turner spirits away again, acting as if nothing has just happened, that Owens finally shouts.

Regardless of Owens' imploring cries for him to slow down, Turner feels calm and renewed. On the day after the worst luck ruined his shot, he has nothing at all to lose. He passes one car, and a foreign car quickly comes into view. Passing the second car coming off another mountain turn, he keeps shifting or bottoming out only when necessary. Even if he doesn't know these roads, he knows the *kind* of roads they are.

A Ferrari is next in his sights, and as it moves somewhat cautiously through a few esses, Turner is on its back bumper quickly. And yet the driver crowds him, refusing to give way, as if enacting some refined code of road race ethics in the middle of desolation. Turner honks; the Ferrari snootily remains in his way. He honks a second time, a long, blaring bugle blow; the Ferrari driver acts like he has ear plugs.

Turner slams his borrowed Nash's long, wide nose into the back of the Ferrari, at a hundred miles per hour, bumping him forward with a jump. The reaction doesn't come fast enough and he delivers another tap, as the Ferrari veers over in a skid, letting Turner fly by. Owens, in his great alarm, finally notices the hint of a smile crossing Turner's lips. Owens hears a faint whirring noise out the window and looks up. The event's official Mexican observation plane is high above, following the Nash. The pilot has circled back from the leader to follow Curtis Turner's climb through the ranks.

Piero Taruffi in his stylish and powerful Alfa Romeo has himself moved up from second to take the lead, but Turner gains sight of him on another long stretch after about 130 miles. Taruffi will be the hardest to pass, and for miles the two cars mirror each other's velocity, with Turner barely inching closer. It will take another fifteen miles until the pair are side by side, and then with a burst, Turner's Nash powers into the lead, and when he gets around the gentlemanly Taruffi, he sees only daylight. He has made up an astonishing twenty-eight minutes in less than 150 miles of driving.

The field leaves the mountain roads and heads for the Guatemalan border as something warm courses through Turner's nervous system. There are ten miles to go before he can claim an outrageous victory.

And with those ten miles remaining, Turner hears a pop and feels an ugly thump as one of his tires begins to shred and wind its way around the wheel, grinding down to the brake drum like a piece of lumber being cut into sawdust. Going better than a hundred miles per hour, Turner discovers the one surefire way to bring the car to a complete stop.

Turner and Owens get out quickly and change the tire. There isn't any great damage to the wheel, but the car won't start without the clutch working. Taruffi passes the Nash, then a second car passes him, and a third. Precious minutes pass and Turner keeps trying to turn the engine over as Owens explores the view under the hood. The task seems to take forever but the engine finally roars back to life and Owens, finally feeling he has contributed something, straps in and is ready for one last push to the finish.

The Nash is underpowered compared to the Olds, the Cadillac and Taruffi's Alfa Romeo up ahead, and there is only so much one can do in ten miles of driving. But after eight miles, Turner has only Taruffi in the distance. Yet that distance is not enough. As scores of Mexican fans stand screaming over the final half mile, no effort of Turner's will change the final outcome, and he watches Taruffi take the victory in the final stage.

But when he and Owens pull in past the Guatemalan finish line, the cheers for Turner reach an extraordinary roar. News of his incredible run has been radioed in and when all the addition is done, the numbers are astounding. Though he "lost" to Tarrufi, Turner has beaten the Italian in elapsed time of the route by an outrageous three minutes and twenty-five seconds. It is the kind of superhuman triumph that makes any outsider instantly question its validity. But those who have seen it react much the way spectators will ten years later, when they watch Bob Hayes run the final leg of the 4x100 meters in the Rome Olympics and cover the distance in a time that would have obliterated the world record. Writing about the event, one automotive historian will eventually observe that "Curtis Turner later became a legend in the wild southeastern world of stock car driving, but it is doubtful if he, or anyone else, ever put on a greater performance behind the wheel of an automobile."

Not surprisingly, Turner's run is a little *too* good. He is, of course, not Roy Pat Connor, and having driven Connor's car illegally, is disqualified from earning the cumulative third-place money the car would have won. But Turner does get a first-place share for winning the final leg. He has, in six days, lost much of his energy and about eleven pounds.

Long after the shouts fade, the record books will show that in the first Mexican Road Race, there were 132 cars starting with fifty-two making it to the finish, and six drivers getting killed in the process. Turner, gleefully enamored of the short-term love of the crowd, ultimately couldn't care less that his and France's Nash finished out of the money. The moment, the here and now, is all that matters.

When he returns home, France and Nash present Turner with a trophy to mark his efforts—it's of a miniature car on a marble pedestal.

"The Nash folks want me to enter the race again next year and I guess I'll do it," Turner tells a reporter, "but I've seen about enough of that rough life for awhile."

He returns to the NASCAR tour for the next Grand National race, at Martinsville, Virginia. Compared to the grueling spectacle of Mexico, Martinsville feels like home. The race is 150 laps on the half-mile dirt course and, after taking the lead from Buck Baker on lap ten, Turner, in his Eanes Motors Olds 88, leads the rest of the way. A week and a half after his magnificent run in Mexico, he becomes the first driver in the short history of NASCAR's elite division to win two races in a row, and for the moment, he sits atop the standings. But that's not what matters most. It's the $1,000 winner's share that will soon be spent on drinks for his buddies. It's the checkered flag, and the celebration that follows. And it's the trophy raised in one hand, and the kiss from the track's beauty queen, as the cheers rain down.

Chapter Four
1950-1953
"There's some damn fine timber down there."

You can tell Bobby Myers is angry by the speed at which his Late Model Sportsman car bounds into the infield at the cramped one-third-mile track. The fenders and body are twisted and bent; it's the metal equivalent of a black eye and a fat lip. A couple of crew guys have to dart out of the way as he skids over the grass and screeches to a stop. Myers can be a scary guy when he's *calm*. When he's angry, it's Richter Scale angry.

Everything is suddenly a little too quiet as drivers strain to hear the muted sound of Myers cursing inside the cab. When he comes out and slams the door, he disappears for a moment and then reemerges, holding a heavy tire iron grabbed from his tool chest. He rushes off with great purpose, his free hand balled into a fist.

"Bobby," one racer calls out; a few others start to chuckle. A trail of drivers begins to follow Myers as he stomps through the infield. Everyone knows where he is headed: He's off to rearrange the brain matter of Curtis Turner.

There are lots of guys who believe Turner deserves what's coming to him: He's somehow planted Myers into a wall again after several miles of the pair beating and banging each other. Then again, if you asked any of those guys to name who started the maddening confrontation between Turner and the Myers brothers, they'd be hard-pressed to come up with a first incident. Turner has knocked both Bobby and Billy Myers out of races and through guardrails, and they've each returned the favor.

But everybody agrees on where most of the action has taken place: Bowman Gray Stadium, a half-mile asphalt track in Winston Salem, North Carolina. Thanks to Winston Salem's location in the heart of North Carolina, and the enormous challenge of trying to best competitors on

Bowman Gray's flat half-mile track with no banking, weekly Saturday night races became enormously popular there almost from opening day in 1949. From 1950 through 1953, Turner and the Myers' each won several feature races and at least one track championship, driving Late Model Sportsman cars, which are smaller than strictly stock and not as haphazardly built as modifieds. But in those years, it was Turner whom the fans overwhelmingly voted for Most Popular Driver. In 1953, he won that title for the second year in a row, in a two-to-one margin over Billy Myers, 9,880 votes to 4,555. The competition between the trio is always spirited and frequently galling to at least one of them at any time. "The Myers boys could go gang up on Curtis and they'd put him in the middle—you know, like putting the squeeze on him," recalls one-time local racer Eddie Bennington. "And when they got almost to him they'd spread out, take it right to the end where you go wrecking it and turn it loose. So one time Curtis, before they get there, he put the brakes on and both of them went on to hit each other. And Curtis won the race."

"We were at Bowman Gray one time," says Glen Wood, a frequent competitor of Turner's and the Myers brothers at the track, even while also owning many of the cars Turner ran there. "This was on a New Year's Day. Curtis was in our car and the way he caught [a turn], it was going to wreck and turn over. It was on two wheels, up on its side, getting ready to go all the way over. So he steers it like a bicycle over to Bobby Myers on the outside, until it got close enough to him, and when it landed, it landed on Bobby and put Curtis back on the wheels—and he won the race!

"One other time over there Curtis was driving our car, him and one of the Myers boys got into it. And at the end, Curtis was mad enough that he just ran into him and crashed out the radiator and everything in our car. After the race was over, he apologized. He said, 'Pop, I was just so mad. I couldn't help it. Just tell me what it cost and I'll pay for it.' First time I ever had anybody say they'd pay for the damages to one of our race cars."

"Sometimes the Myers brothers would just dare Curtis to come to the track," remembers Clyde Conner, a staunch Turner fan living in nearby Yadkinville, North Carolina. "And he'd tell 'em, 'You just wait. Keep driving and I'll be there.'"

Normally, after a race confrontation, a driver can stay mad at Turner only so long; nobody throws a party like he does, and he throws them all the time. Women, alcohol, good conversation, it's a perfect way to douse any bad feelings. But it doesn't look like Bobby Myers will be in any mood to lift a glass with Turner soon.

He charges past other drivers who attempt to repair the damage on their cars, preparing to tow them out for the drive back home. Myers rounds a bend and there is something about his swift movement that attracts attention. Turner, sitting on the back of a truck a good eighth of a mile in the distance, cranes his neck to take a look. Smoking a cigarette, he pushes the shades up on his nose, scratches his shoulder and then leans back, reaching into the truck.

Myers is practically upon him and Turner stretches and sits upright again. The .38 pistol in his hand is now plainly visible, its nose jutting out toward Myers.

"What are you planning on doing with that, Bobby?" Turner asks matter-of-factly.

Myers stops cold; it takes a second but a smile breaks out on his face. "Curtis, ol' man," he says brightly, "I was just looking for a place to put it down."

Giving a stock car racer a gun in the 1950s is like giving atomic weapons to a small country. The results can be combustible and unpredictable, but the simple *threat* of using it is often powerful enough to make someone back down.

Besides, a gun is hardly the weapon of choice for settling disputes: Fists, tire irons, bottles and brute strength are much more effective, and Turner is anything but immune. After a typically spirited battle with Lee Petty during one race, Turner sat on a fence wall, watching Petty stamp toward him, slapping a newspaper angrily against his thigh. "I'm tired of you runnin' into me," Petty said, and when Turner asked, "What are you gonna do about it?" Petty smacked him on the head with the newspaper—which had a tire iron hidden inside. And after Turner ran his friend Tiny Lund off the track at Lakewood Speedway, the towering Lund carried Turner into the lake in the middle of the track and promised to drown him—until Turner kindly offered to pay for Lund's repairs.

Regardless of circumstances, the notion of actually using his gun would never dawn on Turner, but it's good for protection. While he has been busily racking up wins through NASCAR's premier and weekly series through the early 1950s, he has also been pursuing several other businesses, and trying to balance his busy schedule from one vocation to the next, often finding himself starting a race with a fatter wallet than intended.

One car owner of Turner's, Ralph Moody, will later recall a time Turner asked him to hold onto a thick envelope during a race; the distracted Moody stuffed the package inside his t-shirt. The race ended, Turner came to claim it and when Moody asked what was inside, Turner told him he'd been holding several million dollars in cash and checks.

Turner's occasional windfall comes from the one business his father might have suggested he was born for: timbering. He has long dabbled in it, first working with his dad, then harvesting lumber as a sideline to working at his sawmilling business. But he finally makes a much bigger commitment to the business in 1950 when, on a warm Spring day, with nothing much better to do, he decides to buy himself a mountain.

He'd been eyeing it for quite some time. It's a pretty good size, out in Virginia, with plenty of timber on it. Might be nice to own a mountain, he thinks. He'd been wondering how much one should cost, anyway.

Turner takes the plunge and buys the land for $30,000. There is only one problem: no road has been built up into it.

"They told me I couldn't do that for less that $20,000," Turner tells *Sports Illustrated* writer Kim Chapin years later, "but hell, I did it in thirty days for $2,500. Just after that a man offered me $85,000 for the whole thing. Easiest money I ever made. Right then and there I decided to get out of the sawmill business and into timber."

Of all the things Curtis Turner inherited from his father, it's a safe bet the most valuable was an uncanny ability to survey a huge tract of land and estimate with great precision not only how many board feet of lumber you could get out of it, but what the whole piece of land was probably worth.

"I never could get over how he could figure all that in his head," says Ann Turner. "He made more money doing that type of work than he ever did in racing. He got publicity in racing."

During what would become a twenty-plus-year career in timber brokering, Turner's highly public racing name enticed many sales. In times of greatest financial need, he'd return again and again to the potential security of a big timber payday.

Along with helping build and crew on Turner's cars, Paul Cawley joins a group of peers and older Virginia teenagers who look up to Turner in helping his friend harvest or sell timber. Cawley continues to be fascinated by his friend's apparent willingness to attempt anything at all, finding the quality oddly admirable.

"There was this one place," Cawley says about a particular timber tract. "Nobody would have dared to think of getting the timber down because it was on a *cliff*. You couldn't get any machines up there; I don't even know if you could get horses up there."

What you can do, Turner decides, is get as close to the highest point as possible and, in a sense, throw a lasso around the top point in a cliff and pull yourself right to the timber. Turner instructs his friend Acey Janey to back a bulldozer near the peak and then let out a cable winch from the back. When the winch is draped over a rock, Janey begins winding it in. The plan works—until the cable suddenly snaps, sending the bulldozer tumbling back down the road, and vaulting Janey from the truck bed, leaving him cradling several broken ribs.

After Turner checks on Janey and the destroyed bulldozer, he reaches what is, for him, the only logical conclusion.

"Gonna have to use stronger cable," he tells Cawley.

A week later, Turner tries the maneuver again, with much stronger, better secured cable, and Cawley watches the brand new bulldozer Turner has bought chugging slowly up the cliff like a donkey being dragged where it doesn't want to go. Meanwhile, Turner stands with his hands at his hips, the impassive expression on his face never changing. When the bulldozer is pulled as far as possible, Turner's workers have a platform from which to begin felling the trees.

"He'd never let anything bother him," Cawley says. "He'd just turn around and say, 'I won't look back and think about it; just give me a drink.' And then he'd go about his business and do the next thing."

The "next thing" might turn out to be a variety of ventures, many with less than stellar degrees of success. A movie theatre in Roanoke turns a modest profit at first, but will eventually be sold when television's growing popularity brings down the curtain on many local movie houses. And having grown up on a dairy farm, he also makes certain attempts at farming—raising pheasants and later sheep—without the kind of results that might make him consider cutting back on either timber work or racing.

The worst of it comes when he buys a large dairy farm in 1953, and purchases 150 cows from businessman-turned-Virginia governor Tom

Stanley. "Curtis just loved cows," says his friend Charlie Williamson. But when a health inspector discovers a rare disease has spread through both of Turner's barns, all the cows must be slaughtered.

It is a grim task, but Turner does what needs to be done. Because of the disease, his farm is condemned for three years. Though he sues Governor Stanley for misrepresentation, there is no way of detecting when the cows were afflicted, and Turner loses the business and $65,000.

"All those cows had to be put to sleep; it just broke his heart," Williamson says. "He said he didn't think [Govenor Stanley] would pull something like that. But he lost that farm and [about] went broke."

The timber business helps offset the losses and Turner quickly comes to rely on a potential commission from timber to provide the ante for just about anything. "Maybe I would be a success in something else. But timber's all I know," he'll say years later, "and those damned trees have always come through for me."

And he'd go looking for it everywhere. Billy Triplett, who'd begun doing odd jobs for Turner at age fourteen, remembers when Turner took his good friend Acey Lloyd on a boat ride in South Carolina, through a snake-filled swamp that was part of a fertile 10,000-acre timber tract. The land is not hospitable, but the timber is just what the West Virginia Paper and Pulp Company has in mind. Turner buys the land, and turns around and sells it immediately, making a tidy profit as go-between.

"I think Curtis wrote a million-dollar check on a Floyd [Virginia] bank," recalls Triplett. "Of course the Floyd bank never *had* that kind of money. But he wrote the check on the bank anyway.

"He got the West Virginia Paper and Pulp Company to cover that million dollar check by the following Monday morning," Triplett says. "Then he sold it to them. That's the way Curtis did things."

Timber sales frequently bring Turner thousands of dollars in commissions, before expenses. He lives very high on the hog for awhile with that money—it can be like winning ten or fifteen Grand National races in a row. Sometimes it takes weeks for a sale to close; then commissions come in one big chunk, and Turner embraces spending with childlike enthusiasm. Lincolns show up in the driveway of the Turner home in Virginia, and at dinners for fifteen or more, nobody else is permitted to pay for anything. "And he used to like to buy brand new Cadillacs," Triplett recalls.

Turner has new tales to tell drivers and reporters at the tracks, going on about his big-money deals. The stories are good copy, and with requisite exaggeration, it is soon made to seem in print as if Turner is the big wheel in these deals, the buyer *and* seller, instead of the middleman.

"This was back when adjectives were foremost in newspaper writing, and it was twice the wordage of today," says Humpy Wheeler, himself no slouch at drumming up publicity. "I recall Curtis being called 'millionaire lumber baron' or 'millionaire tycoon.' This was when a millionaire was something."

Turner has long known that the appearance of wealth can only make you wealthier in the long run. In July, 1954, a Winston-Salem *Journal* article with the headline, "Turner Wins at Speedway," begins, "Curtis Turner, the Roanoke, Virginia, real estate tycoon who races for fun, became the first professional to win six events on the Raleigh Speedway this season when he copped the twenty-five-lap feature of last night's program."

"He made a lot in the timber business but he spent a lot," recalls Williamson. "He'd get an option on a piece of land, an agreement to buy for so much and he'd have only so much time. And he would find out what he could get it for and then he'd go sell it and [usually] he'd never really own it. He'd sell it while he had the option on it and he'd make this money."

At first, amused by all the publicity he's started, he tries to humbly downplay some of the claims. This only creates more talk, which he can't help but add to. Chasing one big deal after another becomes a passionate pursuit; for a couple of years during the early 1950s, racing is his fallback occupation. When he does make an appearance at the track, it is not uncommon to see him showing up in a business suit, having just come from some supposed negotiation. Business is not always good, but when it is, it's great. "I'll be a millionaire one month and broke the next," Turner tells Triplett.

"He wore suits all the time, and you didn't see a lot of suits in the south back then unless you went downtown to Atlanta or Charlotte," recalls Wheeler. "The closer you got to banks, the more suits you saw. Where I grew up, the only people that wore suits were the mill owners and the bankers and college professors if anyone had any college."

Turner, a seventh-grade dropout with a growing reputation as a successful man who can get things done, is meeting politicians and a different class of businessmen. Racing, and winning, takes on a different meaning, as an exercise for thrilling potential clients. His party lists become more impressive. There are big checks and debts, and more big checks, which, given his joy in spending, feed more debts. It's challenging and at times scary and unpredictable. For Turner, it's an ideal way to make a living.

Ann Turner is a handsome woman, petite and warm, with dark hair trimmed to just above her shoulders. There is a great deal of intelligence, and a hint of defiance, in her bright brown eyes. Talking to her, you get an unexpectedly pleasant amalgam of homespun refinement. And if her personality contains a distinct lack of nonsense, a smile she gives you also betrays a sense of willingness, even a yearning, to let go just a little.

If she doesn't follow that impulse, it's because of a little voice somewhere reminding her that unsettling things lurk around corners. As a child—the product of a broken marriage, raised to a large degree by stern aunts—she came to understand that in this life, there are frequently consequences.

It is her fate, and her choice, to have married a one-man consequence machine. Her husband continually flies in the face of any restrictions he can find. He is frequently quiet and shy, is capable of great sweetness and loving, and yet his actions startle. "All the excitement," she says of Curtis, "came out in physical activity." To Ann, who feels a sense of responsibility for him, her husband's actions smack of the limitless zeal for living. There is money around, there is a house and cars, clothes, and large trophies, and in Curtis she finds an easy strength she wishes she had. Within the uncertainly, Ann Turner feels a tug of security.

If they're not a couple out of Tennessee Williams, they may as well be. There's plenty of drama.

"Mom found him to be so very 'in charge,' very strong and very confident," remembers their oldest daughter, Sue.

But by the sixth or seventh year of their marriage, plenty of seams are clearly splitting. Ann would rather not go to every race her husband competes in. First of all, there are too many of them, and on enough occasions, Curtis will plant someone into a guardrail, or himself be vaulted into the adjoining woods. Going to watch the races is a source of great worry.

Not going creates a different, more frustrating kind of worry. There have always been other women, several of them, and as apologetic as Curtis may sometimes be, there's no sign of it stopping. There are angry accusations and shouting matches. Worst of all, Curtis is out so frequently, going to a race, following a deal, being with friends or whomever, there's no way to create a stable lifestyle. It's clear when they're together that Curtis Turner loves his wife—which is fine if you can catch the two of them together, not arguing.

"Marriage is too much trouble," he will say years later. "If you get married, pretty soon you're all tied down."

By 1953, Ann Turner moves out of the house, the first in what will be a series of separations.

"They had a sweet relationship but it soured as he became more well-known and famous because women were clamoring after him, and they didn't care if he was married or not," says Sue. "That was a problem. And if Mom didn't come with him to every race, I think his feelings would get hurt. It's hard in a marriage when someone's got to do all the traveling and the other person can't keep up and then you're out there alone; you're vulnerable."

It's easy enough to look at Curtis' philandering purely as a cause of the strains of marriage, as opposed to calling it, in part, a symptom. But it's clear to friends by now that Curtis and Ann are not cut from the same cloth and there is emotional distance between them.

In time, Ann and Sue return home. Avoiding talk of their marital woes, Ann and Curtis instead have a number of fruitful discussions about the gray areas of right and wrong that exist in the law. Between overseeing timber contracts, dealing with business associates and fleeing highway patrolmen, Turner has spent more time than he'd have ever imagined embroiled in legal matters. It is his perspective that knowing as much as one can about regulations is the only way to find the loopholes necessary to turn a deal in one's favor. "I love corporate law," he says. "I just get a kick out of reading law and trying to outfigure somebody. It's not what's on the books. If that's all there was to law—reading the statutes—there wouldn't be a need for lawyers, or very few of them. The game is to read between the lines, in a sort of twilight zone, not exactly illegal, but maybe extra-legal." He purchases a Blackstone set of law books and proceeds to fill his shelves with volumes and read his way through them, memorizing decisions and familiarizing himself with process.

In Ann he finds not only a willing quiz mistress, but someone smart enough to bat issues back and forth.

"We'd argue," she recalls, warming to the memory. "We argued about a lot of the cases. I'd see it one way and he'd see it another way."

The process, the knowledge, it all appeals to Ann's sense of self-worth. And even if she and her husband aren't always together, and as volatile as things can be, she and Curtis had fallen in love, and were building a family.

The Piedmont section of the southern United States runs east to west from Hickory to Raleigh; east of Raleigh you're in the coastal plain and west of Hickory, the mountains. From north to south it stretches all the way across North Carolina, up to the edge of Virginia, down to the tip of South Carolina. In the 1950s in Piedmont, you'd be hard-pressed to find a more popular holiday—especially among men—than Easter Monday. This is Bible Belt country, and Easter Sunday is a day of family and prayer . . . as opposed to, say, fishing. With Sunday being not good for anything frivolous, Easter Monday offers an extra chance to relax and recreate on a day that might just carry the first hints of springtime.

Easter Monday is also opening day for racing at Bowman Gray Stadium, which sits in the very heart of the Piedmont section. At Bowman Gray, the season runs through the last week of September, which is when high school football returns.

The regular weekly racing had begun in 1949; it was fair to say, the only game in town. You'd have to travel to Atlanta's Peach Bowl to find this kind of regular weekly show, with premier talent. It is another Bill France reclamation project. Original promoters staged races at the track and ran off with the proceeds. France came in with partner Alvin Hawkins, promising to create profitable, fair-game racing, and the track becomes an important foothold in his growing stock car racing empire.

Bowman Gray is a flat asphalt quarter-mile track that began as a cinder track for foot racers that circled the football field. There had always been stands on either side; the "long" sides, as it were. In the early 1950s, stands are also put in at a short side to complete a horseshoe. By then, the racing had become popular enough to demand the addition. Seating capacity then rose from twelve thousand to seventeen thousand. Three different divisions race for the fans on Saturday nights: Modified, Amateur and Sportsman. Sportsman cars are smaller than Grand National cars; gasoline fuel is required. For the Modifieds, drivers are still permitted to use alcohol in the engine. On a Saturday night, "The smell of alcohol was the prevailing odor in the place," recalls Hank Schoolfield, then a sportswriter for the Winston Salem *Journal*. "That made for a jolly evening. But it was also a very pretty, scenic municipal stadium. There were a lot of flowers around the place. Saturday afternoon, five P.M., an hour before practice, you can still smell them. And you couldn't see the main road for all the trees."

Inside the stadium, however, you don't really care. When the green flag drops on a Saturday night, and the Sportsman cars of Curtis Turner, Billy Myers, Bobby Myers and Glen Wood lead the field around the astonishingly tight turns, the race is essentially right in your lap. Fans sit within a few feet of the track, elevated on stands behind a high fence built on top of a wall. You are up high, looking down to watch the race, and close enough to see the expressions on the drivers' faces when they wham into each other. The racing is very hard going; winning carries great prestige.

"Curtis and I were walking around the rim of the stadium behind the stands one day," recalls Schoolfield. "It was very picturesque, covered in woods. As we were walking around he looked down and said, 'This is a beautiful place. It would have been a hell of a good place to build a racetrack.' He did well though; he won twenty-six races there, including two in the Grand National division."

At the track, all drivers have their factions of fans. It is easy to develop loyalites that, in the stands, may tend to rub the guy next to you the wrong way. Billy and Bobby Myers are aggressive and volatile. In one race at the stadium, Billy smashes into the rail and Bobby, with nowhere else to go, comes along and rams right into him. Emerging from his wreck with a dark look in his eyes, Bobby sidles up to Billy's car and says, "That's a helluva place to park a car, brother." Glen Wood is swift, patient and ingenious. He is famous at the track for, among other reasons, building a car that he drove from the backseat. "His car was a club coupe and he mounted a long steering wheel and built a seat in the back," remembers Schoolfield. "I guess he felt it would be good weight distribution. He won a championship one year doing it."

Turner, however, wills his way to victories, championships and popularity polls at Bowman Gray, as often as not banging and bumping into the lead in the late stages of Sportsmen finals, earning a night's $200 top prize. Clyde Conner recalls a signature Turner move: he'd tap a competitor once and then, if the rival didn't move, he'd knock him out of the way. "He didn't drive dirty," Conner says. "He gave them warning." Turner wins two features in the opening 1949 season, finishing second in the track championship to Tim Flock. But after going winless halfway through the following year, he begins an electrifying run. Winning first on July 8, he reels off three straight and ends the season with five victories and his first title. "That is the year," Frank Spencer writes in the Winston-Salem *Journal*, "that Curtis Turner bolted into the limelight." The next season, the largest crowd ever to attend a race to that time at Bowman Gray reaches, at various estimates, as much as 20,000. The fans, treated to another impressive Turner victory that evening, don't leave disappointed.

Or, at least, many don't. Others are *quite* unhappy, and show their displeasure in seemingly timeless fashion: by creating as much action in the stands as on the track. Conner recalls many Saturday nights spent in the stands at Bowman Gray, watching Turner lovers and haters square off with shouts and fists.

"Curtis was a combination of hero and villain," says Schoolfield. "The fans would get into a fight about what one of them would say. The drivers might be happy but the fans would be fighting."

Sometimes, action will spill over onto the track. According to Brock Yates, "The [Bowman Gray] crowd was so rabid that sometimes, [Turner] had to beat his way out of the race car with a tire iron."

Or action could climb up into the stands from the track. "One night," says Schoolfield, "Turner and the Myers brothers got into a car-bashing and fist-fighting deal. The police escorted Turner to the pit area, and Billy Myers, who was the principle combatant, up through the stands to keep them separated. I never figured out how they got away with that because I'd have figured there'd be trouble in the stands, but they had enough police with them. They escorted Billy out through the stands and out of the place."

The excitement Turner and company generate at Bowman Gray does everything to build the sport's reputation for high-spirited action. It does little, in Bill France's mind, to appease everybody; certainly not folks for whom Easter Monday is decidedly *not* a holiday. But he regards the antics of drivers the way a warden might look at a fight between convicts: Let all the conflict create a good show without thinking of breaking it up— for awhile.

"Curtis would go to the race track and run on Saturday night, and the crowd might grow from a few hundred people to a few thousand," recalls writer Bob Moore. "And France's standpoint is: Okay, I'm doing this for the betterment of the sport. I'm not doing this for the betterment of Curtis Turner."

If there's any one place where the betterment of both NASCAR and Curtis Turner are one and the same, it's Darlington, South Carolina.

In 1948, the same year France hatched his plan for a strictly stock division, wealthy South Carolina contractor Harold Brasington attended America's great race, the Indy 500, at the 2.5-mile speed mecca in Indianapolis. Watching the open-wheel drivers go through their paces for five hundred miles, in front of thousands of delirious fans, gives Brasington the idea that such a track might work in the south. Returning home, he brings up the idea at his Saturday night card game—a rather rich assembly—and eventually gets seed money and begins to raise the rest.

Darlington, population 6,000, with no adequate hotel facilities, is deep in the heart of absolutely nowhere, making it an unlikely site for a speedway. Still, Brasington gets businessman Sherman Ramsey to trade seventy acres of Darlington land for future shares in the raceway. But Ramsey has one condition. There are two ponds on the property. Brasington could get rid of the fish pond, but the other pond, where Ramsey stocks the minnows he uses for bait in his frequent fishing trips, is off-limits. So Brasington's oval takes on a pear shape, with a tight west turn and a wide east turn to keep all the minnows happy.

It takes a year to build Darlington Raceway, a 1.25-mile paved track modeled after Indianapolis, only half its size. Officially open in 1950, it's ready for any takers during the second full season of Grand National Racing. Bill France is interested, but wary. At five hundred miles, with continuously fast speeds, there's a question as to whether the strictly stock cars won't all crack up or blow up well before the long day ends. If so, France's concept of new-car racing will take a hard hit.

But after a rival sanctioning body has trouble filling the field, France steps in and commits his drivers for a race date of September 4, 1950, Labor Day. It will be the first NASCAR race run longer than two hundred miles, and the first race not run on either dirt, sand or highway.

Winning at Darlington could be, for Turner, as lucrative as a sizeable timber deal. For every other race in the 1950 season, the winner's share is $1,000 to $1,500; the Darlington winner will earn $10,510. And since points in 1950 are based on purse dollars, this race could also cement his place in the standings.

Turner comes to Darlington leading the title chase. The season is twelve races old, with seven remaining, and Turner has already won two races in a row twice. In one remarkable three-race stretch earlier in 1950, he led 445 consecutive laps. The week before Darlington, at a dirt track in Hamburg, New York, one of the stops on Bill France's highly marketed "Yankee Trail" of races, Turner held the lead for the first seventy-four laps out of two hundred before blowing a tire. After returning to the race four laps down he proceeded to pass the entire field three times and ended up third, winning a chorus of cheers from the 8,363 in attendance. One week later, Turner wins the pole for Darlington; he'll be the first driver to start first in the race soon to be dubbed the Southern 500.

France and the race's promoters, led by Bob Colvin, organize an enormous effort to drum up interest, including ads in papers throughout the country, radio spots and interviews touting the spectacle of the event. France tries to milk more publicity by mimicing the anticipation of Indy, scheduling two weeks of qualifying to fill the race's seventy-five spots. Even given these efforts, a crowd of about five thousand is expected at the eleven thousand-seat facility on race day.

At least that many people have shown up the afternoon before. By nightfall on Sunday, five thousand more have arrived, clogging Route 151, the skinny two-lane highway leading to the track. Local police, while trying to keep order, are up against a local edict that's never mattered quite so much before: It is illegal to sell tickets for any event on a Sunday, so everybody must wait for the mad rush the next morning. That night, with Darlington boasting exactly one twelve-room motel, people sleep in their cars, find a patch of grass or bunk on the steps of the local chamber of commerce. On Monday, the traffic coming in is historic. Peach baskets filled with cash are piled up on the office table at the track. In many cases, two tickets are sold for the same seat. It takes enormous manpower to assure that, by the time the green flag waves, all twenty-five thousand paying customers have been shoehorned into Darlington for what many expect to be a wreckfest. But what fans end up witnessing is the first race at a track that will ultimately do for NASCAR what the talkies did for the movies.

And lined up in front is Curtis Turner. The track is electrifying, and that alone normally brings out the showman in Turner. But he'd already discovered something during the long qualifying sessions: He loves this place. In the straightaways, you're doing well over 100 mph. This ain't no dirt track; there'll be no powersliding around Darlington. It requires enormous finesse. If you manage to take the turns exactly right, you hug the inside guardrail close and then slingshot off, vaulting up toward the banking and the wall. The ride is difficult and phenomenal.

Turner takes the lead in lap five, and begins to play with the fine line between speed and control. With each turn, he takes the curve a little faster, seeing how far he can safely creep up toward the wall without smacking into it, as a thousand grandstand faces blur outside his window. A little faster and his Olds 88 will skirt along the guardrail, which he barely touches with a quick "Ssshh!", like a swift brush with sandpaper.

But very soon, the smell of burning rubber fills the afternoon. Tires are blowing left and right on the rough asphalt track. Red Byron will use as many as thirty of them. It's a good thing the race has attracted so many paying customers; some crews are raiding the parking lot to borrow tires needed during the race.

Turner is, as always, of a mind that the fastest car will win this thing, and every fifteen laps or so, he passes Johnny Mantz, an Indy-style driver and a friend he and France had just made during the Mexican Road Race. Mantz, driving a car owned by France and Hubert Westmoreland, has qualified dead last but while Turner keeps blowing tires, Mantz, the proverbial tortoise, races steadily on. Having more experience on asphalt than all other drivers at the track, he's acquired tires with a harder compound rubber material, and fifty laps into the four hundred-lap race, he finally crawls his way into the lead.

Turner is having a terrific time heading for a decent finish. But almost three-quarters of the way through, going too fast and trying to make a pass, he loses control of his Olds. The car flips over and Turner knocks his face against the wheel. A ripped shirt, a bloody nose, a cut lip and an early end to the day. Out his windshield, as the caution comes out, Turner spots Mantz making yet another rotation on the track. The race will last 6.5 hours, and Mantz will bring the trophy home, besting Fireball Roberts by nine laps.

The success of Darlington, and it's vaunted position of prominence on the schedule, makes it instantly the sport's proving ground: Winning the Southern 500 is considered about as good as it gets in NASCAR, right up on a pedestal next to a win at the Daytona Beach and Road Course. It will be Turner's pattern to come to Darlington every Labor Day, excite fans and make some noise. In 1951, he leads forty-three laps before engine trouble ends his day. In 1953, he finishes third, and a year later he leads more than half the race and ends up second to tobacco farmer-turned-racing stand-out Herb Thomas.

Turner's increasing success matches his renewed commitment to the sport. Winning Most Popular Driver voting at Bowman Gray in 1952, he returns to a more regular schedule in '53, capturing two features and popularity voting once again. In 1954, Turner loses the title at the small track to his friend Glen Wood, but wins a record six features. By now, however, he has added yet another, unexpected element to his arsenal of thrills: flight.

There are only so many speeding tickets any one person can accrue before he is denied the privilege of getting behind the wheel of a car. It's not that Curtis Turner doesn't understand this, or the irony of being rewarded for driving too fast at the race track and penalized for doing it on the open road. It's not even a question of the injustice of needing to maintain a certain speed on roads he always felt he owned.

It's just fun. It's a lot of fun, and unnecessary, it seems, to not do it. He's always practicing safety behind the wheel. He drives for a living, after all.

Turner sits in the backseat of his Cadillac, staring at the mountain roads rolling past his window at a decidedly reasonable pace. Yet another speeding ticket has cost him his license for a stretch of time in the state of Virginia, requiring him to hire a driver, who is taking him to an appointment to see some land. But his reverie is suddenly broken by the loud growling whir of propellers. Turner's car is passing Woodrum Airport in Roanoke, and the landing airplane gets a little close to the Cadillac as it soars in. The path of the thing is majestic and commanding.

"Hey," Turner calls from the backseat, pointing at the plane with a smile, "what's the speed limit up there?"

The chauffeur squints at the question. "There *is* none. You can go as fast as a plane can go," he says.

"Turn around," Turner answers.

Within minutes, Turner is in the airport's Piedmont Aviation Sales Hangar, laying out several thousand dollars for a plane. "I didn't know nothing about them," he recalled years later. "I'd never been in one. I bought a Tri-Pacer."

The 1954 Piper Tri-Pacer is an ideal starter plane: single-engine, light and without much in the way of instrumentation. Leon Sales, a NASCAR flagman, is always talking about how much fun it is taking a craft into the air and Turner hires him to teach the finer points of aviation on a flight the next morning up to New York.

Turner begins to wonder if Sales is the ideal instructor when he ties a crucifix to the instrument panel, using that to make sure he's always flying level. Clue number two: when the Roanoke airport tower states a baromentric pressure of 29.98, Sales instead dials the altimeter to read 2,998 feet above sea level.

"And I said, 'Leon, that ain't right,' 'cause I knew Roanoke wasn't that high," Turner later said.

In fact, Roanoke is only 1,100 feet above sea level, but Sales—who in fact has not operated a plane solo for ten years—argues that he is in charge.

The plan is to fly into LaGuardia Airport and they appear to be heading right for it without incident . . . until Sales makes a number of calls to the LaGuardia tower, and the traffic controller claims he cannot spot the plane. The pair circle the airport again and again, with Sales' calls getting more panicked by the moment.

"I'm circling right over the runway," Sales shouts.

"We don't *see* you," comes the answer.

The circling goes on for an hour; Turner gazes back and forth between the ground and the ever-lowering gas gauge in the plane.

"Land the plane, Leon," Turner says sternly. Sales is mortified.

"I can't land the plane," he answers. "I'd lose my license."

"Leon," Turner tells him, "you're runnin' out of gas. Your license ain't gonna do you any good if you stay up here much longer."

Sales spies one plane about to land, and another behind him, heading in. He decides to cut the line and land between them. He lowers swiftly, trying desperately to level the plane above the runway; Turner braces himself in the passenger seat. Sales puts the plane down and yanks on the brake. Turner flinches, watching the distant trees come toward him at an alarming rate, until Sales finally gains control.

"That runway must have been two miles long," Turner remembered. "He used up every foot of it."

Turner notices a much larger plane off to one side moving away, and he advises Sales to follow. But the plane is moving too quickly, and Sales, losing sight of it, makes a wrong turn. In his distress, he speeds along a paved road, and then slams on the brakes—to keep from missing a car.

The Tri-Pacer has made it all the way to the exiting highway. Sales, with nowhere else to go, merges. The plane bops along the highway, with its pilot looking for a route heading back, when the familiar sound of a siren fills the air. The police officer races in front, and Sales pulls over.

Turner is steaming. Avoiding moments like this is exactly why he bought the plane in the first place. It is a sight, alright: a policeman walking up to the pilot's side of the plane, staring up coldly.

"Hello officer," Sales says cheerfully. "Would you mind telling me where we're at?"

LaGuardia Airport, it turns out, is miles away. Sales and Turner have landed at New York's Idlewild International.

"Private planes are not allowed at Idlewild, gentlemen," the policeman informs them. "They're not allowed on highways, either."

Sales is issued his ticket, and all of his imploring will not get Turner to take another flight with him. It's up to Sales to get the Tri-Pacer safely back to Roanoke, where Turner meets it after a Greyhound bus ride.

"I came back in and offered to lose $2,500 on the plane if they would take it back," Turner said of his talk with the Piedmont salesmen. "They wouldn't." Instead, a Piedmont captain, Kale Wilson, loads Turner into the plane for proper instructions. After a few days, Turner makes his first solo trip into the open skies. He is a "seat of the pants" pilot, tooling around based more on feel than a real working knowledge of instrumentation. That plan works out fine—until days later, on another solo trip, dark clouds move in on him swiftly and unexpectedly, surrounding him top and bottom. Rumbling and rocking through the weather, Turner again promises himself that if he survives, he'll get rid of the damn Tri-Pacer.

He lands on the edge of an abandoned cornfield, bucking along the thick grass like a bronco rider until a sudden stop.

He sits, breathing heavily in the cab—but the important thing, he soon realizes, is he's made it. There wasn't any panic; only concern. It occurs to him that flying is like driving. It requires a textbook understanding of how everything works, and more importantly, what exactly you need to do to keep things from *not* happening. If he can master all that, he can treat the air the same way he always treated the open roads in Virginia.

Turner reads through the flying manual with as much concentration as he would the law, using Ann again to test him. In mid-November, 1954, he applies for a pilot certificate and takes his tests; figuring it would be more impressive, he lists himself as having completed the 11th grade. On December 23, 1954, he is issued his first Airman Certificate, a private pilot license for single-engine planes.

The plane is an enormous convenience. For brokering timber deals and rushing to make the starts of races, the Tri-Pacer becomes invaluable. At a time when other racers are hardly considering the notion of flying, much less how to afford a plane, Turner has followed Bill France's lead into the skies.

Growing up, coming of age, Turner has seen his world grow larger on the strength of his ambitions; flying his own plane, the world is now limitless. Few things thrill him more than taking off on a clear day and hovering over Virginia, looking down at the Blue Ridge Mountains. These are moments of pure calm; on many occasions, he takes Ann along, and the two of them marvel at life at seven thousand feet. On one occasion, Turner impulsively decides he and his wife should go out for a nice dinner and, after leaving Sue with a babysitter, they enjoy an intimate evening in the Bahamas. For Ann, this is as good as it gets. When her husband is away, there is doubt and loneliness. When he's around, there are parties and plane rides, and the pull to follow him into the whirlwind.

As a timberman, being able to see tracts of land from the sky affords Turner a perspective his dad never had the advantage of. Staring down at pines, oaks and firs, there is a sense of disbelief at his good fortune.

It takes a whole lot for Turner to skip a day in the air. He logs flight time by the hour, building confidence in solo rides. He also flies with much more experienced pilots, watching their demeanor, behavior and conduct in any number of conditions.

"He loved anything with speed," says his sister Dove. "He loved to drive a car until he got his airplane and then he loved his plane more than he did his car."

Turner doesn't showboat; conventional trick flying, turning over and spinning, hold little interest to him. Why do that when you can put your own stamp on things, and develop a method and conduct that's all your own?

Clyde Conner recalls many a mad rush to Bowman Gray Stadium to watch Curtis Turner race. On August 21, 1954, he heads on over after paying a brief visit to his wife, Dora, at North Carolina Baptist Hospital, eyeing his newborn son for the first time. "Fortunately, the hospital was only a few miles from the track," he recalls. "My wife always co..siders that the utmost act of a loyal fan." But there is one somewhat less memorable night where Conner recalls sitting in the stands, staring at the field below, trying to catch a glimpse of Turner. Suddenly, the staccato twirl of a propellor fills the night, heard over the cheers. A small Tri-Pacer plane heads down toward the football field at the center of the stadium; it passes over one goalpost, then dips down toward the field before rising up again over the far goalpost. The delighted throng lets out an enormous roar, interrupted by the public announcer: "Curtis has just let us know he's on his way!" After landing at a nearby airport, a police escort drives him in for the night's Sportsmen races.

This is one of Turner's great joys. Pranks of any sort, while always fun on the ground, take on added significance when practiced in the air. And if you can pull a prank *and* sell some timberland, it's hard to top. Tim Flock recalls flights Turner takes with perspective clients who might have hemmed and hawed too often, unable to decide whether they want to do business or not. On one occasion, Turner, sitting relaxed in his pilot's seat, takes off with two conservatively dressed businessmen who are ready to look at something of value. Instead, Turner positions his plane over a piece of land that's hardly up to snuff, and that's when he decides to switch off the engine. The propellers halt, and in the cockpit, there's no sound but that of the whistling wind.

"Hmm; that's funny," Turner says, looking concerned, while his passengers' faces turn an unappealing shade of ash gray. "Something must have happened."

The plane floats in the sky a few seconds; before it's quick descent is assured, Turner just as swiftly reactivates the engine. The maddening propeller roar is the most comforting sound his passengers have ever heard.

"Are we going to be okay?" one finally asks, fighting nausea.

"We should be fine," Turner tells him.

The businessmen are not quite assured. "Can you just get us back down? Please get me back down."

"Just enjoy the ride," Turner tells him. "In fact, you might want this land right here; it's perfect for what you're looking for."

The businessman barely pauses to look down.

"Fine—can we land now?"

"Sure," Turner says, taking in the view of the land below. "Yep," he says, gestering out the window, "there's some damn fine timber down there."

In the newspapers, they're now calling Turner "the flying lumberman." It is a heady time, as the occasional deals continue to net him tidy paydays. The timber helps take care of everything.

On one June evening, he sits in the stands at a half-mile raceway in Richmond, Virginia, talking to some friends before the start of a race. He's just finished touring the pit area, regaling drivers, crew members and newspapermen with tales of a $3 million deal, and the party they'll all soon be invited to. "We could even start now," he says, clearly feeling the effects of his favorite elixir, Canadian Club and Coke.

He is a presence in the pit area, the only man at the track wearing a brand new white linen suit, purchased to celebrate another commission coming his way.

In the stands, he gets restless talking about his latest conquest. There's too much energy knocking around inside him.

He heads down to the pit area once again, quickly noticing a young guy who's come down all ready to mix it up with the pros. He looks a little too clean-cut and out of place.

It doesn't take long for Turner to talk the kid into letting him behind the wheel. Turner hands the suit jacket to a friend in the stands, loosens his new yellow tie and climbs into the cab.

He is by now "half tuned," about as close to being excessively drunk as one can be. Taking the green flag, Turner starts from the back, and begins to make a typical run to the front, this time with erratic insistence.

It's not about who has the fastest car; it's about who's stupid enough to stay in Turner's way.

Looking at Turner beginning to fill up his rearview mirror, driver Joe Weatherly grins and shakes his head. He shimmies the back of his car a moment, trying humorously to ward off Turner, who continues to stampede his way toward the lead in a bull-like assault. Ultimately, Weatherly clears the way; he has already come to know, much better than most, when Turner is too far gone to ever give way.

When the checkered flag waves with Turner out front, he swiftly parks back in the pit area and returns to the stands. He wants none of the money and certainly not the trophy. The crowd cheers manically, which means Turner already has what he came for.

The next week, the kid is back at the track. Even if he eventually runs the car himself, it's not for lack of waiting. He's returned to Richmond in hopes of finding the guy in the white suit with gold cuff links. He passes the word around the pit area: If the guy with the cuff links wants another chance, he's got just the car for him to do it in.

Chapter Five
1952-1958
"If you don't like this party, don't worry about nothin'. Another party's startin' in about fifteen minutes."

If you've met Joe Weatherly, chances are he's shown you his mongoose.

It's a curious little animal. You might imagine something sweet and furry but, as Joe will tell you, "It's the fastest goddamn thing on earth, and it's dangerous. It'll eat your damn flesh so fast, your face'll be picked clean before you even know your skin is gone."

That's why Joe keeps it locked inside a black wooden box.

"I got him from Africa," he says, as a small crowd gathers around him at the race track—a few women, even a young driver coming to compete in his first race. "I gotta be careful with him." He raises the box so everybody can read all those warning stickers, saying "DANGER!" and "Do Not TOUCH!" And then there's the mongoose tail itself, eight inches of dark fur sticking through a hole in the back. "But don't worry—he's locked up good. You're safe so long as he's in here. Take a look. It's alright."

For some odd reason, this reassures everybody. And like hundreds of others before them, the small crowd leans in a little, everybody trying to get a better look through the screen on the far side of the cage.

That's when Weatherly pushes the button on the bottom of the box.

Through the screen, a spring-loaded "mongoose tail" comes shooting out with a loud "thwack." Piercing screams cut through the air as women run in all directions. The young driver takes off, a shout gurgling in his throat. Chances are he's still running. But you can hardly hear anybody over Joe Weatherly's maniacal laughter.

"It's a wonder he didn't kill people with that thing," says Weatherly's friend, track owner Paul Sawyer. "There wasn't enough money to have bought it from him. He thought that was the funniest damn thing in the world."

When "Little" Joe Weatherly laughs, every part of him jumps and shakes; his compact body, a hair under five-foot-eight, 168 pounds, is all knee slaps and howls. His wide, round face turns crimson under brown curly hair, those small eyes shut so tight, the full lips, normally raised to a cheshire grin, now wide open. Laughing makes Joe's face crinkle up sideways, parted by the lengthy scar that spans from the center of his chin, curving up around his left eye, over to the middle of his forehead like some jagged cross-country highway. "Scars on some people look very disfiguring," says Humpy Wheeler, "but it only made Joe funnier looking." A relative describes him as being "so ugly he's cute." Max Muhleman, a young writer for the *Charlotte News*, dubs him "The Clown Prince of Racing" in the press, and it sticks but good.

Weatherly likes to call things the way he sees them—literally. Open-wheel Indianapolis cars, with their sleek bullet-shaped bodies are "Cucumbers with haywrecker wheels." Choosing, at one point, to farm cattle instead of chickens, he explains, "I won't fool with them chickens. A cow'll outweigh a chicken a bunch." When asked about accidentally turning into another car during a race, he says, "I zigged when I should have zagged."

Weatherly talks in shorthand, the words flowing out in swift bursts that shift from one subject to the next, like Morse code delivered by a madman. He moves the same way. "He seemed to always be in perpetual motion but not going anywhere when he wasn't in the race car," says Wheeler.

Inside the car, punching the gas with trademark Oxford saddle shoes, Weatherly is calm, talented, relentless, successful and in a state of perpetual joy. In the five years between 1946 and 1950, he'd claimed three American Motorcyclist Association championships. After a win, he'd showboat, throw up some dirt and do celebratory runs. Coming to NASCAR in the early 1950s, he stands out once again. Driving the Modified circuit, he wins forty-nine races in 1952, and another fifty-two in 1953 on the way to the national Modified title.

Shake hands to congratulate him and you are apt to get zapped by a joy buzzer.

"My wife would come down on Sunday, she'd cook great big buckets of chicken and Joe would come over," remembers Sawyer. "And he'd pick some chicken out that he wanted and say, 'Goddamn it, leave that chicken,' I'd say, 'I'm not gonna leave it.' And he'd spit on the chicken. He'd say, 'You son of a bitch, now see if you'll eat it.' Joe would do anything. Joe was full of crap and full of fun, but he was crazy as the hinges of hell."

Weatherly fills out a driver information form before a race in Atlanta, and on the line "Occupation other than racing" he writes "Having fun."

Success does nothing to dull the impulse to play a good joke—if anything, time only fine tunes his ability. In the late 1950s, while on the brink of his greatest successes in racing, Weatherly accompanies Lee Petty and other notable NASCAR drivers to a posh off-season dinner at the Robert E. Lee Hotel in Winston-Salem. "It was the biggest hotel in the area," says motorsports writer Tom Higgins. "And it's before dinner, and this waiter comes by, has a tray that's absolutely full of champagne glasses, carrying it up over about shoulder-high. And Weatherly always had this phony snake with him—he liked to throw it around your neck, get a rise out of you. And he threw the snake around the waiter's neck and I vividly remember that tray going toward the ceiling and all those champagne glasses tumbling in the air and the champagne spilling out and falling to the floor with a crash and all the glasses shattering. Well, they raised hell with him, told him, you know, half jokingly, 'Damn it Joe, we're going to have to pay for all those champagne glasses.' He just thought that was uproariously funny. He was quite a character. He was as advertised."

From the moment Weatherly begins racing on four wheels full time in the early 1950s, people keep raising one name to him: Curtis Turner. Turner, he's also outrageous; he'll do things on the race track nobody else will, and in an airplane, forget about it. He's a wild man; throws a good party too.

"Curtis Turner and Joe Weatherly, that's gotta be one of the best, closest friendships that anybody's ever been around," recalls Weatherly's frequent car owner Bud Moore. "They were like two peas in a pod."

In 1951, Turner is promoting races at Victory Stadium near Roanoke, and Joe Weatherly shows up with a Modified Studebaker, ready to qualify.

"I'd heard of him but never met him," Turner later recalled. The pair continue to come upon each other on the local racing circuit and hit it off famously, like two boys who meet on the playground and discover a shared fondness for dodgeball. Kindred spirits, they quickly become inseparable.

They look, at first glance, like two halves of a comedy team: the tall, broad-shouldered, good-looking straight man and his jittery, goofy compatriot who can make anybody laugh. Or perhaps they're Don Quixote and Sancho Panza: the big dreamer with impractical or outrageous plans, and his pragmatic sidekick.

There is always banter between them. The pair can go story for story, and the talk is almost never about racing. Women, partying and flying dominate the conversations, with plenty of whiskey around to make the stories funnier and wilder. "Joe was about half-tuned when we started the party. Then we had ourselves some shooters," Turner will say, referring to his whiskey and Coke mix. "After awhile, Joe was about tuned."

Weatherly, who's not very good with names, sometimes calls people "Pop": It's easier than remembering who's who. When he begins to call Turner "Pop" as well—just because—Turner wears the nickname like some favorite membership badge, and he starts calling Weatherly "Pop" too, for equally incoherent reasons. Soon enough, everybody else is also Pop.

When racing together, they like to make loud "Pop" sounds by whacking each other's cars. Turner will happily tap or brush past anybody else on the track, but he gets an extra thrill from dishing it out to Weatherly.

"He'd root Joe out when it came to it," recalls Leonard Wood. "There was no way he'd let Joe beat him."

Glen Wood remembers a convertible race on the beach at Daytona in the mid-1950s. "Joe's windshield blew out, so naturally with a convertible, it's all open, but when the windshield blows out, look how much less wind resistance you've got. It's just a straight shot. It picked his speed up quite a bit.

"So Curtis is hanging right there with him and he sees this, so he gets his foot up there trying to kick his own windshield out! He kept kicking till he got a cramp in his leg."

"I came from Chicago, and my first race I ran with NASCAR, a Grand National race, everybody told me to follow Curtis Turner and Joe Weatherly, said 'They'll show how it's done on the racetrack,'" says driver

Tom Pistone. "So I kept following them, kept following them, and I kept saying to myself, when are these guys going to back off? And the next thing I knew I was upside down. I went in a corner so deep I didn't come out. That was my first experience with Curtis Turner and Joe Weatherly."

One-upsmanship becomes an artform with them. But unlike the antagonistic relationship Turner has with many other drivers, he and Weatherly share an oddly mature understanding: no matter what happens on the track, the day is a long one, and the night even longer. "They loved to beat each other at the track," says Bob Moore. "And part of their friendship was whoever won the race would have this big thing to hang over the other guy's head until the next race. 'You're no good at all buddy, I beat you by a quarter of a second.' 'Who do you think you are anyway?' Literally they would knock the other guy out of the way to win the race and you expect that's the end of the friendship. But they would just laugh about it and say, okay, it's just part of the deal. Then Joe would tell about four stories and Curtis is laughing like crazy and everything's fine. Or Curtis says, 'Okay Joe, let's start a brand new party.'"

They each race and party very well, and it suits them to try to top themselves in both departments. And in the mid-1950s, in the world of stock car racing, if you plan to race and party, Daytona Beach is the best place to start.

In Daytona, through part of January and into February, there are so many guys named Pop at Robinson's Bar that it's hard to keep track. After a few drinks, it doesn't seem to matter much.

Robinson's is where the party starts every night. Turner, Weatherly, Paul Sawyer and a bunch of friends come in for dinner, Turner and Weatherly having steak and whiskey, and at midnight, the party moves across the street, just past the Castaway Motel, to the small three-bedroom house in the back. Cars jockey for spots out front and the guest list might number more than a hundred on any given night. The country music plays too loud and the police will show up before long; chances are one or two cops will agree to stick around for awhile, courtesy of Curtis Turner's ability to talk his way into other people's good graces. Besides, is there a law against having a good time?

It is just another evening at the Turner-Weatherly Party Pad, and everything is right with the world.

Starting in 1953, Turner, Weatherly and Sawyer rent this small Daytona Beach frame house from Cecil Grant, a lawyer friend of Sawyer's, and turn it into party central, in preparation for the start of the NASCAR season. All kinds of cut meats and extras are brought in, along with case after case of liquor. More liquor will arrive by the day, courtesy of the good folks from Firestone, Ford or other companies whose representatives wouldn't miss these gatherings for anything. The daily toll for entertainment will hit over $1,000.

At one point during preparations, Weatherly stops in the middle of the living room, clutching his skull.

"Isn't it awful, isn't it terrible," he moans.

"What's so terrible, Joe?" Turner asks with a smile.

"The gigantic, horrible hangovers we're going to have two weeks from now," Weatherly says. "I can hardly stand to think of it."

As writer Max Muhleman recalls of the gatherings, "It was a lot like an ordinary home cocktail party, except lots bigger drinks, a lot louder music and a lot more flirting and grabbing."

Weatherly's drinking "glass" each evening is a vase-like object, actually the inside of a lamp, which holds at least two quarts of liquid. "That way you don't have to pit so often," he explains, as he walks through the party with a rebuilt fire extinguisher filled with booze slung over his shoulder. A quick squirt and another guest is satisfied.

Drivers and mechanics, car owners and promoters, writers and reporters, businessmen, timbermen, Bill France and NASCAR officials, in some cases husbands and wives, in other cases gorgeous women and other locals, whomever is around, everybody is welcome.

Chris Economaki, the esteemed motorsports journalist who announced the races at Daytona from 1951-1958, remembers the night Weatherly pushed the guest-list envelope. "He came back with—I don't know whether it was a mule or a jackass," he says. "He brought it to the foot of the stairs, and he had this broom, and he whacked this animal in the behind and it would go up one step. And he'd whack it again and it would go up another step. Well at some point, the animal got halfway up these stairs and now Weatherly had to climb up and he had no way to swing the broom. And there was all kinds of goings-on from top to bottom to hit this animal in the back. He finally got him up, and stuck his head in the room and says, 'I brought my date with me,' and he tugs this animal into the room, and the place just exploded in laughter."

The parties also give Turner and Weatherly the opportunity to, as they put it, "chop some kindling with the honey bunnies." They've placed a scoreboard in one of the bedrooms, meant to keep a running tally of how many women each has brought in—yet another area of competition that will continue between them for years. Like Turner, Weatherly is married; he and his wife Jean share a turbulent union. Though they divorce in 1955, Weatherly never moves his clothes out, and continues to see his wife when he comes home to Norfolk. Weatherly's girlfriend Joanne Michael usually shows up in Daytona during the first week or so of the partying. She is an attractive brunette who's shorter than Weatherly. He calls her Short Track.

There is music and plenty of people join Weatherly and Short Track as they dance in the middle of the room, while shouts and laughs punctuate the evening. And there are the occasional departures to a bedroom. "It wasn't a scout convention, that's for sure, but it was mostly drinking and laughing," says Muhleman. "There were racing oriented people but some were locals, too. People would come over from Robinson's bar—the good-looking waitresses and the bartenders, and some of the good-looking customers. It was just a great place. People weren't having sex all the time, there was just an occasional proclivity or availability for that. And several people would have to sleep over 'cause they couldn't get down the stairs. It was a lot of fun."

Weatherly is practically the evening's entertainment, joking and laughing, playing tricks and cracking up the room. Turner, nursing his Canadian Club, is quieter, making conversation or perhaps sneaking off to a room to take a call for a new timber deal. Maybe there's a tussle, or an argument here or there. A break in the music comes and you can hear the energy begin to deflate in the room, and Turner senses a lull. "Don't worry about nothin' folks," he shouts above the din. "Let's all take a break, comb our hair and then come on back, 'cause if you don't like this party, another one's startin' in about fifteen minutes."

Among the frequent partygoers at the Turner-Weatherly Party Pad is Tim Flock, who's normally about as happy a man behind the wheel of a race car as you'll ever find. But Flock is tense: his car owner, Carl Kiekhaefer, is the last person you'd ever see at the Party Pad, and chances are he'd only show up if it meant dragging Tim out of there.

Kiekhaefer, owner of a Mercury Outboard motor company, is thickly built with furrowed brows over a large ego and a penchant for believing his way is the only way. To help drum up more business, Kiekhaefer begins to pour gobs of his money into the creation of a team of drivers for NASCAR. He decides on Chryslers, hires groups of mechanics and commissions the building of a sleek fleet of white automobiles. And he brings in several top drivers to pilot his incredible machines, making everybody sleep in what looks like military barracks and keeping drivers from their wives or girl-friends on the nights before race days, to fine tune their focus. In 1955, the plan works extraordinarily: Kiekhaefer's cars win twenty-two of the thirty-nine races he's entered. In eighteen of them, it's the happy-go-lucky Tim Flock behind the wheel, and though Flock wins the Grand National title, he can only claim to feel lucky, not happy.

Kiekhaefer at one point yearns to add Weatherly to his stable, but the driver refuses.

"I can't drive for you Carl," Weatherly tells him. "I just can't take the bed checks."

For years, auto manufacturers have supported drivers under the table; with the blazing success of Kiekhaefer's Chryslers translating to sales fig-ures, Ford and Chevrolet decide it's time to jump in directly. Modified great and mechanic extraordinaire Buddy Shuman is brought in to run the Ford program, and Ed Schwam of Schwam Motorsports Company spon-sors a couple of cars for the 1955 Southern 500. Schwam is no slouch at garnering publicity. He has his cars painted purple and dubs them the "Wild Hogs," a slogan that hogs headlines in the motorsports papers. Schwam and Shuman figure the hog drivers should be just crazy and tal-ented enough to steer victory away from Chrysler and Chevy. Out of a slate of top stars in the sport, Turner—Shuman's one-time Modified series rival—and Weatherly are picked as Ford's first factory-sponsored drivers, the linchpins of the motor company's $2 million investment.

Wild Hogs are the right speed for guys like them.

"Curtis was chosen because he was so good!" says Leonard Wood. "The folks at Ford could spot a great driver." And Schwam got perhaps more than he bargained for in the marketing department. "Joe brought a live pig in, and painted him purple, like the car," says Glen Wood. He was leading that little pig around. Somebody said they slipped the pig in the car with him when he qualified, and that it messed in the car—which it would have if you put it in a race car."

Shuman pours everything into getting the Hogs ready for the 1955 Southern 500, and though both cars are strong enough to lead—Weatherly is in front for half the race—mechanical failure knocks them out as Herb Thomas, in a Chevy, wins the day.

Preparations are made to make 1956 a banner year for Ford, with Shuman working overtime. On the eve of the first race, in a hotel room in Hickory, North Carolina, an exhausted Shuman decides to have one last smoke before bed, and promptly falls asleep. An ash falls to the bed sheets and the flames climb. By the time police arrive, Shuman is dead of smoke inhalation.

At the Party Pad celebration in 1956, toasts are raised to Shuman, with Turner and Weatherly vowing to return the following Labor Day to capture the one race their friend tried so hard to win.

But there will be months of racing before then, with Turner and Weatherly concentrating most of their efforts on one of Bill France's more popular ideas. As France writes in a season-preview article for *Speed Age*, "Something new is being added—a National Convertible Championship Division, for late model convertible passenger cars." The sport's growth has led many new tracks to ask France to give them a ride. With the Convertible Division, he can almost double his races for 1956. "The Convertibles will operate as a separate unit, with their own point standings and a separate point fund," he writes. Many Grand National racers will compete on both circuits to help give the division a kick start.

Not that it necessarily needs it. The convertible circuit becomes an immediate hit. Fans can see their favorite drivers' faces as they toil around the turns. They can see everything: gears shifting, a driver's hands crossing up on the steering wheel, even a determined look before the start of a well-delivered bump. When a convertible race is ending, and a winning driver waves to the throng with a smile, fans can see that, too.

The convertible races are filled with action, and in cars that don't hold up as well as the Grand Nationals do. So there's the constant threat of attrition and caked dust building on the faces and arms of the men driving. "It was," says Wheeler, "one of the most entertaining things racing's ever had."

Shuman is gone, and Turner and Weatherly will drive Ford convertibles for former Indy racing star Pete DePaolo. And they are ready for their closeups.

At the moment the fire bursts in the cab of his Modified Ford, licking up from the engine, Curtis Turner can barely see Tim Flock's car way ahead of him on the beach. He can't see Flock himself: All the gear under Flock's hood has pushed his driving compartment to the backseat of the car. After winning the pole at 137 miles per hour for the inaugural 1956 Modified race at Daytona's Beach and Road Course, Flock is going so fast, and is so hidden, he appears invisible.

Inside Turner's car, the thick smoke, and the smell of burning gas and circuits are ever-present. Turner rumbles off the beach and back onto the highway; with one foot continuously mashed on the gas—in essense, feeding his problem—he keeps stamping on the growing flames with his other foot. He turns in toward the beach, then down the long stretch of sand at 130 miles per hour as flames curl up toward the dashboard. Turner stops stamping the fire long enough to hit the brake and send his Ford into a power slide, the fire now visible through the window.

The crowd sardined at the north turn of the course cheers at the sight of him, with many of the 12,000 amazed that he's still running. Earlier in the race, coming into a slide too fast, he'd sent himself into a spin, but in a typical feat of acceleration and control, and without taking his foot off the gas, he regained control after one complete twirl. It looked like something an Olympic ice dancer might have tried, except with a two-ton vehicle.

The fire is another matter, and as he clambers back from the beach to the highway, no stamping will help. The engine finally bursts into flames, smoke billowing wildly. Turner steers into the infield brush, leaps out to the grass and makes a run for it. The car has come to a rest near palmetto bushes, which instantly catch on fire. Black smoke pours from the car and rises as if from a pyre; several parked cars and some nearby houses are in danger of being set ablaze. It'll take crews forty-five minutes to put out the fire, and get the race started again, with Turner's now-unrecognizable car out of the running.

But the next day, Turner is more recognizable than ever, sitting at the wheel of his No. 26 DePaolo Engineering Ford convertible. He adjusts his shades, protecting his eyes after another endless night of partying. Somebody jokingly suggests he overdid things the night before, and Turner shakes his head. "Pop, if you feel bad enough before you start a race, nothing can happen to bother you." Turner hasn't even qualified for the race, which means he'll start back in fourteenth place in a field of twenty-eight. Rows ahead of him he can spot the top of his teammate Joe Weatherly's helmet. Weatherly, in the No. 12 Ford, has qualified with the fastest time, earning the pole.

Once the green flag waves, Turner makes his familiar five-alarm-fire move toward the front. For four laps, Weatherly is steady and in front, cutting through the jutting ruts and onto the ocean-packed sand, his trademark golfer gloves—thin leather half-gloves with all the fingers missing—keeping an easy grip on the steering wheel.

It takes five laps for Turner to gain a better view of Weatherly's helmet. He's upon him after a dash on the beach as he jerks the wheel to begin his slide. Running in a swift parallel to the ocean, the smell of spray and gas mixing in the open air, Turner sees Weatherly sliding right beside him in some strafing formation. Regaining control, Turner makes the pass before the road catches his tires. Come the next lap, it is now Weatherly's turn to watch the spectacle, sending rooster tails of beach airborne in a slide next to Turner's. NASCAR historian Bob Latford, watching from the press area just above the jumping, shouting fans, is amazed.

"I don't know who was taking the cue off of whom, but they came up to the turn almost like they were saying, 'Now!' and then throwing that rear end up to start the drift into the longest broadslides in racing," he says. "It was like synchronized water ballet."

But in this instance, the show lasts only a few laps before Turner puts too much distance between himself and his partner.

When he takes the checkered flag in front, passing one last time the charred brush he'd set on fire the afternoon before, Turner is a full lap ahead of Fireball Roberts, also driving a DePaolo Ford, with Weatherly's day long done thanks to a water pump failure. In victory lane, Turner takes the long, cylindrical, multi-prong trophy from Dede Lund, the pretty Miss Pure Oil, and, his goggles up, hoists the hardware for the grateful crowd. The win is worth a cool $3,525, but most importantly, after years of attempts and near-misses, blown engines and other mechanical abuses all in the name of showmanship, Turner, long considered the most exciting thing on this beach since Sir Malcolm Campbell began setting his land-speed records, has his first-ever Daytona victory.

The only thing Turner and Weatherly seem to guarantee is, given the right equipment, they'll put on a show.

Early in 1956, Ford stalls. Turner has won a few convertible races, but a flood, followed by a fire, wreak havoc on the company's California racing headquarters. The decision is made to move the operation to Charlotte, the heart of stock car racing, and bring someone in to run the division.

John Holman, a successful self-made trucking company businessman, is hardly the obvious choice for the job, but his determination and attitude win over the folks at Ford, and he gets the nod. Thinking a long-term solution is needed to end the reign of Kiekhaefer—whose cars win, at one point, eighteen out of twenty Grand National races, and seven of ten in the convertibles—Holman brings all his cars into the new shop for a week of intense rebuilding.

If the Fords are competitive before their retooling, they come back formidable. Of the sixteen ensuing Grand National races, a Kiekhaefer car wins only once; several Ford drivers split the wealth and deliver seven wins. The turnaround is tremendous.

But it is nothing compared to what will take place on the convertible circuit.

On June 22, Turner brings his convertible to Norfolk, Virginia, and bests the field for his fifth win of the season. The following week, he and Weatherly finish 1-2 in Wilson, North Carolina, and beat the rest of the field by three laps. The drivers have cars that can dominate and they know it. With knowledge comes power—and in Turner and Weatherly's case, it's the power to play some high-speed game of tag. At Wilson, after building a lead on everybody else, the contest now down to the two of them, the race turns into the greatest hits from the chariot race in *Ben-Hur*. The games are fun on paved tracks, but on dirt, with the dust flying in long shoots, it's wild enough to earn the pair a new nickname in the press: The Gold Dust Twins.

"They'd let each other pass the other quite a few times, but when it came down to the last couple of laps, it was no holds barred," says Humpy Wheeler. "It was hilarious to watch them in the convertibles. Those of us who knew what was going on, when they got in a race car, typically the convertibles, you could see they were just playing. In the grandstand you'd hear, 'Man, look at that!' You can't play in a race car unless you're a really good driver, or you're gonna wreck bad. But they would do that. They both were such good drivers that they could."

Through the next twelve convertible races, Turner wins seven times, with Weatherly on his tail in three, the races decided after excessive, spirited metal-banging played out before delirious crowds. As long as they keep winning, nothing else seems to matter. And Turner's wins total has risen to thirteen out of thirty-three convertible races he's entered. The all-time single-season wins record for a major NASCAR series belongs to Tim Flock, who'd won eighteen Grand National races for Kiekhaefer the season before. Turner has fourteen more races to go, and a legitimate chance to top Flock's mark.

On a mid-August day in 1956, Turner and Weatherly plan on driving a Grand National race in the afternoon and a convertible feature at night. The pair take Turner's plane to Elkhart, Wisconsin, and arrive at the Road America track just before the race is to begin. There's a steady drizzle, and puddles mark the 4.2-mile length of the road course. They've missed qualifying and practice sessions and will have to start the race at the rear of the pack.

"Pop, you ever seen this track before?" Weatherly asks, standing in the infield and squinting at the annoying rain.

"Nope, Little Joe, I haven't," Turner says with a grin.

"Well shit, Pop, neither have I."

Turner moves toward his car. "Don't worry 'bout nothin', Pop," he says, "just follow me."

The rain picks up as the green flag waves, and Turner watches a skidding exercise in bumper cars unfold before him. He turns to avoid the action and spots a gathering of shrub pines in the near distance.

"They were about five or six feet high, like small Christmas tree-size," he later recalled. "I thought I could see the road down [through them] 'cause I remembered flying over it on the way in."

Turner cuts through a muddy pass between two trees and bounds back down onto what he figures is the racetrack, cutting off a significant portion of the course. Looking in his rearview, he spots race leader and Kiekhaefer driver Buck Baker gunning to catch him—and Joe Weatherly cutting through the same line of trees. "We went from last to first and second in the first lap," Turner said. The race ends early for both drivers after mechanical failures and they head back to Turner's plane for the flight to Michigan, where officials are trying to hold off the convertible race start time until they get there. With no word on arrival, the cars line in front of the disappointed fans, and a pair of mechanics start the DePaolo Fords in Turner and Weatherly's place.

With fifteen laps in the record books, Turner and Weatherly come speeding in from the local airport. The crowd spots them standing at the fence. They move gingerly on the edge of the turn, looking for a break among the twenty cars roving on the quarter-mile dirt track. Seeing an opportunity, they make a break for it and race across the clay, into the infield. The Ford mechanics are waved in and Turner and Weatherly climb in and take off. They drive like they're in getaway cars.

It is three weeks before the running of the 1956 Southern 500. Holman and the Ford folks have every reason to feel confident; Carl Kiekhaefer is spitting bullets and relishing the idea of Chrysler-powered revenge. Every great driver in stock car racing will be there, fighting to win a battle for ultimate bragging rights at the only 500-mile race around. NASCAR is almost eight years old, and there has never been a more important race, and a greater need to win.

At Michigan, Turner and Weatherly have no chance to win; in fact, they will each succumb to steering problems before the evening is done. But on that evening, as they pass competitors at will lap after lap, and laugh their way through the night, it hardly seems the point.

Early on the morning of September 3, 1956, whatever cars have not made it into the parking lots at Darlington, or onto the nearby grass, or anywhere in close proximity, are lined up on the road leading to the track, the drivers and families having slept in their seats or in the open air. Eventually these fans will have to put their cars somewhere and take the long walk to the raceway, where they'll help make up the crowd of 70,000, the largest in NASCAR history, who have arrived for the large parade and the pomp, followed by the action. Hours later, the winner will walk away with $11,750, more than ten times the average 1956 Grand National winning share.

Given the competition between manufacturers, the spectacle feels Olympian. Tim Flock has departed Kiekhaefer's team, having grown tired of the drill sargeant shenanigans, leaving Buck Baker the biggest Chrysler hope, along with three-time Southern 500 winner Herb Thomas. Baker, with nine wins and a Grand National points lead, will start the race on the pole, after qualifying at a record-smashing speed of around 120 miles per hour. In all, thirteen different auto makes fill the seventy-car field. Flock comes to Darlington with something to prove, driving a 1956 Ford, and hoping to run away with the race, after first helping his brother Fonty in the grueling judgment of the Miss Darlington beauty contest.

Turner and Weatherly have returned to Darlington, their distinctive purple and white Hogs gleaming. Having qualified eleventh and sixteenth, respectively, their cars are among twenty-five Fords in the field. Turner hasn't won in the Grand Nationals in more than two years; in the convertibles he is king, by virtue of fifteen victories. But you can add up all the fans who have watched him win the twelve convertible races he's notched since late-May, and together they wouldn't top Darlington's crowd this afternoon. They'd already cheered for him, earlier that morning, after spotting Turner as he walked around the pear-shaped track, studying each little bump, looking for the best way around.

The green flag waves and in what looks like a signal of the day to come, Marvin Panch, driving a Ford, and Speedy Thompson, in one of Kiekhaefer's Chryslers, make it to the front. The pair trade the lead for twenty laps, before Tim Flock leads for twelve more. It takes all this time for Turner to size up his options and move through the speedy throng. On lap thirty-three, he passes Flock for the lead.

He's led every Southern 500 but one, and his car is among the field's elite. But even casual fans can see there's something different this time. Turner's two-tone No. 99 Schwam Motors Ford makes passes with ease, as if powered in part by his own adrenaline. When he pulls in for pit stops, he gives up the lead, first to Panch, then to Jim Paschal, and to Fireball Roberts, only to return with the same speed and purpose. Just past the midway point he moves in front again and begins to build a dizzying advantage. Four-fifths through the 500-miler, he's ahead by four laps, or 5½ miles.

It is typical Turner, the wild showman who always runs too fast and blows up. He's been in this situation countless times, racing headlong in dominating runs, trying to win without question . . . only to end up losing an engine, or a tire.

In his pit, Ford's head mechanic Pete DePaolo holds up a chalkboard sign with some sound advice scribbled on it: Take It Easy. And something clicks. "The new Curtis Turner appeared," wrote Hank Schoolfield in his *Speed Age* profile, "The Toughest Driver in the World." "When mechanical troubles started telling on the other leaders . . . he played it safe."

Going against intuition, Turner backs off just a little, and maintains a reasonable speed, waiting for somebody to challenge him. With fifty miles to go, his lead is down to two laps, and he waits, ticking off the miles one by one. He passes slower cars, but through his windshield and rearview, he can see other autos fail. It is, he will later recall, "The easiest race I've ever run."

Turner takes the checkered flag for the one race he's always wanted to win. Carl Kiekhaefer's best Chrysler, with Speedy Thompson at the wheel, lags more than two laps behind; and Weatherly finishes eighth, twelve laps off the pace. At age thirty-two, Turner stands at the apex of his sport.

Fans bunched up at the start-finish line pour onto the track as Turner, with one arm stretched out of the passenger-side window, hoists himself out of the car, the mob now coming to circle the Purple Hog. Angry Chevrolet fans shout questions about whether there's a Chevy engine in Turner's Ford, while delirious fans grab under the Hog's hood, stealing the oil stick and spark plugs.

"I can't say that I had any special ambitions to win any particular race," Turner deadpans afterwards. "I'd just as soon win one as another. This is just another race."

But even his staunchest critics know otherwise, Bobby Myers grudgingly among them. "He drove with his head in this one," Myers says, "instead of his foot."

Thousands of racing fans cover the two-lane road connecting Darlington Raceway with the rest of the world, and will be there to celebrate long into the night. But an hour after the action ends, their revelry is interrupted by a plane that pulls away from the track before circling back. Lowering for a moment, the pilot wiggles his wings in salute before continuing off into the distance. DePaolo, still soaking in the glory, watches the flight. He shields his eyes from the setting sun with one hand; with the other, he waves in the distance. "It's Turner," he calls out, and he can't seem to wipe the smile off his face.

"Let's have a party!" DePaolo shouts.

There are only eight more races left in the convertible season. Though he is dominating, Turner has almost no chance of winning the league championship. The point system rewards consistency above all else, and only eight points separate each position in any given race. With Turner having missed several races early on during the Ford transition, and Bob Welborn posting ten more top-ten finishes than Turner, Welborn has a nearly insurmountable lead. All of which means Turner and Weatherly have nothing to lose.

In seven of these final eight contests, the convertible circuit runs races totalling 1,526 laps. Turner or Weatherly lead all but five. Of the races, it's hard to top the action at Weaverville, North Carolina, on September 30. A wreck with twenty laps remaining sends two cars over a dirt embankment; a cloud of dust rises above the track that already boasts poor visibility. Turner is out in front, and one glance in his rearview mirror is startling.

"It was so dusty, you couldn't see nothing," recalls Tom Pistone. "The straightaway got blocked coming off turns one and two because no one could see it, and the cars just kept hitting each other, one by one."

Turner circles slowly then pulls back into the pits where he is soon declared the winner. It'll be the only major NASCAR race ever decided because only one driver is still running.

The 1956 season ends with Turner winning seven of the last eight races. On the strength of that run, he shatters the record for victories in one year, celebrating twenty-two times in forty-seven races. In each of

Turner's last seven wins, a familiar-looking, squinting face is his first sight in the rearview mirror.

NASCAR initiates a new fan-voted award in 1956, an annual selection for the sport's most popular driver. In the inauguaral contest, Turner is the clear winner. It's a trophy he treasures above almost all others.

"Hey Pop, come on—hop on in the backseat."

It is April 1957, and *Charlotte News* reporter Max Muhleman is standing at the edge of the half-mile Charlotte Fairgrounds dirt track as Turner pulls up in a Ford convertible. Turner has been asked to drive the convertible as a pace car for the Grand National race. No doubt this will help drum up more publicity for the second season of the new series.

Muhleman is still new to NASCAR, having reluctantly agreed to cover this sport he originally knew nothing about. But Muhleman's first interview had been with Tim Flock, whose cordial nature, ease with a story and wicked sense of humor instantly won him over. Muhleman had covered sports where participants wouldn't give him the time of day. Stock car racing is instantly refreshing.

But there's refreshing and then there's Curtis Turner, who makes Flock seem comatose by comparison. Still, Muhleman climbs in the backseat and Turner takes off at the correct, reasonable pace, with the engines of front-row drivers Marvin Panch and Buck Baker beginning their low grumble in front of 7,000 fans. Man, Muhleman thinks, this is cool.

"Hey Pop," Turner calls as he's about to turn into the pits, "you wanna make a lap with me?"

"Hell no! I don't want to make a lap with you," Muhleman shouts. "Get in there!"

Turner veers back onto the track and guns the engine, leaving the rest of the field in the dust.

The leap forward sends Muhleman bouncing against the backseat and nearly out of the car. He grabs at the plastic upholstery but it's too smooth and taut. As the car swerves into turn one, he grips the top of the front seat, his legs nearly flying behind him.

Managing a quick glace back, Muhleman can clearly spot Buck Baker's glare, since Baker is annoyed enough to be right on Turner's bumper. "I'm probably the only thing that kept him from hitting us," Muhleman says.

Meanwhile, Turner puts everything he's got into leading the race.

He runs only a single lap before pulling into the pits and letting the grid of racers fly by, and he swings around with a grin. "Hey Pop that was great, wasn't it?" he says.

"He did not mind scaring me at all," Muhleman recalls of times he spent with Turner. "I needed to laugh with him. That was my best chance to end it as soon as possible."

That's certainly the case when Muhleman is around both Turner and Weatherly. On one occasion, he and Weatherly are flying in Turner's plane, and Turner notices his buddy is nodding off next to him up front. He turns back to wink at Muhleman.

"Watch this," he says.

Before Muhleman can even mutter "Oh no," Turner cuts the engine on Weatherly's side of the plane.

"Hey Pop, what's the matter with the engine over there?" Turner asks.

Weatherly wakes up with a start. "God Almighty, Pop!" he yells. "That thing's out—it's out."

Leaning down, Turner cuts the other engine.

"Joe, I think this one's going, too!"

Weatherly, waving his arms, starts looking at all the controls. "Son of a bitch, fuck! Give me the radio!"

Turner sneaks back a look at Muhleman, who is forcing a smile. "And I'm thinking, 'Holy shit! This is the end of me. I'm too young to die,'" Muhleman says. "Curtis thought he and I were having a great time at Joe's expense. And I much more identified with Joe! And it scared me that here's a hell-raising guy like Joe Weatherly: If he's scared, where am I?"

After another few seconds, Turner, howling with laughter, turns the engines back on, while an angry, embarrassed Weatherly swears vengeance.

"The thing about Curtis is these things are never really big deals to him," Muhleman says. "They're just little impetuous things, like some people would decide they needed a drink of water. To you it would be the Event of the Month, and to him it's just another short, brief interlude in his spontaneous life.

"It was a terrible position to be in because on the one hand, you're trying to think of several ways to calm down this mad man. But on the other hand, if you complain too much, he thinks you're such a coward that he won't invite you back anymore."

From the parties to the races, from the flights to the power slides on the beach: to Muhleman, Turner and Weatherly operate outside of whatever boundaries they can. And tagging along is exhilarating.

"It was Bunyanesque, or like Hemingway in Spain," Muhleman says. "It was life in huge slices. Nobody knew stories that I couldn't beat every time I went to one of the races and saw these guys. I sensed that it was an extraordinary time with extraordinary people."

In 1957, stock car racing moves in fits and starts. Though Carl Kiekhaefer has departed from the sport, the manufacturer wars, which had hit a peak at Darlington, inspire an assault of media at Daytona. Never has the Party Pad been so crowded. Officials at Ford, Chevrolet and other makes are embracing the NASCAR marketing juggernaut.

Cars are getting faster. As if to remind people that safety features must keep the same pace, a series of crashes begin to dominate racing headlines, mirroring an increase in wrecks on the highways. On-track accidents are becoming all-too routine, and in a few instances, fans at the races are hurt by either flying parts, or cars somehow bounding into the stands.

Turner and Weatherly remain fixtures on the convertible circuit, where they pick up their 1956 pace. Through the first seventeen races of the season, Turner wins nine times; Weatherly wins four and finishes either first or second in eight of the first ten contests.

But for manufacturers, the situation is becoming more untenable with each crash. The worst of it comes on May 19, when Billy Myers' Mercury splits through a guardrail and past a fence, badly injuring several fans, including an eight-year-old boy. Two weeks later, during a convertible race at Ashville-Weaverville Speedway, Turner blows a tire and his Ford slices through a fence, leaps over an embankment and stops inches from the front row of fans. Incredibly, no one is hurt.

Days later, the Automobile Manufacturers Association issues a statement: All the auto factories are banding together to pull the plug on their support of racing.

For Bill France, the turnaround is startling. Drivers are suddenly given the factory cars they've been driving, but with all promises of future support removed. Ever savvy, he issues a statement defending NASCAR's stellar record for being a proving ground of safety features.

For John Holman, head of the Ford operation, the factory disappearance ultimately proves to be a boon. Ford officials agree to sell Holman all the cars and equipment in his shop for $12,000. He joins forces with the talented driver and mechanic Ralph Moody, and on June 14, Turner and Weatherly become the first drivers of Holman-Moody convertible Fords. Nine days later, Turner gives the team its first-ever convertible victory.

But the factory departure has still created a troublesome void. With Holman and Moody now doing whatever they can to increase business in other areas, they do not have a car for Turner in the upcoming Southern 500. He'll have to scramble to find a suitable ride to defend his title.

Turner has long admired top mechanic Smokey Yunick, whose expertise with Herb Thomas's cars led to all three Thomas wins at Darlington. Paul Goldsmith is set to run for Yunick in the Southern 500, but Turner figures there's no harm in asking.

Turner and Yunick are cut from the same iconoclastic cloth. A World War II bomber, Yunick returned home from Europe, settled in Daytona Beach and began developing his skills as a mechanic. Before long he'd opened a business called "The Best Damn Garage in Town," and proceded to live up to the claim by fielding cars that won two Grand National championships and a dominating number of races on the Beach and Road course.

Yunick never goes anywhere without his trademark flat-top white Stetson and never allows anyone into the mysterious confines of his garage, where he creates cars so swift they can't possibly be legal. Officials typically claim that he's cheating, but usually can't prove it. Yunick typically claims he's being innovative, and does prove it, routinely.

"Smokey was so ingenious, he was definitely the most ingenious mechanical head that we ever had," says Humpy Wheeler. "He was so far beyond. If he'd been working on the moon shot, we'd have been up there in 1950."

Yunick is also a fixture every year at the Party Pad. He can keep up with the best of them.

Turner flies to Daytona and shows up at the Best Damn Garage.

"Smokey, what would I have to pay for you to let me drive one of your cars at Darlington?" he asks.

Yunick lights his ever-present pipe. "I don't know, Curtis. Probably a million dollars."

"I don't have a million dollars," Turner says flatly. "How about five thousand?"

Yunick smiles and leans forward in his chair. "Curtis, I'm kidding. I think I can fix you up a car, a good car. You and Goldy can run as a team."

Turner qualifies third in Yunick's strong Ford, but the pall already covering the season shows no signs of abating at the sport's grandest stage, in front of 75,000 customers.

Twenty-seven laps into the race, Fonty Flock is spun into a wall where he sits, turned around and unable to move, waiting for traffic to pass so he can get out. Seconds later, he looks up through his windshield to see Bobby Myers rounding toward him, boxed in, startled and going over 100 miles per hour. The instant before impact, Flock can see Myers' eyes grow wide.

The crash sends Myers' Pontiac flipping mercilessly, with metal flying everywhere and the engine wrenched from under the hood.

For Flock, the injuries are serious enough to end his career.

By the time rescue workers converge on Bobby Myers, he is already dead.

After a long delay, the race resumes and Turner soon climbs into the lead, where he and Speedy Thompson engage in a riveting battle. For more than 100 laps, they race with abandon, and without incident.

Then Lee Petty joins the leading pack. Trying to move past Turner, he clips his Yunick Ford, sending Turner into a wall. Turner, the wind knocked out of him, angrily limps into the pits to begin a lengthy stop.

Weatherly's day has already been ruined by an early crash, and he's watched the action from the pits during his car's repairs. Turner's crash has him stewing. While Turner waits for Yunick's crew to replace the radiator, Weatherly jumps back into his car. He reenters the race in his battered automobile and promptly uses his bumper to smack the rear quarter panel of Petty's Oldsmobile. Petty's day is completely done, and Weatherly motors back in for more repairs.

"Thanks," Turner says, now able to climb back into the car.

It is frequently that way with Turner and Weatherly and their unique code of ethics. Wrecking is fine as long as it's between the two of them.

It is a formula that continues to work through the end of 1957, as

Turner finishes the convertible season with eleven wins in twenty-nine races, six of those with Weatherly in second. Weatherly himself has made a spirited run for the title, collecting twenty-five top-fives in thirty-six runs and falling just shy of Welborn.

The next season begins with the Gold Dust Twins dominating at Daytona, and Turner winning the convertible race on the beach again. By now, Turner has run in seventy-two convertible races and won thirty-four of them.

But he starts 1958 driving mostly Grand National races for Holman-Moody. In the first six races he runs in the premier series, he wins twice, but there are about twelve thousand fans in Concord, North Carolina, who believe he's won three times. The hundred-mile race there in March ends in controversy as Turner takes the checkered flag only to lose four days later when a complaining Lee Petty claims he's won, and presents his wife Elizabeth's scorecards as evidence. After days of studying the cards, Petty is declared the victor, even though Turner had seemed to lead every lap. "That Mama Elizabeth," he says, "has the fastest pencil in NASCAR."

A March 30 race in Atlanta is rained out and rescheduled for April 13. During those two weeks, Turner and Weatherly make appearances around the city, talking up the race and guaranteeing top-two finishes. On race day, they deliver, with Turner winning by less than a lap in a dirt-track knockabout.

Holman and Moody have two of the most gifted drivers in racing, now operating superior equipment. Although the auto manufacturers have "officially" pulled out of racing, stiff competition for auto-buyer dollars makes Ford and Chevrolet offer some under-the-table support to the sport's top teams once again.

It's one thing if the cars are used simply to win; but to bang, wreck and win as Holman's two star drivers always do makes the man crazy.

His face is rarely redder than on May 10, at the second running of the Rebel 300, the convertible series' annual stop at Darlington.

Neither Turner nor Weatherly had qualified very well, and the Holman-Moody crew spent nearly the entire day before getting both cars into top shape. The effort shows immediately: It only takes nine laps for each driver to hunt Cotton Owens for the lead. Following Owens around a curve, Turner taps his rear bumper, but the force is too strong and both cars collide and swerve as Weatherly dashes just below them and out in front.

Turner and Owens are only temporarily waylaid, and quickly rejoin the chase. Owens will eventually succumb to engine trouble while Turner spends the next seventy-nine laps making swift circuits, brushing the wall, mashing the gas in relentless pursuit of his teammate. A round of pit stops reshuffles the field leaving Weatherly in front, with Turner in second.

On lap ninety-seven, Turner, finally in range, delivers a nudge and a pop and passes his best friend, taking the lead for the first time. For three laps, Weatherly hangs with him, trying to get close enough to slap back, and *he* finally makes another pass. Turner heatedly rides Weatherly's back bumper, making him wiggle whenever possible for the next seven laps before skirting below and smacking Weatherly out of the way. You can hear the popping sounds in every corner of Darlington.

In the stands, 22,000 fans are shouting madly at the action. To anybody unfamiliar with the combatants, it must look like these two guys won't stop until they kill each other.

John Holman doesn't care how it looks. He starts holding up signs from pit road, warning his drivers to stop the shenanigans.

On lap 115, Weatherly dives below Turner as the pair head into turn three, a rail-thin lane hardly big enough for one car. Weatherly whoops madly and slaps the wheel on the way out of the turn. But one lap later, Turner nudges and leans through yet another metal-bending pass.

The drivers each come in for pit stops. Holman is livid. "What are you guys doing out there?" he shouts.

"We're trying to *win*," Weatherly yells before peeling out.

Weatherly is back in front after the stops, leading Turner by a solid half-lap. Once again, his pursuer is relentless. After twenty-five laps, Turner is back in familiar territory: right on Weatherly's bumper, now with twenty-six laps remaining. Turner clearly has the car with more hop to it, and Weatherly plans out his blocking strategy.

John Holman has seen enough. As Weatherly passes the pits on the next lap, he can see the sign Holman is raising, telling him in no uncertain terms to give way to Turner. The lack of uncertain terms come in the form of a string of chalkboard profanities.

Weatherly lets Turner pass and for the final twenty-six laps, he watches his friend's car move further around the track. When the checkered flag flies, Turner is nearly a mile ahead, a lead that belies the fact that this is the most merciless battle of their lives. It'll show the next day and days later, as excited newspapermen become effusive, calling this the greatest stock car race ever run.

Turner swings around toward pit lane across from the start-finish line and emerges with a broad smile, as Weatherly passes him, screeches to a halt and gets out of the car. Standing ten feet from each other, they stare wide-eyed before laughter practically shouts out of Weatherly's throat. Holman stands nearby looking grim, his arms folded.

"That was fun, Pop," Turner says, shaking his friend's hand.

"Damn sure that was fun, Pop," Weatherly answers, slapping Turner on the back. "I can't wait to do that again."

Not everybody is calling Turner "Pop," though. After the Darlington race, and his historic string of successes, someone in the press has invented a new nickname for him, one that he will proudly wear: Turner is now being called "The Babe Ruth of Stock Car Racing." Of course, not everybody agrees. In fact, in many of the South's greatest racing towns, fans will happily correct the misnomer. Babe Ruth, they will tell you, is the Curtis Turner of Baseball.

Chapter Six
1959-1960
"One day I was driving down the road and just decided to build a racetrack."

It is one hell of a steep climb. Bill France, standing at the top, looks out at the expanse with a relaxed smile. Curtis Turner will have to follow him. He lights a Camel and, his arms out to keep steady, trudges upwards.

The banking at the Daytona International Speedway, France's brand new track, is an astounding thirty-one degrees. When you look at it from across the 2.5-mile track, it appears to be steeped even higher, almost like a wall. Each such bank stretches for 2,700 feet. There are two of them on the track, and when Turner reaches the top of the banking next to France, he turns and searches for the other one. The track is so large it's hard to know what to focus on first: the banking, the stands at the start-finish line where cars will come screaming past swiftly, the enormous lake in the infield or the pristine look of the place. The speedway is nearly twice as long as Darlington, and the same length as the legendary oval in Indianapolis.

"Well, that was easy," Turner says, winded, and France, his chin high, can't wipe the grin of pride from his face.

"So, only thirty-one degrees?" Turner asks with a wink.

"I would have made it steeper," France says. "The guys doing the asphalt said that was as steep as they could get it."

Turner and Joe Weatherly have already driven the track, as have many others of the sport's best through these early days of 1959. Doing so is humbling. It is one thing to climb this bank on foot; quite another to reach the speeds that send you up, hugging the rail, only to whip back down, going on average some forty miles per hour faster than stock car racers normally travel. To Fireball Roberts it is "the fastest track in the world." He finds it publicly exciting and privately intimidating. And fellow driver Jimmy Thompson has perhaps put it best: "There have been other tracks that separated the men from the boys. This is the track that will separate the brave from the weak after the boys are gone."

"Isn't it beautiful up here?" France says.

Turner nods. "Congratulations, Bill," he says, extending a hand. "It's gonna be fun racing at a place like this."

A few moments pass and Turner gingerly makes his way back down. He is about a month removed from a trip to the hospital, the off-season price for a chronic disc problem that's seen a few too many wrecks. At the bottom, he looks up at France again, feeling somewhat dwarfed. France remains atop, like a king on a parapet, the final word over all he surveys.

It has taken France six years to build this place. A real estate boom along the already crowded beach, and the unpredictability of tides and crowd control, had long made the Beach and Road course an inhospitable place to run races. France brought up the idea of a permanent speedway on April 4, 1953, incorporating Bill France Racing, Inc., and figuring on a year or two for completion, and a budget of around $1 million. But difficulties arose swiftly, everything from financiers making promises and then backing out, to outrageous budget requests, to the sea of red tape that stalled local government cooperation. Then inflation hit harder in the mid-1950s, severely slowing down the sale of bonds as investments in the speedway. France trudged through days of charming investors, making promises and talking to government officials about all the money the track would bring in, while also running day-to-day operations to make NASCAR grow. Meanwhile, years passed with him wondering when the proverbial traffic would clear enough to let him build. One sneering Indianapolis newspaper referred to the place as the Pipe Dream Speedway.

But money slowly began to acrue. Then a chance meeting with Clint Murchison Jr., son of a wealthy Texas oil man, presented an opportunity. Murchison was in need of transportation back home and France offered to loan out his private jet. A grateful Murchison agreed to have a company representative visit the track and consider investing in it. In time, a loan came in for $500,000. France was in like Flynn. Ground clearing began late in 1957.

One year and $1.9 million later, bigtime stock car racing on the Daytona Beach and Road course is literally swept out to sea. Bill France has created the ultimate speedway and his sport's crown jewel. And he's done it his way, with patience, ingenuity and charm. It is, in fact, the perfect symbol for what France considers the "new" NASCAR, an image-conscious sport of growth, respectability and change, with France the undisputed boss. Daytona is as far removed from NASCAR's early half-mile dirt-track raceways as the Earth is from Mars, and France expects the sport and its players to follow this lead.

In February 1959, the track will see a series of events worthy of its otherworldliness. "Any filbert of the speed sport will literally drool over the various events which run all the way from February 1 through the 22nd," writes *National Speed Sport News* columnist Mace Benner. "Bill France's high banked asphalt speedway promises to break every tradition and speed record in the world of auto racing. It's really worth chucking it all and going."

That first month offers thrills, to be sure, but for some, the track proves horrifically unforgiving. Attempts are made on the closed-course land speed record of 176 miles per hour, among them by longtime NASCAR star and local Daytona hero Marshall Teague, piloting a specially designed auto in which he travels better than 170 mph on one attempt. On the second, he loses control of the car, which flips madly, and vaults him, still strapped into his seat, 150 feet into the distance, to his death.

But less than two weeks later, fifty-nine drivers line up for the start of the first-ever Daytona 500. Turner starts toward the back in forty-third spot behind his friend Tim Flock, who drives an identical 1959 T-Bird—but true to form, he works his way up through the field after the green flag waves. Flock, driving behind the speedy Fireball Roberts, discovers to his amazement that if he hangs right on Roberts' bumper, with Fireball's car splitting the stream of air ahead, he gets sucked along as fast as Roberts is going. Within twenty laps, Roberts has moved from forty-sixth to the lead, but in time, Flock and Turner both find their 1959 tires are no match for the swift speeds of Daytona. Though he ends up spending some time in the pits, Turner still manages to keep running, and ends up thirteenth. In all, twenty-eight cars will succumb to many a mechanical failure.

But for nearly the entire second half of the race, Lee Petty and Johnny Beauchamp will trade the lead, and as they cross the finish line, the race is too close to call. It is a photo finish, but France has not yet installed a camera at the line. For three days, he collects video and photos from around the country, and though Beauchamp had initially been declared the winner, the photos reverse the call, and France hands the first-ever title to Petty. The victor, though satisfied with the verdict, is not entirely enamored of Daytona. Driving on it, he has seen the future, and he's not sure he fits. "There wasn't a man there who wasn't scared to death of the place," he says. "We never had raced on a track like that before." By the next year, the new track will even cause a slight interruption in another February Daytona tradition. "After they went to the big Speedway they got you running so fast and everybody figured we'd knock all that partying off early," remembers Paul Sawyer of the Daytona Party Pad. "So we might party, like, Monday, Tuesday, Wednesday; but once the week ended, they cut it off early."

To Turner, the speedway is like some wondrous, rolling, swift oval, a shiny new toy to play with for hours. Like Darlington, which he'd quickly fallen in love with, Daytona requires only a car, a few sets of tires and courage. He will miss the beach course; in many ways, he made his name there. But why not make your name at the speedway now?

The event itself, the spectacle of the race, is nearly as impressive as the track. Turner has always admired France's ability to play a few notes on a pipe and send everybody running his way. Given all the things Turner and France have each done, and the things they've done together, nothing can touch this.

"If the relatively recent sport of stock car racing were to vote a driver of the decade," writes Dick Pierce in the *Charlotte Observer*, "chances are it would be Curtis Turner."

Pierce sits in the office of Curtis and Ann Turner's expansive new home at 4000 Freedom Drive in Charlotte. In the next room, a good hundred racing trophies are strewn around; on the desk is blank stationery for Turner's National Timber Sales Corporation, which he'd founded in 1955 with partners Richard Phillips and William J. Lawrence. After starting the company, Turner came up with a novel approach to drumming up new business: the creation of a subscription-only newsletter for timbermen. At $100 per yearly order, timber company owners and executives can keep up with various sales, with Turner encouraging subscribers to pass along hot leads.

Pierce's piece is headlined, "Racing Ace Turner Also Timber Tycoon," and by early 1959, Turner, regardless of a great penchant for spending, has his affairs solidly in the black. The newspaper article feels like a welcome: The family had only just moved to Charlotte in December. They'd kept the family house in Roanoke—sitting on ten acres on Laban Road—but Turner has settled home and business operations 150 miles south because, as he says, every time he flew from Roanoke on business, he always seeemed to be passing over Charlotte, which has long been the geographic center for stock car racing.

Turner finds the big timber deal where and when he can. In five years, he'd bought and sold two North Carolina counties, Dare and Hyde, along with 618,000 acres of timberland—half of that in one big-deal chunk.

"That's somewhere in the vicinity of one percent of the entire state," he says with a smile, as a sweet, round-cheeked boy of three-and-a-half with a mop of dark hair, swinging his arms like an airplane, races into the office, making jet sounds, until he is intercepted by his father. The boy, with speed in his genes and expressive eyebrows on his face, is Curtis and Ann Turner's second child. He, too, is named Curtis, but his parents call him by his middle name, Ross. "I want him to go to college, study law and then come with me in the timber business," Ross' dad says. "Frankly, I hope he has no hankering to drive race cars."

Turner has vowed to take things easier on the track because of his bad back. But in the first eight races of the 1959 Grand National season, he competes six times, winning twice and finishing second once in his 1959 T-Bird, despite disc pain that sometimes leaves him hunched over like an odd-looking question mark. When asked about Turner's speedy T-Bird, longtime convertible series rival Bob Welborn says, "You're talking about a driver and not a car when you point up Turner's wins in a T-Bird. That guy can win any race, anytime, in any make of car. He's that good."

When pressed by Pierce to name his most skilled rival on the track, Turner inadvertently lets slip one reason why he's encouraged not to slow down in either vocation.

"I couldn't name one—I'd really stir things up," he says. "But I think Joe Weatherly is about the most fearless driver in the business. Incidentally, Joe's working for us this winter—flying his plane for the [timber] company."

Weatherly had had enough, listening to Turner talk about flying. He'd gotten himself a single-engine plane and taken lessons. Everything about his personality on the ground translates to his attitude in the air: He's frenetic, superstitious and capable of great clowning around. Never very comfortable following flight patterns, he always keeps his plane low enough and flies by following the roadways below. Turner's associate Billy Tripplet remembers Turner landing his plane in Charlotte one afternoon and asking if anybody's seen Weatherly.

"No, why?" Tripplet asks.

"We left at the same time."

Thirty minutes pass and Turner is pacing with worry until the sight of Weatherly's plane comes into view in the sky. When he lands, Turner is there to greet him with a mix of anger and relief.

"Where the hell have you been?" he asks, grabbing Weatherly by the shirt collar.

"I got lost," Weatherly says matter-of-factly. "Yeah, they were doing construction on the roads so I had to follow the detour."

The one thing Weatherly hates is taking chances with weather. "The way Joe put it was, 'I don't want to fly unless I can see some twinkle in the sky,'" recalls Hank Schoolfield. Meanwhile, as timberman Norris Broadhead put it, "Turner could sit in the middle of a hailstorm and be just as calm as a smooth breath." And, says Paul Sawyer, "Curtis flew when the birds wouldn't fly." But together in the air, their planes side by side on a clear day, they revel in hijinks. "We were coming home one time, Joe Weatherly was in his airplane and we were in Curtis', and they got to tapping wing tips," says Turner's close friend, the normally unflappable local Virginia racer Pee Wee Ellwanger. "Now that scared the hell out of me. He was crazy. They've got the little bulbs on the end of the wings, the clearance lights, and they're trying to knock them things out. And they were just laughing with each other. Curtis had just gotten a twin engine. Curtis had a single engine—well, so did Joe, both of them had little single-engine planes and both of them traded and got twin engines."

"The two of them would play tag in the air," says Tom Pistone, another frequent passenger of Turner's. "One would go on top of the other, or the bottom of the other with their wings.

"Or they'd wait for you to go to sleep and then start playing games on you. I'd fall asleep and the next thing I knew, the door of the plane was open and Curtis was trying to shove me out of the plane. He was always trying to throw me out. I was wearing a seatbelt and he'd try to kick me out. He'd be smiling; he was always laughing; it was a big joke. He was playing with you. I remember one time he went straight up in the air and then came straight back down again. He'd tell you, 'hold your breath,' and give you one of them treatments. We used to land the plane in the streets sometimes, find a good empty street. Or we'd land at a racetrack, on the straightaway. The racetrack didn't say nothing because Curtis Turner was Curtis Turner."

Turner also discovers that a private plane is an ideal place to put on the automatic pilot and "chop some kindling." After a high-flying bout of lovemaking with one girlfriend, Turner and the woman fall asleep, waking up only when the propeller shuts down. Realizing he's flown off course and is now over the Atlantic, Turner switches from the empty gas tank to the full one, restarts and turns the plane around to safety.

"But Curtis wasn't the only person to do stuff like that," Pistone adds. "Joe Weatherly was just as crazy as he was. And nothing bothered me; I went along with everything they did."

Although doing so is not always easy for Pistone, a five-foot-three snub-nosed pistol of a driver from Chicago nicknamed "Tiger Tom," who has some success breaking into the sport by making up for budget deficiencies with pure will, and a little help from Bill France. But on April 4, 1959, Pistone comes to South Carolina's Columbia Speedway, ready to pilot owner Carl Rupert's T-Bird, which he's already driven to four top-five finishes in the young season. The only problem is, Turner has also shown up unexpectedly. He's wearing a perfectly tailored brown silk suit and is visibly inebriated. He's also without a ride, which doesn't always bode well for fellow competitors.

"Curtis had had several 'pops' of Canadian Club," remembers Max Muhleman of the day, the memory of which he'll take to the grave. "He said, 'Hey Tom, where's your car?'"

For a car owner and a track promoter, the idea of Turner driving in a suit unexpectedly is an enormous, irresistible boon. But Turner driving the Rupert Safety Belt 1959 T-Bird is almost too much for Tiger Tom to take. He's been given a payoff to let his friend drive, but not nearly enough money to deal with the potential damage a wreck might cause.

"Curtis driving a car was bad enough, but Curtis driving the car drunk was frightening to Tom, and he was having apoplexy when I saw him in the pits," says Muhleman.

Pistone rushes up to Turner, grabbing him by the lapels. "Please Curtis, please! Please don't wreck my car!"

"Tom was a very engaging, funny guy," Muhleman says. "And Curtis was getting the biggest kick out of it. He knew he would do whatever struck him and he loved seeing Tom beg."

Turner takes the ride and starts the race in third, and after Bob Welborn falls out, only driver Jack Smith is up ahead. But coming through the pack at the half-mile dirt track is rookie racer Ned Jarrett, and Turner applies characteristic determination through the powerslides.

Turner inches ever closer to Smith, pushing the car to its limit, when the T-Bird shuffles a little too quickly, and Turner feels the unmistakable movement away from the action and toward a fence. He slams right through it, smacking in a large portion of the front end. Stopped for the day, Turner sits in the cab relaxed, his suit only slightly askew.

"They towed the car back to the pits with him in it," Muhleman says. "Of course people in the stands [went crazy]. And Tom's like, 'Oh, no.' Now he's not being funny anymore."

Weatherly and Short Track have also shown up to watch the action. They'd flown into Columbia earlier that afternoon along with Sawyer, only to find Turner "sitting on the wing of his plane with a honey bunny, waiting for us to come in so he could drive in a suit," says Sawyer.

But hours after the race, Turner is ready to head to a local motel he knows, and he and his lady friend, with Muhleman in the backseat, climb in a "U-Drive-It" rental car, with Weatherly, Short Track and Sawyer in their own rental.

Turner heads down a local South Carolina road, seeing Weatherly up ahead, and something about the emptiness of the road and the sight of Weatherly "leading" sparks a familiar idea.

"Turner comes up to Joe's car and he sideswipes him a couple of times," Muhleman says. "He and Short Track were not amused."

This is not the first time Turner and Weatherly have played late-night bumper cars with U-Drive-Its and it won't be the last. "They used to rent these cars and go down the highway, knock the sun visors off, knock the mirrors off, they'd just body slam each other," says Pistone. "Then they'd come to a red light, Curtis would just shove Joe right through the red light. Joe would shove him, and Curtis would shove him, you know. It was all done in laughter. They wouldn't be going too fast. But there was not a straight piece in the car." It will get to the point where rental companies throughout the South will post Turner's and Weatherly's names at each outlet with instructions never to rent them a car again.

But on this night, it is Short Track who doesn't relish the game, and she cautions Weatherly not to hit back. Turner, reading his friend's expression, gets the message, but he's not done playing.

"We're on a long downhill stretch on this city street," says Muhleman. "I'd been in the situation before and I was always scared. And Curtis says, 'Let's take a couple of these telephone poles.' And I thought, 'Oh God, I hope he means go around them and not take them down.'"

Turner veers swiftly to his left and the car jumps up on the small sidewalk. The rental is hardly the most well-engineered automobile and is not especially equipped for curb-jumping. Muhleman feels the reverberations like a slam in the back, which helps him tune out the woman's yells up in front. Meanwhile, Turner is stoic as usual as he turns to slalom the first pole, then off the curb and back on again to take the second one. "He could make you feel under control when you knew you were not in control," Muhleman says. "I think we only did five or six poles." He takes each a little faster than the one before; it had been too easy the first few times.

What's left of the car then heads up to the motel, the parking lot of which is up on a hill, with a swimming pool adjoining it. The car darts up the hill with Muhleman hunched over, his shoulders tense, his hands gripping any upholstery available; but at least, he thinks, this is the end of it, and he permits himself a sigh. "And that's when Curtis said something like, 'Anyone wanna go for a swim?'"

Turner slams the rental through the low fence, which falls down like some trick door in a wild fun house ride, and vaults it outwards and then down into the pool. "But he only got the front end into the pool, not the whole car," says Muhleman. "It wasn't a very big pool. The car kinda went 'clonk!'"

The ride now over, Turner emerges, helps his date leave the car and then climbs out of the water and smooths down his suit, water running off his cuffs. Muhleman gets out of the backseat to see Weatherly standing by his car in the parking lot, convulsed in laughter. The water ride is another area of one-upsmanship for the drivers. Pee Wee Ellwanger remembers renting a car with Turner and Weatherly, then heading with the pair back to the airport. "Curtis asked him, 'Hey Pop, did you turn in that U-Drive-It?' and Joe said 'Yeah, I turned it in. I turned it in the damn pool!'"

Turner walks over to the motel office, which is, for the moment, empty. Ringing the alert bell and calling "Hey!" a few times yields nothing.

"Either nobody was in the office or they were hiding, and it was probably the latter," says Muhleman. "So Curtis says, 'That's alright, we'll find a room.'"

Muhleman follows Turner to the long row of doors as Turner proceeds to try each knob. Down the row he goes until one turns and opens. "Ahh, here we go!" Turner says. "We'll stay here."

Muhleman catches up and sneaks a look inside the room. "Curtis, there's somebody's suitcase in there."

Turner considers this for a moment. "That's alright," he says, and he reaches over, grabs the suitcase and tosses it out the door. Thinking better of his actions, he neatly picks up some stray clothes and places them next to the case.

"You know," Muhleman says, looking left and right, "I think it might be best if I just wait for the guy back at the office."

Turner and his lady friend will bunk in the room, with the driver managing to sleep through the angry knocking of the displaced motel guest in the dead of night. Muhleman won't see his friend till the next afternoon, at another Grand National race, this one in North Wilkesboro, North Carolina. Turner starts sixth in Pistone's now-repaired T-Bird. At lap 107 out of 160, mechanical problems knock him from the race. Turner is especially frustrated. At the time, he'd been leading for nineteen laps.

Two weeks after his midnight bumper car ride with Weatherly, Turner makes the most important, life-altering decision of his life while heading down a highway in Charlotte. It's made the way many of his decisions are, whether they involve getting married or driving his rental car into a motel pool, passing a competitor on the track or slaloming telephone poles on a dimly lit street. It comes in as a notion, an impulsive thought popping into his mind and, like a dart into the bullseye of a board, hangs there with an attention-getting thwack. Then, without the plodding examination of purpose that can bog down an idea for who knows how long,

Turner simply unleashes the plan. He skips the middle part. He moves straight from notion to action.

"One day I was driving down the road and just decided to build a race-track," he will say years later. "I hadn't planned it or anything. I had the piece of ground, so I built it."

After driving around a huge tract of land a few miles from his house on Freedom Drive in Charlotte, Turner comes home, makes some excited calls and gets ready for his big announcement: the construction of a mile-and-a-half speedway in the heart of NASCAR country.

His plan may be impulsive but it's clear the thought has been with him for years. He'd listened to Bill France talk about the trials, and ultimately the triumph, of Daytona for six years, and his friend's efforts had long given him the competitive itch. In July 1957, France fined Turner and Speedy Thompson $50 each after a tussle at Hickory Speedway, and Turner ini-tially refused to pay the fine, adding one other "threat" to change France's mind: he announced that he and Paul Goldsmith would convert the Packard testing ground near Detroit into a 2.5-mile track, and complete the speedway by 1958—one year before Daytona's opening—with Turner further refusing to race again unless the fine was lifted. France didn't blink, even talking a bit of sense into his friend, as was his style. Eventually, Turner paid the fine and forgot about the track.

But by 1959, the more prescient promoters, track owners and drivers can already smell the future of the sport, and it smells like brand new asphalt. There are already plans to build high-banked paved ovals in California and Atlanta. In 1955, NASCAR had run four of its forty-five Grand National races on paved tracks; in 1959, seventeen of the forty-four races would be on paved surfaces, regardless of purist cries that dirt would be the once and future best test of a driver's mettle. France had addressed the topic in 1956, in an article for *Speed Age* about the future of NASCAR. "What is wrong with auto racing today? There is no need to hide our heads in the sand," he wrote, no doubt with pun intended. "We must face facts. Speedway operators in future years must improve their facilities."

In one moment during a long afternoon drive in Charlotte in 1959, a desire and plan coalesce for Turner. Why shouldn't he, the "Timber Tycoon," become a speedway operator as well?

But he will have to act fast in order to do so. Word has come that someone else is intending to do the same thing in the area: Concord, North Carolina, promoter O. Bruton Smith.

From the earliest days of NASCAR, Smith, an immensely talented promoter with vision, imagination and determination, has made a good living in racing, but he's been something of an outsider looking in. After founding a rival stock car racing ruling body that had dissolved in NASCAR's wake, he continued his involvement through track ownership along with becoming a successful used car salesman in Charlotte. By creating a speedway in the city, he can secure his future.

On April 22, the local press split their time between two exciting press conferences. At his conference, Smith announces he's recently acquired 200.8 acres of land on Highway 21 South, bordering Pineville, for $300,000, land he'd been trying to secure for four years in order to build "the finest speedway in the world." He estimates that another $2.25 million will be spent on construction of the two-mile, high-banked Charlotte International Speedway, which will seat 65,000.

Turner, hardly impressed, reveals that engineers are already at work on his mile-and-a half facility, situated at Arrowood, a property on highway 49, heading toward York, North Carolina. Turner figures on his track costing only $500,000, plus the charge for property leasing. His speedway will house 45,000 screaming spectators.

Both visionaries are asked the obvious question. "No, we won't work together on this," Turner says dismissively. "And regardless of what he does, we plan to go ahead with our own plans. If he builds too, it looks as if Charlotte will have two racetracks." Even so, he also admits, "There's no sense in butting heads over this. There's not room for two tracks here."

Smith agrees. "I'd like to have Curtis throw in with me. He's a good man. Fact is, I'd like to see him as president of this thing."

Smith's words are more generous than Turner's but the rumor persists that both men are playing poker with less-than-stellar hands. Turner has not yet closed the deal to lease the Arrowood property, though it is under consideration by the general manager. "We're sure we'll build there . . . but if anything were to fall through, we'll build somewhere else," Turner says then adds, optimistically, "In fact, we'll be moving dirt within thirty days."

Smith, meanwhile, plans to begin construction "within from six weeks to two months." But a day after the announcement, Muhleman writes that Dabney Coddington, who owns the land Smith intends to build on says,

"No purchase has been made and no contract signed. Mr. Smith made us an offer which we felt was too low." Also revealed in the story is that one of the principal backers Smith mentioned in his plan—his brother-in-law—has not yet been asked to invest the $250,000 Smith said he was willing to give. And an architect's sketch for Smith's track, when studied, looked suspiciously like an exact replica of Daytona.

Turner tersely says he has no need for Smith's help. There's been a vote on the matter by he and his partners: Darlington builder Harold Brasington, Bowman Gray Stadium promoter Alvin Hawkins and North Wilkesboro Speedway promoter Enoch Staley. Says Hawkins, "We don't need any more money. The financial end of our project is already set up, so it follows that we wouldn't stand to benefit by merging." Turner now believes the track will cost more money, about $750,000, and a number of Charlotte businessmen, he says, have already agreed to ante up. "Whatever we might need can be secured through a financier we have contacted," he adds. A day later, Turner is sitting with Muhleman in his Cadillac when the car phone—one of very few manufactured at that time in the country—rings. "Where am I?" he answers the caller. "I'm sitting in the infield of one of the most beautiful tracks in the country. Right now we just call it Arrowood. We'll give it an official name later on. What's important, though, is that besides being beautiful, it's the most exciting track a race fan will ever see. We're not claiming the biggest, the most expensive or the fastest track, you understand—just the most exciting." Turner is considering all kinds of dream designs, ranging from a standard speedway oval, to something like a revolutionary version of the Beach and Road course, with cars going from banked asphalt, to sand, to the road. "It'll take a year, more or less," he says on the phone.

For all Turner's bravado, and the reports of big timber deals, the fact is, he does not have practically any of the funds he claims on paper. It is one thing to put up a good front for the press in order to keep Smith at bay; it's another to actually build this thing. Standing confidently at one point in front of some business partners, he holds up the keys to his Apache airplane and a Diners Club card. "These," he says, "plus faith, energy and work will get the job done. As we say in the timber business, 'The difficult we do immediately; the impossible takes a little longer.'" Turner plans to fly all over the country if necessary to solicit loans to get started. But looking at the situation objectively, Muhleman can sense that matters will eventually come to a head between Turner and Smith.

"I was writing for the *Charlotte News*, which was writing more about racing, but the *Charlotte Observer* was the bigger paper," he says. "Bruton went to [the *Observer* with his story]. My feeling was he didn't have that deal, and was saying 'I'm gonna do it' in order to force a merger.

"I was trying to encourage Curtis to go ahead on his own, saying 'If you can do it…' But Curtis, I didn't realize, was having as much financial difficulty as he apparently was, and Bruton is very clever. I don't think it was about Curtis not wanting to share it. I think he didn't trust Bruton."

But there's one thing Turner has to admire about Smith: he can talk with the best of them. It's hard to know just how much of what Smith boasts is true. The promoter keeps seeking Turner out, trying to get him to listen to reason and join forces. Smith claims he has all the financial backing they both need to get one track off the ground, and enough contacts to make sure the job is done properly. Even if he doesn't, he sounds like the kind of guy who will stop at nothing to see all the money raised. Turner has long known Smith and in a sense, there is much they have in common. Knowing his own financial limits, Turner begins to see the advantage of pooling resources, if necessary. "Curtis had a lot of naiveté and latent trust in people," says Brock Yates. "He was inclined to operate on that mountain ethic of a handshake or your word is your bond and not worry a whole lot about legalities. Some of his problems can be attributed to that."

A week later, Turner and five associates agree to buy the largest contiguous timber track in the state of Kentucky, 71,000 acres, from the Ford Motor Company for $1 million. Turner plans on eventually harvesting and selling the lumber to help pay for the speedway.

By May 7, the most vital piece of the track-building puzzle has changed unexpectedly. Turner and several timber and racing associates reportedly decide to form a corporation—with Turner elected president—to build a 1.5-mile oval that will be called the Charlotte Motor Speedway. But the corporation's first act is to choose a location, and though Arrowood has always been the top choice, the deal has not been concluded as planned. Another area, one that Turner and Richard Phillips have found with a much more reasonable price tag, is chosen. The speedway will sit on half of a 550-acre tract of farmland bordering US 29, just inside neighboring Cabarrus County. With 30,000 seats to start with, Ford Motor

Company talking about leasing the track for testing and the possibility of offering acreage to other industrial interests, Turner's dream is close. The corporation is authorized to issue 1 million shares of corporate stock at $1 per share to help make it all real. The speedway, it is said, will be completed in just under five months. Says Turner, "I hope I can wait that long."

There is a handshake, even broad smiles, and a toast. It has taken several weeks but Turner has agreed to partner up with Bruton Smith in the hopes that two determined fund-raisers will have more success than one. For Curtis Turner and Smith, there is not too much time to dwell on the realities that have brought the two together. For both men, the partnership is an investment, and there's something much more important to raise a glass to: the successful completion of the Charlotte Motor Speedway.

Among the small group celebrating that day is Dan Morris, a doctor-turned-businessman whom Turner has known for four years, since Morris' involvement in a Turner timber deal. In that time he's become one of Turner's most welcome all-purpose "associates," a friend, confidant, party buddy and fellow traveller. Depending on whom you ask, Doc Morris can also be something of a hanger-on, an odd fellow who appreciates a good drink and a well-turned phrase.

Morris will later claim that one can link the departure of Brasington and Hawkins with the arrival of Smith to the Charlotte Motor Speedway team, with Hawkins being especially vocal about Smith's shortcomings. In time, Phillips will also depart, reportedly after a personality clash.

But Turner has accepted Smith, who is fully committed to the project. Together the partners look over the architectural designs for their high-banked oval, and are somehow emboldened by what is a vastly unreasonable deadline: their hope is to run the first-ever race at the track on May 29, in a mere ten months. The event needs to be something exceptional, and the pair agree on two plans: The first race will be the longest ever run in stock car racing, a 600-mile test of will, speed and endurance dubbed the World 600. And with a purse of $100,000, it will hand out the highest payday in the sport's history.

All of which will require money, and the till is not yet full enough to support the venture. Turner and Smith set about selling shares in the speedway, "Literally selling them out of the trunks of their cars for $1 each," says Humpy Wheeler. The funds are only trickling in until Smith produces a series of commercials and mailings to emphasize the millions such a track will bring to the community. Smith sends the mailings and ads not only through North Carolina, but across state lines as well—an act that flies in the face of Securities and Exchange Commission regulations. The move is both illegal and shrewd, bringing in more publicity, and as Morris will later recall, the stock now begins to sell "like peanuts at an Irish beer bust." With money being collected, contractor W. Owen Flowe can get to moving the earth on the 275-acre tract.

Turner, meanwhile, keeps to his original plan, flying his Apache throughout the country, trying to interest any successful businessmen he can find to invest in the track. He also forms the Turner Timber Corporation, selling his interest in the National Timber Sales Corporation to Phillips. He is now president of both the speedway and his own timber company—when he's not busy racing.

With Turner spreading himself ever thinner, a shift of responsibility and power begins in the speedway's Charlotte office. Smith increasingly makes more day-to-day work decisions, while Turner, confident that he still has final say if he ever wants to wield it, is content to let his vice president handle operations. But Smith's growing comfort in his position is a red flag for Morris, who fears Smith is getting more ambitious.

"He's doing a good job," Turner says, assuaging his friend's worry. "And I put him in. He's grateful to me."

"He's making a lot of decisions on his own."

"That's because he's doing a lot of *my work*."

And the work itself is continuing, with tractors, graters and giant dirt movers clearing the land, making huge rivulets of earth throughout the enormous acreage. Turner can't help but tour around the land slowly, admiring the progress. Right here, being built entirely at his urging, he can see the evolution of the entire sport, the beautiful red clay, being prepared for leveling, grading and eventually paving. But the dirt, that's a beautiful thing—even after a rainstorm that seems endless.

"It was just a mess," remembers Muhleman of a day Turner drove his Cadillac to the track to show Muhleman the early construction. "They had graded everything from the highway over to where the racetrack would be and beyond. It was literally a sea of mud."

Though the speed limit is 55, the pair are doing 40, just gazing at the land. Turner, wearing a silk suit as he frequently does, points out various areas to Muhleman.

"Boy, that is a mess over there," Muhleman says. "There won't be any equipment getting into that for awhile."

Turner eyes him strangely through his aviator sunglasses. "Aww, Pop, that ain't a big deal," he says. "It's not so hard to get through."

And Turner floors his Seville, sending the car vaulting over a ditch and landing with a "Schoom!" into a gloppy sea of mud, covering half the body of the Cadillac in slop. The wheels spin but the tires gains some footing and Turner keeps the car moving forward, as comfortable here as on any open road.

"And we're sliding and he's laughing. And all of a sudden I feel something wet hit my knee. And it's mud coming back through the air conditioning outlets," Muhleman says with a chuckle. "And we're looking across, it's coming out a little bit in the middle and on both ends! And I'm saying, 'Curtis, we're gonna get stuck out here in the middle of this!' And I only had one decent pair of pants and shirt and tie in my life back then."

Turner courses left and right, slipping and speeding. He watches Muhleman survey the land, and he feels the glee of something beyond ownership or accomplishment; it is the pride of a father playing in the backyard with his boy. This place is muddy, unweildy and vast, but it is his, and it would be hard for Turner to love anything else quite this much.

The pair travel for what seems like a mile before hitting solid gravel and turning toward the road, heading back for the office, as if after a short detour on an afternoon drive.

"We need to get this place dried out so we can get the machinery back out there," Turner tells Muhleman, who stares straight ahead.

"Well, you certainly did your part today," he says.

"Yeah," Turner says, staring up over the windshield. "Better take this in and get it washed."

If there are any power issues going on in the front office of the speedway, they're instantly rendered moot the moment Owen Flowe comes in one afternoon with the terrible news.

Wearing a look of extreme distress, Flowe takes Turner and Smith on a tour of the land they've planned for their speedway. Drilling has commenced and Flowe's crew has come upon a totally unexpected glitch: a solid line of rock below the surface of the farmland.

A core-drill report had been commissioned for the land prior to building, and had revealed what were believed to be boulders below the ground. Flowe had agreed to remove the boulders for eighteen cents per yard—a number long figured into Turner and Smith's budget—and he swiftly began to get that difficult work done. But the "boulders" turned out to be half a million yards of solid granite.

"Eighteen cents a yard ain't gonna do it for this," Flowe says.

"What will?" asks Turner.

"I don't know. I'll let you know after we start with the dynamite."

The job will cost $1 per yard, TNT not included. "It cost $70,000 worth of dynamite just getting through the first turn," Turner later recalled.

"Bruton and Curtis made a giant mistake," said Smokey Yunick. "If they'd have searched North Carolina for the worst possible place to build a racetrack, that's where they built it."

The whole project, Turner figures, will cost a good half-million dollars more than expected.

But the pair have made a schedule; Flowe keeps blasting and Turner and Smith continue looking for money. On September 29, they fly to Daytona to meet with France to firm up their place in the 1960 Grand National schedule.

France has been keeping up on Charlotte's goings-on, and he's a little wary.

"It'll be finished," Turner tells him brusquely. "It'll be beautiful and fast— and the race'll be 100 miles longer than anything else you've got going."

"It's an ambitious schedule," France tells him.

"It's gonna be just fine," Turner says with a smile. "On May 1, we'll be done. You'll come and stand on *my* banking."

Turner watches his friend chuckle and he and Smith shake hands with France. It had taken France six years to build Daytona. Turner wants to prove he can do his in eight months.

Pee Wee Ellwanger works for Piedmont Airlines in Roanoke during the day. Lots of evenings and weekends you're likely to see him on the tracks of the local Virginia racing circuit. But there are plenty of nights when, after dinner, he'll get in the car and start driving. Maybe he'll head to Greenville where, for two years, he and Curtis had spent a lot of their time, living, partying, just having fun. Or he'll head out even farther south or west. Anything he can do to collect a loan, he will. "I'd take off and be gone all night," he says. "Curtis had different places where he had to meet the track payroll. He'd borrow five or ten thousand dollars to meet the payroll.

"See, when they hit all that rock, that's what [did] it," he recalls. "Up until the very last, he did everything he could think of to get the money."

Creditors are lining up to sue in order to collect. Flowe's creditors threaten the same. And it gets harder to borrow more money the conventional way when word of all these money problems reaches the banks. Debts continue to pile up and a halt is put on the sale of stock shares until all the solid rock is blasted out, and it can be proved that the track will be viable.

Turner and his partners are constantly on the road, raising enough to stay one step ahead of the debt, calling in markers, making promises and offering collateral. This is when Turner begins a unique practice of exhausting desperation: he'll write paychecks on a Friday evening and then spend the weekend in a mad flying rush around the country, collecting money to cover the checks and be at the bank the moment it opens Monday morning. "He was getting money from people who lived down here, in Martinsville and Stuart (Virginia), and he had two guys in Charlotte and one in Greenville," says Ellwanger. Loans also came in from Washington D.C. and everywhere else Turner can think of. "A lot of people donated to it."

Racing is now both a good distraction and a way to crank up the publicity machine. In December, Turner is one of three NASCAR drivers to race a sportscar at Sebring. He finishes second in his group and gets to talk all about being the "speedway president."

He sells off various small businesses and gets rid of a great deal of land, putting the money into the speedway. One week, he sells seventy-five acres of Atlanta Airport for $75,000—exactly what he'd paid for it—in order to meet payroll. In a sense, he's doing what he'd done in 1942, at age eighteen: making all those extra moonshine runs to pay his workers. That was seventeen years earlier, half a lifetime ago.

If the pattern is the same, the practitioner has gotten more inventive. Turner makes a deal to purchase $3 million worth of timber and mineral lands in Kentucky and West Virginia, but does something that's never been done in the United States: requests that $2 million of the money be paid through notes, purchased by the public, that can then be converted to stock.

But no idea is as fertile, or as odd, as the one he raises one morning to Doc Morris over breakfast.

"A few nights ago," Turner says, "I was sitting on a rail fence in the mountains of Virginia, just thinking and looking at the moon. I took to wondering if there were any timber up there, and if so, how I could get it down."

The notion arises from Turner reading an article about the space race, and wondering why governments were the only players in that game.

"Somebody's gonna go to the moon," he later tells Muhleman. "I think private enterprise can get there first."

After delving a little further, he discovers that several companies are in the process of developing communication satellites for launch. Those companies will need a way to get the satellites into the sky, and Turner—while building the speedway, making million-dollar timber deals and running some races—leaves his moon plans aside and resolves to build the missiles that will take them there.

As Morris will later recall in great detail, several aircraft companies offer great advice and support, but Turner's plan really takes hold when he learns about the Vaga project, a $28 million contract the U.S. government had made with a San Diego company called Convair, to build eight missiles. After pumping $11 million into the project, the government dropped the Convair contract, believing the Vaga missiles would not be as technologically advanced as they preferred.

Turner heads to San Diego to meet with the Convair board. Walking into the conference room, he's surprised to find the table filled with company executives, ready to hear his vastly technical explanation for project completion.

"I felt," Turner says, "as out of place as a drunk at a Baptist temperance rally."

But for Turner, this is simply another exercise in charm and determination, and after a long meeting, all parties agree in principle that the project can be completed if the remaining $17 million can be raised. Turner's next stop is Washington, D.C., where a NASA board of officials is ready with their own questions. Like Convair, however, NASA is cooperative, even agreeing to rent out the use of the Cape Canaveral launching pad, for $1 million per launch.

Turner sees the potential for $50 million in profits from this venture, enough to pay for new speedways in half the states of the union. But getting there will require half that in capital, enough to pay for launches, liability insurance, and to settle the odd but suddenly pressing legal question of who owns the rights to particular areas of space.

What Turner really needs is a quick way to raise $25 million. Reaching into his pocket to pay for lunch one afternoon, and finding a single dollar bill, he instantly wonders what would be wrong with advertising on the little white border around the currency. Wouldn't, for instance, Ford Motor Company be willing to put a coupon ad on the edge of each bill printed in a single month, at five cents per bill?

"I don't see why the government wouldn't let me do this," he ultimately tells a congressman friend. "This satellite project will benefit everybody."

"Everybody?"

"Better communications for the American people, clearing a path for the U.S. government—yes everybody."

"Curtis, this'll take an act of Congress; you don't have that long. Plus defacing a dollar bill is a misdemeanor."

"I'm not talking about defacing the bill," Turner says, getting his ire up. "I'm talking about helping the country. You think anybody cares about that little white border? It's wasted space."

"I don't think you can do it."

"You know what?" Turner says. "I've got a tip for you. Maybe the U.S. government should advertise on the bills. If you did that, you'd liquidate the national debt in no time."

Turner has spent $40,000 on the wild goose chase in space, and can't afford to devote any more time or funds to something other than the speedway. He will watch closely when, a year later, President Kennedy prepares a bill for congress, allowing private enterprise to sell stock to the public for just such a venture, leading, a few years after that, to the launching of the first Tel-Star satellites.

"Curtis never really had a system," says Muhleman. "I think Curtis was, in his mind, a pioneering achiever. Dream a big dream and do it. Do things that people didn't think could be done—pretty much like his driving style."

"He'd been down to Cape Canaveral about ten times and negotiated with the space authorities to rent a rocket to launch that first satellite," says Smokey Yunick. "Did all the paper work, did all the funding, and [someone else] started the company.

"He was a pretty good businessman when he decided to be. He thought good enough that he could run a big corporation. He had the balls to risk an awful lot of money on a new idea. *His* idea didn't happen, but his *idea* did happen."

At the end of 1959, the stockholders for Charlotte Motor Speedway elect a seven-member board—a collection of well-known businessmen from throughout the Carolinas—to officially run the track. Included in the group are Turner, the speedway president; Smith, its vice president and general manager; and G.B. Nalley, a businessman and timberman with whom Turner has conducted some of his most lucrative deals. Several posterity photos are taken of six of the members. In most of the pictures, five of the men, each clad in standard business attire, pose in varying states of discomfort, as if this is the one unwelcome responsibility of their deal. Only Turner, in a dark custom-cut suit with a lightly colored, uniquely patterned silk tie, sits amiably in the center of the limelight.

The photos mask the nearly plague-like circumstances that continue to befall the construction. There are twenty-six tons of equipment being used to move what will be three million cubic yards of earth to get the track ready, a situation the local hornets in the area find inviting. "When we finished clearing the worst stretch, at one point we only had four workers left on the job," Smith tells a reporter. "And their eyes were all swollen shut from multiple hornet stings." After the hornets clear out, it's time for the sting of winter, and North Carolina is suddenly hit harder than it has been in decades, thanks to three significant icy snow storms. The storms push the track work back for a month, time that Turner and Smith cannot afford. Every week, every day is another exercise in resolve. "But it was always, 'Everything's gonna be alright,'" says Muhleman. "That was one of Curtis' favorite sayings."

After only a year in Charlotte, Turner has emerged as one of the city's most reknowned businessmen, a local hero with the best interests of Charlotte's future at heart. Even his sprawling home has been featured on local television, after a lengthy redecoration. The TV exposure is a triumph for Ann Turner, but Ann misses the airing, being in an area hospital giving birth to the couple's third child, their daughter, Priscilla.

If success and fame are elixirs for Curtis, they're anything but for Ann. Always a reserved and shy woman, she is more uncomfortable and out of her element than ever. And she increasingly grapples with something deeply troubling, thoughts and feelings that have been festering for many months. Each stress in her life serves to scrape at a calm veneer, and begins to uncover the signs of mental illness. In several years' time, the condition will grow much more serious, and be diagnosed as paranoid schizophrenia.

"There are pictures of Mom holding Ross when he was young, about three or four," her oldest daughter Sue recalls of the late 1950s. "It looked to me like things were already beginning to affect her. Just the expression on her face. I could see little bouts of it starting, right around the start of the Speedway."

The move itself from Virginia causes great distress. On moving day, Ann had spent nearly the entire flight to Charlotte in tears. The idea of being separated from her roots hits her particularly hard, and is part of the reason why Curtis ultimately agrees not to sell the house in Roanoke.

For a time, Ann moves back to Virginia, living separately from Curtis in what has become something of a pattern. Other women are plentiful and available for the "Babe Ruth of Stock Car Racing/Millionaire Lumberman." If Ann is away, she doesn't have to see it all so clearly. But that, he might sometimes counter, is part of what makes him do it in the first place.

"There were some unhappy times, disagreements and falling outs. I could have done without that," Ann recalls. "Curtis didn't want to get in a fight with me. He'd usually disagree, and say things like, 'I don't want to talk about it.' So I finally decided, well, if you're not going to talk about it, I'm going to find somebody who *can* talk.' But I didn't say that out loud."

In fact, Ann doesn't have much in the way of confidants, and won't stray in their marriage. Part of her dilemma is that there isn't a great deal that she is willing to say out loud.

"She had an attitude of handling it that, to me, when I look back at it, was a double-edged sword," says Sue. "She seemed to handle it, but what she was doing was not handling it. It was all inside."

Though Ann has been vigilant about keeping the fights out of earshot, Sue remembers one particularly ferocious one, the yelling getting so loud she finally rushes to the kitchen to call the police. "Dad found out I had done that, he came in and I dropped the phone, ran out of the kitchen and hid in the yard," she says. She remembers hiding in the trees, watching her dad run around the house a few times searching for her, before finally cooling down and going back into the house.

Ann and the kids want for absolutely nothing. There are always new clothes and jewelry; inside Ann's closet are plenty of dresses that still have the tags on them. When Sue is old enough, new cars will be available, courtesy of her proud father. On occasional family vacations, Ross remembers traveling in style, flying in Dad's plane. But any kind of traditional family life remains elusive. *Make Room for Daddy* it clearly is not.

"The first time Mom and Dad separated, when I was five, and Mom went back to him, it was because she kept giving him chances, so he kept trying," says Sue. "I'd say, what did you go back for? And she'd say, he came back and he was so sweet. He would try, just try to do better."

After an argument, or a separation, Curtis returns, his hands frequently filled with expensive gifts and eyes full of charm. One day, he comes home and slips a beautiful rhinestone-studded watch on Ann's wrist. He tells her to redecorate the house in Virginia, and the one in Charlotte, to spare no expense. And for a little while, everything is okay. But then the arguing begins again, the disagreements lead to anger and silence and Curtis is gone, and Ann is home with the kids, but in a marriage without stability. More rumors continue to dog her. And you can see that by the look on her face.

Speedway construction has hardly begun by the start of January, 1960. One can now spot the outline of the first turn. The grandstands area is little more than a large mound of dirt. Turner and Smith have light poles erected so crews can work around the clock. With ticket sales at a lower rate than hoped, Smith invites the public to an open house in late January, a plan that is an immediate success. "We were busy selling reserved grandstand tickets and answering hundreds of questions about the construction," Smith says at the time.

Another open house is scheduled for each ensuing weekend, and the buzz throughout Charlotte grows louder. After the snowstorms have come and gone, the race fans return in the spring. But what they see as late as mid-April is still a head-scratcher: there are no grandstands, no guardrails, no garage stalls and, most significantly, no paving has been done for the 1.5-mile track.

Even though progress throughout late April and May is extremely fast, it is clear that the track won't be nearly ready for the first race on Memorial Day weekend. Tickets have been sold, flyers, advertising—it's all been planned, but running the race before everything at the track is entirely finished would be like begging for a disaster.

Turner and Smith ask France for a new date, and the only available one is a mere three weeks later, on June 19. The two partners guarantee they'll be ready.

"It was the hardest decision I ever had to make," Turner says.

"It's a very wise move," France replies.

France remains hopeful but skeptical: he'll believe it when he sees it.

The track's contractors are starting to feel the same way about their payments. The several paving and building companies, working twenty-four hours a day, are feeling ill-used, and schedule a meeting amongst themselves to discuss the possible use of legal action. Turner gets wind of the idea but finds himself without nearly enough ready capital. He is up against a wall.

"The contractors were going to try to throw me into receivership," Turner later recalled. "I'd paid out at that point about $900,000 and they thought I wouldn't be able to finish paying them."

He has one more trump card to play. As he later put it, "I knew this Mafia guy in Memphis, Tennessee."

Turner flies out to Memphis after recalling that his well-connected friend once boasted of his book of cashier's checks. The man is willing to part with one and Turner writes himself out a check for $250,000. "It was drawn on the Bank of New York, and there wasn't a bank by the name the check was drawn on," Turner recalls. "But it was a nice *lookin'* check."

He flies back after a long night and is just in time to surprise the crowd of construction company heads—"and each one had their lawyers"—stretched around a conference room table.

There is immediate animosity upon having Turner crash their party. One company head threatens a lawsuit. "We understand you can't pay us anymore," he says. "We're going to have to pull the curtain on you and your track."

Turner circles the room, staring bitterly at his hired hands. "You all want to get paid?" he asks. "I guess that's because you've all done such fine work."

Turner moves from man to man, pointing out the gaps between progress promised and completed. The pavement isn't nearly as thick as it should be at this point. The concrete in the grandstand is not up to specifications. The dirt-moving contractor hasn't moved as much dirt as he's claimed.

There is loud outrage, which Turner shouts above. "Now as far as paying you, which is why you're here in the first place, I have $250,000 in my pocket." Turner offers up the impressive check, with its sprawling script typeface. "But I'm not gonna pay you until you get all this work straightened out."

"Then I got brave," Turner remembered later. "I hadn't endorsed the check—it was made out to me—and so I just passed it around." The check passes muster with every lawyer in the room, each of whom inspects it the way an audience member carefully yet distractedly glances up a magician's sleeve.

"Everybody went back to work to finish that racetrack, on the strength of that check," Turner said. "I've laughed at them lawyers a lot of times since then about it."

With the workers running triple shifts again, Turner and Smith can plan on receipts for the first race covering the majority of expenses, not to mention all the prize money. As confident as they've been in the outcome, the two men are amazed to see the track now taking shape with astounding speed. One day before the first practice sessions are to be run at Charlotte Motor Speedway, only a single short straightaway remains to be paved.

That's when Owen Flowe decides he's had enough. There have been too many broken promises, and too much pressure from creditors of his own. He literally pulls the plug on 20 massive bulldozers, leaving them blocking the path of the pavers. "Tell Turner I'm not moving these machines till I get paid," Flowe says to one of his workers. "You tell him I want $75,000 in real money or I'll plow up this whole damn track."

The local police sheriff tells Turner that, since his track is private property, there's little he can do about Flowe's threats. Turner's lawyer Joe Greer has a better answer: "It is your property, and it's being invaded," Greer says. "You have a right to protect it."

Turner gets off the phone and nods darkly to Smith. "You up for this?" he asks.

Moments later, Owen Flowe hears tires screech on the nearby gravel. But only when Turner, Smith, Turner's younger brother Darnell, longtime friend Acey Janey and driver Bob Welborn emerge from the shadows does Flowe see the glint of firearms.

"Put 'em up, Owen," Turner says, standing in his suit, cocking a rifle, with Smith doing the same by his side. Slowly, Flowe and his workers lift up their hands. The entire scene looks like some odd reenactment of a Western bank heist, and Turner can't stop the slightest grin from crossing his lips. He looks over at Smith; chances are this is not what the promoter banked on when the two men merged. Janey and Darnell hot-wire the bull-dozers. It takes the better part of an hour for the large equipment to be moved but after that, the paving continues all through the night.

June 12, 1960 is a warm day in Charlotte. The sun is not very oppressive, but to the newly minted asphalt surface of Charlotte Motor Speedway, it might as well be, as the tonage of cars whip their way around the oval for practice. While the few thousand onlookers try to spot their favorites in the track's first practice session, many are also noticing something else. As competitors enter turn two, they swerve to avoid brand new holes in the track, the asphalt coming up in chunks, shooting off tires and bouncing down the banking.

Great lines of paving unearth themselves throughout the day. Drivers have come to see the new track, to get some experience riding and to try to find the most productive line through turns and straightaways. All too quickly, it's established that the best line is one that will not leave you buried in a ditch.

That night, crews begin reworking the surface, with more practices and qualifying scheduled for the next day. Fireball Roberts wins the pole in the afternoon, but this is after still more road cracking and repairs. Turner and Joe Weatherly will each drive 1960 Holman-Moody Fords. Turner qualifies third, which means he'll start in the front row for the race.

For the drivers, the riding at the speedway is a conundrum. They'll be competing for the highest purse ever offered in a race—but is it possible that the track will last for six hundred grueling miles?

In the weeks leading up to the first World 600, Turner and Smith, and all the drivers, make as many safety preparations as possible. Smith deploys dump trucks to ride around the surface to try to cement it down further; Smith himself even gets in a truck one evening to help out. Meanwhile, drivers wrap mesh screens around the grills and windshields to deflect the road chunks.

Bill France is eager to inspect the surface himself, and he's wary. He's kept abreast of every challenge, and all the odd solutions Turner and Smith have made in order to get to opening day. There has been no need to make grand comments or to intervene. France knows better than most the challenges inherent in building a track. He just never had to resort to gunplay.

Turner knows something all too well: According to NASCAR rules, prize money must be held in escrow prior to race day. It's a rule France established in the sport's outlaw days when promoters ran off with gate receipts without paying the drivers.

"Well, we got it done," Turner tells France with a smile as the two men stand at the bottom of the track banking, while crews continue to press down the surface in the days before the race. "A little late, but it still took less than a year."

France, like a prison warden, nods with his fists on his hips.

"Curtis," he says, "you're short $75,000 in prize money. We need to have that before the race."

"Bill, I know the rule," Turner says. "I'll be honest: we're short. The race is Sunday; Saturday, I'll take in enough in gate receipts that I can give it to you then."

"Curtis, if I don't have that money by two o'clock tomorrow afternoon, there isn't going to be a race on Sunday."

Turner tries to argue his point; given everything he's needed to do in order to create yet another big track for France's cars to run on, given their long friendship, isn't this the least France can do? Rules are rules, he is told. The sport is a professional one, and requires everybody to respect that. "You built a nice track," France says. "But we can't run a race here without having the money first—and in cash."

Turner stares at France. "You'll get it," he says.

France walks off and continues to look over the repairs. Turner remains behind. "That was the first inkling I had," he later recalled, "of Bill France trying to cause me trouble."

Turner has just one last provision for an emergency such as this. Nothing has been more annoying during the construction than a perennial lack of control: over time, track conditions, anything. And every time he turned around, he was always dealing with the endless red tape of financial institutions.

So a few months earlier, he had bought a bank.

"It was a small bank," he later said. "It could only loan $12,000 to any one person. So I borrowed $75,000."

After a flight to Lynchburg, Virginia, Turner visits his friend G.D. Smith, president of the Bank of the Big Island. Smith writes out a cashier's check to Turner, in exchange for a three-day note that Turner plans to cover first thing Monday morning, with gate receipts.

"I got a cashier's check made out to me for $150,000 and I kited a $75,000 check for the prize money and deposited one up there in the Bank of Charlotte," said Turner. "It was the only way I could do it."

The next morning, Turner and France meet up again at the Bank of Charlotte.

France looks closely at the cashier's check, then nods to the bank's vice president, Dewey Godfrey. "You're backing up this check?"

Godfrey has been friends with Turner since the start of the speedway. But on this day he only cares about one thing: his belief that the track will be good for the city.

"To me," he tells France, "this is cash."

In eleven years, Bill France has poured his considerable efforts into making stock car racing worthy of the name NASCAR, a sanctioning body with rules to govern professionals, instead of something ragtag and disorganized. He'd first established his reputation as the man in charge on June 19, 1948, disqualifying the winner in the first-ever Grand National race for rules violation. Eleven years later, almost to the minute, he stands at the Charlotte Motor Speedway, watching Curtis Turner, who'd run in that first race, line up in the front row at his own track, with both men hoping this day will add to a fine history.

It takes Turner seventy-nine laps to get to the front. By then, Pistone has already led for eight laps, Junior Johnson for five more. Several more racers see their engines or tires blow, with everybody keeping a close watch on the ever-changing obstacle course created by asphalt.

"The first race, the track just tore up," Pistone says. "It was like a dirt track, and that hurt Curtis tremendously."

But once in the race, his only concern is getting around and staying up front. Nobody knows this place better than he does. It's been designed exactly how he wanted it to be, and each lap in competition is a gift of purpose and accomplishment. He races past spots that remain unfinished, or where endless blasting occurred, and lengths of chopped asphalt. It's rough, but it's all his.

What a triumph it could have been to come away with a win, to have one hell of a good time with some of the winnings and them pump what is left of the $27,000 winner's share back into the speedway. But less than halfway through the 400-lap race, while sitting in third place, his engine blows, sending him to the sidelines.

Turner climbs to the press box and watches the cars swerve and speed around. He finds Bruton Smith and they share a moment of relief: it looks as though the race will make it all the way through without any breaks for repair.

Fireball Roberts, Marvin Panch, Ned Jarrett, Tom Pistone, Joe Weatherly, Turner . . . the list of casualties grows, leaving number-two qualifier Jack Smith ahead by several laps through the waning stages of the race. But a sharp piece of metal, perhaps from a bumper of a competing car, slices into his gas tank, ending his day.

With Smith out, Joe Lee Johnson, the defending NASCAR Convertible Division champ, inherits his own sizeable lead, and for the last fifty laps, no driver or pothole will threaten him. When he takes the checkered flag, he does so with a four-lap advantage. Johnson is one of sixty drivers who started the race, and one of only twenty-three who end the day still running.

In order to win the race, Hank Schoolfield will later report, "Johnson survived a grueling battle between automobiles and flying asphalt."

Turner, his off-white pants still streaked with dirt and grease from the race, joins Bruton Smith in the winner's circle as Johnson latches onto the five-foot-tall trophy created for the race. Cheers rise from the crowd, and Turner looks out at them through tired eyes and dark sunglasses. The crowd had been announced at about 70,000, but looking at the stands, attendance is patchy. The actual number of fans will be a little over half that. Then Turner gazes out over the track, which is almost as patchy. When the receipts are all counted, how much will he and Smith's speedway get for all this effort, and what will result from the first impression it has left?

"You know, people were really disturbed about how that race turned out," says NASCAR star driver Junior Johnson. "I think the success of that racetrack basically hinged on having a good day, and they had a pretty bad day."

Turner goes back to the on-site ticket office and he and Smith stare at the piles of cash in the main room.

Staffers stuff the money into bushel baskets, and the baskets are then loaded onto Turner's plane, where Ann Turner is waiting.

"I knew from his demeanor that something was awful wrong," she remembers. "He was disappointed because it didn't make everything the first race. And I thought that if he'd be patient, the thing would make plenty of money in time.

"He took the bushel baskets full of money and flew it from Charlotte right out to the bank. He didn't even want to count it all. He just took the money and set it down in the bank and went on out."

Chapter Seven
1960-1961
"He lost everything he had."

On February 14, 1960, Bill France stages the second-ever Daytona 500, and Junior Johnson captures the race by twenty-three seconds. His win is a shocker, even though Johnson is considered a top driver in his sport. But with eight laps remaining, the rear window of then-leader Bobby Johns' Pontiac somehow pops out, creating an air suction gust that momentarily spins him. Johnson then swerved around Johns to take the lead for good.

The win comes one day after the Modified-Sportsmen race is run at Daytona. About ninety seconds into that contest, a car driven by Dick Foley sets off a massive chain reaction that will create what is reported to be "the most spectacular accident in the history of automobile racing." In all, thirty-seven cars come crashing together, seventeen of which flip and roll, with twenty-four cars knocked out of the race for good. The race is stopped for thirty-nine minutes as debris is cleared and eight racers are taken away for emergency treatment. Anybody watching these events is well within his rights to believe that in stock car racing—as the cliches go—not only is anything possible, but one must expect the unexpected.

By this time, Johnson is a little more than two years removed from serving his eleven-month prison sentence for moonshining. In 1961, after notoriously being one of the last remaining homebrew holdouts in the sport, Johnson retires his bootlegging cars for good. In the annals of stock car racing, Johnson quiting his whiskey runs may be about as stark an indication that "anything is possible" as the flight of Johns' window had been.

By 1961, the years of racers strapping themselves in with ropes and chains is long gone. Drivers who can now earn a decent enough living in NASCAR are part of a growing roster of stars ever more familiar to the public, and at least willing to try riding the sport's slow and steady evolution to greater respectability. Historian Greg Fielden recalls that, "In the early years, stock car racers were said to be a direct reflection of the failure of the education system." By 1961, drivers are gaining experience racing on longer, faster tracks, and seeing more professional looking microphones thrust in their faces before and after a race, not to mention the new presence of TV cameras. And they're responding, more and more, as professionals. You'll still see fists flying at some tracks—when the situation calls for it—but perhaps more frequently, you'll hear arguments about safety and a sense of fair play, a tug of responsibility, and entitlement, as befits sportsmen in a nation of prosperity, and in a sport where, in Indianapolis, drivers of a different style of racing are revered as gentlemen.

Bill France has pulled his sport up to this greater level of maturity. Drivers and promoters have come along willingly, playing the game France's way and seeing the benefits thereof, or else not at all. "I guess back then he had to be hard-headed but it was like you were behind locked gates in prison [because of all the rules] sometimes," remembers Paul Cawley, who ended his runs on the local Virginia-track circuit after being penalized severely when someone accidentally used his pit passes without his knowledge. "You might as well go stay at home if you didn't follow Bill France."

Among the drivers France can count on to help grow the sport, few can match Curtis Turner for on-track bravado and off-track vision. In the stable of racers, Turner is wild, but when that energy is put to good use, it's a beautiful thing for France to watch. In early December 1960, Turner, driving a Wood brothers-prepared Ford, sets a new track record at Daytona International Speedway, at 153.335 mph. What better publicity can France get than that? The present and future of the sport, France knows, will be built on the success of new track builders and savvy promoters. Driving stars are the raw materials that help bring fans in. In Turner, France has not only an ally, but someone who, like himself, fits all three categories.

"Bill France had been a racer and he was a much better racer than he ever got credit for," says Fielden. "And he learned a working knowledge of what was needed in the sport and so he gathered all that information and he was the man to do it. Curtis Turner had a similar path. He raced but he didn't have the business expertise. But while Curtis was a good businessman—he needed to be to pull off some of the things he did in the timber business—Bill France had an iron fist and a velvet glove that was needed at times. Curtis didn't, and I think Bill France commanded more respect than Curtis. Bill France also aligned himself with good-quality people, which was one of his finer points. He had a far vision."

Turner's vision in 1961, meanwhile, is clouded by nagging debt. The bushel baskets of cash he and Bruton Smith netted the previous May after the World 600 covered the purse handed out to the participants, without making any dent in monies owed to creditors. Building Charlotte Motor Speedway had seemed like a grueling ascent up a huge mountain with jagged edges and pitfalls at nearly every turn. It is frustrating, even humbling, for Turner and Smith to discover that they've really only gotten to one ledge. And like in an Ian Fleming story, if they're going to escape any higher, they'll have to keep climbing, while eluding the sharpshooters on their tails. The sinking feeling gets no better in October, after the track's second race, the National 400. Tom Pistone crashes at 130 miles per hour in a pre-race tire test, and Grand National points leader Rex White, who'd been on the track at the time, blames the crash on the speedway surface. "If you ask me, the track stinks," he says. France takes a trip to Charlotte and declares the place safe. "There are some rough spots in the third turn," he reports, adding he's sure they'll be smoothed out by race time. "I'm sure every driver out there has driven on tracks a lot worse," he adds. The bad press contributes to a lower attendance, which doesn't even hit 30,000—despite such promotional efforts as Smith's announcement that one lucky fan in attendance will have a brand new house built for them near the speedway. The growing list of creditors, who've heard promise after promise, are less than pleased.

Turner is discouraged but he's too busy plotting to dwell on it. Besides, he usually finds a way to be oddly inspired by discouragement. The speedway in Charlotte is the biggest thing he's ever tried to do, and he's taken it further than anyone might have expected. And if he and Smith share anything at all, it's the growing belief that everything will still turn around, and the track will grow into a solvent, thriving business.

"Curtis was always very, very positive," says his longtime friend Domer Reeves. "You never saw him down. And he headed back against the wall so many times. I never saw him despondent. He always seemed to be up, like he knew there was a deal around the corner for him somewhere."

Between the two races at Charlotte Motor Speedway in 1960, Turner considers many deals and rescue options, from timber buys to loans.

Some options will help keep the lenders at bay, others are little more than footnotes.

One deal, however, grows into something much larger than anybody could have predicted. No one knows it at the time but the deal will send NASCAR hurtling toward the most incredible detour in its history. And when all the smoke clears, it will have altered the fortunes of Turner's life forever.

William R. Rabin seems an ideal choice to set up the books for Charlotte Motor Speedway. Rabin is both an accountant and a lawyer, and creditors are willing to listen to him as he creates a more workable schedule for loan payments.

There's another part of Rabin's appeal: he has wealthy friends, and Turner is happy to receive some introductions. Among those friends is Jimmy Hoffa, president of the Teamster's Union.

The Teamsters have been trying to set up unions for professional athletes, and Hoffa's representatives talk to Turner about an exchange: they'll loan Turner $800,000 for the speedway if he'll use his considerable influence to discuss the possibility of a union among his fellow drivers. There are any number of health and payment benefits drivers are entitled to, Turner is told. And with the Teamsters helping to negotiate with NASCAR, major victories can be won by just signing with the Sportsmen's and Entertainers Union.

Turner talks to a number of drivers about the possibility, but with speedway debts hovering around $1 million, there's really only one victory he's interested in: the relief that can come from the $800,000.

Turner ultimately rejects the plan. There are other items he and Smith are attempting to negotiate, like having an NFL football game played at the speedway. Then there are Turner Timber Corporation deals to go after. And toward year's end, there's the inevitable trek to Daytona for a couple of months, give or take, of partying, driving, phone working and more partying. When Turner sets the speed record at Daytona that December, he and Joe Weatherly have something else to add to their one-upsmanship game. In 1960, Weatherly had made his first serious efforts in the Grand National circuit, winning three times, including the Rebel 300 at Darlington where, two years earlier, he and Turner had waged their most memorable war.

Turner spends a typically lengthy period of time in Daytona. He's absent from the day-to-day struggles of the speedway for stretches, then flies in for meetings and to sign some checks before heading out again. This, he will argue, is the best use of his time: mixing with NASCAR promoters and drivers, flying off at a moment's notice to meet a potential investor, being the face of Charlotte Motor Speedway for the world. The track is his baby, but he's the kind of father who runs off to follow many dreams, and then returns, chagrined, with gifts.

In a sense, Turner's absense suits Smith. Building the perfect track in Charlotte had been his idea as well, and it's one he takes a great hand in shaping as he heads to the Speedway office every day.

There's no denying Smith's expert promotional savvy, and his own ability to sell stock and raise the track's profile. And when Turner is away, it's more natural than usual to feel a sense of ownership of the place, and a little bitterness as well.

"Bruton had a natural opportunity to—and probably needed to—consolidate the administration of what they were doing," says Max Muhleman. "Pretty soon people would see that, well, maybe I'm working for *this* guy really. There was a time where Curtis felt that he could see a power play coming here. And that started conflicts, most of which took place behind closed doors, but it went that way."

What had started out as a reluctant relationship has grown into a marriage of convenience. Turner and Smith have come to accept each other's responsibilities, moving in tandem whenever possible. They get along the way some trench fighters do, overcoming major onslaughts cooperatively, then bickering through the lulls. What they may lack in friendship, they make up for in a grudging respect.

"They got along *okay* because, number one, they were in a very strained environment," says Humpy Wheeler. "There was a lot of tension, which always happens when you don't have enough money. Who's going to spend money for what? Who's going to sign the checks? Looking at it from the outside in, Bruton was more of a builder, and Curtis just wanted to get the money and get it done. Bruton's a good promoter and Curtis was trying to get the money, and it was just so difficult in those days."

"Their friendship was not really a friendship. It was two businessmen teaming up for a project," says writer Bob Moore. "Each of them wanted to be the man in front. But again, they both realized—for lack of a better term—

that they needed each other. And to complete this project, they both had to do some wheeling and dealing. So to say that Curtis shouldn't have done what he did or Bruton shouldn't have done what he did, it's pretty hard to say that."

"Curtis had a lot of ideas and they all represented an expense," adds Muhleman. "And Bruton's trying to think of how to raise some money, acquire ownership, equity. Eventually somebody had to pay somebody.

"But Curtis was less concerned about that. He was the entrepreneurial half. He just knew everything was gonna be alright."

Turner knows this down in his bones because he has a lifetime of proof. Go to Daytona, take a pretty Baby Doll to some motel, win a race— or if you lose a race, win the next one. Lose your driver's license? Learn to fly a plane instead. Or build a track and get the money to pay for it later. How else would he operate? Everything always does turn out alright, to his satisfaction. It is the priviledge of a life fully lived, and enjoyed—up to this moment—without consequences.

For Turner, one more advantage of working on the speedway is that it has given him an opportunity to spend some time with Darnell.

Curtis' little brother, Darnell Lloyd Turner, is 13 years Curtis' junior. It is, to say the least, not easy being Turner's younger brother, but the long gap practically puts them in different generations. One might call Darnell a younger, less outrageous carbon of Curtis, a tall, handsome, dark-haired, soft-spoken kid. Darnell has learned the timber business, working with his hands alongside his father. And like his close friend Bruce Sweeney, Darnell looks to Curtis as a hero. So with extra effort needed for the Speedway, the twenty-four-year-old joins the crew of local Virginia friends who head to Charlotte to help out. There, he gets a close-up view of his brother's vaunted lifestyle. There are parties filled with people who regard Curtis with something bordering on reverence. Curtis always pays the tab for everybody when they go out. And there are pretty women whom Curtis can charm right into a bedroom, or a car, or anywhere else for that matter, and Darnell is captivated by it all.

"He tried to follow in Curtis' footsteps," Sweeney says of Darnell. "And he had pretty big shoes to fill."

Darnell even had the chance to feel heroic himself, helping to subdue the "Owen Flowe Gang" that wouldn't pave the last straightaway. He'll have a lot to brag about when he gets home to Virginia.

One late-winter night early in 1961, Curtis is tied up with business and he asks Darnell to pick up a woman friend who lives nearby.

"Just a friend of yours?" Darnell says with a smile.

"A little Baby Doll," Curtis says. "We're going out a little later."

Darnell settles into the nice new 1960 Ford he's been driving and heads out onto the highway. He cracks the window open: there's a hint of spring thaw in the crisp night air.

When he pulls up the gravel drive and walks toward the front door, the shrill shouts of an argument put him on alert. The closer he gets, the easier it is to make out what is being said, and when the name "Turner" is called loudly by a man inside, Darnell shifts his feet on the walk—and then there are more shouts, and a pounding charge toward the front door, followed by the cocking of a shotgun.

Curtis had joked with Darnell about this woman and her jealous husband. But she and Curtis had been discreet, remaining convinced that her husband suspected nothing. Rumors, however, had been flying and by now the man has heard all he needs to hear. Seeing a shadow by the front door, he's ready to exact some revenge on the tall, dark-haired man waiting outside for his wife: his rival, Curtis Turner.

The door opens and two shots ring out. Darnell spins but before he can make it back to the car, a bullet rips into his hip. He clambers into the front seat and manages to get out to the road, but the pain is immense.

Curtis waits in his office, glancing at the clock. The phone rings and the woman is hysterical. Her surprise and relief to find Curtis on the other end distracts her a moment—someone has been shot.

Turner is normally so low-key that the sight of him now—his eyes big and menacing—is startling. Nobody knows where Darnell is. Curtis rushes to his car and heads for the woman's house with some speedway friends in tow. Halfway there, he spots two headlights pointing into the woods.

"Curtis got out to the highway and they found Darnell laying on the side of the road," says their sister Dove.

Curtis drives, possessed, to the hospital and doesn't relax until he watches Darnell being wheeled into surgery. But the waiting room offers no relief from his impatience. For one of the few times in his life, he is utterly unapproachable.

He's been close to harm's way over a woman any number of times before; it's almost like a sport. He's made middle-of-the-night calls to friends to spring him from trouble and has hidden in forests to avoid detection. Paul Cawley recalls finding him once, freezing, after he'd been sitting up in a tree for hours. But he's always managed to avoid something like this.

The surgery is a success, but Darnell will have some lingering effects of the injury. Through his recovery, he manages a survivor's smile, as if he's taken one for the team. He insists there's no hard feelings. For Curtis, however, all the assurances don't matter.

"If it had been me, that would have made me crazy, too," says Charlie Williamson, Turner's longtime friend from Roanoke. "It really messed Curtis up—it was the worst thing because Curtis had been dating her. He never really got over that."

Turner is able to keep the Darnell story away from the police and the newspapers; that kind of publicity would deal another ugly blow to the track at a critical juncture. Preparations are being made to turn the coming World 600 into a two-weekend-long money-making bonanza, the kind of event that will thrill the creditors. Like at the Daytona 500, Turner and Smith arrange for two one-hundred-mile qualifiers the week before the big event, which will further milk attendance figures. But first comes the May 6 Rebel 300 Convertible race at Darlington. It will be the nineteenth race of the season, but only the fifth time Turner has suited up all year.

He has been little more than a journeyman driver through 1961. He lasts all of six laps in February's Daytona 500 while Weatherly, his one-time Gold Dust Twin, comes in second behind Marvin Panch.

In one of the two Daytona qualifying races, Lee Petty and Johnny Beauchamp, two years removed from their epic finish-line battle, stage another late-race duel, but this one has horrific consequences—the pair lock bumpers and end up sailing over a guardrail at 150 miles per hour, hurtling toward a lot below. Petty's injuries are severe enough that there is fear for his life. He survives but the crash effectively ends the three-time champion's career, leaving the family business' primary driving duties in the hands of Lee's son, Richard, who'd finished second to Rex White in the 1960 standings.

Richard Petty, at age twenty-three, is thirteen years younger than Turner. Buck Baker's son Buddy is two seasons into his own career; David Pearson comes into 1961 as defending rookie of the year; and Fred Lorenzen, the Chicago-born United States Auto Club champion, is back for his second season of NASCAR racing, finishing fourth at the Daytona 500. When Lorenzen gets his first-ever Grand National win at Martinsville the following April, he is behind the wheel of a Holman-Moody Ford. Ralph Moody has seen something tenacious and extraordinary in Lorenzen, the handsome northerner with the ready smile, dimpled chin and the look of NASCAR's first-ever pin-up idol. Like Moody, Lorenzen is a Yankee, and the first bona fide star to not emerge from the standard dirt track route. "He was the golden boy," says Humpy Wheeler. "He just didn't look like your normal Carolina/Georgia stock car driver: Had all his teeth, looked good, all that kinda stuff. He looked like Robert Redford." Despite the differences, part of what has drawn Lorenzen to the sport is his longtime reverence for Moody's first-ever Ford factory driver.

"Turner was a great racer," Lorenzen remembers. "I used to listen to races on the radio in the backyard of my house: Curtis Turner in Darlington, battling Joe Weatherly and Fireball Roberts. He was the biggest man down there."

But it is Lorenzen who has Turner's old ride in what is now the only convertible contest of the year. The racing series where Turner achieved historic success lasted all of four seasons and is now gone. But Glen and Leonard Wood have a speedy 1961 Ford waiting for him, and they're only too happy to help out. The winner's share for the Rebel 300 will be $8,420, a fine payday that could come in especially handy.

Turner may still be president of Charlotte Motor Speedway but people are pulling at him from all sides. The two main creditors for the track, Henry Morgan and James McIlvaine, hold a second mortgage on the speedway and they've threatened to foreclose. And while it's one thing when creditors are voicing the loudest threats, it's quite another now that shouts are coming from the board of directors.

After the first Charlotte race, there'd been calls for Turner's and Smith's ousting, but the pair have always kept their positions, thanks in large part to the protection of the rest of the seven-member board. With recent shifts among the directors, Turner and Smith are barely hanging on. Now among the seven—along with longtime Turner friends G.B. Nalley and G.D. Smith—are three new appointees: local businessmen Allen Nance and J. Lewis "Virgil" Patterson, and a blustery thirty-two-year-old Louisiana lawyer with the rather neon-bright name of C.D. "Duke" Ellington, whose specialty is finances. Ellington had been brought in at McIlvaine's suggestion, and in April, over the objections of an outraged Bruton Smith, Ellington is handed the General Manager title, one of Smith's two positions. Meetings are now bitter affairs. Everybody is digging in, waiting to see who will start the next inevitable battle for control.

But Turner still holds an ace: any boardroom coup will require a majority vote, and G.D. Smith, Nalley and Bruton always vote his way in a block.

It is getting harder for Curtis Turner to keep his head above water. Every time he raises himself up, there comes the inevitable scream and another waitress flies past his head into the pool.

He finally hoists himself out of the shallow end. "Damn," he says looking down. With each step, his leather shoes are making squishy sponge noises.

Darlington Raceway is only miles away, the Rebel 300 days away, and the back of the motel is sanctuary. The pool has taken on an oddly bluish tone. "It turned whatever color it did from the dye in our shoes and socks," recalls Tom Pistone of the several-day party. Most folks are staying away from the deep end. They still haven't fished out the police car.

Thankfully, Turner's Canadian Club and Coke hasn't gotten wet.

But all is not entirely carefree. Turner joins a discussion at poolside; apparently, "Fearless Freddie" Lorenzen has not come out of his room, and the contention is that he may be a little chicken. The accusation disturbs Turner immensely. "No, don't worry about that," he says, rising heavily out of his chair. "I'll go get him."

"I'm comin' with you, Pop," Joe Weatherly says enthusiastically.

The crowd gathers at the pool fence as Turner gets into his Ford, with Weatherly in the passenger seat. "Now remember, Pop," Turner says, gunning the engine, readying to put it into drive, "It's all about getting it at the right angle."

Lorenzen is in a first-floor room, the door facing the back. Turner slams his car into Lorenzen's door diagonally, buckling the frame and sending the door cracking off its hinges.

"Freddie," Turner calls, getting out of the car. "You in there? Some of the guys said you were too chicken to come out here, but I wouldn't have none of that."

Lorenzen slowly appears, his head going up and down, surveying the damage. At poolside, the cheers ring out.

"After that," remembers Pistone, "everybody was involved."

A fifty-five-gallon drum of water is filled up on the roof and soon water is cascading down upon drivers and other motel guests, who were also fair game for tossing in the pool. "It was a two-day affair and nobody took off their shoes," Pistone adds. "Oh, it was bad, it was bad."

And it is all prologue for the three hundred miles of convertible driving on May 6.

The race is a blazingly competitive affair from the beginning. In the early going and through the first half, the lead changes hands between some of the sport's best and brightest: Lorenzen, Turner, Weatherly, Fireball Roberts, and local North Carolina dirt-track favorite Ralph Earnhardt. But an early blown tire puts Lorenzen down, and for lap after lap, he slowly makes his way back to the front to challenge two of his heroes, Roberts and Turner, running one-two.

Roberts holds the lead for forty laps until tire trouble sends him into the pits, giving Turner the top spot with less than twenty laps to go. Lorenzen inherits second place, and the slaps and pushes the two have exchanged for miles suddenly feel like part of a hasty dress rehearsal before a great performance. At Darlington, where Turner had solidified his fame only four years before, the 32,000 in the crowd are standing, the cheers split between the older favorite and the fair-haired boy. With each lap, Lorenzen climbs up the high part of the track, and Turner slaps at him, keeping him at bay. Given the convertible view, fans can see Lorenzen jostled with each metal slam, but his arms remain relaxed and he's still coming. The race has inadvertently turned into a bitter contest for the ages.

Lorenzen hangs back, plotting his moves and remembering all the advice given by Moody, a man who knew Turner's style on the track better than just about anybody. "I was the pilot, he was my radar gun," Lorenzen says of Moody. "Before the race he said, 'We're coming to the biggest place and Curtis Turner's up. Look out because Turner will do anything to win. He'll run your rear end right out of the joint. Stay away from him. Stay ahead of him or behind him, but don't stay with him.'"

Lorenzen, who'd gotten frustrated at first with Turner's expert blocking, had tried passing him high and low, until Moody held up a sign that read "W.H.T." Lorenzen figured it out: "What the hell are you thinking?" And he understood it was time to work Moody's strategy: try to pass Turner high every time—until the very last moment.

"My car was by far faster than his at the end," Lorenzen says. "And I was younger—young blood. I stayed away from the parties. That's why I had the edge on those guys. The next day I'd be fresh, I'd have had eight, nine, ten hours of sleep, they had four, five, six hours of sleep, and I was ten years younger than them. That's how I had my hidden horsepower: age and sleep."

With three laps remaining, Lorenzen again goes high, and Turner drives him up until he's rubbing against the guardrail. By now, Lorenzen knows he has enough horsepower to make a move. With two laps to go he fakes high yet again. Turner has read this page in the script for eighteen laps and instinctively moves up for the block. The moment he turns his head to the right, Lorenzen veers down hard and plants his car on the bottom of the track.

In the grandstands, the roar is deafening, and for many, it's a shout of amazement.

The shock of the move burns at the center of Turner's back. Like a prize fighter tagged by a mysterious uppercut, he feels a momentary lapse in his reflexes. He moves left, and locks his Ford hard against Lorenzen's, neither driver letting up. Slam follows slam, back and forth like pendulum swings. But Lorenzen has horsepower, and the fastest route on the track. With one more slam, he sends Turner skidding up the track and powers into the open air.

Turner's been duped. This is all Moody and he knows it. There's no way Lorenzen would have come up with that fake on his own.

Now Fast Freddie has to keep Turner in his rearview. And as hard as Turner pushes the pedal, Lorenzen remains that much ahead of him.

"If I could have caught him before he got the checkered flag," Turner angrily tells reporters moments afterwards, "I guarantee you he never would have finished the race."

Lorenzen takes the checkered flag with a lead of six car lengths.

Nobody, apparently, has told Turner the race is over. Lorenzen keeps sprinting until he slows to a crawl right in front of the Holman-Moody crew on pit lane, and that's when Turner rams him like a kid playing bumper cars. Moody watches the scene and a little smile crosses his lips. Lorenzen jolts forward but then gives the car some gas and waves to the crowd.

"It was the race of my life," says Lorenzen. "Turner bumped me fifty times and I bumped him fifty times in the last twenty laps.

"Then the crowd came over the wall, and I was the new hero. They wanted a change in the South, you know? A young kid who was nobody they knew—they liked that. And people like to watch somebody get knocked down off their throne."

Lorenzen has also knocked Turner out of first-place money, which the veteran had been fixated on. Suddenly that feels like the least of it.

"Curtis seemed to be able to irritate the younger guys," says Humpy Wheeler. "Young drivers have to go through a period of intimidation. But Freddy parked Curtis, which is something very few people ever manage to do. That's when Freddy went from here to *here* in the fans' minds."

"Lorenzen knocked Curtis aside," Max Muhleman remembers thinking that day. "He put a dent in the armor."

In the three weeks that follow the Rebel 300, Charlotte Motor Speedway hosts four events for the sport's elite, and the fans turn out: 45,000 fill the place for the big show on May twenty-eighth. And they get their money's worth: in a huge upset, David Pearson, the fabulous second-year driver, wins the World 600, racing for the first time in a superior piece of equipment, Ray Fox's Pontiac. Turner starts the race in twentieth place but finishes forty-fourth, undone by a wreck one-third of the way through.

All the revenues are tabulated, and according to Ellington, CMS brings in $408,270 for the several weeks worth of racing. It's a significant step forward for the track. Debt that had reached $1.5 million after building was completed has now been reduced, by Turner's estimation, to $875,000. With those numbers, Turner travels to New York and returns elated, with a bank's promise for a loan of $750,000.

1. A dapper Curtis Turner sat for a portrait at age twenty, with pen and comb at the ready.

2. By his early twenties, Turner was already a success story, and a fun guy to party with.

3. The Chief Boson's Mate, standing in his Navy uniform, stationed near the Virginia coastline.

4. Curtis and Ann Turner eloped after his honorable discharge and began a life less ordinary.

5. Turner keeps the pace in a Ford, riding on the gleaming dirt in front of ever-growing crowds.

6. When not on the track, Turner enjoys his other great vocation, among the harvested timber.

7. Frequent partners and friendly rivals, Turner and Bill France shared a great mutual admiration.

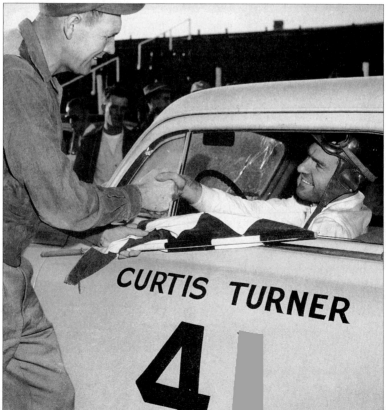

8. ABOVE: Turner (right) and France with their "upside-down bathtub" Nash, looking for a short-cut in the first Mexican Road Race, in 1950.

9. RIGHT: Little Joe Weatherly, the Clown Prince of Racing. "Joe Weatherly," said a close friend, "was crazier than the hinges of hell."

10. BELOW: At the quarter-mile Asheville Speedway track, fans witness the typically startling competition between Joe Weatherly (12) and Curtis Turner (26). This one ain't over yet.

11. The No. 99 Wild Hog outdistancing the field on the way to a win in the Southern 500 in 1956

12. An early view of Turner's grand dream, the Charlotte Motor Speedway.

13. Turner and his Charlotte Motor Speedway partner Bruton Smith give a lady friend a guided tour during construction of their track.

14. Turner sticks to the road during his record-setting run on the Pikes Peak Hill Climb in 1962.

15. Darlington President Bob Colvin, who'd worked hard for Turner's reinstatement, watches his friend remove the "Outlawed" tag from the Raceway's trophy case.

16. Driver-turned-owner Glen Wood always felt indebted to Turner for recommending him to Ford. When the ban was lifted, Wood and his brother Leonard returned the favor.

17. Just another night at Turner's Charlotte house, in the days leading up to the first-ever Rockingham race in October, 1965.

18. Curtis sleeps off a hard night of partying hours before the start of his comeback performance at Rockingham.

19. LEFT: Dirty and grinning, and nursing a broken rib, Turner accepts the prizes of his remarkable comeback win.

20. BELOW: Turner at the home office desk where many his timber deals started. A sign above his complete sets of Virginia legal books reads, "The ladder of life is full of splinters, but they always prick the hardest when we're sliding down."

21. BELOW: Turner's impressive collection of hardware took up a wall in the den. He often gave trophies away for the asking.

22. When he needed a friend to help set him up with a car, Turner frequently sought out Smokey Yunick, the iconoclastic master car owner/builder who considered Turner a brother.

23 and 24. Dick Ralstin captured the tail end of Turner's horrific crash at Atlanta in 1967 before rushing to help his friend out of the car. To commemorate the event, Turner signed one of the photos.

25. At a party with Bunny. For Turner and his Sweet Thing, life felt like one endless party.

26. Professor Turner teaches the art of the 180-degree spin at his Safe High Performance Driving School. The school allowed Turner to spend time at his beloved Charlotte Motor Speedway.

27. Turner poses with the first graduating class of the performance driving school. Sitting atop the car, from left, are his daughter Sue, and girlfriend Bunny.

28. ABOVE: The Turner family home, at the top of a 10-acre hill on Laban Road in Roanoke, nestled among the pines. From here, Turner could watch the planes leave from and return to nearby Roanoke airport.

29. RIGHT: Losing flying and driving licenses were inconveniences but few things sidetracked Turner quite like badly breaking his leg.

30. BELOW: The remains of Turner's Aero Commander litter the side of a Pennsylvania hill.

31. Turner's six-foot-long grave marker. From his cemetery plot, you can hear the planes taking off from nearby Roanoke airport.

32. The first Turner family gathers to remember old times, and acknowledge how far they've come together. Clockwise from left: Priscilla Gauldin, Tyler Turner, Ross Turner, Sue Wright and Ann Turner.

33. Bunny kept a close watch as Curtis Jr. made a brief but spirited attempt to reach for his own stock car glory.

34. The 1968 *Sports Illustrated* cover featuring the Babe Ruth of Stock Car Racing.

Sports Illustrated

FEBRUARY 26, 1968   40 CENTS

KING
OF THE
WILD
ROAD

CURTIS TURNER

McIlvaine and Morgan, however, have made up their minds. The speedway is a money-making proposition but it has its troubles, and those troubles start at the top.

They've heard enough of Turner's and Smith's unique business practices, of SEC violations and investigations, of kiting checks and gun battles on the front stretch, and suspect loans. All this might even be forgivable, part and parcel of building the speedway, but the fact is Turner and Smith, while creative and intelligent, do not, according to the creditors, have gumption enough to bring the track from where it is to where it could be. They're plenty savvy, but this is now about solvency. And the creditors have three members on the board who are ready to back them up.

Turner and Smith, however, can see the future, and there's no way it'll be harder than the past. The hard part is over. This is now a question of patience, and so far, patience and savvy are paying off.

"Everybody saw that it was a money maker," Turner will recall later. "And they all got hungry."

One week after the World 600 runs, McIlvaine and Morgan come to Turner with a deal. They have decided to foreclose on the track, and throw it up for auction.

Turner stares at them incredulously. "The track made over $400,000 last month."

"It made less than that," McIlvaine tells him. "It made $367,000. Ellington thought the higher figure would help get the newspapers interested. It seemed to work."

"I have a loan coming for $750,000," Turner says emphatically.

"We're not interested in the loan," McIlvaine tells him. "We're interested in the future of this track and seeing it succeed."

"Yeah," Turner says. "I know what you're interested in."

But the creditors are willing to make a deal: If he and Smith resign, they'll promise not to foreclose. "You've got a lot of stock tied up in this place," they tell him. "If we foreclose, what happens to all that stock?"

Turner can see where this is headed. If he resigns, he'll save his stock—and what about all the other friends he's pulled into this thing? They could lose all their stock as well. But if he resigns, it's all over.

"No," he tells McIlvaine.

"We can throw you out if you don't."

"No you can't. Only the board can do that."

There is another option: he could help vote Bruton off the board. Ellington has already been doing half of Bruton's job and it's time for a change.

Turner smiles. "Now why would I do that?"

Turner leaves his office, his mind roving and his mood dark. He has to get the loan first. After the bulk of the debt is gone, Turner can then think of more stopgaps, maybe new timber deals.

Bruton Smith isn't surprised to see McIlvaine and Morgan show up.

"I'm not going to resign," he tells them. But for him the pot is sweetened: He could switch his position on the board's vote. If he'd help vote Turner out, he'd take over as president of the speedway, the job he's always wanted—and they wouldn't foreclose. He'd run the place with the board's support.

The deal is a tempting one; it's a smart one as well. If there's one thing he and Turner both believe, it's that nothing is more important than the survival of the speedway. And he could have his cake and eat it too.

But he knows it's not that simple.

"I'm not ready to vote Curtis out of the speedway," he says.

The following Wednesday, Ellington calls the board of directors together for a meeting. There is, however, one significant absence: the speedway's president.

All the participants are testy. It is illegal in the state of North Carolina to hold a corporate board meeting without all members present, and tempers are short as Ellington and Nance go over all the reasons why Curtis Turner is a detour to the continued progess of the speedway. He's the man not willing to read the writing on the wall: Morgan and McIlvaine are going to put the track up for auction unless Turner resigns. When that happens, they'll all lose money and their positions. There's only one way to go with this, Ellington concludes.

The next afternoon, on June 8, another board meeting is held.

"Nice of you fellas to invite me to this one," Turner says, glaring around the conference room at Charlotte Motor Speedway. He has heard about everything: the meeting, the discussions with Smith, all the plans behind his back.

Shouts and accusations fly from one side of the table to the other. But Turner's position remains the same. "I'm staying," he says flatly.

"Then we'll take a vote," Ellington answers. A silent count is taken on the motion of whether or not Curtis Turner should be forced from his position of president of the speedway. "No," Turner writes on a slip of paper, and hands it across to the speedway secretary.

Ellington opens all seven papers and lays them out on the long oak table.

Three are opposed; four are in favor of Turner's departure.

The silence lasts only a moment before Ellington asks that the decision be recorded. Turner looks around the room, at G.D. Smith, at G.B. Nalley, and he settles on Bruton, who shakes his head. There is no reading the expression on his face.

Turner packs his briefcase, going through items in his office. Details are worked out and McIlvaine and Morgan are brought in for final arrangements. Turner resigns his position; the creditors then request that Smith resign as well. But he is immediately retained as the speedway's promotions director. Nance is the new president; Ellington now owns both of Bruton Smith's former titles.

Turner stands outside the glass door of what had been his office. The nameplate, reading Curtis Turner—President, slips easily from its frame. Turner throws it in his bag and walks outside, greeting the press as nothing more than a shareholder in the speedway corporation.

"You might say I was between the devil and the deep blue sea," he tells an angry Muhleman, who takes notes for his *Charlotte News* story. "On the one hand there were creditors determined to auction the speedway unless I resigned, and on the other there was my old partner Bruton Smith, who was ready to help vote me out if I refused.

"Of course I resigned, if for no other reason than to protect my stock and that of people who had invested in the track because of me," he adds, heading to his car, trailed by reporters. "But I know for a fact that Bruton Smith agreed prior to Thursday's board meeting that he would vote against me. Four men, of course, control a seven-man board, and until Bruton decided to change horses, the balance of power had been in our favor. Bruton, you'll notice, is still with the speedway."

For the two visionaries who'd sunk all their time, sweat and finances into this one great idea, and had worked to make it come together despite biblical obstacles, it is an ignominious way to part. The question of whether Smith cast the deciding vote or not would remain a debated issue in some corners, but never in Turner's mind. Could it instead have been one of Turner's close friends, G.D. Smith or Nalley?

"I don't know how many of those were *close* friends," says historian Greg Fielden of the stormy situation. "There seemed to be pretty wild goings on that could skirt the edge of etiquette and legality."

Years later, Smith will continue to deny the assertion. "I talked with Curtis and told him the board wanted him out, that I refused to vote against him and that I would resign if he would," he'll one day tell writer Bob Myers, but Smith's next statements are particularly vague.

"We resigned, and that kept me from having to vote against him.

"Then the directors turned around and rehired me. I stayed until I put the corporation under Chapter 10 of the Federal Bankruptcy Act. In retrospect that was foolish. If I'd put it under Chapter 11, I could have retained control."

Standing in the parking lot on June 8, Turner looks back at the guardrails and the visible line of asphalt track heading off into the distance. Bitterness rises in him like bile as he sighs and shakes his head.

"I tried to build it, as they say, on a credit card," he tells Muhleman. "It was a gamble that backfired. But I'm sure I could have carried it through smoothly if I hadn't put too much confidence in the wrong people. That was my biggest mistake."

Years later, upon greater reflection, he'll admit to what may have been an even greater flaw.

"I never kept books on the Charlotte Motor Speedway, or other places. I just figured we'd sit down one day and figure it all out," he'll tell *Sports Illustrated*'s Kim Chapin. "Didn't sign any notes. I just figured if somebody needed the money I'd give it to them and when they got it they'd pay me back. I guess I just like everybody, and trust people until they give me a reason not to. I guess maybe you'd think I'd learn by now."

Turner goes home from the speedway and puts down his briefcase. He stuffs a few items in a bag, giving single-word answers to Ann's questions. "Where are you going now?" she asks, and he heads for the door. In a moment, he is gone.

"He disappeared," says Charlie Williamson. "He still had this house up here in Roanoke and he came here and then he was gone. It was maybe a week or two."

The Blue Ridge Mountains of Virginia, when seen from the air, are a blanket of green, with brilliant starbursts of swaying treetops, and mountains like cascading folds. Turner takes his plane down close, almost brushing against the top leaves of the trees, close enough to smell them. He lands at Roanoke airport and drives straight for the woods. Those same mountains, seen from deep within the forests that cover them, offer a trek to nowhere, except for someone like Turner, who knows exactly where he's going. Turner trudges in with a numbing amount of liquor and cigarettes and lets himself get lost for awhile. He's never one for drinking alone, but something tells him he has no choice: it's the right thing to do.

"I don't know where he went," says Ann, "but he went out in the woods somewhere and just contemplated life in general."

"He lost everything he had," remembers writer Bob Myers. "He said, 'I had half a million dollars when we started the speedway. I must have flown my airplane a mile for every dollar trying to borrow capital. We ran out of capital and I was left with little more than a stand of trees.'"

It takes at least a week of hanging around, going out to see some friends and heading back for the woods, before Turner wakes up from the fog and is ready to rejoin the living. He leaves with a renewed sense of purpose, and he senses the difference when he flies over the trees once again on his way to Charlotte.

"He came back and he was better," Ann says. "He was ready to do whatever it takes."

Now at stake for Turner is his reputation and his speedway, along with at least $200,000 in lost personal savings. Getting it all back will require a more imaginative plan than it took to build the place.

He is being sued by one creditor for $90,000. Owen Flowe is also suing him. But the most pressing matter is the track.

On July 12, 1961, just over a month after being ousted, Turner holds a noon meeting in Winston-Salem to announce a revolutionary plan that is guaranteed to shake up motorsports: the introduction of pari-mutuel betting on stock car races.

This is the first pronouncement of his new company, Turner

Investors. The company has a three-fold purpose: to organize betting on auto races in states where such activities are legal (and work to get betting legalized in North Carolina); to acquire capital stocks of existing corporations; and to buy and sell real estate, timberland and mineral rights. The company plans to incorporate when $300,000 worth of stock has been sold.

"Curtis," says *Charlotte Observer* writer George Cunningham, "legal betting on auto races in North Carolina—that's a pipe dream."

"I know," Turner says, "but it's legal in Kentucky, Louisiana and Florida. We're looking to hold our first experimental race somewhere in the South within the month."

Everybody assembled understands that the betting is secondary; the desire to "acquire capital stocks of existing corporations" is paramount. Cunningham asks the obvious question: is this specifically directed at the speedway?

Turner smiles. "No comment," he says.

And what about Bill France?

"Bill France is not personally against this idea," Turner says, in reference to the betting. The pair haven't discussed the matter but a year earlier, NASCAR ran a race in Canada where "open pool" betting had taken place, and fans could wager on win, place and show finishers. Surely that means something, Turner figures. However, France has always frowned on the idea of betting, and he'd had no control over that element in the Canadian race.

"France was vehemently opposed to that. He always had a real strong objection to anybody suggesting gambling getting involved with automobile racing," says Hank Schoolfield. "Curtis was trying to raise money, that's all. And though I wouldn't have been made privy to such a thing, I suspected that it involved some relationships between Turner and underworld people involved in the pari-mutuel betting business."

For Turner there is a deadline to meet: Duke Ellington has announced that in order for the speedway to survive, a loan of $850,000 is needed within sixty days.

Clearly, Turner Investors will not have that money available but this is only part one of the grand plan. The loan offer from the Teamsters had been laying dormant for weeks but Turner is ready to revive it.

"He went to the union and met with all those guys—gangsters I called them," remembers Pee Wee Ellwanger. "That's what they looked like."

"I need $850,000," Turner tells Teamsters Vice President Harold Gibbins in Gibbins' Washington D.C. office. For a year and a half, union representative Nick Torzeski, under the direction of his friend, Teamsters president Jimmy Hoffa, has been working to create the Federation of Professional Athletes (FPA), in order to branch out the Teamster influence to include all pro sports. Gibbins agrees to the loan, provided Turner helps sign up drivers.

"The Teamsters can offer the drivers all kinds of advantages they've never had," Torzeski tells him. "And if NASCAR gives your drivers trouble, we'll be there to help negotiate, and to protect them."

Turner weighs the obvious downside of getting involved with the Teamsters. Hoffa is an electrifying presence, the country's most powerful labor leader—not to mention the target of Attorney General Robert Kennedy's relentless legal crusade to expose the union leader's longtime association with organized crime. Wherever Hoffa goes, legal woes and scandal frequently follow.

But this isn't about Hoffa and his reputation. It's about securing a loan. Helping out his fellow drivers in the process could be a good fringe benefit. And Turner will have won back the track.

He does not go into the process naively. He is, however, at a point of desperation. There are no friends or creditors lining up with checks for $1 million. And, as Humpy Wheeler remembers, "You couldn't borrow any money for a speedway at those times because no government entity would help you do it like they would an NBA team or football team."

Turner sees the negatives as important, but secondary.

He nods at Torzeski. "Sounds good," he says.

He reads through Torzeski's brochures. There's a pension plan, death benefits, health and welfare benefits, a scholarship fund for children of deceased drivers, compliant procedures that can carry some weight and assurances of adequate safety.

Turner knows NASCAR already has much of this in place, to varying degrees—they have no pension plan or scholarship fund—but he also knows that the way to the drivers is through their wallets.

"When France first started this thing, what was the purse size for a 100-mile race?" Turner asks Fireball Roberts and Buck Baker days later.

"It was $4,000," Roberts says, sitting in the front seat of Turner's car on a late July night in Bristol, Tennessee. The Grand National circuit has come to town for the July 30 race, the Volunteer 500.

"That's right. And this year, for a 100-miler, the purse is still the same. But it costs $6,000 to build a good car—twice what it did back then. Everything has gone up but the purses. Even NASCAR membership. Ten years ago, that cost five dollars; now it's twenty."

All the talk of better money and benefits stirs the two drivers up, and they are among the first to sign membership cards that state a willingness to join the FPA, and give a $10 initiation fee. Roberts is especially intrigued. In 1958, the year after Turner enjoyed his monumental racing success, Roberts gained his own exalted status by entering only ten of the circuit's fifty-one races and winning six, including all three of the super-speedway events. He'd gone from struggling to winning a small fortune, from running in his own lackluster equipment to driving for top owners. He's already won a few races in front of his hometown Daytona Beach fans at Bill France's new speedway and is now driving for Smokey Yunick. Through his own amazing run, the fact that enough good friends are barely eking out a living in the Modifieds hasn't been lost on Roberts.

During the next week, Turner, Roberts, Baker and Tim Flock, pass the word along and help bring in drivers and mechanics.

Turner, with all his enthusiasm, has little trouble talking his fellow drivers into the deal. "He was a good salesman and he convinced a lot of us that that was the way to go," says Ned Jarrett. In 1961, only the most fortunate drivers get to pilot factory cars, or rides sponsored by a car owner or local businessman willing to put up enough money for a long 50-race season. There are no big corporations lining up to paste logos on the sides of stock cars.

With each positive reaction, Turner grows more confident that the one person he really needs to bring in on this will understand.

He races in early August at Bowman Gray Stadium, and spots Bill France at the track.

"I called Bill out and told him I thought I could borrow $850,000 from the Teamsters Union and that they wanted me to organize the drivers. I thought he'd cooperate with us."

France listens to Turner's proposal, all couched in the exciting possibility of him regaining control of the Charlotte track. France nods at each thought, his face impassive.

"He didn't say much," Turner recalled years later. "He didn't say it was good or bad. He said he'd have to give it some thought."

Bill France spends two days in Washington D.C., listening to congressmen, lawyers and businessmen advise him on a plan of action against the threat of the Teamsters Union. With each new revelation, his resolve grows stronger and his mood darker. Junior Johnson, after speaking with Turner about the union effort, alerts officials at his sponsor, Holly Farms, knowing they've recently had labor problems, and sensing that the union could be devastating to racing. During his Washington discussions, France gets a call from Holly Farms officials, who tell him drivers are being signed up. Adding insult to injury, Fireball Roberts, whom France has long considered a friend, has been named president of the new federation. Turner is the organization's new secretary-treasurer.

The final straw comes on Wednesday afternoon, August 9, while France is meeting in Charlotte with promoters from the sport's four major tracks: Charlotte, Daytona, Atlanta and Darlington. Word comes of a quote from Torzeski to the *Charlotte Observer*. By signing up a majority of the drivers, the Teamsters Union, Torzeski states, has now gained control of the NASCAR Grand National circuit.

Later that evening, twenty-three drivers, and several car owners and mechanics show up at Bowman Gray stadium for one of the shortest races on schedule, 37.5 miles on the crowded quarter-mile track. The race itself will take less than an hour to run. The meeting beforehand, led by France, will take longer.

There is no Turner, Roberts, Flock or Baker at this meeting; none of these drivers have been officially "invited." Word has been spreading of France's meetings, and his great resistance to the union plan. There is a mood of impatience in the field house room; some drivers appear embarrassed, others defiant. Ned Jarrett can see the mix of controlled anger and determination in France's face. "You could tell he was rattled by the circumstances that necessitated him to be there," Jarrett recalls.

Turner, meanwhile, is a little rattled to find himself on the outside of a locked door.

He and Flock have come to witness all the commotion first-hand.

Flock follows as Turner moves around the field house to an open window; he can see France standing behind a desk. Turner bends a bit at the knees, out of sight but well within earshot.

Sounding even more like a stern father than usual, France begins by reminding all assembled that before he began the National Association for Stock Car Auto Racing, the sport was in chaos. For these last thirteen years, however, there have been guaranteed purses, the appearance of insurance and the creation of major speedways that each promise bigger paydays. The future, as France paints it, is a bright one indeed.

The new union activity, he says, will destroy all that. Without France constantly looking out for their best interests, there will be no ruling structure. Haven't things gone well enough in the past? Drivers can't have it both ways.

"And gentlemen," France says, "make no mistake: before I have this union stuffed down my throat, I will plow up my 2.5-mile track at Daytona Beach and plant corn there instead. I will also tear up all the tracks I have an interest in in the state of North Carolina."

"Gentlemen," he says, removing his glasses and loosening his tie, "I won't be dictated to by a union."

He begins to pace around the room, telling them of his discussions with senators and justice department officials, going on about the Teamsters' reputation.

Form a union, he says, and much of what has been gained will be lost. "If you unionize, any support from the auto factories will be withdrawn. And all you car owners: if you hire a mechanic, as you will, then you'll have to pay him time and a half on Saturday and double time on Sunday.

"The union you want to join has a pension plan? I tried a year ago to get a pension plan for you people," France says, glaring around the room. "I was unsuccessful because drivers are independent contractors. All retirement plans are based on weekly earnings, on an employee-employer relationship. This does not exist in NASCAR, where every driver—every one of you in this room—is an independent operator and does not get a weekly paycheck." Given that, France reminds them, the drivers can't even legally form the union they've decided so hastily to join.

He is, however, willing to meet everybody halfway. He has decided to appoint a committee of five NASCAR officials who will hear grievances by drivers and renew efforts for a pension plan. The committee will include two of the sport's most respected racers—Lee Petty and Ned Jarrett—along with car owner Fred Lovett, France himself and NASCAR Executive Manager Pat Purcell. But Jarrett, France says, staring at the driver, can only join the group if he agrees to give up any designs to join the union.

Torzeski's quote is still ringing in France's ears, and he moves back to the front of the silent room. "There's another thing," he says, his ire building. "After the race tonight, no known union member can compete in a NASCAR race. And if this isn't tough enough, I'll use a pistol to enforce it. I have a pistol and I know how to use it. I've used it before.

"Why am I barring union members from the races? To protect the drivers who do not sign up. And why is that? A Fireball Roberts or a Curtis Turner will drive alongside you on the track and say, "Hey, you signed up yet?"'

Turner, he reminds all assembled, has been known to knock a driver or two out of the race on a whim. "I'm not going to let this happen. I'm protecting NASCAR drivers by not letting union members compete."

France pauses a moment. "You can call this a safety measure," he says.

Flock watches Turner, who drops his gaze a moment, squinting, paying as close attention as possible.

"And Curtis Turner talks about purses?" France says. "Ten years ago, Darlington Raceway paid $25,000 for its Southern 500. Today it pays nearly $100,000.

"And then there's this talk of pari-mutuel betting," France says without mentioning Turner again. "We know it won't work with auto racing, which is a clean sport. We've never had a scandal and I will fight any pari-mutuel attempt to the *last*."

France's jaws are set tight as he looks over all the faces in the room. He shakes his head.

"If this union you have was really such a great thing then I'd *join* it," he says.

Outside the window, Turner's eyes raise up, and he reaches for a card in his jacket pocket, and sticks a hand in through the window.

"Here's your application," he says.

He can hear the footsteps charging toward the window. When he looks up, France is glaring at him with venom. The look does nothing but harden something inside Turner.

France grabs the card and slams down the window and locks it. It takes him a few seconds to collect himself but he reaches for his briefcase and snaps up the top, and flips through papers in a folder on the inside in the silence.

"I have one offer to make gentlemen," he says, smacking down the top of the case. "Any driver or mechanic who will sign this card I have here, killing their application in a union, can come back to NASCAR," he says. "We welcome them."

Everybody can hear that outside the field house, the gathering crowd of several thousand race fans is milling about, ready to watch a brilliant mid-week dogfight. At the end of the race, if all goes well, the drivers can expect a check for doing what they love.

Ten drivers and mechanics step up quickly to sign France's card, a show of support that, while it humbles France a moment, also strengthens his bitterness at having to do this in the first place. Among the ten are Jarrett, Junior Johnson, current Grand National points leader Rex White and Glen Wood.

"I signed this union paper but I didn't consider everything," Jarrett admits later. "All of us drivers have beefs but this was going about it the wrong way. The grievance board that Bill France appointed is a better answer than the union."

But it is the ultimatum that had the most powerful effect.

"France made it very clear that he'd shut down NASCAR, and do whatever had to be done, but he would not succumb to the union or any drivers who had wishes of doing it that way," recalls Jarrett. "He changed a lot of our lives that day."

Moments after the meeting disburses, the drivers and mechanics go about getting their cars ready for the race, but in the garage and in the stands, everybody is abuzz with talk of the union, which has been boiling over for days. Soon, the "newly welcomed" drivers will take to the track, while France is surrounded by a collection of reporters. Somebody asks him whether his welcome mat might also be tossed down for Turner and Roberts as well.

France considers this a moment. "Maybe. Just maybe," he says, rubbing his lower lip. "If they make an affadavit and swear on the Bible."

Years later, Curtis Turner will look back on this particular moment in his long history with Bill France and recall—in a detail as important to him as anything to do with the Teamsters—that France had said he needed to "give it some thought."

"The next thing, during the middle of the week [France] made a statement to the newspapers that he was against it. He didn't even call me, and tell me what he thought. From that day on I never did talk to him much."

And yet the fact that Turner had begun talking to drivers without first mentioning it to France must have done its own share of damage. "It actually hurt Bill France's feelings that he was not told that they were going to do anything like this," says Buddy Baker. "Then I think it became more personal."

Whatever may have been solved by a long talk between old friends, or a strategic meeting about raising money for the Charlotte Motor Speedway, is suddenly beyond words once Torzeski talks about the Teamsters taking over the sport France has spent fifteen years molding. A bitter war of words rages between Turner and France in the press. Turner calls the ban on union drivers a violation of the Sherman Anti-Trust Act, and he vows to speak to Jimmy Hoffa about an injunction to suspend all NASCAR races.

"The majority of the drivers aren't as dumb as France thinks they are," Turner tells the *Observer*'s George Cunningham. "They've heard empty promises for fifteen years, and all that has resulted is drivers getting leaner and promoters getting fatter."

In a written statement given to drivers and reporters, Turner lays out the advantages a union association will buy the NASCAR members. It calls for greater purses, death and health and welfare benefits, a scholarship fund and a much more proactive approach to safety. And yet almost every point also takes a jab at NASCAR's present leadership under France. "The insurance program currently offered professional athletes is totally inadequate and serves no purpose other than a burial," he writes at one point. "The drivers are spending [on cost of living, tires and repairs] twice as much as they can win (if they come in first) while the promoter is charging admission for your practice and time trials, plus the race. We feel the drivers should get forty percent of the time trial money," he continues. And in one final swipe, and an attempt to remind everybody of his own credibility, he writes, "France states the drivers don't realize the money invested in these tracks. I know, because I built the best one in the nation and paid the largest purse, and I also realized a field of race cars represents over a half million dolars while damage to the tracks is a small percentage of damages to the race cars. Bill France knows we are right. He's already begun to make you more promises."

The *Charlotte Observer*, in a commentary rife with sarcasm, states, "We have read that Jimmy Hoffa, out of the kindliness of his heart, has offered to take professional athletes into his Teamsters Union. He has chosen Curtis Turner, the All-American boy, to pass out pamphlets. Turner . . . is always on missionary work. Only a few weeks ago he was attempting to set up pari-mutuel betting for stock races.

"Bill France, the NASCAR president, has been quoted as saying: "No known union members can compete in a NASCAR race, and I'll use a pistol to enforce it." Boy, think what this will mean to fans. You can buy a ticket to a track and not only see smash ups, but gang battles between pit stops."

The piece prompts France to write his own lengthy editorial. "A recent newspaper story suggests that I might be some kind of rootin' tootin', hootin', shootin' cuss, waving a pistol and itching to shoot up anyone who might disagree with me. HONEST, I'M NOTHING LIKE THAT!" it begins. "But I am an American who believes in our constitution and our laws—and bearing of arms to repel invasion is part of our great American Heritage. For fourteen years I have had the honor and responsibility of heading, as president, the building of a house called NASCAR. . . . WE HONESTLY FEEL THAT OURS IS A RECORD OF SOLID ACHIEVEMENT AND PROGRESS FOR OUR MEMBERS AND FOR THE SPORT. AND WHEN, OUT OF A CLEAR, BLUE SKY, in a period of continuing growth and progress in the sport, I am suddenly confronted with the fact that a few of the boys who have grown to stature and respect in the sport as NASCAR members, and with the help and support of NASCAR over many years which have been good and profitable for them, engage in activity which is disruptive—and actually poisonous to the sport—I HOPE IT'S NOT TOO HARD TO UNDERSTAND WHY I MIGHT BE A BIT MAD."

In a 48-hour period, each instance of "he said/he said" between France and Turner continues to swiftly erode fifteen years of friendship, and makes any kind of reconciliatory conversation unlikely. "They were close friends," recalls motorsports writer Bob Myers. "There was genuine affection between them. But Bill France absolutely shuddered at anything that he felt remotely threatened NASCAR."

A day after France's Bowman Gray speech, Turner's union effort suffers a startling blow: Fireball Roberts resigns from the federation, and his post as president. Roberts admits he was worried that Turner's threat of an injunction on NASCAR races could put a great economic strain on hundreds of less fortunate racers. And though he bitterly admits that "just because I've done something France doesn't like, he can ruin my career overnight," he's also grabbing hold of France's olive branch of forming a committee to address driver concerns.

He's not alone, and nobody is less surprised by this than France himself. In the old moonshining days, the credos were clear: never interfere with another man's business and keep outsiders out. That mindset bred a company of individualists, drivers who held onto what was theirs, who raced hard and knocked their way past competitors whenever necessary. Social thinkers might one day refer to them as "a herd of independent minds." It is a hard group to form into a Brotherhood.

Still, seeing his old friend Roberts' turnaround is a great relief for France; and Bibles, affidavits and grumblings be damned, he decides. "As far as I'm concerned, he is welcome to race for NASCAR as long as he pleases. I know he'll be welcomed back by his fellow drivers. I think in future years Fireball will regard this move as the best thing he ever did for sports in America.

"We have won round one. But we've got to win all the rounds and we will."

To Turner, it seems like the worst kind of gloating.

"I understand that Bill France has been talking about pistols and threatening my life and Fireball Roberts' life," he says in the newspapers. "I guess Fireball decided he didn't want to get shot."

More and more drivers join Roberts in renouncing their union ties; ultimately, only Turner and Tim Flock are tagged with the ban. And France has given no indication as to how long he plans to uphold the suspension.

Flock has had his own contentious dealings with France in past; when France disqualified Flock's winning car because of a technicality after one Beach and Road Course race, Flock drove to France's house and angrily slammed and shattered his glass front door. But Flock has won two Grand National championships, and figures maybe he can do some damage control by talking sensibly to France. The NASCAR president listens incredulously for a moment before lashing out. As Turner will later recall, "France said to him, 'I don't want you; I'm after Turner.'"

Turner won't even talk to close friends about the depths of his bitterness. Given the increasing ire in each tirade, Turner and France seem headed for a major face-to-face confrontation, and all signs point to a showdown at the Sunday, August 13 race at Asheville-Weaverville Speedway. Racing fans have read all about the battle; the place will attract quite a crowd, from the faithful to the curious. France, now feeling much more secure, seems to welcome it. "I hope he does show up," the NASCAR president says, though he's the first to remind anyone that Turner is still banned from running the race. "The sooner it gets started and out in the open, the better we will be."

But Turner will not show up at Asheville. Days earlier, with no press around and little fanfare, he'd gone to a smaller track to test his luck. Expecting the worst, he got it.

At the driver credentials window, he is told, for the first time in his life, that he won't be permitted to compete.

"Sorry Curtis," the track official tells him. "I'm afraid I can't let you in."

"I know it," Turner says, behind his sunglasses.

"It says here your presence on a NASCAR track is no longer welcome."

It's one thing to read that in the newspaper. To be hit with this news head-on is outrageous. To be stared at, or worse, to have other drivers avert their eyes, is surreal.

He walks away, holding his tongue; in a legal sense, this action is just what he needs, evidence that France is singling him and Flock out. Turner is convinced he has no shot at the Teamsters loan unless he maintains his membership in the FPA. But for all he knows, the racing ban can continue, based entirely on France's whim.

Five years earlier, Turner had won more races than anybody else in stock car history. He'd walked away with the Southern 500, the fans streaming through the stands, climbing the wall and mobbing him on the track at Darlington. It had given him and France a good reason to celebrate.

"If early in this union situation, the two of them had sat down in the back room—the old cliché—and just screamed at each other, it probably would have been settled," says Bob Moore. "But soon it took on a whole different level. And when your friend basically tells you to disappear, and 'I never want to see you again,' that hurts. What happened between Curtis and Bruton, Curtis wasn't happy about it but I don't think it was completely unexpected. But for France to say that, the idea had never crossed Curtis' mind."

They are like the last two players in a round of poker that has become too rich for everybody else's blood.

Turner stews for a week over his lost driving privileges until he and Flock threaten to sue their way back into NASCAR. Turner Investors Inc. will now "promote racing all over the Southeast" through the Midwest Association of Racing Cars (MARC), putting Turner's company in direct competition with NASCAR. And he's still fixing to get back his speedway.

France, meanwhile, remains stoic and noncommunicative. Despite all the bait, he's not nibbling.

On September 11, 1961, Frank E. Hamilton Jr. of the Tampa law firm of Hardee & Ott submits a nineteen-page complaint on behalf of Turner and Flock in the Florida Circuit court, Volusia County, asking for $200,000 in damages for each driver, along with earnings lost since August 9. There, in legal papers, is hard evidence of the ban, beginning with the litany France delivered at Bowman Gray stadium. By barring the racers from competition, the complaint contends, France has interfered with their "right to work," a right promised in the Florida constitution in 1944. The court papers do acknowledge that NASCAR claims the right to suspend a member whose actions are deemed "detrimental to the best interest of stock car racing," but "the [NASCAR] contract does not specify that membership in a labor union is detrimental [or] not detrimental," and that France and NASCAR have read into the contract provisions that aren't there. At issue in the case will be whether or not France has the right to do so. The court papers ultimately call France's actions "intentional, wanton, willful and malicious." Turner is also armed with the services of Jack Wiley, a St. Louis attorney hired by the Teamsters, and more importantly, a $100,000 Teamsters cash fund to fight the fight.

Ten days later, France's attorney Louis Ossinsky, and Charlotte lawyers Bob Sanders and J.W. Alexander make their own statements. France's lawyers have done some work with the Kennedy's, and the bad blood between Jimmy Hoffa and the Kennedys has no small presence in the courtroom in Volusia County.

According to Ossinsky, the entire complaint made by Turner and Flock should be dropped because the claims are "vague, indefinite, uncertain, irrelevant, redundant, repugnant, immaterial and contain scandalous matters."

Judge Robert. H. Wingfield listens to the list with a frown and a shake of the head. He glances at Turner and France, both of whom are making this appearance in his court, with their respective wives, to lend credence to their claims. Everybody is civil, but neither man will look in the other's direction, as if somehow magnetically repelled. Even Annie France and Ann Turner, old friends and frequent double-dating partners, with their husbands back in Virginia, in the days when the men promoted races together, are forced to be cordial at best.

Ossinsky is tall and flamboyant, a presence in any courtroom, "the kind of man who could make you mad, though you couldn't help but like him," according to a colleague. An excellent lawyer, you could still see the form of the Georgia college footballer behind his now-bulging midsection.

There is, Ossinsky insists, no proof in Turner and Flock's "vague statements" that France is operating some kind of conspiracy. "And there is talk of a contract between the plaintiffs and my client," he adds. "There is no contract.

"Each and every count of the complaint fails to allege how, when, and under what circumstances my client conspired to affect their rights."

Flock is practically in a state in his seat in the courtroom, and must be motioned to remain calm by Hamilton. Flock and Turner, it is pointed out, are not officially employees of NASCAR. "I will read from the NASCAR rule book," Ossinsky says before thumbing to the words "NASCAR members are not employees of NASCAR and are independent contractors." But these drivers are nonetheless subject to the ruling body's rules and regulations, along with any other rules that might be added at any time during the season. And item 16, Section 4 clearly states "NASCAR members agree to abide by official decisions."

In other words, France can make up his mind and remake up his mind to enforce whatever suits him.

"And your honor," Ossinsky concludes, his face twisted with a smile, "this honorable court should not be used to settle differences between members of NASCAR."

Hamilton sits calmly, listening to Ossinsky speak, occasionally pushing his glasses back up on his nose, or permitting himself a gap-tooth smile beneath his red hair. At five-foot-seven, he is a good six inches shorter than Ossinsky, and being much more slender he looks shorter still. He is, looks aside, about as focused and sharp a lawyer as one will find in Tampa, with a brilliant memory. Hamilton doesn't cross-examine so much as he slices and dices for information with incredible subtlety. One steps down after being grilled by Hamilton thinking they've done alright, only to then realize just how skillfully he has turned the tables.

During some of the statements, Turner is distracted, flipping through Turner Investors papers and several notices sent to stockholders of the Charlotte Motor Speedway. He will travel back and forth from this courtroom, a mere 20 miles from the brain center of NASCAR in Daytona, to Charlotte, trying to win back his speedway in the heart of stock car country. Turner remains an optimist; for the past five months, each growing disappointment has led to a greater sense of inevitability, the belief that a turn-around of fortunes is due any moment. "Curtis wasn't a quitter," remembers his friend Henry Mason. "'You always keep digging, you keep going,' he said. He told me one time, 'even if you're sinking in the ocean, if you could hold your little finger up, maybe somebody could still see you.'"

He is back in Charlotte, discussing the case with Doc Morris when a call comes in from Hamilton. The lawyer has spoken to Jack Wiley, the Teamsters attorney, about the proposed loan for the speedway.

"What do you mean proposed loan?" Turner asks. There are several meetings coming up in the next few weeks tht will decide the fate of the track. Turner has kept to his side of the bargain, attempting to organize the drivers.

"I wish it were that easy," Hamilton says.

Wiley calls a few moments later to confirm Turner's worst nightmare: two years earlier, congress had passed an amendment to the Taft Hartley Act, later known as the Labor Relations Act. According to this amendment, it is now forbidden for a labor union to lend money to any person who is attempting, on their behalf, to bring new members into that union. Turner slams the phone down, pacing the room in a state of shock. "I didn't know until after I'd gotten into court that they couldn't make a loan to me if they wanted to," he recalled several years later, still vexed by the memory. "We had already been banned and filed suit against NASCAR. Taft-Hartley or some damned thing."

Turner has every right to feel duped and put-upon. That he would somehow not have been advised of this beforehand seems preposterous, even pathological. But thinking this way won't do him any good. He immediately begins working the phones, like he did when he first lost the speedway, calling G.B. Nalley, Richard Phillips and anybody else he knows he can lean on. Later that night, he gets in his plane and flies to New York. By morning, there'll be some investors looking at a familiar face, with an incredible hard-luck story to tell.

The flyers go out in the first few days of October: on the 23rd, a meeting will take place to decide who ultimately controls Charlotte Motor Speedway. Money will do all the talking that day: the track is now $900,000 in debt and in grave danger of being put on the auction block. The lost Teamsters loan sticks deep in Turner's craw.

There are now only five members on the board of directors: Nance, Ellington and Patterson, and the remaining Turner allies Nalley and G.D. Smith. If Turner can fill those last two board spots with people loyal to him, he can affect a change with the stockholders, many of whom are longtime friends he'd brought in. His plan is to attend the stockholders meeting on Wednesday, October 11, call for a vote and work his way back in. One week later, on Wednesday the 18th, he will have raised enough money to save the speedway, and win the confidence of the more than 2,000 shareholders. The cash isn't in his pocket yet but it will be.

"We are prepared to ask the stockholders to accept our proposal," he tells the *Observer*'s Cunningham. "Under our proposal, the speedway will remain the property of the present stockholders. But there will be two conditions," he adds evenly. "One: resignation from the present board by everyone except G.D. Smith and G.B. Nalley. Two: An agreement that I remain as president and member of the board for the term of the loan." The loan, it is reported, will come from Turner Investors, which is being backed to some extent by "interests in the North."

It is the best Turner can do, and it feels uncomfortably like déjà vu. He will log hours and hours in the air and cover this loan, and win back the track with pure will if he has to.

But it won't even be that easy.

"You know you're not the only party trying to win the speedway back," Doc Morris tells Turner at the house in Charlotte.

Turner pores through papers on his desk. "Yep," he says, without pausing. "It's like old times."

Bruton Smith, still with the speedway, and still allied with present management, has made his own proposal. His plan starts with 120 stockholders who will be asked to put up $5,000 each, for $600,000. The rest of the money will come from track earnings: the next National 400 race is set for Sunday, October 15. As with Turner's plan, Smith does not have the money yet either.

But on Monday morning October 9, two days before Turner is set to call for elections, Smith's attorney William E. Poe; and John Dillon, a television official some speculate is working with Smith; are, curiously, elected to the Charlotte Motor Speedway board of directors, presumably giving Ellington and company a landslide majority in all speedway decisions.

The legality of the vote is immediately called into question, since only Ellington, Nance and Patterson are in the room to vote. "G.D. didn't go to the meeting because nobody told him there would be a vote involved," Turner tells his local lawyer, Pat Cook.

"Which is illegal, of course," Cook says.

"And Nalley just left for vacation in Bermuda," Turner adds. "You think Duke Ellington didn't know that? There's no way this election can hold."

G.D. Smith is getting sick of the shenanigans. "This was not the right thing to do," he tells Cunningham for his *Observer* piece. "After I find out all the angles, I will let the stockholders know my feelings.

"I admit, my sympathies here lie with Curtis," he adds. "But saving the track is the important thing. If present management comes up Monday night with money to save the speedway, I'm for them. That is, unless Curtis also comes up with the money. Then I would side with him."

But nobody, it turns out, has the money, only a series of elaborate plans and a world of bitter backbiting masking good intentions. Everything about the building of Charlotte Motor Speedway, everything faced by

Turner and Smith—leading, ultimately, to their own face-to-face battle—has been combustible, until at last the board delivers the troubled track to Federal District Court. In December, Turner will stand in a room with many of his fellow stockholders to hear that the track has been placed under Chapter 10 bankruptcy protection, where Federal District Judge J.B. Craven Jr. will practically serve as guardian, helping it get on its feet. Craven will ultimately reject yet another bid to foreclose. "There is almost a probability that new money will come in to make it possible to pay off the creditors," he'll say, all but guaranteeing the track's chance for future success.

But no defeat is more bitter for Turner. "Curtis had lots of big ideas and got a few of them six or eight feet off the ground, but very few of them were ever brought all the way home," says Max Muhleman. "His thought was, 'I didn't get to the moon, the dollar bill didn't happen. But this other child has every chance of living a full and successful life and it's mine! I conceived it, and now I'm gonna lose it? After I brought it in?' I'm sure that's what went through his head."

The track never would have been started without Turner; and never would have been completed without Smith. And now it will have to thrive without either man.

"The happiest triumph and biggest disappointment in my dad's life: in my opinion they would be the same thing," says Ross Turner. "It would be building the Charlotte Motor Speedway and then losing the Charlotte Motor Speedway."

Doc Morris sits in the audience at the Volusia County court, craning his neck to get a better view of Turner. Morris is five-foot-ten, his salt-and-pepper hair pulled back over a kindly, undistinguished face, with eyes that are a little droopy from too much time spent living at Turner's house, and trying to keep his hours. The former doctor is scribbling notes on a pad, collecting background for a biography he now plans to write about Turner, who sits impassive as always at the plaintiff's desk. Like Turner, Morris is an optimist. But it is getting harder for Morris to see a completely satisfying outcome for this current part of his friend's story.

It is October 20, and Ossinsky is reading the response to Turner and Flock's original charges made against Bill France and NASCAR. As Turner listens, the futility of this whole exercise, the unreasonable actions and reactions work their frustrations upon him, beginning when Ossinsky takes issue with Turner's claim that he and Flock had long been members in good standing of NASCAR.

"It is admitted," Ossinsky says, "that the plaintiffs *from time to time* have been members in good standing."

But Ossinsky's comments quickly get bizarre. "My client admits to having presided over a meeting at a NASCAR-sanctioned race in Winston Salem," he says of France's night of incendiary comments. "But neither plaintiff was present. Consequently, none of Mr. France's statements are material to this case. And furthermore, Mr. France denies making any of these statements whatsoever."

Turner blinks and shakes his head. Up on the bench, Judge Wingfield looks up, listens with half an ear and then stares back down again, as if lost in thought.

Every allegation, every paragraph is denied; either that or Ossinsky offers his fantastic knowledge of the NASCAR rule book. Turner and Flock, he reports, had five days to dispute their suspension after it was issued, and ten more days to appeal to the NASCAR commissioner. Turner and Flock hadn't even known there was such a thing as a NASCAR commissioner.

"That's fifteen days," Turner whispers to Hamilton. "I guess I'm a little past that deadline."

"Shame on you," Hamilton deadpans.

"Maybe I should have had the rule book memorized," Turner says, but he winces the moment the words cross his lips.

During a break in the proceedings, Hamilton senses something in Turner's silence. "What is it?" he asks.

"I just never figured on all of this," he replies, waving a hand at the courtroom, the suit, everything.

"You and Tim brought the suit," Hamilton says. "And you had every right to—you're not wrong. Remember that."

"I know. But I never saw Bill France pushing me to it. Me and Bill have history. We're close friends. I think the world of him. I'm mad as anything—and I still *like* the man. I'm not mad at him. I just wanted to get my track done. And I figured nobody would understand that better than him." Turner tosses his Camel to the ground and stubs it out. "But the things they're sayin' in there are ridiculous."

"It's what they're supposed to say," Hamilton reminds him.

Turner nods. "France said those things at Bowman Gray."

"It was in all the papers," Hamilton says.

In the weeks that follow, depositions are taken from drivers, officials, track owners, even Ellington and Bruton Smith. France spends considerable amounts of resources to prove his points, beyond just trying to counteract any damning testimony. He attempts to enlist more drivers, owners and mechanics to lend credence to his side of the story, feeding his determination to wipe the matter off the records. He even seeks out Smokey Yunick at the track before a race; getting Turner's good friend Yunick to testify against him will strike an immediate blow, and while France's NASCAR inspectors have ripped apart more cars designed by the innovative Yunick than anybody else, he figures a friendly conversation to clear the air might work wonders.

Yunick quickly cuts France off; he can't even look up at him. "Hell, I was the first guy to have a mechanic's license in the union," Yunick says, tinkering under the hood of a car. But the NASCAR president pushes his point until Yunick stands up and glares back.

"Where have you been for the last ten years?" Yunick nearly shouts. "Curtis and I are brothers. Why in the hell would I testify for you when Curtis is in trouble?"

France nods, his lips curled down into a frown. "Well, that's fine—"

"Shit, I'd lie for Curtis and I'd lie against you," Yunick says, rolling a wrench in his hands. He smiles at the irony of Bill France acting like he needs his aid. "You're not gonna get any help from me," Yunick says. But then he shakes his head. "And I'd guess you won't need it."

The signs that things might not work out in Turner and Flock's favor start piling up. Flock will later state that, during Curtis' three-and-a-half hours of testimony, the fifty-seven-year-old Judge Wingfield appeared to be only half listening. "He spent the whole time reading comic books up there," Flock bitterly recalled. He and Turner had felt it best to bring this suit in France's backyard, and now wonder if perhaps they should have rethought this, given how much pride the NASCAR president has brought to the community, and his contacts among local government officials. Would the outcome be more of a lock in their favor had they sued in North Carolina?

Judge Wingfield opens up November 28 for a final, bitter day of testimony. "However you wish to spend the time, I leave up to you," he says to all concerned.

Doc Morris is in court when, during the morning session, newly crowned Grand National champion Ned Jarrett comes in as a late witness. It becomes clear to Hamilton that Jarrett has not been briefed about all the statements in the case; he's there to confirm that one cannot hold up racing as a sole means of financial support, arguing against the right to work claim. "For instance, I own a wholesale lumber business in addition to my racing," he says.

But Hamilton, having heard much about the honest reputation of "Gentleman Ned," brings up the driver's meeting at Bowman Gray. Yes, Jarrett says, France threatened to plow up his tracks. Yes, he admits, France threatened to use a pistol to enforce his decrees.

As Morris will later write in *Timber on the Moon*, his biography of Turner, "Jarrett had not heard France's testimony and testified to the truth which made France look like a prevaricator. Both the faces of Bill France and his wife were studies in contempt of Curtis."

When the day's testimony is done, Turner's eyes are bright with triumph.

"We really got him," he says to Hamilton.

"You did," Morris says, walking up to the two of them, "but you didn't see his face. Bill France was hurt today."

"We've been hurt all along."

"Yes, but I don't think it'll work in your favor in the long run," Morris says. "I'm telling you, this humiliated him. He was embarrassed. He's never going to get over this as long as he lives."

"He might have to reinstate us now," Turner says.

"But he'll never forgive you."

"I just need to drive for him, Doc," Turner says, moving back toward the court. "That's all that matters."

On November 28, Wingfield renders his decision: the Plaintiff's request for an injunction against Bill France and NASCAR's right to prevent them from working is denied. Curtis Turner and Tim Flock remain, effectively, suspended and blackballed from NASCAR.

For Judge Wingfield, the crux of the case appears to be Exhibit A: the NASCAR rule book. Whether Turner and Flock knew all the rules or not, they have agreed to abide and be governed by them. Wingfield never says whether he finds those rules suffocating or fair; it becomes clear to Turner that this is hardly the point. Wingfield refuses to make this a case about the rule book. Ultimately he seems to agrees wholeheartedly with Ossinsky: his court is not the place to settle differences between members of NASCAR.

Perhaps the right place is the National Labor Board, or maybe it's for a higher court than Wingfield's. The judge at least acknowledges this—while he denies the injunction, he doesn't dismiss the case outright. The fight isn't over yet.

But as he had done after the very first Grand National race, France has now managed to not only wield his power, but build upon it. By quelling what amounted to a riot, he has never been stronger.

"I still won't believe it," Flock says, standing later that night in Turner's Charlotte home, pouring himself a scotch.

"It don't matter," Turner says. He is past disappointment, ready to work at turning over the decision. "We'll get 'em."

Both men are thirty-seven years old. Flock is one month younger than Turner but he's leaning much closer to retirement. He hasn't driven full time in the Grand National circuit since 1956. His second and last Grand National championship came in 1955; he has run only fifteen top-division races in the five seasons since. Flock is prone to ulcers, and can still feel a bitter heat in the pit of his stomach recalling the horrific injuries both his brothers sustained behind the wheel. But he looks at Turner, still in the prime of his career, wondering when his friend will get to drive for NASCAR again, if ever.

"You know what I think, Tim?" Turner says, downing some Canadian Club.

"What's that?"

"We could've won this case," he says. "Funny thing is, I bet if we had a union, we would have."

A month later, Turner gets a call from the Ford Motor Company officials with whom he's been working at buying and selling timberland. The Ford men are in a bind over the perpetuation of the Turner lawsuit.

"Ford had 76,000 acres of beautiful timber in the upper peninsula in

Michigan on Lake Superior," Turner related several years later. "I was trying to sell it; they wanted $7 million for it."

Along with being the first-ever Ford factory driver, Turner has also
become invaluable to the company for his timber brokering skills. The
deal has long worked well, but Turner's legal troubles with NASCAR are
creating a nightmare for the car makers. They offer an ultimatum: drop the
lawsuit if he wants to continue these off-track dealings with them.

Turner sees this as his final way out. "I didn't have nothing to gain by
going ahead with the lawsuit," he recalled, "'cause I couldn't get my money
[from the Teamsters]."

To Turner, dropping his suit is a good-faith message to his old friend
France. Along with that, Ford will put in a good word. Turner has now
withdrawn from the union, dropped the lawsuit and done whatever he can
to get back into France's good graces.

"I figured France would reinstate me right then," he said.

But no phone call comes in from the Daytona Beach headquarters.
And when Turner calls France's office number, he's told to leave a message
that isn't returned.

Ultimately, the message is returned, in the daily mail. Soon after the
case is dropped, a letter arrives at Turner's home from Daytona Beach. He
opens it to find an official decree. Curtis Turner, it states, will not be reinstated. He is, effectively, banned from NASCAR racing for life.

Turner sits in the office at his Charlotte home with several business
deals pending and a desire to complete none of them.

It's been three years since he cavalierly announced his decision to
build Charlotte Motor Speedway.

He starts to make phone calls, talking to drivers and track owners,
lamenting his uncertain status and acknowledging now that it's actually
quite certain. And though he almost never feels sorry for himself, he permits the impulse for a few moments when Morris comes in and refreshes
both their drinks.

"I've been banned," Turner says, "from my own track."

Chapter Eight
1962-1964
"He never was the same after that."

The car is doing nearly a hundred miles per hour when the mountain road disappears. It is lost beyond the twenty-degree incline leading to the horizon, and Curtis Turner has to trust that something safe and gravelly waits on the other side. There has to be a switchback coming, some corkscrew turn he can screech and swerve around. Turner leans in to follow the wall of rock, which cuts off his sight. For some reason, this makes him press on the gas, going a little faster. Why put on the brakes, ever, before it's truly necessary?

And it is, in an instant. His hand resting easy on the emergency brake, now jacks the lever back hard and the rear of Turner's Ford spins halfway around, with the front end locked like it's some pivot dug deep into the ground, just as Ralph Moody promised it would. Then Turner unhooks the emergency brake and is back on the gas, heading over the Devil's Playground. Passing the "scenic mountain view" adjoining the curve, he barely catches sight of a 700-foot drop to eternity, one of many that make up the Pike's Peak International Hill Climb, Colorado's 12.42-mile gasoline-powered exercise in fast and dangerous upward mobility.

But something else truly startles Turner when he hits this curve, and it pokes at the back of his neck like a voodoo pin—for one subliminal half-second, Bill France pops into his head. Turner can practically see him sitting in the passenger seat, as he did back in Mexico, on another mountain twelve years before.

Turner pushes the thought away, lost again in his instincts. Exactly one year earlier, on July 4, 1961, he'd first started trying to enlists drivers for the Federation of Professional Athletes, promising them higher purses

—hell, who doesn't want more money?—and better benefits. And what better place to stress the importance of death benefits than at Pike's Peak?

Turner had qualified for the race in 1960 without finishing. In '61, he came in second in the stock car division to Louis J. Unser, which is akin to winning anyway, since nobody beats an Unser in what has long been called the Race to the Clouds. But on this day, July 4, 1962, he ascends again, winding swiftly around a course that climbs to 14,110 feet, with 156 separate switchback turns, heading now toward the so-named Bottomless Pit that lays 1,500 feet below the summit.

Turner is something of an anomaly here, a man in a Stetson in a cap-wearing part of the racing universe. The Peak course is the haven of the midwest or beyond, with the Unsers from Albuquerque, and everybody else in Turner's division from Colorado or California. But nowadays, he goes where the races are, where his reputation preceeds him, and his suspension from NASCAR isn't worth the paper it's printed on.

For someone who had never been much of a fighter by nature, Turner had put up a good one, an admirable battle for his professional life. But it's all over and done with. It's like a race that's had too much banging; now that it's finished, it's time to laugh about it and start a brand new party.

Turner knows it's much more complicated than that, even though it shouldn't be.

"I had an extra $70,000 to spend on that court case that I never used," he reminds his friend Bob Colvin, promoter at Darlington Raceway. "France knew that and I figured when I withdrew the suit he would reinstate me. Instead he banned me. Man doesn't even answer my calls now."

So Turner figures it's time to start some parties without him, and run with a different crowd. There's always a guarantee with Turner that everybody's sure to have a good time, and who's going to be the one missing out on that?

Turner's Courtesy Motors Ford charges up another hill, around a bend—and into a snowstorm. For the next half-mile, he squints through the wipers, slipping on a couple of turns. The sky then clears as quickly as it had clouded up, but he is now barely on pace. The year before, Unser had won the stock car division title, running the jagged course in exactly fifteen minutes. A new barrier is ripe for breaking, but Unser won't be the man to do it this year; he has skidded and slammed his Chevy into a trailer on the side of the road. Frequent winner Nick Sanborn and newcomer

Parnelli Jones have manhandled the route, with Sanborn finishing a half-second slower than Unser's record time. Turner remains, still clawing his way up the mountain.

One month earlier, Jones had won the Indy 500 pole and finished seventh, becoming the first man to drive better than 150 mph at Indianapolis. Now he awaits the outcome of this race, but he has a good idea who will win. He'd seen Turner make his way through a horseshoe turn lower on the mountain. Turner had gone in way too fast, skidding until he'd slung two tires over the edge of a straight-off. It took a mix of speed, momentum and sheer will to keep that car going until the two lost wheels were back on solid ground. Jones then watched the Courtesy Ford continue its charge, moving off like a spectre. "That," he said, "was the most spectacular damn driver I've ever seen going up that mountain."

Finally past the 14,000-foot point, Turner rounds the final turns and in a burst, speeds beyond the finish post at the summit. When he skids to a stop, he can hear the cheers and see officials running his way. He's driven the course in 14 minutes, 55.5 seconds.

To win, to set a record, right now these things are like icing, something sweet and decorative to coat the sheer joy of racing and competing. Dirt, gravel, asphalt…snow, he couldn't care less. "That race was right up his alley," says Dan Gurney, the open-wheel driving legend who knows and loves the Pike's Peak course. "It's dirt, and it is something that can't really be learned down pat, like something you go over and over again. It's a place where Curtis' natural gifts would show up."

Asked to assess his performance afterwards, Turner is matter-of-fact. "I would've done a whole lot better," he says, "if it hadn't been for that snowstorm."

Back in Charlotte, George Cunningham of the *Observer* sees Turner's victory in Colorado as a good story, and more fuel. Cunningham is the most vocal of several national motorsports writers fighting for Turner's reinstatement. He writes entry after entry in his "Motor Beat" column, charging France with letting his heart, not his head, decide his ex-friend's fate. What's done is done; it's time to move on.

"The reason for France's failure to reinstate Turner is believed to be the considerable expense inflicted upon the NASCAR boss when Turner filed suit," Cunningham has written. "How better could France recoup than by having Turner running at France-owned tracks at Daytona Beach,

Winston-Salem and North Wilkesboro. The name Curtis Turner would draw more fans to races at these tracks."

Four days after the Hill Climb, and nearly a year after the start of Turner's ban, the *Observer* publishes Cunningham's open letter to France. "I have been bombarded by readers who are also dyed-in-the-wool stock car fans," he writes. "By an overwhelming margin, they say you should reinstate Curtis Turner (and Tim Flock) to your organization, which is rightfully billed as the auto racing world's largest and finest.

"I say by an overwhelming margin. That may be the understatement of the year, for the actual tally according to the mail I have received is more than 800 for Turner and just five against him. I need not remind you of this, however, for I suspect that your mail on the subject has been even larger and more one-sided than mine. I can't ignore my letters. Can you yours?"

France offers no response. NASCAR is in the midst of a boom. Five years earlier, the Automobile Manufacturers Association had agreed to stop offering assistance in stock car racing—which didn't prevent factories from continuing to give under-the-table support to race teams. But in June 1962, Ford decides to jump back in formally. There is no disputing the notion that auto racing helps sell cars. Chrysler, wanting to keep up, opts to return as well. With manufacturing aid out in the open, competition is stellar, boasts are the rage and manufacturers are busy working on larger, faster engines to race with. It is France's task to keep the playing field level; with Detroit's return, the last thing France can afford is the bitter backtalk of favoritism. And there are safety concerns as well, which must keep pace with technology or else tragedy can lead to another ugly boycott. France has long been the master of this kind of paternal rulemaking.

And as he ponders these decisions, he is listening to the circuit's drivers more. He has to. For France, it is another safety measure. After the union episode, listening is a good way to avoid a costly mishap.

"France would listen when we put our concerns on the table, and that was something new," says Ned Jarrett, acknowledging one big benefit to come out of Turner's union efforts. "That was better than what we had had before. The grievance committee sort of fizzled out, but the precedent had been set: maybe there was a need for NASCAR to listen."

Curtis Turner figures he'll try anything. But trying anything keeps bringing him back around to the wheel of a car.

"He always used to tell me, 'It gets in your blood, and once it does, there's nothing you can do to get it out,'" says Ross Turner.

In late 1962, Turner takes Ann and the kids to Florida, trying his hand at the hotel business. It helps to be there when the year changes, to see some old friends getting ready for Daytona. It's also a good excuse to visit Daytona's "Best Damn Garage in Town," to see Smokey Yunick.

It's been awhile. As close as they may be, Turner and Yunick are race-track friends, and only one of them is now at the racetracks.

"Did I hear right, they're making a movie about you, Curtis?" Yunick asks with a sly grin.

Turner chuckles. "That ain't no big deal."

Turner had recently gone to Hollywood to negotiate a start date for *The Checkered Flag*, a film based on his life, to star John Bromfield, best known for his TV role in *The Sheriff of Cochise*. The movie is budgeted at $500,000 with some filming to be done at Charlotte Motor Speedway—in the unlikely event officials will allow Turner and the crew the access. Turner will be one of the producers, and everything will require money, which Turner doesn't have.

"Smoke, I want to ask you something."

"Of course you do, Curtis," Yunick says. "Why else would you be here?"

"I want to run at Indianapolis, in the 500."

Yunick frowns and rubs his chin. "Curtis, I got a better idea," he says. "Why not just get yourself a gun, walk out there to the parking lot and shoot yourself. It'd save us both a lot of time and money."

"C'mon, Smoke—"

"Curtis, you know what you're gonna do. You'll get up there and try to dirt-track that ol' car on rock hard tires and antique suspension—you ain't gonna last no time at all."

"I'm not gonna do that," Turner says, shaking his head. "Look, Smokey, I need this. I gotta do something."

There's a quality in Turner's expression that switches something inside Yunick. He's sad for Turner, and more bitter than ever about France.

"You want to go so bad, okay," he says with a grin. "It's a dumb shit idea but we'll do it."

Decades later, remembering the moment, Yunick says, "I owed it to him.

"I had this very innovative car, the Fiberglass Special; they called it the Python," Yunick continues. "The wheels leaned into the corner. It probably never would have won the Pulitzer Prize for engineering but it was totally different. And I thought that since Curtis didn't know what it was supposed to feel like, he might be able to master it. He was a master at driving ill-handling cars."

The pair aren't in Indianapolis more than a few days when Yunick introduces Turner to a young blond woman he's met by chance. Yunick has already spent a night with her; Turner spends the next ten nights. "I think I'm gonna marry her, Smokey," Turner tells him.

"Dumb son of a bitch fell in love," Yunick later recalled. Turner buys himself a new suit and takes the woman to the finest restaurants, and returns to the hotel room each night to find Yunick asleep in the next bed. "I got tired of sleeping out in the car, so the third night I said, 'You'll have to do your screwing while I'm sleeping.'"

This is business as usual for Turner, life lived the way its always been and for the time being, he swiftly and gratefully gets lost in it. His family is now back in Roanoke.

Turner is in debt. He's at the hub of an investigation into a supposed $40,000 missing from the books at Charlotte Motor Speedway, a controversy that will ultimately take years to clear up. And Robert N. Robinson, a trustee appointed by Judge Craven with the task of reorganizing the track and getting it ready for sale, questions the validity of Turner and Bruton Smith's stock. Robinson asks Craven to "cancel, expunge, deny and disallow" the 50,000 shares each man received for their promoting efforts, saying they were "invalidly issued." Turner can't even afford his own room in Indianapolis; Ed Martin, a successful friend in the auto sales business who's also a car owner, is helping to pay his way for a month.

And if he wants to keep living this renewed style he's grown accustomed to, he'll have to qualify the Python for the Indy 500. Parnelli Jones looks like a good bet to win the pole once again, and this time, Jones should go faster than 151 mph.

"Curtis, if you don't figure out how to get this pile of shit going a mile or two faster, they're gonna cut all the buttons off our coats and send us home," Yunick says at the track during practice.

Turner is defensive. "What would you suggest?" he yells over the sounds of horsepower.

"Try going a little faster."

Turner straps into the Python and makes his way out of the pits. He gets around the 2.5-mile track once and can feel the confidence build. Just hold the speed a little longer in the straightaway—that's what he's thinking when one of his tires grazes a patch of oil, and starts to send him places he doesn't want to go.

"Don't fight the car in a skid." Parnelli Jones and Dan Gurney had both told him that, trying to give him advice on driving open wheel as opposed to a stock car. But Turner reflexively tries to save what is now beyond saving.

The Python practically leaps into the wall. Pain reverberates through Turner's shins up into his back, till it bangs in his skull.

"When one of them Indy cars breaks loose," he says later on, "all you can do is hang on and pray."

"What took me two years to build, Curtis took apart in about one second," Yunick says. The fact that Turner is still intact seems miraculous. Yunick winces when he visits him later in the hospital.

"How are you, ace?"

Turner raises his thick eyebrows lazily. "I just hate what I did to your car."

"I know it." Yunick sighs. His friend has nineteen stitches in his right leg; he's badly scratched and he'll be mighty stiff by morning, but incredibly, nothing is broken. "You know, I think we need to go think about this for awhile."

Turner squints. "In Las Vegas?"

Yunick considers this a moment. "Yeah," he says.

Las Vegas, for Turner and Yunick, lasts for five days, a blaring, yet strangely relaxing, bleary-eyed coda to a great escape, even if Turner can barely move. Months later, he returns to Indianapolis, this time to stay.

And he's come with Ann and the kids. "We bought this grandiose house," recalls Sue. "And he did participate up there."

Turner had moved his family from Florida back to Roanoke, then to Denver and to Roanoke again, and now Indianapolis, in the space of two years. Sue's high school years are spent in half semesters in different parts of the country. The family lives extravagantly, and Turner happily pays all the bills. But at each location, he is like a frequent guest, staying for one week out of four, or sometimes a few days more. For the six months the family is in Denver, he is there only a few weekends.

Indianapolis becomes a base of operations, and it almost seems a little odd to have Turner around so much. Sue is a teenager now, in tenth grade, the independent oldest child of parents living independent lives. The family moves and travels and important, exciting people are always coming to the house. To Sue, it is a whirlwind. Though this is her life, she is aware of the gap between life in the Turner home and everywhere else, where parents are together for family meals and go to church on Sunday. Her father is revered, and everything about him seems larger than life, but it's those qualities that have kept him away from home, and away from family.

"I don't think we had much strength in character as a family in those days," she says.

Third-grader Ross Turner is now being drawn into the whirlwind as well, seeing it from the view of a kid taken for a magic ride. He is in his dad's Lincoln one afternoon when a young guy in his twenties, driving a Thunderbird, pulls up next to them at a red light. The two men look at each other and Ross can hear the engines begin to roar.

"All I remember is that we started racing this guy in the streets of Indianapolis," he says. "And we were two abreast on a two-lane back road. We were racing, and I finally remember the guy actually going off the road, and Dad kinda feeling like, well, there goes another one.

"I was afraid for about five seconds, and then I was really in it," Ross says. "I was holding on. I wasn't pulling for Dad, I was pulling for me! But I wasn't afraid, I was excited. It was an adrenaline rush, a testosterone rush, and it was just fine. Those first five seconds I was thinking, 'we can't do this,' and then I was thinking, 'Don't stop, don't stop!' So we kept going. My Dad could put cars in places they didn't belong."

"He did his own thing," says Sue, with admiration. "And to him, the whole idea was that 'nothing is impossible.'"

But life with Ann remains a challenge, regardless of how much time he spends at home. They've experienced too much incompatibility and separation, and in a number of ways, Ann is too far from home.

"At that point, they really didn't seem to be getting along," says Ellwanger, who had also moved to Indianapolis with his wife, and continued to work with Turner. "I mean they didn't fuss or fight, but Ann was, I don't know, mentally she had changed."

She has changed to the point where she follows her own need for escape. At times, she walks out of the house, leaving the children for a day or two at a time. At times she may appear fragile; at other moments, defiant. She'll respond to the treatment of a doctor, and then feel lost again.

As supportive as Turner tries to be, he is dealing in yet more unfamiliar territory. When Ann is herself again, the strain between them still remains.

Things are much different in Indianapolis; Turner is clearly out of his element. "We didn't do much partying," says Ellwanger. "The people up there were funny. We knew Ed Martin and all that bunch from racing, but it wasn't as much fun. We didn't know anybody."

Turner has begun to drink more on his own, a consequence of dealing with his own debt and stress. Sometimes Ann joins him, drinking more on her own as well. At times, it is a sadly combustible combination.

But sometimes, it takes an argument for the pair to see the long path that keeps bringing them to the brink of separation after eighteen years of marriage.

"I don't know," Ann says one evening, sitting across the kitchen table from her husband. "I don't regret anything. And I'm not sorry that we keep trying."

Turner shrugs. "I can't believe we're in this thing," he says.

Ann sighs. "Gosh," she says. "I wonder what's next."

From his base in Indianapolis in 1963, Turner runs fourteen races in the United States Auto Club (USAC) series, winning twice and leading all but one race; he finishes fourth in points.

"It was just fun to watch him drive," says Leonard Wood. Ford Motor Company continues to lend support to Turner's efforts, and Wood remembers a Wood Brothers-prepared Ed Martin Ford Turner drives in a Sherryville, Indiana USAC race. "He went in a turn behind three cars and he weaved his way through all three in one turn!" Wood says. "And then on a restart in that race, Paul Goldsmith was on the outside pole, Norman Nelson was on the inside pole and Curtis was sitting third. Nelson backed off to let his teammate, Paul Goldsmith, take the lead so Curtis wouldn't get him. And Curtis just goes down on the infield over the asphalt humps and everything else, and comes out side by side with Goldsmith! I mean, you can't explain how good he was at working traffic. He could be slower than the guy, run up on him in traffic, and then just pass him."

As much fun as it may be to run USAC, the pot isn't nearly as lucrative as it is in NASCAR, and the cars and drivers Turner is most comfortable competing with are back east.

And it's made quite clear that he's still not welcome back in that club. He promotes some races at Virginia International Raceway, a road course in Hannibal, Virginia, with some success. But, says writer Bob Latford, who runs public relations for Daytona Speedway at the time, "when Curtis tried to put a race on there, Bill France countered that by scheduling a bunch of races in area tracks."

Turner and France still aren't speaking, unless one counts these kinds of angry economic gestures. In August, 1963, Turner announces his plan to begin constructing a $1.5 million 1.5-mile track near Greenwood, Indiana. The idea is to make the track identical to Charlotte Motor Speedway, "except the two turns will be more like an elbow, and it'll be banked," he says. Like CMS, it would have seats for 40,000, and if Turner can get it built with the help of Ed Martin and other area businessmen, his plan is to run USAC races on the track, starting with a 600-miler on July 4, 1964, the same day France will run a race at Daytona.

Turner continues to investigate a number of other businesses, "but the only things he knew were timber and racing," says Latford.

Timber remains Turner's solid foundation, his one reliable safety net in any storm. Timber puts him in a twin-engine plane, flying high above acres of trees. If he can't race where he wants to, he can fly anywhere, and nowhere is as satisfying as above a sea of "bushes," trying to make a deal for a patch of land. Curtis' father was right about that. The things they can't take from him are the timber and the art of the deal.

"What!?" says Norris Broadhead, a Meridian, Mississippi, business-man, looking out Turner's airplane window at 6,000 acres of Georgia timber. "Hell, Curtis, I ain't gonna give you that much money for that."

Broadhead's father owns vasts tracts of land, and the family business has moved into oil drilling and hotels. But Norris' father, like Curtis', had been a sawmiller all his life, and he knew nothing so well as timber. Norris is young—at thirty-two, he's seven years younger than Turner—and he's as outgoing as his father is quiet, making him an ideal representative for the business. And he loves few things more than the twice-monthly phone call that comes in from Turner, who's ready to show him a piece of land, followed by a memorably good time.

"I was always careful about the people I did business with because I was from a different part of the country," Broadhead says. "And I had a lot of confidence in Curtis. I didn't trust him a damn bit but I had confidence in him."

Turner listens to Broadhead's offer for the Georgia land and says, "Pop, there's no way they'll take that."

"You take it to them and see," Broadhead shouts over the engines.

Turner has no time to wait. The faster a big-money deal happens, the quicker he gets commissions. "Everything he ever sold, he was desperate to sell it," says Broadhead of Turner's perennial debt. "But yet he was always very, very calm. And that's what instilled my appreciation of him being a pilot. Everytime you asked him about the weather he always said the same thing: 'Pop, it's C.A.F.B.' It could be storming all over the place but he wasn't scared of it. Always 'C.A.F.B., Pop. Clear as a fuckin' bell.'"

Turner sells the Georgia land to Broadhead, who will wait two years and sell it for a more than $1 million profit. Meanwhile, Turner has long gotten and spent his $100,000 commission. Like G.B. Nalley and several others with whom Turner does business, such deals make Broadhead count his good fortune, but that attitude frequently has less to do with money than a growing level of respect for the way Turner manages to make everything look so C.A.F.B.

"Guy like me sitting in that office on my ass ain't going to find no deal," Broadhead says. "But Curtis out there, wandering around in the world, he's going to run into one every day. That's the reason Curtis Turner's who he is. He's the one with the grand dreams."

But in 1963, each grand dream that makes some profit pays for other grand dreams long gone. "In the last ninety days, I've made more money than I have the last three years," he recalls later in the year. "I sold 16,000 acres of land in Virginia for a profit of around $100,000. Of course I used most of my share of the money to pay some debts. But the wolf at the door isn't howling quite as loud."

There is a nasty chill on this late January morning in 1964, and Curtis Turner sits in the back of an airplane, gripping the neck of a fifth of Canadian Club. It is just after dawn when the plane takes off, heading from Indianapolis to Norfolk, Virginia.

Someone asks if he needs anything and he shakes his head cordially, but in such a manner that it's obvious he is to be left alone. He unscrews the cap, and with each sip, he remembers something else. And he wonders if there's anything he's forgotten.

"Hey Pop! Gimme that hose!"

It is the mid-1950s and Turner is leading a race with Joe Weatherly in second, and when Buck Baker turns his car over, the caution comes out and Turner reaches for his water jug. He takes one sip and is startled. In a second, he figures out the taste: mint julep.

In the next car, Weatherly is laughing so hard he's nearly crying. "Gimme that hose!" he yells. Turner moves closer, leans over and tosses the bottle, which Weatherly grabs the way the driver for a bank heist catches the loot. He takes one swig of the drink he spiked, and his laugh gets louder. The bottle volley will continue all race long, with every caution. "By the time the race was over, we was both about tuned," recalls Turner.

Another time, at Wilkesboro, Turner slams Weatherly hard and powers on by for the lead. A few laps later, Weatherly is back and knocks Turner clean off the track. Before the checker flies, with neither driver in front, Turner delivers one last lick. It's a typical exchange but Turner knows something's wrong when the race ends and Joe is joking, carrying on. "Hey Pop, jump on, let's go get a chaser." Turner is wary, but he climbs on Weatherly's motorcycle. In a matter of minutes, Weatherly, the former motorcycle champion, is slaloming along the back road so fast that Turner pleads with him to slow down. "Pop," Joe shouts back, "You promise you won't never hit me that hard again?" Turner is quickly relieved. "Pop," he yells, "I promise I never *will* hit you again."

On the plane, Turner allows himself a little smile. He takes another sip of Canadian Club. It goes down like water; it coats his belly but has no sting. He's been drinking too much. Either that or other things have been stinging far worse.

It is August, 1961, and Turner, fighting for his professional life, boasts of all the drivers he's signed to the union. "Only three of the top names in the sport remain unsigned, and we haven't contacted them yet. Only by one driver have I been turned down. I promised those that signed that their names would not be revealed until the time was right."

Later that night, the first night of Turner's ban, the one driver who turned him down flies from Darlington to Roanoke, and shows up at Turner's old home track, Virginia's Starkey Speedway. He will take over and drive the William Mason Modified car Turner had been scheduled to run before his suspension. Glen Wood, who heads the field, and Turner's friend Charlie Williamson watch as Joe Weatherly methodically straps himself into the Mason car.

"Joe didn't join the union because he was working for Darlington Raceway at the time," Turner later recalled.

Wood will win the Starkey race, with Weatherly in second.

It is coincidence, but the astounding phase of Joe Weatherly's NASCAR career begins exactly one month after Turner is ousted, as if the two men had tried squeezing together past a door jamb, with Turner now letting his friend through. Weatherly ends the 1961 season on a tear, winning five of the last nine races, including an amazing come-from-way-behind victory over Richard Petty at Charlotte Motor Speedway in October. He climbs to fourth in the final standing, having won nine of 25 starts for his rookie owner, Bud Moore. Had Joe run the whole season, he might have creamed the field—the kind of thing he seemingly could never do with Turner forever up front, almost always keeping him back.

Moore had seen Joe and Curtis play bumper cars with rentals—often from the backseat—and marveled at their friendship and fortitude.

"Joe would say, 'Boy, my head's killing me today,'" Moore recalls of the typical Weatherly hangover. "He'd take four or five Bufferins about forty minutes before the race and climb in and get with the program—and do damn well."

In 1962, Weatherly starts all but one of season's fifty-three races, winning nine times with thirty-nine top fives. He is among the circuit's most popular names, his days as the shadowed half of the Gold Dust Twins now a five-year-old memory. He is especially bankable at Darlington, where he still works some promotions with Bob Colvin, who considers Weatherly practically a son. In 1962, Darlington stages the thirteenth Southern 500, but the vastly superstitious Weatherly refuses to run a race associated with that number. Colvin changes the name, and Weatherly finishes tenth in the "12th Renewal Southern 500." One month later, he does something Turner has never done in the Grand National division: he wins the championship.

A year later, General Motors boycotts most of the season because they consider the engine limit rules imposed by Bill France unfair. Moore runs only half the year, leaving Weatherly to pick up races in some awful cars, which he still gets the best out of. Fred Lorenzen wins most of the lucrative superspeedway races, and becomes the first NASCAR driver to pocket over $100,000 in a season. Weatherly, driving for nine different owners, manages a miraculous feat of consistency. He wins only three times, but is good enough in the last race on the road course at Riverside, California to beat Richard Petty in points. When Petty falls out early, Weatherly clinches his second championship in a row.

During these years, you might see, before the start of a race, the spectre of two guys in the back of the garage, hanging around, laughing. When you look again, one is gone.

"Every once in a while, Curtis would show up," says writer Bob Moore. "Since he was banned, he wasn't supposed to be there. You figured he and Joe would see each other later in the evening. It was one of these friendships between two completely different individuals, who just hit it off extremely well."

But it is a friendship suffering from attrition. The way Weatherly figures it, Turner's absense is his own damn fault, whatever he was trying to do. Weatherly got bounced by Turner hard as hell on too many occasions, and now there's no forum to return the favor. There are times Little Joe feels like the younger brother, doing battle with an older sibling's reputation. But now Weatherly is the champion. He is NASCAR exec Pat

Purcell's favorite representative for the sport. As Paul Sawyer says, "Joe was *it*."

One night Weatherly walks into Robinson's bar in Daytona Beach, sees Turner and keeps walking. "Joe got mad at Curtis for the union deal," says Ellwanger. "Joe comes in, had some gal with him, and walked right by the table. I know he seen Curtis, but didn't speak to him. That hurt Curtis' feelings I think more than anything, 'cause he always thought a whole lot of Joe. They were good friends but also very competitive. Curtis didn't say nothing about it but you could tell it hurt."

But just as it had happened on the track, whatever their ill feelings, nothing lasts long. "Joe would fly to Roanoke to see Curtis or vice versa," says Sawyer. "They weren't together every weekend but Joe stayed in touch. That friendship never, ever dwindled."

Or the phone will ring in Turner's house at 4 a.m., with Turner reaching to get it.

"It's just me," Weatherly says on the other line. "I had to pee, figured I'd call."

Turner knows Weatherly is thinking about retiring. He and his girlfriend Joanne—"Short Track"—have been living together for a few years in Midway, N.C., and Joe's even bought a cow farm. With his divorce final from his wife Jean, he plans to marry Joanne in late January 1964 in Daytona. Maybe after one more year on the circuit, it'll be time to give it up. Now that, thinks Turner, will be a party.

Weatherly returns to Riverside for the fifth race of the season, driving a Bud Moore Mercury and leading the points. Several laps into the race, he gets caught in a pile-up and radio's in to tell Moore he's lost second gear. When Weatherly pits, Moore tells him he wants to park the car, and the driver is incensed.

"Put in a transmission," Joe shouts, practically jumping up and down. "Just put it in!"

Weatherly knows every point counts in the title chase and Moore obliges. There is a red flag while the track cleanup goes on, and when the new transmission is in, Weatherly is only two laps down.

"He was running the car awful hard," says Moore. "He was running like he was goin' to try to make those two laps up."

It is one thing for a car's brakes to hold up through a 500-mile speedway race. At Riverside, a track with eleven turns, even the best brakes can fail you. By the eighty-sixth lap, Weatherly can feel his are fading as he heads through the esses. He makes a hard left going into the fifth turn followed quickly by a hard right into six. He's only going about sixty miles per hour, but he's in a skid, the car rolling toward the retaining wall.

There are many things Turner and Weatherly have in common; one of them is a fear of fire. That's one reason Weatherly doesn't always like to wear a shoulder harness when he races—just in case. It's easier to escape from the car that way.

But on this day, there will be no fire. Only the sound of Weatherly's Mercury broadsiding the retaining wall. The angle and force of the blow jerks his head, slamming it into the wall at 60 miles per hour.

At the moment of impact, Weatherly is killed instantly.

Turner is in Indianapolis, listening to the race on the radio when he and Ellwanger go out to pick up chicken for family dinner. When they return, there's a phone call. It's a reporter, looking for a comment from Curtis on the death of Joe Weatherly.

Days later, Turner's plane lands in Norfolk on the morning of the funeral. He has consumed the entire fifth of Canadian Club, and he is stone cold sober.

He meets up with Joanne, who had been in California with Joe. She'd gone back to her and Joe's house in Midway, only to find the place had been padlocked, with much of her and Joe's belongings and their memories locked inside.

"What can I do about this?"

Hank Schoolfield, who'd spent several evenings at the house with the couple, hears Joanne imploring on the phone and shakes his head.

"Joanne, you can't do anything. You're caught in the middle of something."

Since the couple had never married, all Weatherly's possessions are inherited by his mother. In time, she will sell the house, wanting nothing at all to do with it.

Hundreds of people are at the funeral. Turner is a pallbearer. Joanne is not allowed to sit up front with the family, even though she had become Weatherly's family.

When it comes time to choose the headstone, a friend of Weatherly's suggests something only a practical joker like Joe would appreciate, and it is accepted. The several-foot stone, with the words "Clown Prince of

Racing" etched in it, is carved in the odd shape of Riverside Raceway.

But after the funeral, Turner and Joanne huddle together, consumed by their grief, and their disbelief.

"During the ban, I don't really remember Turner being depressed," says Smokey Yunick. "There was just more parties, more drinking and more activity in the timber business. But Joe's death—that affected him badly. He never was the same after that, never the same easygoing hell-raising guy that he was before Joe passed away. It didn't change Curtis' driving; he still drove just as hard and strong and reckless as he ever did."

Turner leaves the funeral, shaking his head. "He was only going but sixty miles an hour," he says, and he knows he's said it a hundred times.

Turner keeps walking, wiping at something on his face. "There's four hundred ways that little bastard could have made a living," he says, "but I don't guess he'd been happy doin' anything else."

Every once in awhile, Turner picks up the phone and calls the NASCAR office in Daytona Beach. He leaves a message, but knows enough not to wait for a call.

There are petitions in the press, supporting his reinstatement. About once a month, another southern motorsports writer runs a piece catching up with Turner, wondering what he has to do to get back in. A Kannapolis, North Carolina, racing fan named Kenneth Moss sends a letter to fifteen newspapers. "I think I speak for all Curtis Turner fans when I say we are begging you to help us get him back in NASCAR," he writes to the journalists. "After all, you wouldn't go to a movie or anywhere else, pay your hard-earned money to get inside and then miss the main feature."

It is 1964, and just as it seems to have done everywhere else in the country, a growing youth movement has begun to creep to the top of NASCAR's Grand National standings, a climb that began the moment Fred Lorenzen beat Turner outright at Darlington in 1961, and made his name. Lee Petty's twenty-six-year-old son Richard, runner-up the previous two seasons to Little Joe, wins the Daytona 500 going away, and seems poised to win a title, with David Pearson, twenty-nine, ready to challenge. Buddy Baker, Cale Yarborough, Lorenzen, these are the names on many fans' lips, the new challengers to Junior Johnson and Ned Jarrett, who are both thirty-two. The youngsters make the veterans feel older, and the death of their contemporary Joe Weatherly forces much more profound issues to the surface. "The new names, the new tracks, things began to happen that would make the sport take shape in a different way," acknowledges Jarrett.

Curtis Turner is forty; he hasn't driven a Grand National race in three years, and doesn't expect to enter another. You can see that in his face, a little plumper now, and a quality of resignation in his eyes.

"It was beating up his spirit," Ann Turner says of these days. "Nobody could get along with him for a while. Not me, the children, nobody could. Nobody knew what to do for him."

"The ban just devastated him," says Turner's friend, the writer Marshall Spiegel. "It took a lot out of him. It was about as serious as Joe dying because he became a different animal. He was sure he'd never drive NASCAR again. He talked about the ban incessantly."

In mid-May, Muhleman reports that Turner has retired from racing. "The man *Sports Illustrated* once called 'The Babe Ruth of Stock Car Racing,' the most legendary figure the sport has ever seen, a race driver who became one of the greatest chargers ever to sit in any kind of machine because his only philosophy was 'never quit,' has decided to give up." Turner has come back to Charlotte, back to the house on Freedom Drive, making it the center of his business, and just about the finest spot in town for a party. But sitting with Muhleman in the office of his house, he acknowledged that running USAC costs more than he gets paid for victories. "I've got a wonderful opportunity to go into a full-time partnership in the timber business with G.B. Nalley, a very successful multi-millionaire contractor in Easley, South Carolina. I'm going to do it."

Turner's not alone: Fireball Roberts is thinking of hanging it up as well. He's thirty-four, and Weatherly's death weighs on him. He says as much to Jarrett on the eve of the World 600 at Charlotte Motor Speedway in late May: There are ways to make a living other than racing, he reminds Ned.

But Roberts suits up for Charlotte, and for the first several laps, he hangs back right behind both Johnson and Jarrett. On the seventh lap, those two cars ahead lock bumpers. When Roberts swerves hard to avoid them, his Holman-Moody Ford spins and heads backwards into a concrete wall. The car catches the wall on an edge, and it suddenly spins, flipping over onto its roof. The impact with the wall ignites Roberts' fuel tank; the car is immediately engulfed by flames, with Roberts caught within a plume of black smoke.

The fire reaches Jarrett's car as well, but he manages to pull himself free and races over to help Roberts. The sight that greets him is startling.

"My God, Ned, help me!" Roberts cries from inside the car. "I'm on fire!"

Jarrett reaches in, his hands burning against the flames, and helps pull Roberts out. The driver is transported to a local Charlotte hospital. He is burned over 80 percent of his body.

For six weeks, Roberts makes tremendous improvements. But after a June 30 operation to remove burned skin, he takes a downward turn and falls into a coma. Two days later, Roberts is dead.

Within four months, the sport has lost its champion and its most beloved superstar in track crashes. There is an immediate outcry for better safety measures to match the increasing speeds of new engine designs. The drivers are jittery, and NASCAR officials grapple for a plan of action. Do they make the cars slower, or the tires stronger?

Tire companies begin an extensive series of tests, and Pontiac driver Jimmy Pardue, a rising star on the circuit who'd been runner up to Petty at Daytona, heads back to Charlotte Motor Speedway on September 22 for a ten-lap test. On the seventh lap, while travelling faster than anyone ever has at the speedway, one of his tires blows and his car bangs through a guardrail, vaults off a 75-foot embankment and lands 150 yards in the distance. Two hours later, Pardue is dead.

Bill France stands in his Daytona Beach office, staring out the window at his track, the centerpiece of the sport. His grief is consuming, but he knows there is only so much time for it. He is in a quandary: He has to slow the cars down. It's been only two years since the return of factory support to NASCAR, and any change in engine rules is bound to alienate somebody. But when it comes to certain things, France can see he has no choice.

Curtis Turner admits the place looks different. It's brighter and newer, even sleeker; it has evolved several beautiful steps in the right direction. There are even a few things he doesn't recognize about it. But there's nowhere on earth he feels more at home.

He stands in the infield of Charlotte Motor Speedway, pointing up at the first-ever double-deck grandstand in a NASCAR superspeedway.

"That was Bruton's idea, a few years ago," says Richard Howard, now the general manager of the track. "But I don't have to tell you that."

"I know it," Turner says. "But I'll tell you Pop, you made it happen."

In the wake of bankruptcy, court ownership and debt, it is Howard, among all the stockholders, who has emerged with the greatest chance to produce the glory days that ought to come for the speedway. He is a bear of a man, with a warm smile, a prodigious belly and a contented nature, the last quality a result of a successful furniture business and a happy family. The affection he feels for this place extends to Turner, and standing in the infield, he wears a look of eternal satisfaction, like a rich uncle walking through his brother's house on Christmas.

Turner is here because Howard has made something else happen. The National 400 NASCAR race is set to run October 18; one week later, the Automobile Racing Club of America will run the ARCA 200 at the track. Turner is eligible to run in ARCA, and he's agreed to race.

At first he said no to Howard again and again. He hasn't raced in five months, hasn't driven a stock car at a superspeedway in four years. And this is not the way he ever wanted to come back here.

But there's not going to be another way, so he might as well.

Come race day, there isn't a moment Turner takes for granted. The typical ARCA race might draw a few thousand; 11,000 people are in the stands, the majority of whom have come to see Turner behind the wheel. It doesn't matter if the competition is inferior and the cars have about fifty horses less than the NASCAR machines. It is a slice of the past, and right now, everybody in racing can use that. Especially Turner. He sits in his Holman-Moody-prepared car and everything is alright.

Turner starts the race in second. By lap two, he is in the lead, coursing around the track with confidence and skill. Of the twenty-five cars in the field, he has lapped all but two by the time he pulls in for gas and tires at lap seventy.

When he returns, there's a familiar face up front. Tiger Tom Pistone, who's been out of NASCAR for several years, is about twenty-five seconds ahead. With each lap, Turner and pole-sitter Jack Bowsher eat into

Pistone's lead, and Turner can feel some rust falling away with each circuit.

Two-thirds through the race, Bowsher loses his clutch and crashes, and two laps later, Pistone has to make another pit stop. There are thirty laps to go, and Turner's pit flashes him the "EZ" sign. Thirty more laps, at 125 miles per hour, taking in the cheers and the sights, with a lap on the field.

Afterwards, standing in victory lane, track president A.C. Goines asks Turner to address the crowd. But the cheers go on and on.

"It wasn't a grind at all," Turner tells a group of reporters after walking up to the grandstand press box. "I'm tireder from climbing those steps to get up here than I was from the race." He allows the hint of a grin. "I was having a ball out there," he says.

It is the same old Turner—and old is what someone suggests he is, as everybody else laughs. "It's true that I'm an old man, but only when I look at the calendar," he says, adjusting his driving suit. "But I get plenty exercise in my timber business. Last week I flew 7,000 miles."

George Cunningham, still doing what he can to help usher in the driver's return, asks if maybe this race is the start of more, but Turner shakes his head. "Naah, Pop. I don't have any plans. Besides, it all depends on that man down at Daytona Beach. And I haven't been in touch with him.

"I'd like to run another year or two," he adds with a shrug, and he smiles at Cunningham. "Little chance that's gonna happen, right?"

All the attention is a welcome distraction, but it's temporary. So far removed now from the life of regular racing, he runs his timber business and flies wherever he can, but there are too many afternoons he finds himself alone in the house. Then it can be quiet enough to hear echos of a great party, even the far-off infectious laughter of Little Joe Weatherly. Against the wall in Turner's display case sit the same exact trophies.

Occasionally the phone will ring in Dove Carson's California home in the middle of the night, and she'll roll out of bed and pick it up in the living room.

"Curtis would call anytime he was lonesome about two or three o'clock in the morning," she recalls. "We would talk late at night when he didn't have anything else to do. He would just tell me, 'Oh, I've got an option on this land and I've got an option here.'

"He enjoyed having us visit him, and showing off his planes, his home. His life was just to be around people, people he cared about. He was a lonely guy but he didn't like to be alone. He had to have somebody with him all the time."

Writer Bob Myers visits Turner in his house in Charlotte frequently in the afternoon. Myers now covers racing for the *Observer*, after the departure of Max Muhleman, who'd been extremely close to Fireball Roberts. The pair had been collaborating on an autobiography, and the death of his friend devastated Muhleman, who left Charlotte and found work in California.

There are days Myers comes in to find Turner alone. "Where you been, Pop?" he'll ask. "I've been waiting for someone to show up."

The pair sit together in the grand, empty den. "I'm so lonesome," Turner says. "We're gonna start a brand new party when that clock gets to five," he says, pointing to the clock behind his desk. The clock has only one number on it—five.

One month after the ARCA race, Turner is down in Daytona on business, and after a night of fine food and copious drinking, he and John Griffin, a partner in the newly formed Carolina Atlantic Timber Company, are on the main strip, with a cool chill coming in off the water.

"How far are we from the old beach course?" Griffin asks, and Turner gives him a curious look.

Moments later, the two men stand in the overgrown grass at the edge of the south turn, and Turner listens to the sea churning in the distance. It is pitch black, like a museum after hours, housing something long since forgotten.

Griffin shakes his head. "This place ain't the same anymore, is it," he says.

Turner squints. His night vision adjusts and he can see out into the Atlantic. Far down the sand, ten years in the past, he and Joe Weatherly would broadside in tandem and take the north turn like ballet. And the crowd would stand and stamp their feet, with the yells, and the engines, and the surf and churning wheels sounding like a brilliant bullrush, stamping out all thought and fear. Turner raises his eyebrows with a smile.

"Oh no, Pop," Turner says, walking slowly back to the rental car. "It's the same place, alright."

They get in, and Turner vaults down onto the sand. Building up speed, he counts the timing in his head and tosses the car into a slide that goes on for yards. Then back up to the pavement in the darkness and around again. With the windows down, the ocean smell pours in, a smell he'd hardly noticed before at that speed.

Back up on the road again, a bright light switches on in the near distance. It's another car, giving chase, but then the lights on top begin to flash, and the siren blares.

Turner pulls onto the bank and the police car screeches to a stop behind. Turner knows there's trouble when both deputies angrily get out of the squad car. One of them comes up with a flashlight, shining it right in the driver's face, a spotlight in the darkness.

"Who the hell do you think you are?" he yells. "Curtis Turner?"

Turner smiles. He drops his head, and chuckles through his nose. Apparently, not everybody has forgotten.

"Well, Pop," he says to the deputy, "what seems to be the problem?"

Chapter Nine
1965
"I'm plenty thirsty for racing and it's been a long time between drinks."

This is not the way Bill France wants to spend his afternoon. It is Saturday, July 31, 1965 and he is in a room in downtown Atlanta on the receiving end of a lecture. His son Bill Jr., now a NASCAR vice president, and Pat Purcell are with him. But Charlotte Motor Speedway President A.C. Goines, the track's general manager Richard Howard and Darlington promoter Bob Colvin are doing the talking. The facts, France is told, are speaking for themselves.

After a few years of growth, 1965 has been disastrous for NASCAR. The 1964 season had ended with blow after tragic blow. Drivers shouted to the press about the need for more attention paid to safety in their cars. Fred Lorenzen even threatened to stop racing.

The rule changes France issued were meant to keep the drivers out of harm's way, and the playing field level among manufacturers. Both Ford and Chrysler were affected, but Ford got off easy. Chrysler, on the other hand, could no longer use their powerful Hemi 426 engine, with which Richard Petty cruised to the 1964 championship.

With no Hemi, Chrysler's hopes were sunk, and the angry manufacturer opted to boycott the season. The top young stars France had been banking on—Petty, David Pearson and Bobby Isaac chief among them—would be out of rides for the year, with a few of them running on the rival USAC circuit. In mid-January, George Cunningham of the *Charlotte Observer* previewed the year with a story titled "Ford Versus Nobody." The Fords were set to run roughshod throughout the season.

Many incensed fans stayed home. At the Daytona 500, Ford cars captured the first thirteen spots, and only 58,682 people showed up to see it, a drop from the 69,738 attending in 1964. The faithful booed Bill France during pre-race introductions and one report called the crowd "the largest mob of uninterested sports fans the world has ever seen." About 10,000 came to the April Martinsville race, down from the 23,500 who attended the previous April. During driver introductions at Darlington's Rebel 300 in May, the largest ovation from the crowd of 15,000—half the audience from 1964—was reserved for Richard Petty, standing around in street clothes, ready to watch the action he yearned to participate in. "What we need is personalities," France told the Bristol (Tenn.) *Herald-Courier* the day before the race. "If we still had Little Joe and Fireball, it wouldn't matter if they were all driving Fords."

To bring some personalities back, France eventually compromised on the rules, and on July 25, Chrysler agreed to return for the last quarter of the year. But attendance remained stalled at the larger tracks, causing Atlanta International Raceway president Nelson Weaver to think about spurning NASCAR in favor of USAC.

"The damage is done," an angry Colvin tells France. Fan trust is remarkably low and there is no iron-clad guarantee that another manufacturer won't pull the same stunt. In other words, nobody is happy.

"The fans will come back," France says.

"When?" Colvin says. "What's going to bring them back?"

"I suppose you have an idea?"

"We do," says Richard Howard with a smile. "Bring Curtis back."

France stares at each man in turn. "I don't like your idea, gentlemen," he says, settling deeper into his chair.

The tension in the room spills out into angry shouts hurled back and forth, each side imploring the other for logic and understanding. Something, Howard says, has to be done.

"This is good business, Bill," A.C. Goines says. "It's smart. Don't tell me you haven't thought about it."

France doesn't say anything. A week has hardly gone by without the name Curtis Turner creeping into mind. Bill Jr. looks over at his dad. He knows that look: he can see the wheels turning inside his head.

"I'll tell you Bill," Howard says. "Curtis won that race at the speedway last October and the place went crazy."

"People love the man," Colvin says. "Either that or they hate him, but everybody wants to see him race. We can't ignore GARA."

The time being right to challenge NASCAR, several promoters have banded to form the Grand American Racing Association, with Turner joining in as their main draw. It's still early, but eager crowds are standing in line for tickets to see Turner tear up short tracks once again. At a time when attendance is taking such a hit at NASCAR tracks, fans at North Carolina's Concord Speedway can't get enough of him. If this is Turner's way of attracting NASCAR's attention, it's working.

"You know how much he'd love to come back," Howard says. "'I'd give $10,000 to rejoin NASCAR.' That's what he said a month ago. He's always talking about it."

None of this erases what Turner did, France maintains.

True enough, he is told—which is why he's been out for four years.

For the men in the room, there is no holding back. Given the fiscal state of the sport, France no longer has the luxury of his personal bitterness, which is clouding his normally reasonable nature. This anger is costing everybody money, and it will cost him most of all.

"How great would it look," adds Colvin with a smile, "to finally welcome back an 'old friend?' The man doesn't have to win races; he just has to show up."

"It's a goodwill gesture," Howard says.

"It's *time*," Goines adds.

France looks around the room with a blank expression, and heaves a sigh of annoyance.

Curtis Turner, Charlie Williamson and Bob Myers are sitting in Turner's Lincoln in the infield at Concord Speedway. There'll be no racing for Turner tonight: rain will cancel the evening's GARA event, and the lines of prospective ticket buyers are already heading for their cars. As they pass, many greet him; that big Lincoln with the huge bullhorns on the front of the hood have become a public relations dream for the new series.

"Why do you need one of these things anyway?" Williamson asks as he lounges in the passenger seat. He is gesturing at Turner's car telephone.

Turner shrugs. "Guess I must be mighty important, Pop," he says.

The phone is impressive, and there aren't many like it in the country. He'll be on a timber sale—and business has been mighty good for his

Carolina Atlantic Timber Company—and letting a prospective buyer make a call on the phone doesn't hurt.

Turner stretches in the drivers' seat, watching the crowds walk off. He's disappointed. Racing for GARA has been for pleasure. Physically, he's out of shape. It's been nine months since the ARCA race at Charlotte Motor Speedway, four years and two months since he drove Grand National. Races in both those series are much longer than in GARA, and driving at Concord tires him out much too easily. It's almost like runnng an exhibition. GARA promoter Tom Cole tells *Charlotte Observer* writer Mel Derrick that at one race, "Turner hadn't been around that track ten times before he had hit every other car. If he couldn't pass 'em, he'd nudge 'em on the side. If he could pass 'em—but they wouldn't move over—he'd pop 'em in the rear."

"You ever seen all the equipment he needs to makes that phone work?" Williamson asks Myers, pointing a thumb to the back. "Shit takes up half the trunk."

The phone suddenly rings and all three men laugh. "Probably some baby doll," Williamson says as he picks up the phone, but his face quickly gets serious. "Yeah, he's right here.

"Bob Colvin," he says, handing over the phone. Turner listens and squints a moment but then his eyes get wide.

"C'mon, Bob; please don't fool me," he says. But Colvin hands the phone to Pat Purcell who confirms the news—Curtis Turner is back in NASCAR, if he wants to be.

Turner can't keep the grin of relief off his face. "I do appreciate it," he says, "I really do."

"Let's get out of here," he shouts as he hangs up the phone and tosses his racing gear into the trunk. "This is not a NASCAR track and from now on, I'm legal!"

Myers, Derrick and several other reporters who'd devoted many a column inch to stories about Turner join more close friends back at the house where the liquor is flowing. "I feel like a fellow who just got out of jail after a four-year term," he says.

"You know, I never was interested in the union, I was desperate for money," he adds later on, pouring himself another drink. "Bill France did what he had to do and I'd have probably done the same. He had his interests to protect, and so did I."

France's statement to the press isn't quite so effusive. "We feel that Turner has paid the penalty for his actions by sitting out for four years of NASCAR racing," he announces. "If he desires to become a NASCAR member, all he has to do is apply for membership through the normal channels. He will be treated as any other driver and enjoy the full privileges of NASCAR—as long as he's a good boy."

"That suits me," says Turner. "I guess I just pulled my time, but I'm not going to question Bill's reason," he says, grinning broadly. "I'll be back on track as soon as I get a car—I want to run all the races. If Glen Wood'll get me a car, I'll be up there with the leaders as long as I stay in the race, I can promise you that. And you can count on me being a good fellow from now on. I don't want any more trouble. I'm plenty thirsty for racing and it's been a long time between drinks."

Turner can file his application at the nearest NASCAR office, and he flies his plane to Reynolds Airport in Winston Salem. A Modified car is waiting for him to race as soon as he wants at Bowman Gray Stadium, where he'd once brought so much triumph to NASCAR, and where his membership had been taken away.

Alvin Hawkins and Hank Schoolfield of the stadium have come to the airport to greet him.

"Welcome back, Curtis," Hawkins says, putting out a hand. "I just want you to know I've been pushing for this for a long time. We all have."

"I appreciate it, Pop."

"Should we go inside and get this done?" Schoolfield asks.

Turner takes out a pen. "Let's do it right here," he says.

Schoolfield laughs and hands over the papers, and Turner signs them on the wing of his plane, the pages flapping madly in the wind.

Turner stands in his living room, talking on the phone, and he can't stop squinting. Newspapers are strewn all over his desk, each one trumpeting Turner's return to NASCAR. The *Observer* prefers to cover his every move, as if he were running for president. Radio spots, TV reports, all the racing press of course, fans showing up by the thousands, doubling the crowds for non-Grand National events at Bowman Gray, then Hickory and North Wilkesboro, just to see if Turner still has the stuff. The Southern

500, once considered Turner's domain, is a month and a half away. With the Chrysler boycott recently ended there would have to be plenty of opportunities, even encouragement to join the fray. But here is John Cowley of Ford racing, telling Turner he can't give him a ride.

There are all kinds of reasons, Cowley says. Ford has committed only so many dollars to the year's prime rides; they can't switch now, with the season winding down. And with the Pettys, Pearsons and Isaacs of the world back in the running, all their dollars are going toward the challenge, with Fred Lorenzen the top name on Holman-Moody's Ford factory team.

"I guess you're telling me this is Freddie's doing, now that he's the big gun," Turner says. "Maybe Freddie is worried I might be planning to give him one more lick, like I owe him or something. Tell you the truth, I do, and I just might."

"It has nothing at all to do with Fred Lorenzen," Cowley tells him.

"I know what it has to do with, John," Turner says. "You think I'm too old and washed up."

Doc Morris is alone in the room with Turner. Years later, writing Turner's biography *Timber on the Moon*, he'll woefully recall the incredulous look on his friend's face, the stooped shoulders, and the jaws working tensely.

Cowley keeps talking but Turner cuts him off. "I understand," Turner says, "understand better than you think. I've been a Ford man forever, till now, apparently. So thank you and goodbye, Mr. Cowley."

Turner hangs up and paces around the room. "Too old," he says. But Turner does understand: Ford has enjoyed historic success. The day of Turner's reinstatement, Richard Petty wins at Nashville to give Plymouth, in race number thirty-five, only its first NASCAR win of 1965. Ford doesn't need the forty-one-year-old Turner to chase new glory against Petty. Lorenzen had won the rain-shortened Daytona 500, a superspeedway race in Martinsville and the World 600 in Charlotte; and between Ned Jarrett, Marvin Panch, Dick Hutcherson and Junior Johnson, Ford has the season in the bag, powered by Holman-Moody and the Wood Brothers teams. Hiring Turner, looking purely at the numbers, makes no sense.

He can feel the pride drained out of him. It's that number, forty-one years old, that bothers him now, because it means four years of prime driving time lost. Whatever the reason, the punishment didn't fit the crime.

"I guess I'm washed up," he announces, his voice filled with sarcasm. But given this reception, he has to wonder. The sport is younger, the tracks faster. In only four years, speeds at Daytona have gotten higher than 171 mph, fifteen mph faster than when he last ran there.

He sits at his desk, making phone calls, getting in touch with every owner he can think of, along with sponsors, promoters, anybody with a good few dollars and a car. He didn't get reinstated to sit on the sidelines. But each call yields nothing.

Turner gets in his plane, trying to make connections that way, as if a Grand National ride were the equivalent of $25,000 he needs to have in the bank by Monday morning. He goes to a dinner in Darlington three weeks before the Southern 500, and everybody is delighted to see him, but even John Holman, who's never one to pull any punches, can't help out.

"Curtis, I'm sorry. We've got nothing for you," he says.

"Does that come from you and Moody?"

"That comes from Ford," Holman says. "There's nothing in the till."

Finally, he receives two responses from his calls, and they're head-turners. Bob Colvin has lined up a Plymouth Fury for the Southern 500, one prepared by Red Vogt, a master builder from the old days.

"A Plymouth?" Turner asks. He can't recall the last time he's even been inside a Plymouth.

But strangest—and in a way, most gratifying—of all is the call from Lee Petty. Richard's not running for the championship, and they're still getting themselves up to where they want to be. Lee offers Turner a ride in his son's number-43 Plymouth. The "Petty blue" 43 car has already become, for young NASCAR fans, a most welcome sight up front, with the always-smiling, good-natured Richard at the wheel.

Turner shows up at South Carolina's Piedmont Interstate Fairgrounds in Spartanburg on August 13 for practice and qualifying. Lee gives him whatever directions he can.

"Nice car," Turner says, eyeing the sleek Plymouth. "I was always used to chasing your cars, Lee."

Petty smiles. He's lost a half-step since the horrific Daytona crash that ended his career four years before. To Turner, this gesture of Petty's wipes away a bunch of the bad blood between them.

"Just take care of this one, Curtis."

Turner walks around, getting a good look. He knows what he's going to find on the back bumper but it startles him nonetheless: two yellow stripes; rookie stripes.

"Crazy isn't it?" Turner says. "Richard's more of a rookie than I am."

"Richard's a champion," Lee answers. "You're the rookie."

"I know it," Turner says. It's one of the first things he'd been told: according to the NASCAR rule book, if you're away from the sport more than three years, you have to wear the rookie stripes.

"Believe me Curtis, you need it," Lee says. "It's not like it was when we were driving."

"Speak for yourself, Lee," Turner says. "I'm still doin' it."

Everybody in the garage greets Turner warmly enough, but many of the faces are unfamiliar. He's a curiosity. Some reps from Ford have shown up, ready to check him out. The whole day, which should be a party, has him a little worn out before it even begins. Maybe it's this car; everybody expects somebody else, the new superstar of the day. And then there's that stripe.

"Curtis Turner—rookie," he says, strapping in.

"Curtis went through something, and this happens within the fraternity itself," remembers Humpy Wheeler. "A guy's been out for 4, 5 years, I don't care how great he is, everybody questions his ability to get on the racetrack then and make a comeback, because this is something you have to do over and over again to be good. So there was that question."

Turner feels that question within. But there are 8,000 fans in the stands, an extraordinary number for qualifying; the year before, only 9,000 had shown up for the race itself. And half the crowd has come just to watch Turner run.

Each practice lap he goes faster than the one before as he broadslides into turns. The race at Spartanburg is two hundred laps on a half-mile dirt track: if that's not a fine welcoming for Turner, nothing is.

But he has to qualify first, and it's not going to mean anything unless he can blow everybody away.

"Driving the number-43 Plymouth is Curtis Turner," comes the loudspeaker call. Whatever else announcer Buddy Davenport says about the car, the ban or Turner himself, is swallowed up by the shouting embrace of the crowd.

The fastest time so far has been around 26.5 seconds to turn a single lap. In practice, Lee Petty had timed Turner at 26.1. On his pre-qualifying lap, he's determined not to turn a lap any slower, careening around the third and fourth turns, barely keeping all the wheels on the ground as he passes the flag stand and gets ready for his timed run.

With each practice lap, he's expanded the circumference of his line, seeking out that extra bit of speed, and he won't stop till he turns the ultimate lap.

That's all he's thinking, until he eyes the patch of mud at the edge of turn one.

He slides toward the mud and the car spins, the back end smacking into the wall, cracking something central to the frame of the Plymouth. The car comes to a rest with a thud. As fast as he was going, his day ends even more quickly, before it begins. Things could not possibly have gone any worse.

Turner apologizes again and again to Lee Petty, and heads back to his Lincoln with Doc Morris and Bob Myers. "I can't believe it," he says. "I wrecked the kid's car."

Now this is cause for concern, Morris thinks. Turner has never given a second thought to killing anybody else's car.

"The place was packed with Curtis Turner fans," Myers says. "That says something."

"Some show I gave 'em," Turner says, putting the Lincoln in gear. The car is silent a moment. "Ahh, it's alright, I guess," he says finally.

"There'll be another ride," Morris tells him. "You've got the Southern 500 coming up."

"Yeah." Turner shakes his head. "Maybe they'll all figure it's just some kinda rookie mistake."

Everywhere Turner goes, he meets another track promoter willing to take some credit for getting him reinstated. "I talked long and hard to Big Bill all through these years," they say. "I kept telling him, 'What are you crazy? Let Curtis back in!'" Turner thanks them all, but notices that none of them are willing to give him a ride.

Bob Colvin doesn't take credit; he doesn't have to, since he had almost everything to do with it. Joe Weatherly's death had hit Colvin hard, and having Curtis back helps. Smart promoter that he is, he's brought the press and photographers to the main trophy case in the Darlington Raceway office.

"You have the honors, Curtis," he says, and Turner reaches into the case. A nameplate with the word "BANNED" had been placed against Turner's Darlington trophy. Turner removes it and the pair shake hands.

"I'd *like* to have the honors, Pop."

Colvin smiles. "Don't keep asking me, Curtis."

"C'mon, Bob. Just let me judge the beauty contest." Turner opens the idea up for consideration by the press. "Hey fellas, who's better than me to judge the Miss Darlington beauty contest?" Turner and Weatherly had performed the grueling service several times. Every year, they'd pick a sweet favorite and then spend the next week consoling a number of the losers.

Colvin has done what he can for Turner. Just getting him out on the track to be seen has got to help, even though this Plymouth he's going to drive in the Southern 500, it turns out, isn't worthy of its driver. Car owner Sam Fletcher had run the car sporadically to try to make a dent in Ford's sweeping season. It hadn't been on a track in two months.

But being back at Darlington for qualifying feels entirely different from Spartanburg, no matter the car. Here, at the hardest and sweetest track in the world, Turner is confident. In a field of forty-four, he turns the eighth fastest lap in qualifying.

He'd been spending days at Darlington, conducting tire tests for Firestone. Each lap run had pushed him closer to the track record. He was scraping more rust off with every turn.

Junior Johnson and Fred Lorenzen qualify to start in the first row; right behind Turner are Ned Jarrett and a feisty, frenetic twenty-six-year-old from Timmonsville, South Carolina, named Cale Yarborough. Yarborough has the sense of entitlement that comes from youth, and from scraping his way toward the top and not being willing to look back. He could almost be another younger Myers brother, and Turner also sees a bit of himself in Yarborough. For good reason: as a kid, Yarborough had worked at Holman and Moody before getting the chance to drive, and had come to Darlington for the races, where he rooted hard for his idol, Curtis Turner. And now here he is, one row behind him.

There is no Richard Petty at Darlington, nor David Pearson or Bobby Isaac. Plymouth is still getting its superspeedway cars where they need to be. But there is Turner, making his first start here in four years, and at driver introductions, that's enough to make 50,000 fans extremely cheerful.

The mood turns somber quickly, however, and the tone is set for a wreck-filled affair: two laps into the race, driver Buren Skeen's Ford is broadsided by Reb Wickersham, a hit so hard it knocks Skeen's seat to the other side of the car. Skeen is removed from his Ford after several minutes and taken to the hospital. Nine days later, the injuries, which include a basal skull fracture, will prove fatal.

Turner tries to keep pace when the action resumes after Skeen's crash, but it's clear he doesn't have enough car to be a threat in a field filled with factory-supported Fords, which Turner watches roll on by. He works his way past some competitors, but in a race filled with attrition in even the best cars, his wheel bearing gives way after fifty-one laps. In the final tally, he'll end the day in thirty-fifth.

It's a curious feeling, to exit the car that day for good. He's tired, but not nearly as tired as he would have been had he finished, and he'd have given anything for that exhaustion.

He sits on the wall, breathing heavily, and when he looks up, it takes him a second to greet John Cowley, standing before him with Ford racing liaison Jacques Passino.

The pair had been roaming the pits of the top factory drivers since the start of the race, talking about Turner.

"The first time I ever saw him on dirt," Passino had said, "I was dumbfounded."

He recalled the beauty of seeing Turner set records in Ford convertibles, the exhilaration of all those wins, and the frustration at how many more times it seemed Turner blew up for no good reason. And there was the time he'd flown with Turner here to Darlington in weather so bad you couldn't see a damn thing. But the driver, sensing they were close to the track, had said, "Start looking for the wire."

"What wire?" a panicked Passino had asked.

"There's a radio tower down there with some guide wires on it," Turner told him calmly. "I know, it's probably a little hard to see 'em." But Turner had found them, and landed the plane on a tiny grass strip behind the track as if nothing were amiss.

"That's just the way he is," Passino reminded Cowley. "Fearless."

"And he's a Ford man," Cowley said.

"Yeah, he is."

The Wood Brothers pit was nearby; with Glen Wood packing up after Marvin Panch's blown engine forty-two laps into the race.

When Ford had first entered stock car racing Turner became their star attraction. Then the company began lining up the best teams to build and field their cars and Turner, who had Ford's collective ear, recommended the Woods, and pushed the issue strongly enough to see them get hired. During Turner's ban, the Wood Brothers won the 1963 Daytona 500, became the fathers of the swifter modern-day pit stop and made their name.

Glen Wood is normally a quiet, unassuming man, about as humble as you can be and still be a master car builder. But he's been annoyed at Cowley: the idiotic sight of Curtis Turner in a Plymouth makes him irritable.

"What do you think of Turner?" Cowley asks him.

Wood stares at him incredulously.

"You think he can still drive?"

"I'm *certain* he can," Wood says. "Look at him out there. That car ain't fit for him."

"What would you say if I asked you to build him a car, and have him drive for you?"

Wood can't contain a smile. "Sure we would," he says.

And now Cowley and Passino give the news to Turner: he should go talk to the Wood Brothers. Ford is giving him a car to drive for the four remaining major races of the season.

Turner jogs over to Glen and Leonard Wood's pit, the sting of the early exit now almost gone. "Curtis," Glen says, "I guess you heard the news from Cowley."

Turner shakes Glen's hand. "I had a rough day today, Pop, that's all. Nothin' to worry about. I think once I'm in one of your cars, I'll do just fine."

"I'm sure of it," Glen says reassuringly, looking slightly perplexed.

"We'll build you something good, Curtis," Leonard adds.

"It was just the wheel bearing today," Turner continues. "Damn thing just wasn't that good a car. Can't trust a Plymouth anyway."

Glen is embarrassed enough to put a hand on Turner's shoulder.

"Curtis, you don't have to prove anything to us," he says. "We know you can drive a race car."

Turner smiles, and a twinkle returns to his eyes. "I appreciate that, Glen. It's been a little rough."

"Curtis, we wouldn't even be in this business if it weren't for you," Glen tells him.

"We'll make you the car," says Leonard, reaching for an errant tire. "All you have to do is go out and do what you do."

In the two weeks following Darlington, Turner runs two dirt-track Grand National races in Fords owned by Junior Johnson. At Hickory, he starts on the front row, right next to pole-sitter Johnson, but an overheating engine knocks him out after thirty-five laps. Then he starts fourth at the Rural Fairgrounds at Richmond but finishes second to last, watching the steam rise from under the hood once again.

The Wood Brothers have their number-47 Ford ready for Turner at the September 26 Martinsville race. After that will come North Wilkesboro, Charlotte, and then the brand new track at Rockingham, North Carolina. All four tracks are paved.

Marvin Panch is the Wood's main driver, but creating the right car for Turner is an effort the brothers take to heart. At Martinsville, Turner qualifies sixth out of thirty-seven. The field is full once again: Richard Petty has the pole, with Bobby Isaac next to him starting second, and Johnson, Pearson and Lorenzen taking the other top spots.

Turner likes Martinsville, a challenging half-mile paper clip with tight turns connecting mad-dash straightaways. It's a track where, as Buck Baker likes to say, "you can knock someone out of the way and then say 'Excuse me.'"

Several laps in, Turner winds his way through traffic and passes Bobby Isaac, leaving Johnson and Petty up ahead. Isaac is making only his first start of the year. He has a strong Dodge, and Turner is in his way.

Isaac is not a youngster. At thirty-two, he is five years older than Petty, and two months older than Ned Jarrett. But he'd risen to the Grand Nationals late, in 1963, and like any other non-Ford driver in 1965, is hungry for a return to form. A mess of straight dark hair slants down onto his brow under his helmet, and his round olive-skinned face is twisted in a scowl as usual. He'd been brought up in a sawmill in Catawba County,

North Carolina, and grown into a slight but brutally honest man of very few words. "He's the kind of guy," says his friend Humpy Wheeler, "who you didn't mess with." He tests Turner high and low from one lap to the next, and the veteran blocks each attempt.

Both men feel a great urgency: Junior Johnson is running away with the race. On lap forty-five, Isaac has had enough, and brushes Turner's rear quarter panel as he gets in tight to make a pass. But Isaac has moved up the track just a fraction too high. Turner swerves and the force of his car makes both slide. Together, they slam in diagonal tandem into the four-foot concrete wall at turn three. Twenty some-odd miles into the race, and the day is done for them both.

Turner is incensed, seething at so boneheaded a move by a kid messing up one of his last few chances of the year. He's out of the car as fast as he can curl through the side window, and moves up the track shouting, while Isaac calmly extricates himself.

"What are you trying to do, deliberately wreck me?" Turner says, his fists at his waist.

Isaac, now face to face, glares up at Turner. "Why should I wreck you?" he spits. "I don't even know you."

"What are you talking about?" says Turner, but his squint softens. He turns around, shaking his head. Isaac's words are more of a blow than anything Turner has felt from the crash.

"That moment defined how things had changed," recalls Ned Jarrett. "Bobby was part of the new group coming along to take over the sport, so to speak. Things like 'who was well known or popular,' that didn't matter to him. And he really didn't know who Curtis Turner was. It was like things had really passed Curtis by."

Back in the pits, Glen Wood raises his shoulders. "You can't be serious," he says. "Bobby Isaac knows your name as well as he knows his brother, if he has one."

Turner stares back at his wrecked car, it's right front corner still stuck to the wall, and he wonders what else he could have done to keep Isaac behind him.

"Curtis was determined that, 'Okay, all you young whippersnappers out there, I'm going to show you I can still drive,'" recalls Bob Moore. "Curtis was going to show Isaac he couldn't push and shove on him. It's like he was saying, 'I didn't allow this before, I'm not going to allow this again.'"

Marvin Panch has won both Atlanta events in 1965. Johnson has twelve wins in thirty-two races, and Jarrett and Dick Hutcherson are battling for the Grand National title. At Holman and Moody, and the Wood Brothers shop, the premier Ford factory teams are tooled and retooled, just as Turner's Fords had been ten years before. The Woods are very meticulous with Turner's car, which is a terrific gesture. Turner understands he's been hired by Ford because he "belongs in one," and how could they pass up that kind of product recognition opportunity? He's got a good enough car to win at any track. But first he'll have to get passed Ford's finest.

After Martinsville, Turner starts making the best of what he's got. He starts eleventh at North Wilkesboro and finishes fifth, one spot ahead of Panch, with Johnson, Yarborough, Jarrett and David Pearson in front of him. It is the first time he's raced 250 miles in years. Finishing, and not feeling like he's ready to die, is encouraging. And he'd passed Pearson and several others. It didn't matter that they eventually passed him back; his ability with the car is a good sign.

"At least I finished one," Turner tells the Woods afterwards. "Now I hope I can win one."

Everybody is heading back to Charlotte for the National 400, and Turner throws the kind of party that indicates he is back in every sense. Leonard Wood makes adjustments to the car and Turner comes out to test, looking a little overdone.

"Don't worry, Pop," he tells him. "I drive better with a hangover."

Being back at his track nearly one year after his ARCA triumph, running in Grand National in a Wood Brothers car—this is the way he'd dreamed of doing it all along.

But a week before the race, Turner's number-47 Ford is clipped in a practice crash, and no matter how Leonard tries, he cannot get it handling right. He sends Turner out to test, knowing that any other driver would come back with a list of complaints.

"Rides just fine, Pop," Turner says, stretching a little.

The Woods are fielding cars for Panch, Turner and open-wheel star A.J. Foyt, and Leonard knows Turner's is the least of the three. The 35,000 diehard fans in the stands couldn't care less: the field is packed with

Fords, and Curtis Turner, the man who built their track, has as good a chance as anybody, they figure. Cameras will capture his efforts throughout the day: Dynamic Films, Inc. has resurrected the idea of a film of Turner's life.

But the going starts in devastating fashion, an echo of Darlington: Harold Kite, a friend of Turner's from the MARC series, making his first NASCAR start in nine years, is killed in a five-car lap-one crash. Turner has to squash this from his mind, and look ahead to the cars out front: Yarborough, Lorenzen, Darel Dieringer and Johnson.

The race continues, the laps pile up and after a hundred of them, Turner passes Lorenzen and holds the lead in a Grand National race for the first time since his return. Two laps later, the lead is gone, but he remains among the front few cars, trading spots, inexplicably biding his time, being just patient enough from one moment to the next among the sport's most impatient men.

He begins to feel something in the grooves in the speedway pavement, a jostling that gets worse with each bump. One more hard bump and the dread hits home: he's lost his shock absorbers. It's two-thirds through the race; as is his style, he hadn't bothered to have Leonard Wood fully adjust the seat brace. Rolling over a pebble now at 140 mph is magnified fifty times when the edge of the seat gouges deeper into his ribs.

Foyt holds the lead for forty laps, then Turner, and Lorenzen. Dick Hutcherson creeps up alongside Turner, while Foyt and Lorenzen do remarkable battle up front. For fifty miles, the leaders seek whatever advantage, while Turner holds back, with every jerk of the wheel sending him flopping then pounding down, the brace stabbing into his side. Then with one powerful bounce, the brace juts into him, snapping one of his ribs, turning a dull ache into the kind of shooting pain that makes you want to stop breathing—all at 140 mph.

Hutcherson moves up. Now he, Foyt and Lorenzen are side by side by side, the outside cars running inches away from the gravel edge. Any human mistake and all three will go tumbling. For laps this goes on, an exhausting sight, with Turner holding back in fourth, ready to help push the fastest man through, then skirt around, take the final lead and head on home.

The tension of so precise a run can only hold so long and Foyt is first man out. On the high side, he makes his run on turn three with six laps left. Lorenzen, in the middle car, drifts up an inch or two; Foyt's Ford wiggles and Turner lifts off the gas for an instant. Like magnets, Foyt's car is drawn up against the guardrail, which he rides for yards. Lorenzen blasts off, catching Hutcherson and Turner off guard, and the trio are stuck in single file.

Turner can only wish for a car like Fast Freddie's, but he doesn't have it. And the crowd, having been on their feet for an hour, stomps madly as Lorenzen continues his swift run and takes the checkered flag in what may just be the greatest race anybody's ever seen.

It's certainly up there for Lorenzen, who exults in victory lane. He's relieved to be done with this one. And when a reporter brings up Turner, he hardly lets him finish the question.

"Curtis Turner is *back*," Lorenzen announces. "His physical endurance is amazing. His reflexes and skill have not been hampered by age."

Turner tools his Ford down pit road, his eyes misty from pain. His fist bunches up the uniform over his broken rib, but that won't make him feel any better.

"Great run, Curtis," Glen Wood says, but Turner is motioning for Leonard with the worst kind of grimace. For the first time since they've known each other, he actually has a comment to make about the car.

"How about putting some *shocks* on this thing!" he shouts.

The accolades pour in about the amazing battle at Charlotte, and though Lorenzen and Foyt get most of the press, Turner's showing is also cited. But that's done. Turner has two weeks to get ready for his last ride of the 1965 season: the American 500, the premiere race at the newest track in NASCAR's growing empire, the million-dollar North Carolina Speedway in Rockingham, the fastest one-mile track in the United States.

Petty, Pearson and Isaac; Johnson, Lorenzen, Jarrett and Yarborough . . . Ford, Plymouth, Chevrolet, Pontiac, Dodge, for the only time all year, everybody will be racing together, looking for a chance to end the season the sweet way, by stuffing someone's bragging rights down somebody else's throat, after months of rancor and bitterness.

Turner is hurting all over. Four hundred miles at speed will do that to you under any circumstances. And it's been too long since he's had to concentrate on anything for four hours, with the harsh vibrations running off the steering wheel, into the muscles in his forearms. One day after the race and his hands are still shaky. Thankfully, his aching rib is feeling okay. But it's hard to argue with the annoying perception: he *feels* like an old man.

Turner flies home to Roanoke to start getting his body into shape. He walks through his lengthy yard with a large pair of shears, using his hands, cutting bushes, trimming, working his fingers, "trying to build his muscles for holding the steering wheel again," says his old friend Paul Cawley, whom Turner invites over for company. It's been a few years since Cawley has seen his onetime racing buddy, who is looking worse for wear. "Curtis was bending his body this way and that, trying to build his strength back up," Cawley adds. "He was so glad to get back."

Turner is happier still when he arrives at Rockingham. Glen Wood will be putting him into the red number-41 Ford with the white top, which Foyt had raced in Charlotte. Foyt can only drive stock cars when the schedule permits a break from his Indy racing, and Rockingham is out for him. Turner will be driving the only car that could have challenged Lorenzen at the end in Charlotte.

Turner qualifies the car in fourth place on the Friday before the October 31 race; only Petty's Hemi-powered Plymouth, Johnson's Ford and Pearson's swift Dodge are timed faster.

Turner's car feels terrific; the driver himself does not. It's not as if he's been using any therapy available to treat his broken rib, unless the rec-ommended regimen includes ample amounts Canadian Club, followed by exercise, sex and more Canadian Club. He's been up late partying with Roanoke and Charlotte friends, proving he can still accomplish things his way, and he's logged a few hundred miles in the air, showing off timber tracts in Georgia.

The rib has behaved through everything, until he is behind the wheel again, hitting bumps at 115 mph. On practice-day Friday, he comes into the pits after only thirteen laps. The pain is excruciating.

"There are few injuries that hurt more during a race than a broken rib," says Humpy Wheeler. "When you break a rib, it affects those inter-costal muscles between the ribs, and once you're into turns you can hard-ly breath. You've got a load going down and a load going sideways that's just tied to your rib cage. Nobody figured Curtis was gonna last real long in that car."

Turner is sure he won't, unless something is done to ease the pain. On Saturday, he flies to Charlotte and heads to Presbyterian Hospital. The discomfort of driving with a cracked rib is rivaled only by the darting ache of having doctors examine it, but when they're done, they apply an excessive amount of tape to help hold everything steady. Meanwhile, Leonard Wood is at the track, building and attaching a fitted brace on the car seat designed to put pressure on Turner's shoulder and cushion the injury.

Turner is pretty much ready to go. Only one more activity is required to get him set just right.

"He partied the whole night before!" recalls Glen Wood, laughing. "The morning [of the race] he's at the track, laying on the hood of the car, sleeping it off."

By mid-morning on October 31, Rockingham is already too warm for comfort. A sellout crowd of 48,000 has travelled in on Highway 1 with their windows down, taking in the rich honeysuckle from dense blooms in the woods beyond the Sandhills roadside. Then inside the stadium there's a fine new introduction of oil and gasoline, the wondrous building blocks of adrenaline.

Turner wakes up from his car-top nap and feels the snug grip of adhesive tape along his belly and back. The rib is pretty tender. The Wood Brothers have a couple of relief drivers in mind in case Turner can't continue at any point.

Leonard Wood is looking more serious than usual. "I want you to listen to me Curtis," he says. "There's lots of sand on this track; it's gonna wear out your brakes. The way I figure, the driver with the best chance of winnin' will be the one who conserves those brakes."

"You want me to take it a little easy, Pop? I can do that," Turner says, nodding.

Leonard isn't entirely convinced. "You've got a very fast car, Curtis. You don't have to worry about that."

"I know it. Don't worry."

"And this is a handling track, Curtis," Glen Wood continues. "You've got to be on your toes all the time."

The cars are lined up by noon, and the day is a scorcher. Inside Turner's Ford, the temperature is already close to 100 degrees. The brace fits perfectly, but the green flag waves, the cars rumble to get up to speed, two cars crash before the first lap is run and there's nothing he can do to stop his ribs from killing him.

Or maybe there's one thing. He can keep running. Running, once the green flag comes back out, is a pleasure unlike anything he's felt in more than five years. He knew it in practice and the car is better now. Even among the class of the field, the best of the sport, he knows it, and everybody else does too, with some sixth sense. He holds back. He can pass Junior Johnson for the lead but it's too early. He and Panch, Johnson and Isaac, they start trading the lead back and forth, for miles at a time. Fifty-eight laps in, Petty is collected in a crash that also slows Pearson down. Johnson blows an engine after 150 miles; Fast Freddie loses his about halfway through. Bobby Isaac will follow, all of them running too hot, too fast.

Turner takes over the lead from Panch at the 175 lap mark and is out front for the next one hundred miles. The ride is slowly tapping his energy, even given some reserve of will he has. The car is a glorious machine, it makes him feel humbled and nearly invincible. And still, he holds a little bit back, using a finesse block here or there instead of a burst of speed. Several drivers in the frustrated field end up blowing their engines. Turner has this track figured out. He'll drop down low to force someone behind him to go lower still, on a slower groove. Or if someone goes up high, he forces them too high to race past him. Other drivers keep trying and then backing off.

When he comes in for pit stops, even Leonard Wood can only say, "Just keep doin' what you're doin.'"

"How are you holdin' up?"

"It hurts," Turner says.

The race goes on for hours. By three o'clock, the blazing sun starts to set at a very bitter angle that hits drivers directly in the eyes when they come off turn four. Turner's windshield has no special coating, nothing to keep the glare from pouring in, and the sand and salt make visibility grimy. He begins to dread the fourth turn.

A quarter of the way through the race, Jim Paschal had pulled into the pits, bequeathing his Petty Plymouth to fresh driver Richard Petty, who leads for eighty-three miles after Turner goes in to pit. Turner has to fight the urge to reel him in.

The pre-race strategy is working, but Turner can still feel his brakes loosening up. With seventy-five miles left, Ned Jarrett falls out. And even given their fine cars, Panch and Petty will not contend unless something odd happens. This battle is between Turner and the kid fifteen years his junior, Cale Yarborough.

Turner pits and when he returns, Yarborough's lead is only five seconds. If the race goes the rest of the way without a caution, Yarborough will have to take one more stop for fuel. All Turner must do is wait, and hope that he doesn't blow a tire, or run out of gas. The heat inside the car is mesmerizing.

With fifty miles to go, the sand has finally ground away his fan belt. It starts slipping and the engine heat skyrockets, the water temperature hitting well over two hundred degrees. Turner instinctively steps on his brakes. They're slipping, too.

Yarborough keeps eyeing his rearview, waiting for a challenge. Turner eases up, going just fast enough to stay with him. Yarborough is forced to pit for fuel with twenty-five laps to go. When he comes back, Turner is leading him by eleven seconds.

It is almost 5 o'clock in a race that began at noon. In the press room high above the track, Bob Moore watches his friend's car intently, listening to the shocked talk among the writers. "No way Turner lasts," someone calls out. Yarborough has the mark of greatness about him; everybody can sense that. It's a matter of time, another writer yells out. "The old man's gotta run out of steam."

"Maybe," Moore says, "but it's one hell of a story if he doesn't."

It's a story that raises 48,000 to their feet in the grandstands, people leaning up on their toes with shouts, arching toward the effort. "The fans really got into it," remembers writer Tom Higgins. "They stood there cheering him on every lap."

With less than ten miles to go, his lead still better than ten seconds, Turner comes off the second turn hard and banks his Ford off the wall, swerving for an instant and getting back on the gas. A cry erupts from the stands and Yarborough hovers, tasting the kill.

"Five bucks says Yarborough wins," someone yells in the press room, but then the place gets dead silent, except the growing growls and whispers of plenty of the writers nearby. "C'mon," Moore hears himself say. Turner's run suddenly looks erratic. Moore is finding it hard to believe Turner isn't fading.

Five laps to go, and again, Turner goes into the second turn too fast, smacking the wall harder this time. He jerks the wheel left and recovers, feeling the tape ripping at his skin, and the pain in his ribs bulging. His hands are swollen, the temperature in the car is high above a hundred degrees. In the rearview, Yarborough's car hardly seems to be growing, like a mirage. All Turner has to do is keep it there, and drive true for five more laps, five more miles, and as he does, the closer he gets, the more he knows everything's going to be alright.

When Turner crosses the finish line in front, the roar envelops the brand new track, and Turner closes his eyes as if admiring the sounds of a storm. In the pressroom, Bob Moore can't help himself; he leaps up once and claps as he races outside, heading down to do his postrace interview. Walking through the grandstands, he stumbles a moment. The cheering is like an earthquake.

Turner drives into the flower-strewn victory lane, and he sits there, listening to the sound of his heaving breath inside his helmet. He climbs out gingerly and paws at his sweat-soaked driving suit pocket for a Camel. His hands shake furiously with exhaustion. He gets the cigarette and it takes several tries before he is able to light up and the moment he takes that first puff, the strong hands of Glen and Leonard Wood are on his shoulder.

"I thought I had it won before I started," Turner says, needing every effort to get the words out. "I know no car was better than the one Glen Wood had prepared for me. And—" Turner pauses, making sure everybody is listening "—I knew better than anyone else that I *wasn't* over the hill."

Glen Wood whoops at the answer. He is the last man on earth you'll ever see drunk, and Turner sees it's the last thing he needs at the moment, and a smile comes to his haggard face.

"I guess you could say this one means a lot to me," Glen says. "There never was one doubt in my mind about Turner's ability."

"Now, I was *warned* before Curtis joined us that he was over the hill," he adds, and by now everybody is laughing. "But I didn't believe it. The race at Charlotte and today prove that Curtis and I weren't out of our minds when we teamed up."

Every move now feels justified. Tom Higgins remembers getting a quote from Yarborough after the race, his face "as red as a pickled beet. He was burning up, he was right on the verge of heat exhaustion." And he has nothing but admiration. "Turner drove a beautiful race," he says. "He's lost none of his old form." Yarborough soaks himself with a cold towel. "He's still a great driver," he adds. "I don't think there's much doubt about that."

There are kisses from the beauty queen, and there is a glorious trophy with an eagle perched on top. And there is the normally quiet Leonard Wood with a warm grin on his face. "A race driver just don't forget how to drive," he says.

In the stands, the cheers continue. It's a tribute to Turner that for the first time anybody can remember, nobody leaves the stadium through the entire trophy ceremony. They're all standing, and to Turner, the sea of arms is as stirring as the surf at Daytona Beach.

"We're gonna go home after this," he says, huffing through the words, "and we're gonna start a brand new party every fifteen minutes. I think Little Joe would like that."

"People left there just shaking their *heads*," remembers Humpy Wheeler of the day. "It's the most sensational thing anybody ever saw him do. Just the fact that the guy is still sitting there at the end, and with a busted rib. There's no telling what determination he had in him. And it took over five hours to run the race. I mean just sitting in a chair for five hours, doing *anything* for five hours is hard."

Partying for forty-eight hours, however, is something Turner has trained hard for. After all the writers file their stories, they converge on Freedom Drive, joining Turner and Ellwanger, Doc Morris and a house full of guests.

A day or so into the festivities, Bob Moore hovers nearby, watching Turner tell another tale about the race. Somehow, his stature has grown still larger to Moore. There will be no taking this away from Turner; just as he'd lost all those years under suspension, there is now some spark of what he's gotten back.

"But listen, Curtis, I've got a question for you," Moore says, and Turner settles in next to the writer.

"I was sure you were running low on energy those last few laps," he prefaces, and Turner responds with a sip of Canadian Club and soda.

"Those last few laps, you went into the wall—twice. Now you didn't slam into it; it wasn't bam! it was more like hmm!, like you brushed it hard. So I want to know: did you do it on purpose?"

Turner raises his eyebrows with a grin.

"Because I'm figuring you're saying to yourself, 'You people think I'm falling asleep out here, don't you? You think I'm getting old. Okay, I'll hit the wall, keep on going and still win the race.' It's like you got too far ahead and wanted to make it exciting for people. You hit the wall and it woke everybody up. So?"

Turner smiles like the cat who ate the canary.

"Does that smile mean Yes?" Moore asks, and Turner has to chuckle.

"I didn't say that," he says, and he stands up and looks at his watch. "I don't know about this party," he says, and a roar rises from the crowd in the room. "Listen, let's all go and wash our faces, comb our hair and come right on back. Another party's startin' in five more minutes."

Moore shrugs on the couch. "I'm sure he did it on purpose," he tells another partygoer who'd been listening in. "It's almost like he hits the wall and then all of a sudden, by doing that, he's right back in the groove again, as if hitting the wall is what did it. It's like at that moment, he's back to being Curtis Turner again."

Chapter Ten
1966-1967
"I don't want to build the car that kills Curtis Turner."

Dan Gurney has a face that belongs on U.S. currency. A sandy-haired, straight-living California racer with an easy smile and chiseled jaw, Gurney can drive and win in anything: Indy cars, sports cars, Formula One cars. Every January, when the NASCAR tour heads west to Riverside Raceway, the 2.6-mile road course eighty miles east of Los Angeles, Gurney tags along, hops in a Wood Brothers-prepared Ford and beats everybody else. The stock car stalwarts are tired of this treatment, but as they head back for the January 1966 race, they don't see any way to stop it, given Gurney's immense road-course skills. Semi-retired driver-turned-car owner Junior Johnson, who will field Fords for A.J. Foyt and Bobby Isaac, admits, "We got about as much business bein' here as a one-legged man in an ass-kicking contest."

On his first practice day at Riverside, Curtis Turner walks through the garage area wearing a firesuit, a Stetson and a smile. His face is a little pink and soft; he's maintained a typical late-night agenda here in California. Having attended a party at Frank Sinatra's one evening, followed by others the next night, he tells friends that out in California, "these guys really know how to *party*."

Turner has never once raced at Riverside, and his only experience on the track so far has been riding around in his rental car, slowly checking out the course's eleven snaky turns. None of this concerns him very much. People keep talking about how grueling the track is—"This race is murder," says Ned Jarrett. The way Turner figures it, come race day, there'll be cars, and turns, and laps, and everything will be fine.

And that has Dan Gurney concerned.

"Curtis showed up with about a week's growth of beard and he looked like he hadn't had any sleep for four or five days," recalls Gurney. "He looked like he wasn't going to be able to go twenty miles. But that was part of the game."

Gurney had met Turner at Indianapolis, watching his aborted attempt to qualify Smokey Yunick's car. "I already had enormous respect for him," he says. "He drove with a flare that was hell bent for election. Competitors are sizing each other up all the time, under every situation. Some of them can win that sizing-up contest and the other guy fades. Curtis was strong at that. You're talking about a really dangerous business and if you can convince your competitors you're crazy enough, that's a big advantage. A guy like Curtis might say, I'll match you one dangerous thing after another.

"And in the end, he probably volunteered to come to Riverside and see if he could 'do something about Gurney, this road racer,'" Gurney adds. It was the sort of thing a guy like Curtis would have loved to do."

The Wood brothers had planned on cars for Gurney and his perennial Riverside challenger Marvin Panch. But Turner had told them he was also going to run, period, and the Woods refused to refuse him because they understood why. Turn six at Riverside is where Joe Weatherly got killed, and there are rules about things like that.

If anything, Turner is more vindictive about this place than ever. He's waited a long time. "He was bound and determined; he was going to beat Riverside," remembers writer Marshall Spiegel. "During the ban, he would say things like, 'That goddamn race track killed my friend.' It was a vendetta." Beating Gurney will be the icing.

Winning, however, will be a challenge: Turner, being last man in the Wood stable, must drive the lesser machine he raced at Charlotte the year before. "We did all the things you're supposed to do with it," Leonard Wood recalls of the car. "We fixed it as good as you could fix it." But when Turner walks into the garage and stares at the three Fords, he knows.

"Is this the one I ran in Rockingham?" he asks, tapping his car.

"Nope," Wood says glumly.

"This the one Marvin drove at Rockingham?" he asks hopefully.

Wood presses his lips. "Nope."

Turner is quiet a moment, drumming his fingers on the roof. But then he shrugs confidently. "Shoot, I like road coursin'," he says, and Wood has to laugh.

The car is wheeled out for practice, and Turner looks out at the gleaming pavement and the kind of veering turns that once made moonshine running so pleasurable.

"How 'bout getting in there and checking the seat out, see if it fits?" Wood says.

Turner sticks one foot in the door and says, "She's just right."

Glen Wood is out among the track's infamous esses, waiting to see Turner fly off into the dirt again and again in his first practice lap. "But that wasn't the case," he recalls. "Curtis come up and run sideways just almost off and then almost off the other way, and finally he evened that thing up. And he broke the track record before he'd come off the track the first time, and he'd never driven anything at speed til then. I thought that was the most unusual thing I'd ever seen."

Turner feels like a guy brought back from the dead. It's been three months since his big Rockingham win. His comeback, says *Stock Car Racing* magazine, brought a legion of fans back to a sport devastated by death and tainted by boycotts. Right now, every race is like being able to ante up at the card table. He lives for the love of the deal.

Turner doesn't feel his age so much as the years lost. He plans to run every race there is in 1966. The last time he saw a new NASCAR season through to its end was 1960, and he hardly ran at all. That's the year he and Bruton built the speedway. Kennedy was winning the White House and January meant drinking shooters at Robinson's bar with Weatherly and Fireball, getting about half tuned and then chopping some kindling in the nights leading up to Daytona. Life was a little more predictable then. Now everybody seems to be looking for an upswing, pining for something new and a break from grief. Vietnam is a horrific, constant sight on TV.

Thanks to huge new contracts, there are more sports to watch on television as well. In football, the AFL and NFL are heading for a merger, and suddenly, big money abounds. In sports in general, there is a shift in the balance between what we revere as a game, and what we must admit is a business. New national heroes are being molded and raised up every day. Image, it turns out, is everything.

NASCAR wants in on this new age. For fans, that means a rich new year of Petty and Pearson, Yarborough and Isaac.

And then there's Turner, that rookie driver from 1965. *He's* brand new, too.

At Riverside, Pearson qualifies well enough to win the pole. The next three slots are taken up by the Wood entries of Gurney, Turner and Panch.

Ten laps into the race, Gurney moves to the lead and begins taking things relatively easy. To him, Riverside is six or seven races in one; it requires patience and pacing. Turner is in second, trying to push Gurney to go more quickly through the esses. He thought this guy was supposed to be fast.

Gurney is unsettled by Turner's frustration, sees him on his bumper one minute, then back a few car lengths from one lap to the next. If this were a boxing match, Turner would be telling his opponent to start hitting back. In the pits, the Wood brothers are holding up signs asking Turner to even his pace. In the packed stands, 73,000 fans are imploring him to do anything but.

By lap thirty-seven, Turner has had enough, and it happens almost without thinking. He overdrives the car going into the esses, skirts to the right of Gurney and goes darting off the road, across the dirt and grass, through the apex of the curve.

"He was in the wrong line and he was going too fast," remembers Gurney. "But he was going to get in the lead."

Turner bounds down, his Ford tilting into a small ridge, and standing on the gas at eighty-five miles per hour, he vaults into the air, slams back down onto the course and takes off.

"It was the first time," Gurney recalls with admiration, "that anyone's ever passed me while airborne."

Turner swings through the rest of the esses and is on his way. "The hell with it," he says out loud, "I came here to race."

For thirty-four laps, the two Wood drivers trade the lead through pits stops and the creeping traffic of lapped cars. Turner's moves are erratic, just this side of disaster, and Gurney is astounded by his fluid movements of instant recovery.

Panch, Yarborough and Foyt are out with transmission problems, and blown engines end the days of Petty and Tiny Lund. No matter how much abuse Turner may mete out through each ess and turn, his Ford moves forward. But Gurney has taken off now, like an expert endurance runner with a great kick.

Pearson has designs on the lead as well and three-quarters through the race both he and Turner sense that their duel only keeps them further from Gurney. A standoff is inevitable.

They tangle, and Turner sails straight into a fence. He is enraged in the pits, squirming while the crew pries and slices the crumpled fender off his wheel to return him to the fray. For the only time all day, he thinks about Weatherly, and he wishes he didn't have to.

"Slow it down a bit," Leonard Wood says. "Take it easy."

"Sure," Turner says, and he peels out of the pits with a great lurch.

The team has done its best, but Turner is struggling to keep control and regain some ground. Trying to avoid a slower car, he spins and slams backwards into a concrete wall. Fuel pours from his tank and he is sent into the pits for repairs. He reemerges but he is two laps back, running in fourth place, when Gurney takes the checkered flag at Riverside for the fourth straight time.

After the race, after the celebration, Glen Wood tries to console Turner, but there's no need. "It's alright Pop," he says. "We'll get 'em next time."

Next time is a month later in Daytona. For Turner, there are practice sessions, a Modified race, qualifiers, a Grand National and the rejuvenating power of a familiar place and a good party. Here, everybody remembers him again.

But almost everybody still wonders about him. He looks more than four years older since the ban, plumper and softer, as if all the inactivity has taken a toll.

There's an afternoon he isn't running well in a Daytona Modified practice session. One of the Ford reps comes by the pits and suggests to the Woods that maybe Turner has lost some of his skills. Leonard Wood looks at the guy as if he's just told him he's using the wrong lug nuts.

"Curtis Turner hasn't lost *nothin',*" he says angrily.

Wood spends the day turning all kinds of adjustments and when he's done, Turner can put that Ford any place he pleases. Tiny Lund runs beside him in one corner, forcing him up into the marbles during the next practice session, and Turner swings through and passes Lund before he's back on the straightaway.

The next day Turner wins the Permatex 300, the richest Modified race on the schedule, beating Panch by two miles. At one point, he passes pole-sitter Jim Hurtubise by sneaking his Ford way down on the apron, as low as it can go. The move takes him by the pits and Glen Wood sees Turner do something that makes Wood blink: he sticks his hand out the window and flashes an "okay" sign, pulling his maneuver at 180 miles per hour.

"He could have blown his hand right off," Wood says with a smile. "But he just wanted to say everything's okay."

Turner stands in his office, talking on the phone, waiting for the punch line. But Ralph Moody won't deliver it.

"Wait a minute," Turner says. "I just got back into this thing. You've got to be kidding."

Moody is not—ten races into the 1966 season, Ford Motor Company has decided to boycott the remainder of the year.

Bill France had let the Chrysler Hemi engine back into NASCAR at the end of 1965, and Ford, feeling the need to counter the threat, tried to get France to approve its single-overhead cam 427 engine. When France said no, so did Ford, and the edict went out: Turner, Ned Jarrett and Bobby Isaac would be the first Ford drivers to sit, for the next three races. Until France reverses his decision, Ford drivers will continue to remain on the sidelines.

Ford knows exactly what this will do; they've already seen how the Chrysler boycott shifted a year's fortunes. All they need is for their united front of drivers—Turner, Jarrett, Lorenzen, Yarborough, Isaac, Panch and Dick Hutcherson—to keep the pressure on, and they'll be able to get NASCAR to readjust the balance once again.

Racers, promoters, writers and owners line up on both sides of the issue, with everybody hoping for a speedy end, which does not come. For France, the question is an all-too-familiar one—will he allow himself to be dictated to?

Richard Petty is fed up. "The car companies are like Russia, Red China and the United States," he says. "An agreement is almost impossible."

"The sport has become large, but it is not grown up," writes Hank Schoolfield in his *Southern MotoRacing* editorial. "It will not escape such problems as long as it can be controlled by car makers."

Irritated fans immediately produce a boycott of their own, with attendance taking a nosedive. Weeks go by without a Ford entry from Holman-Moody or the Wood Brothers.

Turner is climbing out of his skin. He's enjoyed only eight months of racing since his return. And in his last start, he'd finished second to Pearson at Hickory's small dirt track, losing by seconds.

He plays some golf. He goes back to setting up timber deals. He plays more golf. And he keeps on the phone, talking to the Wood Brothers and several drivers. He'd just spent four years being banned for sticking to his own principles, he tells Glen Wood. It's ridiculous to now be banned by sticking to someone elses, even if it's Henry Ford's. Besides, Ford is only planning to pay him $600 per month on retainer. You can get twenty times that winning at Darlington.

Turner's friends know what he is like when he's frustrated, even irritated. But this is the first time they can recall him being angry.

"Hell no, I don't like NASCAR's ruling at all," he says. "But I don't want to have to quit because of it. Hell, I want to *drive*. If I wanted to sit around on my tail all day long, I'd *retire!*"

Everybody he talks to can sympathize, but nobody seems to understand quite like Smokey Yunick, who stays away from NASCAR and Bill France's rules for stretches, only to return with another faster car meant to give technical inspectors fits.

"I'm damn tired of doing nothing," Turner tells him.

"*You're* doin' nothin'?" Yunick says.

"I didn't say I had any spare time," Turner says. "But I'm a race driver, not a damn golfer. I've got two or three years left and I need to be racin'."

"Then race," Yunick tells him. "Darlington's coming up."

Turner is quiet for a few seconds. "You got any ideas, Smoke?"

"Always."

Three weeks after being told to sit down, Turner becomes the first factory driver to defect from the Ford cause. "Others may be able to sit around," he says in an announcement, "but I've got to make the most of the time I have left."

Several promoters agree to help sponsor Turner's ride; he had brought fans back before and could do so again. But people stay away from Darlington in droves; a dismal crowd of only 12,000 shows up, with 5,000 of those being Boy Scouts admitted for free. And midway through the race, Turner's Smokey Yunick Chevrolet breaks down for good.

His movement into the middle of this issue has created a firestorm. All sides seem eager to use his defection to their advantage, and all he wants to do is race and win in the best equipment available.

There may have been a time, years ago, when he'd sit down and talk these issues over with Bill France. That could never happen now. Turner recognizes the way France has been treating him since his return; he's overly gracious but standoffish all the time. There seems to be no chance of them ever growing close again.

Turner had promised to be "a good boy" when he returned. But what has that earned him? The potential breakdown of a fifteen-year partnership with Ford, all because of NASCAR's rules.

"I'm fed up," he says after learning he may have to miss the next Charlotte race. "Ford was one hundred percent right in pulling out of racing. Why should they have to run with a handicap? And promoters complain about the absence of Ford, but when they meet with Bill France, they take no stand. They sit back and listen and then come out supporting him one hundred percent.

"Racing has gotten too big and involved for one or two men to rule and regulate," he says, delivering a well-placed dig. "I think there should be a governing board set up consisting of people in every phase of stock car racing in order to resolve the problems."

He runs at Charlotte, in a car normally fielded by rookie driver Bobby Allison, but blows an engine nineteen laps in. Several days later, he finds out he has bigger problems than this when Charlie Williamson calls from Roanoke.

"Ann's disappeared," Charlie says.

Turner flies home from Charlotte and walks in to find neighbors in the house, helping Sue look after Ross and Priscilla. Sue had gotten up early and having found her mother missing, spent the morning making panicked phone calls while watching her siblings and getting herself ready. In a few hours, she'll have to head over to school. Today is her high school graduation.

Turner calls members of Ann's family, trying to get a lead on where she might be. He'd wondered if something like this might happen. He and Ann had hit a new low lately, growing as distant as they'd ever been. Midway through Turner's ban, Ann had gotten pregnant for the fourth time. After the reinstatement, Turner and Ann were swallowed up again, each in their own lives. Tyler was born in August, 1964.

Ross comes over, an eleven-year-old with thick eyebrows and a sad but pensive expression. Turner rubs him on the head awkwardly; he can see Ann in his son's face.

"Where'd Mom go?" he asks.

"Don't you worry," Turner says. "She'll be back soon."

It'll be another day before they find out she's run off to New York, and a day after that till they can bring her home and get some help. But now Turner stares off into some distance in the white tile kitchen, with the sounds of his children running through and yelling, and the somber feel of a funeral. Something blue and shimmery crosses his gaze. He looks up to see Sue in her pleated graduation gown, staring down at him.

She has shifted into some other place of mind. For years, dealing with the uncertainty of a house so much different from any of her friends, she's been buffeted by the most stable measure she knows: the passing semesters of school years. Sue has attended school in Roanoke and Charlotte, then Florida, back to Roanoke, Denver in the second half of ninth grade, Indianapolis in tenth. Now back at Roanoke these two years, it's been a relief to have the comfort of the same friends she's always managed to come home to. Turner stands slowly and stares at her in befuddlement.

"Daddy," she says, looking distressed, "let's *go!*"

It is an extraordinary thing for Turner to see Sue graduate, something he'd never come close to doing. Somebody takes a picture of the two of them together, Sue in cap and gown, her father in his fine suit. They share a bemused smile.

He's heard again and again that of all his kids, Sue is most like him. She's not afraid to push some limits. It has put them at odds too many times, with Turner the kind of man whose life is too frequently recounted in anecdotes and newspapers stories, and his oldest child fighting for more time on his radar.

A few weeks later, they go together to pick up a rental car Turner needs. On the way back, Sue in the family car, Turner in the rental, they are side by side at a stoplight on Peters Creek Road in Roanoke. Their eyes meet, and something instinctive makes Sue gun the engine. A cheshire grin crosses her dad's lips, and he grips the steering wheel the way a gun-slinger grabs the pearl handle of a pistol.

At the green, they jet down the road at once, with Sue swerving slightly but gaining control—and then the lead. She has the much better car and she knows it. Or else, how could she win?

They turn off the road, heading for home, when the familiar blare of a police siren fills the warm afternoon. Fear's bitter taste fills Sue's mouth and she takes the clearest route home, screeches to a stop and runs inside to hide—a ticket for her and she figures she's finished.

Turner is on her tail the whole way, watching her maneuver and ricochet, and by the time he stops, she is already running into the house.

The policeman, it turns out, had been a bag boy at a supermarket in Floyd years before; for him, writing Curtis Turner up would be like disrespecting his elders. Otherwise, Turner would have had to explain that here in Virginia, on a sunny afternoon, it's just not right to give a man a speeding ticket when he's out trying to catch up to his daughter.

Brock Yates, the editor of *Car and Driver*, has flown several times in Curtis Turner's twin-engine Comanche, but he's never seen anything like this. Dominating the view through the windshield is an enormous thunderhead, a classic bilious summertime storm that looks like one of those H-bomb test pictures, with lightning curling inside it. At present course, the plane will begin heading into the heart of it in about a minute, which gives Yates enough time to begin contemplating his mortality. Richard Howard, in the front passenger seat, stares ahead wide-eyed; and a lawyer friend of Howard's, tagging along for the flight, sits in the back next to Yates, looking chalky and continuing to chain smoke. All three men have the same thought: Everything would be so much better if Turner would just wake up.

Turner is blissfully asleep. Yates can hear the faint sound of snoring. They'd gotten on board in Atlanta half an hour before, heading back home to Charlotte, and twenty minutes after takeoff, Turner put on the automatic pilot, told Howard to wake him if disaster struck, tilted the seat back and went to sleep. Knowing how skilled Turner is in the air, neither Howard nor Yates can figure out if this storm is to be considered a "disaster." And neither man is particularly in his right mind.

No wonder—it has been one hell of a few days. The party at Turner's house in Charlotte on August 1 had lasted through the night and come next morning, with vicious hangovers in their heads, they'd all flown to Atlanta for qualifying. At the track, Turner drove one of the oddest-looking cars anybody had ever seen, a Chevelle built by Smokey Yunick that sat noticeably off-center and was undoubtedly some kind of hardly legal aerodynamic wonder. Miraculously, the Chevelle had been approved by NASCAR inspectors, and Turner then took it onto the track, where he shattered the Atlanta International Raceway qualifying record, circling the 1.5-mile track at 148.331 miles per hour, while the headache pounded reassuringly in his skull.

They'd begun the flight back home the same way as usual, with Turner foregoing any actual flight preparations and checklists and simply taxiing and taking off. In the air, the foursome had enjoyed several shooters of CC and Coke before Turner covered his eyes with his beloved straw cowboy hat. The hat has a small bite mark, a few straw grains chewed out of the brim by the dog of a woman artist he likes to visit often.

Yates has come to admire and respect Turner, both for his sheer force of will and his enormous presence. As Yates' friend Max Muhleman had discovered, there is a sense with Turner that life is forever some vast human adventure, spearheaded by the man in the aviator shades and the deep, soft, friendly drawl.

The first small rumbles of the storm wake Turner up and he rubs his eyes and looks ahead. Yates sighs with relief, but Turner simply drives his plane right into the heart of the storm, pushing the cowboy hat down on his forehead and steering headlong into this next great challenge.

The plane careens and bolts through the hollering winds. It's tossed like a leaf, pulled in up drafts and down drafts. After a few minutes, hail smacks the windshield. Turner is relaxed but determined at the controls. Next to Yates, the lawyer puts a second lit cigarette in his mouth and groans as lightning is followed much too quickly by thunder.

"Hey, isn't this dangerous?" Howard shouts over the wind, looking down at Turner's dangling seat belt.

Turner shrugs. "Yeah, it can get dangerous if the windshield blows off and you gotta duck down behind the instrument counter," Turner says. He looks over at Howard with a wink. Howard smiles crookedly. His lawyer friend yelps and lights another cigarette. Lightning flashes and runs across one wing of the plane. Turner raises his eyebrows.

"Look at that," he says. "Lightning's dancin' all around us, like a greased onion."

Yates is partly terrified, partly thrilled. There is, with Turner, an assumption that all will be well when you're in the air, if for no other reason than Turner refuses to permit any other outcome. And if not, there's nothing Yates can do about it; there is a certain comfort in futility. But as ugly as this storm is, Turner has spoken of flying through much worse: landing on an ice patch at the edge of a cliff, landing in mud and needing to broadslide the plane in order to stop, needing to skirt just below a little bridge in order to touch down on a small air strip. Perhaps this one hardly rates.

The vicious tossing lasts for fifteen minutes. Then Turner can see the hint of a clearing and he sails on past the storm, and continues his northeast climb into Charlotte. When he lands and shuts down the engine, Howard's friend pushes his way out the door of the plane. Yates expects he will vomit. Instead, he falls flat onto the tarmac, his lips pressed to the pavement.

"Thank you," he cries. "Thank you."

"My God," says Howard, getting out of the plane and bending to his knees, "it's nice to be back on the ground."

"Yep," says Turner casually.

When he returns to Atlanta days later, Turner finds himself wrapped up in a different kind of turmoil, now coming to a head in NASCAR. Junior Johnson had brought his Holly Farms Poultry Ford to the track on qualifying day, with Fred Lorenzen breaking ranks and making his first start of the season. Johnson's Ford is a work of abstract art equal to Yunick's Chevelle, with everything from the windshield to the roofline to the front end being either sloped or lowered. Given its shape and bright color, the car is nicknamed the "Yellow Banana." More important, it had also passed NASCAR inspection, with Lorenzen qualifying third. Defending Grand National champ Ned Jarrett, who has announced his plan to retire at the end of the year, had been one of three drivers whose more conventional-looking cars *hadn't* been deemed legal by NASCAR. The yelling and complaining about the inspection follies will continue long after race day. Bill France goes so far as to admit the rules were bent. The implication is that letting stars like Turner and Lorenzen into the race only encourages other Ford drivers to return.

Race day doesn't last very long for either Turner and Lorenzen. But by then, Ford has reversed their landmark decision: they've agreed to return to NASCAR full time, this attempted boycott ultimately undone by Turner and others crossing the picket line.

For the second straight year, the season will finally end with all manufacturers back in and playing by the rules. In that spirit, Johnson is "encouraged" to refine his Ford before the next race. And he'll have himself a new driver when he gets there.

Johnson's got it good for a first-time owner: he'd been able to keep Holly Farms as his sponsor after moving out of the car. Holly Farms is an anomaly, one of few non-auto companies willing to invest in NASCAR for the long haul. And on top of his driving success, Johnson has made a career of knowing how to keep the Wilkesboro, North Carolina, company happy, and their respectable reputation unsullied.

Fred and Rex Lovett run Holly Farms and Fred's wife is a big fan of Curtis Turner's. After the ban was lifted, and Johnson retired from driving, Mr. Lovett wanted nothing more than to see Turner behind the wheel of the Holly Farms Ford.

An offer is made and with Smokey Yunick having taken his Chevelle home, Turner is grateful for the opportunity. But there's a company image to keep up, and Turner is no Boy Scout.

"Don't worry about me, Pop," Turner tells Johnson. "I'll do whatever I need to do."

He needs to match the company image, and be presentable at the track. Among other things, he's got to show up wearing a proper driving suit.

South Carolina's Columbia Speedway is not your average half-mile dirt track. The first turn is notoriously dicey; many a famous driver has taken it too fast, and found himself being launched into the parking lot, flipping end over end.

Practice begins at 6 P.M. and qualifying will follow, with the green flag waving at 8 P.M. By 7:20, Turner is still a no-show, and Johnson is doing a slow burn.

The field is nearly done qualifying when Turner's Lincoln finally screeches to a stop and he emerges, walking casually to his pit stall. Johnson stares at him, perplexed.

"You gotta have on a driver's suit," he says in his slow drawl.

"I *do* have on a suit," Turner says.

Turner is in an impeccably tailored brown silk three-piece business suit, with a white shirt, wing-tip shoes and a dark tie. "The tie was nothing showy; Curtis knew how to dress," remembers Humpy Wheeler, there at the race as a rep for Firestone Tires. "I was watching all this in total amusement. This was so Curtis; you couldn't ever get mad at him." Adds Johnson, "The dang-blamed suit probably cost around $500."

Turner takes off his jacket and hands it neatly to a pit crewman, loosens his tie and puts his helmet on. He'd just come from a personal appearance for Ford, signing autographs at a supermarket. "About halfway through the appearance I started having a tap," he later recalled. "And soon I was half-juiced. I got to the track about five minutes before the race began and figured what the hell, I'll drive with what I got on."

Johnson gives Turner last-minute instructions, and Turner speeds off to qualify, barely making it out to run his timed lap. In the field of twenty-six, he qualifies second.

Turner passes pole-sitter Bobby Allison before the first circuit is run. In the 200-lap race, he leads the first 134 times around, broadsliding and darting, outpacing the field.

He pits at one point for gas. "I'm thirsty as hell," he announces, and one of the crewmen hands him a cup of what he figures is Coke, only there's not enough in there, and he sniffs it.

"That ain't Coke," he says, looking at an inch or so of bourbon.

"No it ain't," says the crewman laughing.

Turner considers it a moment. "Well, shit," he says, downing the cup. He returns to the race, still in the lead until his right front tire suddenly blows and he bangs into a wall. He steers the car into the pits for a lengthy stop, watching the field set him back a few laps but he's calmed by another inch of bourbon. And when he reemerges, Turner passes car after car, making back his laps with less than fifty miles to go. He is about tuned. "On track, nobody'd come near me," he later said.

J.D. McDuffie wrecks in the final going, and the race ends under caution. Turner has made it all the way to third, and takes the checker right behind Pearson and Petty.

Buddy Baker finishes eighth, having spent the race chuckling at what he'd seen. "Some people said Curtis may have had a drink or two before getting in the car. I will tell you it didn't affect his driving whatsoever," he says. "I've never seen in my life Curtis do anything halfway. He partied like a wild man and he drove like a wild man."

And he climbs from the car, pats down his shirt and greets reporters. "Holly Farms told me that if I was gonna drive for them, I had to wear a suit," he says, adjusting his silk tie. "They wanted me to be a gentleman driver and I figured this is the first step. You've gotta look good, you know."

Bowman Gray Stadium brings up all kinds of memories for Turner. He'd made his name there in the early 1950s, fighting his most stirring battles against Bobby and Billy Myers and helping draw tens of thousands to the tiny quarter-mile. He'd been banned from there in 1961, and signed his reinstatement papers right around the corner from the track four years later.

On August 27, at what will become the wildest Bowman Gray Saturday night of his life, Turner shows up wearing an imported pale yellow dress suit. What had worked before, he figures, will work again. Having done his share of shooters, he arrives late and qualifies the Holly Farms Ford in fourth, behind Petty, Pearson and Bobby Allison.

It's hard to get a fix on Allison. On the one hand, he's the very essence of the young, modern racer, a good-looking twenty-eight-year-old with jet black hair, piercing eyes and a subtle cinematic grin. He eschews dirt tracks; to him, large paved tracks are the future "and the big tracks are not going to be dirt," he says. "Dirt is history." On the other hand, he's a throwback, a three-time Modified champion who's stunned everybody with the success of his tiny home-built Chevelle; he's a fiery, determined driver not long removed from his days racing in Alabama where he and his younger racing brother Donnie sometimes only had enough money to eat peaches every meal for three days.

Allison has spent no real time with Turner; he's seen him around, knows he's a tough, entertaining competitor. He considers him "a neat guy." They're from vastly different worlds but both, when pushed the wrong way, will eagerly strike back without compunction.

So when Turner spins Allison out on lap eight of the Saturday night race at Bowman Gray, something hard and vengeful awakens inside Bobby. He is crooked on the track, and needs to let all twenty-three cars go by before he can proceed. And when he does, his life's mission becomes catching up with Turner.

It takes him about a hundred laps; by then, Turner is leading the race, masterfully blocking the pursuit of Petty, Pearson and Tom Pistone. It is hard enough to pass at Bowman Gray; with Turner, it will require something miraculous, or at the very least extremely imaginative.

Allison moves into second and Turner veers to block him several times. Pistone tries Turner on the high side and Allison dives to the bottom. The cars are three abreast on a track that barely accomodates two. Pistone loses room and smacks against the retaining wall and Turner and Allison press against each other, forcing their cars together like swords in a swashbuckling duel. When Turner's Ford spins, Petty finds daylight between them and grabs the lead.

Now it is Turner's moment of frustration. While all other cars are at speed, he moves slowly, waiting for Allison's No. 2 car to come back around. But the young driver still hasn't let go of his own bile. Instead of taking Turner's bait he plows into him hard. When Allison tries to regroup, Turner clips him once more, and Allison spins to the infield.

By now the crowd of 15,000 are practically dancing out of their seats, screaming at the battle. Everybody knows Turner likes to mix it up with the rookies a little. But Turner in his big Ford and Bobby in his little Chevelle, this is mythical.

The yellow flag comes out, with NASCAR hoping to clean up debris and let tempers cool. No such luck.

"NASCAR threw the caution," remembers Allison, "and Curtis was slowed down to a crawl. I simply put my car in first gear and drove right into the side of his car and pushed him into the wall, along the back straightaway of the racetrack. And of course that cost Curtis his place in the race, the guy behind him went around and filled in behind the pace car, and so once I had him stopped against the wall, I let the entire field go by, and I backed up and attempted to start away. With that, he put his car in reverse and backed into me, very much like the old destruction derby. And that damaged my car a little bit more severely. So I put my car in reverse and I backed around in a circle and backed into him. And then he put his car into first gear and drove into me nose first. And so then I backed away from him and drove into him."

The banging goes on for a slow and mesmerizing ten caution laps. Both cars look like exhausted brawlers with Turner's No. 26 Ford clinging to the edge of the infield. The Chevelle will not do more than twenty mph, but with all the power that such speed possesses, Allison piles into the back of Turner's car one last time, and winds up nearly on top of him.

A slew of fans jump the fence and surround the cars, and several police officers rush out to keep them at bay, and separate the drivers. NASCAR officials quickly join them, coming to the scene to disqualify both cars—not that either car is capable of the slightest movement.

Turner gets out of his Ford and without a glance back, makes the slow walk to his street car, with Allison, winded and angry, staring after him. Turner drives off to Smithfield airport, gets into his plane and before heading for home, flies over Bowman Gray, making one last low sweep to dip his wing and say goodnight, to the roaring approval of the crowd.

By then, Junior Johnson has finished supervising the hauling away of the Holly Farms Ford. "Well you can write down one thing," he tells Hank Schoolfield. "This will be the last time Curtis Turner will ever drive a car of mine."

"It was really embarrassing for Holly Farms," Johnson remembered years later. "It wasn't the image they wanted because although Turner was popular, so was Bobby. And Holly Farms wanted to sell chickens to Bobby Allison's fans the same as they did Turner's. It's like biting the hand that feeds you. Besides, they didn't want to be part of no ruckus."

But there is no ruckus. NASCAR fines each man a token $100 for "rough driving," and a still-steamed Johnson tells Turner, "next time *I'll* pay the fine and *you'll* pay to fix the car." A week later, Turner is preparing to drive Johnson's Ford for the very last time, in the Southern 500. During practice sessions in the days before the race, he seeks out Allison in the garage.

"You and I need to be friends," Turner tells him, holding out a hand.

Allison is instantly disarmed. "I'm having a party at my house next Wednesday and I want you to come," Turner adds.

"From that day on," Allison remembers, "he was my friend, self-proclaimed: 'I'm Bobby Allison's friend.' He was great at shrugging these things off."

Not everybody is quite so accomodating. Ford and Chrysler are now thrust back into the sport's manufacturing wars and with few races left in 1966, much pride is at stake. Turner's prime days with Ford are long gone. When Ford racing manager Jacques Passino looks for the next great hope, his model isn't Turner, it's Lorenzen. And Cale Yarborough has inherited the prime Wood Brothers Ford.

Turner is still perfect, however, for Yunick, who has his black-and-gold No. 13 Chevelle ready for the driver in mid-October at Charlotte Motor Speedway. Turner qualifies third in the race, with Richard Petty starting fourth. Gordon Johncock, driving for Junior Johnson, qualifies second; on the pole, driving a Ford for Holman-Moody, is Lorenzen.

Turner is joking with a group of drivers in the garage area when, looking at Lorenzen, an idea hits him.

"I bet I'm gonna lead the first lap," he says.

There is laughter and there are boasts back and forth and someone says, "I'll take some of that action."

Before the betting is done, thousands of dollars are laid on the line. This appeals to Turner, a nice little challenge, a little man-to-man combat. He walks up to Lorenzen and the two stand toe to toe, with Freddie nervously running his hand through his hair.

"Well now, I just might have something on this, too," Lorenzen says.

Turner nods. "Pops, if I have my bumper even with you, and I'm on the inside going into turn three of the first lap, don't you turn left on me."

On race day, by turn three of the first lap, Turner is exactly where he says he'll be; having gone by Petty and past Johncock, he is even with Lorenzen, riding so low he's on the apron. And that's when Lorenzen does turn left.

"Well, that made me mad," Turner later recalled.

Ninety-three laps into the race, Turner will blow his engine and retire early. But it won't feel quite so bad when he remembers lap one, turn three. That's when he'd given Lorenzen a solid nudge. Nothing too hard. Just enough to get him a little shaky, with Turner flying on by to the start-finish line.

To Smokey Yunick, being scrutinized at the track by the press and NASCAR inspectors is a bit like going to the dentist: you've got to sit there patiently the whole time, but you don't have to pretend you like it.

The factory wars are at their height at the start of 1967. The high-price teams have brought their stout machines—their Fords, Plymouths and Dodges—to Florida to do battle on the grandest stage of all, Daytona.

There's not a factory Chevy in the bunch. Yunick has his Chevelle, but the outsider insists that General Motors had nothing to do with it.

"It doesn't belong to them," he says gruffly. "It belongs to me."

Nobody is surprised. The black-and-gold No. 13 Chevelle looks smaller and smoother than anything else on the track, and everybody is a little shocked by the sight of it. In mid-December, Yunick and Turner had spent several days at the speedway, with Yunick making adjustments and Turner taking laps. In all, Turner had run five hundred miles of practice, reaching terrific speeds. Yunick has squeezed as much extra horsepower into the engine as he can, creating something brilliant and formidable. Who knows what the factories will show up with?

On qualifying day, it's assumed that LeeRoy Yarbrough's record of 178.66 mph will be history. Rain early on Sunday morning February 12 promises to slow the track and keep speeds down. But David Pearson still manages to turn laps at 178.695, and Richard Petty, in a beautiful new Plymouth, ratchets the record up to a blazing 179.068.

Turner gets behind the wheel, a large man shoehorned into a little car, waiting his turn and listening to the numbers.

"Smoke, we went much faster than that in practice," he tells Yunick.

"You know it and I know it, Curtis—and this isn't practice," Yunick says. "You got something you wanna say, you can say it out there."

Turner, three months shy of his forty-third birthday, hits the track and begins turning his laps, hitting his marks, feeling about as empowered behind the wheel of a car as he ever has. The Chevelle is smooth and incredibly swift.

Mechanics and factory reps are in the pits, watching him jet around, but it doesn't hit anybody until the public address announcement: Turner is driving better than 180, the first time anybody's ever driven above that speed at a closed course in a stock car.

Don Naiman, then the manager of Smokey Mountain Raceway in Tennessee, squints at the Chevelle still motoring in the distance. "Where did that car come from," he asks friends, "and how is he driving it like that?"

All necks are craned now in the direction of Turner, and when he finishes his laps, the announcement rings: he's qualified the car at 180.831, nearly two seconds faster than Petty, and earned $5,000 for himself and Yunick.

Firestone rep Humpy Wheeler stands in the infield, smiling at the number. "That might have been the most incredible qualifying feat in the history of American motorsports," he says now. "Curtis Turner on the pole, at the height of the factory wars—everybody was completely astonished. And yet at the same time, you just sat there and said, 'Oh boy, they pulled one over on everyone.' It wasn't a surprise but it *was* a surprise because you figured he was too old to do it. It was probably his vengeance on everything."

And it is also a bit of an embarrassment. Days later, *Indianapolis Star* sports editor Bob Collins writes, "Turner is something of a problem to NASCAR public relations writers who, in this era of big purses, are trying to drum up an image of clean-cut, golly, gee-whiz youngsters racing stock cars over the Southern circuit. Somehow, Curtis doesn't fit . . . he believes that clean living went out with Jack Armstrong. He has been called, appropriately, "the last of the good old boys."

And now he's on the pole for the sport's biggest race, so speed is not a question. As Lee Petty and the Wood Brothers start talking about the need to draft with Turner, lest he run away with the race, there are whispers that the car won't be able to last 'til the end.

Yunick wonders the same about his driver in the days leading up to the race, reminding him at a party at the Castaway Motel that he'd better take it easy.

"Smoke, the last time we raced at Daytona, you told me I needed to go to bed by ten, said you'd call to make sure I wasn't out partying. And you never called. I wasted a whole evening."

Yunick rolls his eyes at all the laughter. "Curtis, I'll be happy if you get two hours sleep Saturday night."

"Two hours?" somebody yells. "Why, Curtis is liable to lose his competitive edge lying around that long."

On race day, it's clear that the car, not Curtis, has lost its edge on the longer runs. After 143 laps, with Turner already a lap behind, the Chevelle blows an engine. The twenty-six-year-old IndyCar star Mario Andretti, driving a Ford for Holman-Moody, beats his teammate Lorenzen for the win.

Yunick and Turner skip the next four smaller races; a month after Daytona, they're at Atlanta International Raceway to challenge for the $21,000 winner's share available at the Atlanta 500.

If Yunick's Chevelle is again the class of the field, Turner's Rockingham runnerup Cale Yarborough, now the prime driver for the Wood Brothers team, is a close second, in a new Ford.

Through the early practice sessions, the two drivers keep sizing up each other's rides. Turner is defiantly quiet but when Yarborough comes by, his comments surprise Turner.

"It looks like you're sideways all the way around the racetrack."

"What do you mean?" Turner asks defensively. "Car's fine to me."

"You have plenty of horsepower but how are you keeping it straight?"

To Turner, who never met a car he couldn't handle, there is nothing wrong with Yunick's ride. If there were, suggesting a change in the set-up never would have occurred to him anyway.

And the idea that Yarborough might be telling him how to do his job is annoying, and motivating.

At practice on Wednesday, March 29, Turner is in the pits, timing his exit so that when Yarborough comes off turn one, he can head out behind him at a good speed, and then see how long it'll take to make a pass. It'll be a good way to see how fast the Chevelle is—and to have Yarborough see that as well. Turner exits and goes by the Ford before they've even gotten to turn three, and he tucks himself into line. Everything feels great.

The cars are moving in tandem, curving together into turn four, when Yarborough sees a plume of smoke puff from the back of Turner's car. Before Yarborough can react, the Chevelle abruptly turns right, and everything normally associated with real time is instantly frozen.

Turner slides and hits the concrete retaining wall with the force of a roundhouse, and the car ricochets backwards into the air, sailing some twenty feet upwards. Yarborough, without taking his foot off the gas, glides right below Turner's car, missing part of the fender by three inches. Yunick, glaring from the pits, sees the rear bumper of the Chevelle reach high above the last row of grandstand seats, and he starts running.

Turner grips the wheel, bracing himself. The car is dead silent in the air. As the trajectory shifts and the Chevelle falls earthward, he clamps his eyes shut, waiting for the inevitable sounds of breaking glass.

The car crunches down on its nose and begins somersaulting end over end, and then twists like a gymnast in midair and barrel rolls six times, landing upside down on a guardrail and flopping over one last time, landing in an arc a few feet from Turner's friend, Goodyear Tires racing PR manager Dick Ralstin and his friend Chuck Blanchard. Pee Wee Ellwanger is there in seconds, as are Yunick and his crewman T.A. Tombs, and from all parts of the track, drivers, crewmen and car owners rush to turn four, with something cinching tight in their bellies and one thought in their heads: No, not another one.

"Pops, are you alright?" yells Ralstin, who's trying to undo Turner's belts.

Turner sits with a grimace, his eyes still shut, hands maintaining their death grip on the wheel. "Is it over yet?" he says.

Everything's twisted in his brain, like wires shooting currents, and he can't hardly hear a thing until someone yells, "Get him out, it's on fire!"

Flames burst from under the hood and Turner tries to lift himself but the tension and the fall rattle in his belly and he passes out. The five men claw him through the side window. By the time he's out, he's being supported, but is miraculously on his two feet, and he is taken to the infield hospital.

He arrives by ambulance; the ride has left him awake and lucid. He is bruised and battered, and his neck and back are stiff. Aside from that, he is whole and unharmed.

Yunick can't stop looking at the car. Every time he does, it frightens him, and brings back visions of the Python at Indianapolis.

After checking on his driver, he's asked about the crash, and he wants only to forget it all. "We're through, Curtis and I," Yunick says. "I'm not gonna build the car that kills Curtis Turner."

There will be no figuring how the Chevelle broke at high speed. Yunick is convinced Turner went too fast into the middle of turn three and broke the watts linkage upon impact with the wall. Turner doesn't see it that way.

In Turner's house in Charlotte a few days after the wreck, the two are still arguing about it in the middle of a brand new party, which is feeling a bit subdued, considering the stakes being discussed. Norris Broadhead leans against the wall of the den, watching Yunick sit down at Turner's desk and light a pipe when Turner says, "Smoke, you gotta get me that car fixed."

"Curtis, I ain't giving you another car you son of a bitch," Yunick says sternly. "Hell, you're too damn old, your reflexes ain't no good."

"You crazy bastard, there ain't nothing wrong with my reflexes. You know I'm good as I ever was," Turner says, leaning over on the desk.

Yunick sucks in a long puff, blows it out and sighs. "That's bullshit," he says. "Curtis, if your goddamn reflexes had been any good you wouldn't have wrecked."

"You're crazy as hell, and you don't know," Turner says, trying to keep the frustration out of his voice. Yunick knows his friend well enough and a grin sprouts on his face.

"Curtis, I'm sorry," he says. "You and I ain't gonna race no more because I think you're over the hill. I don't expect you to agree with me but you're gonna have to, about driving my car because I'm not gonna let you *drive* the damn thing anymore. I don't want to take the chance on killing you because I have too much fun at the parties."

Turner stares at him glumly, shakes his head and turns around. He pours another drink and starts talking to some other friends, still trying to figure a way to get Yunick to change his mind.

The following Monday morning, back in Daytona, Yunick opens his inner office at the Best Damn Garage in Town, and takes one last look at the beaten Chevelle. He hears a grinding noise and opens the garage door, and motions the pickup truck in, and looks for a safe place for them to hook up the No. 13 for its trip to the wrecker.

Chapter Eleven
1967-1969
"He kissed me on the forehead and he said, 'I'm gonna marry you.'"

Brock Yates remembers when he first heard Curtis Turner talk about marrying again.

In June 1966, during the Ford boycott, Turner, John Griffin and Yates had traveled to Virginia International Raceway, where Yates and Turner each drove in the track's Trans-Am event. Accompanying Turner was Audrey Blankenship, his pretty, dark-haired, eighteen-year-old assistant. The driving day ended early for both Turner and Yates, and the foursome returned to Turner's Piper Twin Comanche plane, which stood at the edge of the racetrack, pointing against traffic and now blocked in by a sea of parked cars.

Griffin shrugged. "Looks like you're gonna have to wait for the race to end and this lot to clear before you can take off," he said.

Griffin, Turner's Carolina Atlantic Timber Co. partner, is several years older than him, with gray hair and the worry lines of the classic pessimist. Though Turner didn't have any viable options to fly out, he loves few things more than proving Griffin wrong.

"Now Pop, don't look at it that way," Turner replied with a grin. "The glass is half-full, not half-empty." And he pointed to a little adjoining strip of grass running next to the track for about fifty feet that then dipped down and rose again, before rolling level some fifty yards and jutting sharply downward toward a drainage gully and a fence. "That oughta do it," Turner said.

Yates smiled at the preposterousness of the idea, but with Turner, he knew not to question. He and the others strapped into the plane—with Turner letting the seat belt dangle as usual—and Yates watched while cars on the track veered away for a moment from the sight of a large twin-engine plane seeming to move in their direction.

"Turner revved the hell out of the engines—no pre-flight check, he just started driving it," Yates says. Turner bore down over the controls, the plane bumping and hopping along the grass, with Griffin raising his feet up to brace himself. The Comanche started to build speed before it rolled downward, screaming now toward the fence, and at the moment of no return, Turner yanked the controls. The Comanche jerked upward and Yates' body snapped back as the landing gear barely whispered past the top of the fence. Turner laughed—even he's surprised. "I didn't think we were gonna make it," he said.

"I have no idea how we did it," says Yates. "I remember looking out the windshield and thinking there was no possible way this could be done."

Yates might have said the same thing for Turner's plans to marry Blankenship.

Their relationship was relatively new. For awhile, Turner had been dating Betty Skelton, perhaps the only woman in America who could "keep up with him." A daredevil aviatrix, Skelton's best-known maneuver was to fly her plane upside down ten feet off the ground and slice through a ribbon stretched between two poles. She'd also set several land-speed records at Daytona Beach.

There were other women, in different cities, from Atlanta to New Orleans, San Diego and back to Charlotte. There were racetrack beauty queens, a shrimper's daughter, a timberman's daughter and a painter among many others. He'd proposed to a woman at Niagara Falls, getting so caught up in the moment he'd gone out to buy a ring. But no prospect seemed quite as right as Audrey Blankenship.

Turner proposed to her early in 1966. Ultimately, he came up with the perfect way to tie the knot.

Turner's idea called for Audrey to join him in his Camaro on the front stretch of Charlotte Motor Speedway. He'd found a preacher willing to hop into the backseat and marry the pair while the forty-two-year-old would-be groom made laps around the track at 140 miles per hour. The preacher had his concerns but was willing to table them in order to see the happy couple wed. No doubt the ceremony would attract quite a crowd to the speedway. And then Turner and Blankenship could have one hell of a party. The wedding would be a brand new start, a fast, easy, uncomplicated turn, like when Turner and Ann had eloped nearly twenty years before.

It had been a nice pipe dream for awhile, and Blankenship, a very sweet girl, loved it and loved Turner. But before long, the relationship ended, because Audrey knew full well that there were too many obstacles for any of it to happen, none of which involved a Camaro or a speedway.

Ross and Priscilla had been living with their dad at his house in Charlotte since Ann's episode the day of Sue's high school graduation. Ann soon returned to Roanoke, and the kids shuttled back and forth to visit, while Tyler lived with family friends in Virginia, and Sue was off at college. Odelia Williams, the longtime family maid, remained at the Charlotte house during the week, taking care of the kids.

Months pass; it is early 1967 and the family arrangement shows no signs of stopping. The kids have gotten used to the idea that living at their father's is an adventure, an exercise in unreality, beginning with the strict instructions that Ross and Priscilla can't come into the den when the parties are going at full strength—a plan that works except for the times they manage to sneak their way in. It seems as if there are always people in the house, and all of them are unfamiliar: businessmen in suits, obvious hangers-on who simply stay for a few days of partying.

Sue recalls being at the house one evening and her father asking if she'd like to talk to Elvis—he's met the singer during his travels. Turner dials and Sue talks to Presley; though a Beatles fan, she is cordial. But the extraordinary idea that her dad has Elvis' phone number is not lost on her.

Nothing about the arrangement is stranger or more unsettling for the kids than the lack of their mother's presence. Turner and Ann are still married, and while Turner has not yet sought to end the union, whatever connection they've had has all but snapped. Since Audrey's departure, Turner has gone back to joking that he won't ever get married because it's too much fun being single. No matter how much he and Ann might have loved each other, they also share years of rancor and bitterness, of blame and promises and guilt. Most of the time, it's easier to not have to think about it anymore.

In late April, 1967 Turner sits in his Carolina Atlantic Timber Co. office, with its gold carpeting and drapes, gold and white scenic painting on one wall, and a bar beside the gold vinyl desk chair. The office is on the top floor of Charlotte's new Home Federal Building, and on the street outside is Turner's gleaming $20,000 Rolls Royce complete with a polished wood dash and red leather upholstery. Turner is being interview by Kay Reimler, the *Charlotte Observer's* Women's News Reporter, who's writing a story to be called "Curtis Turner—Playboy of Southern Stock Car Tracks."

"Is that car something you always wanted?" Reimler asks about the Rolls.

"Naa, I just never had one," Turner says.

Turner admits he doesn't spend much time in the office, or racing for that matter. "There's never been any money in racing," he says, "even if you win."

It's been a month since he'd totalled the Chevelle in Atlanta, parted with Yunick and seen his Grand National prospects seemingly dry up. For now, Turner is usually busy flying, trying to make the next sale for timberland or anything else. His fortunes are like night and day, a series of vast highs and lows. The timber business that had once produced extraordinary deals is not nearly as steady or lucrative. "Eonomic times were changing and those big deals were not moving as quick as they had been," says timberman Norris Broadhead. "Money had gotten harder to get ahold of. People like me had to go borrow money to buy these things."

Turner spends a great deal of time trying to sell a piece of G.B. Nalley land in West Virginia to the Catholic Church, a sale that never materializes. He also continues to speculate: buy land and hold it for a set period, hoping to sell before the lease runs out. Doing so often requires borrowing more money from the same timbermen or investors he does business with, sometimes owing twenty percent interest. He finds himself overextended. There are other options, such as branching out into the airport business. And an old partner of his from Virginia, businessman Hugh Rakes, dangles some "one last big score" opportunities.

Two days after speaking to Reimler, less than a month after nearly losing his life at Atlanta International Raceway, Turner negotiates to bid on controlling shares of the track. He is like a gambler betting on every horse in a race, figuring it's only logical that one will eventually come in a winner.

And then enough do, just like that. Turner is impulsive and shrewd, relentless and well connected. To counteract the difficulties, he quickly buys and sells interest in a slew of businesses: a Chicago-to-New York truck line; three motels, a nightclub and two liquor stores in Florida; a mirror company in Galax, Virginia; the Sort-Rite Co. of Harlingen, Texas, the world's largest maker of seafood processing equipment; several factories; and his timber deals. There is a barrel next to his desk filled with maps of large tracts throughout the southeast. Strom Thurmond is only one of the U.S. Senators and Congressmen whom Turner considers a friend, and Turner frequently comes to know where interstate roads are being planned months or years in advance.

"I remember him talking with presidents," says Turner's sister Dove. "He and Lyndon Johnson had a deal going about some big building Johnson had influence over; it wasn't entirely on the up and up," she adds, laughing.

He'll have close to a million dollars one week, and spend it freely, living big. Along with his new Rolls, there are Cadillacs, his Aerocommander, a Mustang, a Jeep and plenty of other cars to raise a certain profile. Or he'll keep giving money away. Fans might recognize him in a hotel and say hello, and then find their entire bill covered.

The rapid swing in fortune, the appearance that at any time he can live the life he's grown accustomed to, creates the air that makes Turner seem richer than he is.

"A lot of people would throw ideas at Curtis on the assumption that he could fund them himself, that he was a multi-multi millionaire, which he was not," says Bob Moore. "Instead of Curtis saying, 'No, I don't have $10 million,' he would take on the idea, and then go to somebody and say, 'Okay, will you loan me $100,000?' There was a lot on his table but not always a lot being done or accomplished. Everyone had this image of Curtis being wealthy. Curtis was a businessman, like a lot of businessmen, just paying his bills. He always wanted to find the next big thing for himself to do. What he really wanted was to start a new racetrack or build a racetrack or own one or run one."

The Atlanta Raceway negotiation ends before it really begins, but Turner believes to his core that another racetrack opportunity will come along when the time is right. If not, something else will happen; it always does. "Even if you're drowning and have just your little finger wiggling above the water, there is a million-to-one chance someone might just see you—as they have seen me," he is always saying. That confidence is frequently the first step to keeping business coming in—that and a wad of $100 bills in his pocket ready for the peeling. "He was good at talking people into doing things," remembers G.B. Nalley Jr., a timberman and son of Turner's longtime friend. "He should have been a psychology teacher."

It is midnight, and there are seventy people dancing around, or talking, singing, joking and drinking in Turner's living room in Charlotte and he is holding court behind the long bar, fixing some shooters. More people are coming in all the time: racers, local writers ready to enjoy a post-deadline party, friends, even friends of friends. "Anybody was welcome," says Henry Mason. "Women were coming in and out and the music was going. Curtis never seemed to meet a stranger. He'd say, 'Come in and have some fun, want a drink? Get your shooter.'"

Robert Griffin, who'd decorated Turner's golden office in town, has also done the job in the party room, but in quite a different style. On the wall behind the bar is a mural featuring a smiling caricature of Turner with a golden index finger and a crossing pair of checkered flags, next to several scantily clad beauty queens; on another wall, a barely dressed waitress stands holding a tray, with the words "What'll you have?" scrawled across her legs. When the lights go off and Turner puts on a decorative fluorescent light, the girls on the walls magically lose their clothes.

That's been known to happen to the real women at Turner's parties as well. "Oh man, you'd see a lot of talent there. It was like the Playboy mansion," remembers Buddy Baker. "You know, everybody's having a good time and everybody's drinking and if they wanted to go to the bedroom, they did. It looked like Hugh Hefner was having a party when Turner had one.

"It was wild, but you'd have to know Curtis Turner to know that he actually didn't do all the wild stuff. He just opened his house up to people, and said come on, we're having a great time tonight. Women danced naked on tables, and that was the least of it."

In its heydey in the late 1950s and early 1960s, the Turner parties developed a legend in their own time that continued into the mid-1960s and beyond. There were plenty of evenings when each of Turner's four bedrooms were in use at some point. Of course, as Bob Moore points out, "that only needs to happen once or twice for people to believe it happens every single night, and it didn't happen every night." But it happened often enough, and the potential that it could sometimes drew the curious.

For Turner's friends, the house on Freedom Drive is the ideal place to joke around, maybe chip golf balls with their host and enjoy the hours. Who didn't want to be a regular at Turner's house? On any given night, Turner's friendly competitors, from Tiny Lund and Bobby Allison, to Junior Johnson and Fred Lorenzen, might show; followed by half the sports staff of the *Charlotte Observer* and *News*; sponsors; timbermen; Firestone and Ford representatives; mechanics; and perhaps Cale Yarborough, Buddy and Buck Baker: a motorsports who's who. The parties are not, as Brock Yates points out, huge, Hollywood-style affairs, full of sophisticated chatter. "They were just constant," he says. "They were laid-back, ongoing affairs. That basically fit Curtis' profile. Curtis liked having things going on in his life."

But by the late 1960s, the character of the room feels different for Turner. Instead of seeing who's there, he'll notice who's not. There are too many standouts who won't be coming back, guys he misses, like Little Joe and Fireball.

"Hey," Turner says to Bob Myers.

"Hey," Myers says with a big grin.

"Let's go to Daytona," Turner says, and he gets up, motions to Pee Wee Ellwanger and one or two others, and with the party in full swing, the small crew exits, hops in Turner's Cadillac and heads to the airport. Back in Turner's house, it takes awhile for anybody to notice the host is gone, and somebody else starts a brand new party.

In his plane, flying over Charlotte, Turner mixes and downs some shooters and relaxes, letting the stars and the darkness, the laughter and chatter buoy his spirits.

It's something he likes to do frequently: pick up and fly to Daytona, or to South Carolina, Las Vegas, anywhere the mood hits him, right in the middle of the biggest party in town. He's flown friends into the Grand Canyon just because it's beautiful and you can get down really low and slalom some of the jutting rock formations. Turner's friend Domer Reeves remembers flying on a whim to the Grand Ol' Opry; before their arrival, there are four front-row seats waiting for them at the Ryman Auditorium. Bob Moore recalls leaving for Daytona with Turner one night at 4 A.M. and being on the beach by dawn, with Turner saying "Let's fly back" after about an hour. Other times they'd stay for a day, with Turner buying everybody a change of clothes. Some nights, instead of flying he'll grab a Doll Baby and drive a few miles to the Hornes Motel on the corner of Freedom Drive and I-85, and stay there for awhile. Or he'll head to the motel for a few hours and sleep off the effects of the last party, before going home for more partying.

There are times Turner wishes it would all slow down, times he wishes he could just sit in the middle of a forest for awhile, but there is a flow to his life that makes it practically uninterruptible. Besides, slowing down only makes him antsy.

That's why there are planes. Nothing is more relaxing than life at 5,000 feet. As fast as his plane travels, there's also a calmness, no matter the weather. He's never appreciated that more than in these days since July 23 when, after an incident in Easley, South Carolina, the Federal Aviation Authority had suspended his license. It was that flight with G.B. Nalley over Easley, Nalley's hometown, when after several passes as low as a hundred feet, he'd landed the Aerocommander in a parking lot between two churches, and pulled down several telephone lines upon takeoff. The FAA had given Turner ten days to appeal the suspension; Turner sent his letter back on the eleventh day. Not that he'd planned on appealing based on his infraction; he explained to FAA officials that he'd landed after hitting the prop control lever by mistake, a version of the story the FAA just wouldn't buy. So Ellwanger or any number of other friends sometimes has to start out at the controls before Turner takes over in the skies.

Turner lands in Daytona and he and his friends drive into town in a rental car and eat, drink and hang around. After a few hours, with the day beginning anew, Turner decides to head home, and the party hops back on the plane and rises through the wind once again.

Turner is quiet, settled into the pilot seat. He turns around a moment, almost wishing someone had a thing or two to say, but in the exhaustion, all is quiet.

It's been a rough week, and though he'd hoped it would, Daytona hasn't made it much better.

He'd gone to see Darnell a few days earlier. In the years since his brother had gotten shot during the building of the speedway, Turner couldn't help but see the moment in his mind whenever they spent time together. Darnell held no grudges, but physically, the wound had left a mark, and Turner sometimes wondered how much the incident had changed them both.

Darnell had moved around after that, spending time in Virginia working with their father, then going wherever the jobs were. Most recently he'd been cutting timber in Maryland.

Darnell had gotten into an argument with someone there, the kind of disagreement that frequently blows over, but this one hadn't. And without warning, Curtis was getting another phone call: Darnell had been shot once again.

This time, it would be very bad. Bleeding profusely, Darnell was rushed to the hospital, where emergency room doctors discovered his blood pressure skyrocketing. "It was the first time I ever heard of a doctor 'bleeding' someone," remembers Dove. "His pressure was so high, they had to cut a blood vessel, and it squirted to the ceiling in the hospital."

The trauma leads to a massive stroke. Physically, Darnell is partially paralyzed on his left side, and will remain so for the rest of his life. But the stroke has also caused brain damage. "It left him in a really bad state," says Bruce Sweeney, one of Darnell's closest friend. "After he got out of the hospital, he didn't know anyone or anything." Adds Dove, "Sometimes he was like a four-year-old and sometimes he was like a twelve-year-old."

"I went with Curtis to visit him in the hospital," remembers Charlie Williamson. "Curtis told me about it and it just really hurt him bad. But there was nothing he could change."

It is a hard truth for Turner to accept, especially upon observation. Darnell sits in a chair, barely acknowledging him and hardly knowing him anymore. He is only thirty years old.

Sitting one row back in Turner's plane on the way back from Daytona, Bob Myers moves up and switches seats with Ellwanger. They're getting closer to the airport in Charlotte and Myers can see something distant in Turner's expression. He looks out the windshield and after a moment, he nods.

"A pretty impressive sight," he says, and they look down at Charlotte Motor Speedway, curving like some tiny bullseye in the distance.

"It is," Turner says, and he grins. It's his first grin all flight long.

He instinctively veers in that direction, and the track slowly grows bigger through the windshield. Moments later, he drops down low and with cheers behind him, lands his plane on the far straightaway and rolls into turns three and then four, and back to the front straightaway. His headlights illuminate the grandstands and he gives the Aerocommander some gas, and runs through the next turns.

One more lap and he's off again, lifting out into the night, heading for the airport.

"The asphalt is lookin' pretty good," he says. "Pays to check on it every once in awhile."

One of the first things Carolyn Vance notices is the briefcase.

Turner walks into the Bank of Charlotte on a warm Spring Saturday afternoon in 1967, holding his briefcase, which seems about as big as a suitcase, all beaten up and battered, the kind where the top flaps over and you pull the handle up through the center. It looks as if it's seen almost too much use.

Turner walks around, trying to spot the teller he normally goes to. He scans the row of windows and his eyes finally stop at Vance, and they stay there. By the time he is in front of her, he's taken a check out from his jacket pocket. And after a cordial deep-voiced greeting he says, "I need this cashed, and I want big bills."

Vance has been called "Bunny" by everybody since age five. She is now twenty, a trainee in the bank, a pretty, blue-eyed brunette from the little town of Spruce Pine, North Carolina. Trainees are not supposed to cash any check over $25 without first getting permission from bookkeeping. But that doesn't seem to make sense when it's Curtis Turner handing you a check for $7,500.

Bunny doesn't mention this to anybody. She silently counts out the money and puts the stack on the counter with a covert grin.

Turner takes the bills with a smile, a "thank you" and a lingering glance. Two days later, he is back in the bank, and this time, he doesn't go looking for anybody else.

"I nearly got fired on Saturday because of you," Bunny tells him.

"Is that right," Turner says, grinning.

"That was a large check."

"I'll have to try to make it up to you."

On Wednesday he is back again, and asking for Bunny's number.

"No sir," she says. "Uh-uh."

"Why not?"

"Because, that's why."

But Turner keeps coming. "He came in three days straight," Bunny recalls. "And I was rooming with three girls in an apartment in Charlotte and they were saying, 'Bunny, give him your phone number, you crazy thing, what's wrong with you?'"

It's hard to imagine giving her phone number to a man twenty-four years older than she is. That never would have flown at home where Bunny was the baby in a family of eight, and her late father Virgil had been a prison warden. But she's been to a few races, and Turner has always been her favorite driver. And now she looks forward to seeing him in the bank. "He walked like John Wayne and he had a soft-spoken yet powerful voice that had a calming effect on me," she recalls. "Maybe that's how he just hypnotized people. His eyes were blue-gray and he had beautiful skin and the most perfect set of teeth you have ever seen in your life."

Bunny ultimately agrees to the date and Turner says he'll pick her up for dinner. He does, in a limousine.

She settles into the back with Turner and John Griffin. "John was real old; he had all these wrinkles in his face and I thought, dear God, what in the world am I even thinking about?"

The limo heads to the airport, where Turner's plane is waiting, and he opens the door for Bunny to climb aboard.

"And where might we be going?" she asks.

"I've got a race to go to in Atlanta," he says. "I figured we'd go there, have some dinner."

Bunny stares at him as if he's got six heads. "I can't do that. I've got to go to work."

"You'll be back in time," Turner says. "You'll see—it'll be fine."

Bunny has never been on an airplane, much less a small private plane. But they head out and Turner spends the flight showing her what the world looks like from the sky, taking her past timber tracts and fields, cities and towns. When they land, another car is waiting to take them to dinner at a fine restaurant in Atlanta. "It was beautiful," Bunny recalls. "It was country come to town. And I felt just like Cinderella."

After dinner, they head to the Peach Tree Inn in Atlanta, where Turner checks in. Walking up to the room, Turner puts the key in the door and Bunny asks, "Is this my room?"

"This is our room," Turner says.

"No, this is *my* room," she says sternly. "This is not *our* room."

Turner squints at her, but then he smiles.

"I'm afraid you're gonna have to get a second room," Bunny says.

Turner chuckles, but he turns and heads back downstairs to the front desk.

"I don't think anyone had ever dared do that to him before," Bunny later recalled.

She is already settled into her room, behind the locked door by the time Turner comes back up and knocks.

"Yes?" she says, her voice a little muffled.

"Just me," Turner says.

"Did you come to say goodnight?"

"Well, I figured we could talk a little first."

Bunny pauses. "Okay," she says. But the door doesn't budge.

"You could let me in," Turner says.

Inside her room, Bunny smiles, nervous as she is. "I can hear you just fine," she says.

They talk through the door, laughing and joking for an hour. Turner moves off to his own room and returns after awhile, still trying to get in. But Bunny hadn't been allowed to date until she was seventeen, and her older brothers had then needed to approve of any boy she met with. She'd never even read *True Stories*, and here she is at a motel, after a plane ride and dinner with Curtis Turner. No sir, the door is staying closed.

But there's something sweet about him sitting there, talking to her, trying to get in but in a way not so much caring about it anymore.

Come morning, they head to the track in Atlanta only to find it empty; the race had been rained out after an early morning thunderstorm.

Bunny finds it all vaguely suspect, not to mention nervy. All kinds of crazy thoughts go through her head: What is she doing here to begin with? She doesn't know this man. "Did you just make up some crazy story to get me to come here with you? What were you thinking?"

"I was thinking I was gonna race," he says, looking dejected.

So they spend the day in Atlanta, with Turner giving Bunny a grand tour before they fly home to Charlotte. He is gracious and kind, and he tells her about his life, about business and racing, and though Bunny braces at first with every bump, she quickly gains a level of comfort in the air.

"You're not afraid of anything," Bunny says, as much a statement as a question.

"Not too much—you're as safe in the air as you are in your own home," Turner says. "But I am scared of fire. I'll say that."

"I'll bet you've had some bad wrecks," Bunny asks.

"Yeah, but none up here," he says with a smile.

By the time Turner walks Bunny back to her apartment, she's been won over.

They stand at the door and Turner leans down and kisses her on the forehead. "I'm gonna marry you," he says.

Bunny smiles up at him. "You think so?"

"Yeah," Turner says. "I'm gonna marry you."

But Bunny doesn't hear from him for four days. Each day, going to work at the bank, she gets a little more steamed and a little less forgiving.

On the fifth day, roses arrive at the bank, and Turner calls from Texas with a slew of apologies. He is stuck there on business and wanted to let her know he hadn't forgotten about her.

The next day, more roses arrive. Turner's in California. The following day, more roses, and a call from New York. By now, Bunny is giddy, and the bank is aromatic.

They make plans for the following weekend and Turner picks her up when the bank closes at 5:00 P.M. And when Bunny emerges, she's startled.

"Do you like it?" Turner says with a big smile. He's standing in front of a dark green Corvette.

On their long first date, Turner had asked Bunny what her favorite car was.

"I've always been a Ford fan," she'd told him. "But I've got to say, I've loved Corvettes for my whole entire life. They're just so beautiful."

It's a beauty, alright. "Yes, it's very nice." Bunny says.

"It's for you."

Bunny is wide-eyed, but as flattered as she is, something troubling immediately registers. "Look, I don't know where you come from or what you mean to do but I was taught not to accept gifts from men," she says, but she keeps walking around the thing, studying its sleek lines, with a smile building on her lips that finally turns into a giggle.

"You wanna try it out?"

"*No* I'm not gonna try it out. I'm sorry, but I can't take this," Bunny says. "You're gonna have to take it back."

Turner laughs. "I can't take it back; I bought it."

They stand across from each other, the green Corvette parked between them. Finally Bunny shrugs. "You're gonna have to."

Turner stares at her, this girl not far removed from the days when she'd gone to drag races with her big brothers. They'd race their fast cars against kids from neighboring counties. Occasionally the stakes got very high, and they'd race for titles. Lose the race, lose your car. And sometimes, the Vance boys put their kid sister Bunny in the car, letting her race. She had the spirit in her; she loved to go fast. And it made her brothers laugh uproariously to see the faces of the guys who'd lost to this girl.

"Alright," Turner says finally. "Can we still go to dinner?"

"Sure, that's fine," Bunny says, and as she looks at this handsome man, who would make such a gesture as this, the ludicrousness of the moment, and her refusal hits her. They both start to laugh.

"It's beautiful and I love it," she says. "I just can't accept it."

"That's alright," Turner says, moving toward her. "These little bitty things are like coffins. I was worried about you drivin' it anyway."

Turner is driving a Camaro down a dirt road near Charlotte Motor Speedway. He is dispensing driving tips but he might as well be offering life lessons.

"One thing to remember is that you can steer your way through anything," he says to his passenger, adding that it's necessary to be prepared. At any moment, disaster can strike, and it pays to know how to react.

The passenger, auto writer Bill Kilpatrick, is listening with half an ear. He's distracted, watching Turner doing seventy mph in the dirt, heading toward a set of traffic cones.

"Or you might hit a skid," Turner says. "In a skid, you've got to hang in there all the way." And with that, the founder, chief spokesman and head instructor for the National School of Safe High Performance Driving stamps on the brakes and cuts the wheel over hard. The Camaro's tires teeter for a second before the back end slides through a textbook bootleg turn, spinning around perfectly until the car is facing the opposite direction.

"When you're in a skid," he says matter-of-factly, "you've got to keep *driving* that car."

Kilpatrick, who's there to write about the school for *Popular Mechanics*, nods with exhilaration, nausea and relief.

"Now you'll try it," Turner says.

A half-dozen drivers have plunked down $475 for a week's worth of instruction at the only school designed to teach the fine art of speeding and maneuvering in a stock car in the country. Ambulance drivers, firemen, police officers, salesmen, would-be racers, even moonshine runners, anybody who can benefit from knowing the right way to brake the car, and when not to, make up the ideal client list for Turner's latest brainstorm. In order to pass, students have to master high-speed 180-degree front and back spins through pylons that are twenty-four feet apart. When they have trouble doing so in little race cars, Turner performs the maneuver for them in a Cadillac. Students must also drive swiftly over a sharp pipe to see what a tire blowout feels like. Turner has rented space at the speedway, and now Monday through Friday, at his leisure, he can tool around on a Honda scooter, and get into a car and teach anybody how to slalom on his old straightaways.

The speedway is about the only place where he can legally get behind the wheel of a car at the moment. A few weeks after the school's first sessions, Turner is stopped for doing eighty mph in a sixty mph zone, an infraction which, in North Carolina, leads to an automatic suspension of his license.

He'd lost his license for a year in 1963; this is the eighth time he'd been caught speeding in North Carolina, Virginia and Georgia since 1960. Between this and what happened in Easley, he isn't legally permitted to drive or fly. "I don't even have a hunting license now," he tells reporters.

But he does have a car for the upcoming National 500 at Charlotte Motor Speedway, his first Grand National race since the Atlanta crash. This is big, promotable news. NASCAR, however, is hyping a different story. On October 1, Richard Petty had won the Grand National race at North Wilkesboro, giving him an astounding ten victories in a row, and twenty-seven for the season, besting the record mark Turner had put up between his Convertible and Grand National runs in 1956. Petty will go for eleven straight at Charlotte and his dominance, toothy smile, ease with a reporter's microphone and a strict policy of never refusing to sign his swirling autograph upon request will soon earn him the nickname "The King of Stock Car Racing." It's fitting: NASCAR popularity is beginning to expand further beyond its southeastern borders, and for officials of the sport, Petty is the ideal ambassador.

But Petty is not whom *Sports Illustrated* reporter Kim Chapin comes to see in the days before the Charlotte race. He follows Turner, watching his typical pace for several days, and seeing him among 250 revelers at the house on Friday before qualifying. Petty, a family man, is not the type to show up at such a gathering. He may have the gaudier statistics, but as Chapin will eventually write, "It is Turner's style that made the legend grow." Turner is one of only three drivers set to race at Charlotte who also appeared in the first-ever Grand National race eighteen years earlier, in 1949. But nobody else has had so many close calls, near misses, daring slides, and incredible triumphs matched by too many blown engines, like a car that dies in the valiant attempt to win. Nobody has earned so much affection and made so much trouble. And regardless of the sport's vaunted youth movement, it is Turner who best represents the times. The sport, like the country, has seen too much death, followed by too many attempts to keep pushing the envelope. But then there's Curtis Turner, the ultimate survivor, flipping a million times at Atlanta, and coming out of it with a sore back and a request for a Camel.

Come the following February, during the week of the Daytona 500, with Richard Petty set to defend one of the greatest racing seasons in history, and Curtis Turner not even able to find himself with a ride, Turner becomes the first NASCAR driver ever to grace the cover of *Sports Illustrated*. The accompanying story is called "Curtis Lives!" This too is fitting: With guys like Richard Petty, the sport has a future. But thanks to guys like Turner, the sport has its history.

Neither Turner nor Petty wins the race at Charlotte. Turner loses his clutch after eighty-two laps and Petty blows an engine with sixty-six laps to go, which is about when Buddy Baker takes the lead for good.

There are only two races left in the 1967 season and Bobby Allison wins both, driving a Holman-Moody Ford, and muscling his way past Petty in the last contest.

Turner is making timber runs and now trying to sell coal mines, flying somewhere else on a daily basis. And there are the parties, and sliding runs in classes at the speedway.

And Bunny Vance is with him practically everywhere. There is something unique about how they interact; anybody who normally travels in Turner's circle can see that quickly. Though it's clear Bunny adores Turner, even worships him, there's nothing new about a woman looking at him that way. But he dotes on her. It's beyond buying her fine clothes and jewelry and keeping her happy, beyond even genuine affection. He's not joking about being single so much anymore.

"There was this old gal in the airport who worked for Hertz rent-a-car," remembers Henry Mason. "This was a little problem Curtis had, renting cars. Anyway, she had slid Curtis a car for some deal he needed. And I was standing there after he'd been up to the counter when he walked away. And this old gal, great big old gal, kind of an ugly complected woman, she looked at Curtis and looked at me and said, 'He is just the most handsome thing in the world. I just love him. But you know, he's just not husband material.'"

"Fun was written all over him and women fell all over him," says actor James Garner, a friend of Turner's who also took the Driving School classes. "All he had to do was turn his head and some woman would meet his eye and that was usually all it took with him."

Oddly enough, Turner appears to be attempting to reverse the view. He finds an enormous relief in being with someone entirely separate from anything that had come before in his life, and someone unmotivated by anything other than seeing him happy.

"Deep down there was an insecurity about Curtis," Bunny remembers. "There was this little boy side of him that needed to be loved and protected. He really felt like I could protect him, and that's what was so crazy. He said, 'I feel safe with you.' It would amaze me when he would say that. This was Curtis Turner and that's the side of him I don't know if anybody else knew but me."

It is inevitable, not to mention understandable, that the closer the bond between Turner and Bunny, the more neglected Ann and the kids feel.

Sue first meets Bunny at Charlotte Motor Speedway, when they both spend a week taking Turner's driving performance course. Sue loves every second of the classes, doing 360s and 180s on wet and dry pavement, going around the track at 100 mph and finding another opportunity to bond with her dad. But there is immediate tension between her and Bunny. Watching her father getting serious with a woman just about her own age, while he's clearly prepared to end things with her mom, is the last thing Sue wants to see happen—a fact she doesn't exactly try to hide. Bunny can't help but feel threatened.

But Turner has been ready to make this change for a long time. It has taken meeting Bunny, however, for him to finally embrace it.

In 1968, he begins divorce proceedings against Ann. He has already bought Bunny a ring.

For months, Bunny has been getting peppered with questions from her mother, but has hidden the level of her seriousness, fearing a negative reaction. "There was that big age difference," says Bunny's brother Danny Vance. "That didn't work in the south."

When Bunny finally opens up about the plan, her mother calmly suggests a proposal of her own: come to the house and spend a week to talk it all through. After that week, if she still wants to get married, she'll have her mother's blessing.

It is a warm if awkward homecoming for Bunny, even given how close knit the relationship is. When the topic finally comes up, Bunny starts listing all the positives on the ledger. Her fiancé is warm and gentle, she says; he's larger than life. He has a wild reputation, but with her, he is, of all things, stable.

Bunny's mother listens and nods. She already knows her daughter's heart, but she has one practical question to raise.

"What are you gonna do when he's older?" she wants to know. "What are you gonna do when he's in a wheelchair?"

Bunny doesn't spend more than a second on her answer. "Push it," she says.

The Roanoke County Court grants Turner a divorce on December 17, 1968. Three days later, after hearing Turner and Bunny talk on and on about a wedding, their friends Domer and Carol Reeves suggest an evening trip to the big farmhouse in Chester, South Carolina, owned by Probate Judge Haddie Y. Harden. Harden had married the Reeves' years earlier.

For Bunny it is comforting that Harden, a white-haired woman in her eighties, looks so grandmotherly. Domer and Carol are there as witnesses but Harden focuses on the young bride, who is now all of twenty-two, marrying a man exactly twice her age.

"If you're worried about the age difference, don't be," Harden says to Bunny and Turner as the two couples sit in her ornately decorated parlor, along with Harden's husband. "My mom and dad were years apart, and they had and raised eleven children, educated all of us—we're all in the law, or medicine. Set all that aside because it does not matter."

The moment the ceremony ends, the celebration begins: The couple head to Bunny's mother's, then to Charlotte for a few days and back to Bunny's mom for Christmas. Then on to Daytona for some pre-race partying—even though Turner won't be running; and out to Los Angeles and finally back to Roanoke. It is about as spirited an introduction to married life and as cramped a honeymoon as Bunny might have imagined.

Life is a big whirlwind machine. If Turner takes pride in squiring his pretty young wife, buying her several-hundred-dollar dresses and minks and making her happy, Bunny is equally grateful to have married a famous husband who is this gentle and considerate. If he's out, a night never passes without him calling to check in with her at around 7 P.M. A week doesn't go by without roses being delivered. At parties, he'll sometimes grab a tablespoon and, along with Carol Reeves, duet on one of his favorite songs playing on his juke box, the Ernest Tubbs-Loretta Lynn country hit "Sweet Thing"; before long, that's what he's calling Bunny.

"I know he was wild, and he sowed his wild oats," says Bunny, "but everybody said the same thing: that he changed. That he was different after we met. So if that's true, it really makes me happy."

"The best thing that ever happened to Curtis was Bunny: I firmly believe that," says Turner's friend Dick Ralstin. "Bunny loved the guy. And if anyone ever understood Curtis, Bunny came as close to it as anyone. You talk about a diamond in the rough, well, that's Curtis. And Bunny knew it. And Curtis was as good to her as a man could be.

"I don't want to say Bunny could put up with his shenanigans because she could get upset with him, but it was always for his own good. I mean there was never any doubt: You know that Bunny loved Curtis Turner. And Curtis knew quite a few women but Curtis loved that woman more than any he'd ever known."

He is forty-four; the brightest klieg of the limelight is no longer fixed on him, and he is past the need to prove something vital to anybody. If everybody has their moment of compromise and realization, where they are finally ready to consider the idea of settling down and being happy, then as Chris Economaki once announced to the cheering crowd during races at the beaches of Daytona, it's time for Turner.

Occasionally, he will still run some local race, putting on what amounts to a dirt track exhibition. After one race, he's in the infield, surrounded by fans, with Bunny standing above him in the bleachers. Pretty women swarm around him, the kind of roster that at one time would be an invitation to a long and enjoyable evening. A few of them are flirting, even dangling hotel room keys. Turner grins at them all cordially, and grabs one key for a moment.

He looks up at Bunny, who's taking in the whole scene with a knowing smile. Turner jingles the key like a trophy.

"Sweet Thang, can I go?" he calls up to her. And Bunny shakes her head with a laugh.

"Nah-ah," she shouts back with a wink. "Not this time, Curtis."

Perhaps Bill Jennings should have known better.

Jennings, who runs the concession stand at Roanoke's Blue Hills Golf Course is among the party of twelve playing golf, drinking, partying and laughing late into the evening with Turner at a course in Boone, North Carolina. Turner is a regular at Blue Hills, often playing until dark, and Jennings is now a friend, and this group has followed Turner around for some late-night putting under the lights. Jennings is also a longtime racing fan, and he's between shots when he works up the nerve to say, "You know, I've always wanted to ride around the Daytona track."

Turner squints, and a small grin comes to his lips. Danny Vance shakes his head with a laugh.

"Curtis did anything you wanted," he remembers. "If you mentioned something, you'd better be ready to go."

At 2 o'clock in the morning, Turner drives Vance, Jennings and Jerry Vance, one of Bunny and Danny's brothers, to the airport and the foursome hop in Turner's Aerocommander, en route to Daytona Beach.

Bunny is home for this trip; she's not a big fan of these occasional late-night excursions of Curtis', but it helps to know Danny is along. Danny has always been Bunny's favorite, and he and his wife Betty are now in Roanoke, having moved into a small house bought for them by Turner. Turner and Bunny are living nearby; they've switched their base from Charlotte to Roanoke, with Turner having given up the house on Freedom Drive. Most of their time is spent at the Laban Road house Turner has long owned, with a sprawling ten-acre front yard that slopes steeply downhill; in winters past, he and Weatherly, and sometimes Ross, would sled down that hill at break-neck speeds, riding on a detached car hood turned upside down.

Meanwhile, Ann and the kids are sharing an apartment across town, the second floor of a house on Williamson Road.

In Daytona, Turner rents a Caprice and takes his party to the old Beach and Road Course. He tours everybody around the circuit, riding from north turn to south turn, taking the long stretch of road, building some speed and timing his exit back to the sand, the happy memory of the act feeling warm in his hands, which rest easily on the wheel. On the beach, he spins and spins again, to the fear and delight of Jennings, and all is quiet and calm out in the ocean while dawn creeps over the horizon. Turner loves the joy of driving these familiar stretches but the place has the washed-over look of long abandonment. "They haven't run here in ten years," he says, raising yet more rooster tails in his old haunt.

After a few bloody marys and a quick visit to see Smokey Yunick in the Best Damn Garage in Town—he and Turner are starting a new timber deal in South America—Turner drives out to the Daytona International Speedway. It is just before seven in the morning when Turner enters, offers a vague explanation to the man at the gate, and rolls out onto the track. Turner manages to do a quick warmup lap before the security guards scramble in his direction. Yes, they know who he is and yes, they know this is just for fun. "But you'll have to talk to Mr. France," the main guard tells him.

Turner and France had patched things up well enough after the ban. France liked ending all major disputes the same way: by taking out a long, tassled Indian peace pipe and smoking it with his foe. The act always pro-vided a nice goodwill photo opportunity. He and Turner had smoked and shaken hands, and Turner genuinely anticipated a continued easing of ten-sions. But France remained short and cold around him. Given the earlier part of their history, Turner finds France's awkwardness, after all this time, mystifying, and unnecessary.

But walking up to the Daytona offices, reveling in the majesty of this place, Turner feels only pride in his friend's accomplishments. In nearly a decade since its opening, Daytona's reputation for prestige has skyrocketed. The track is now the centerpiece of a sport generated by the power of factory-built competition played out on superspeedways. In 1959, out of forty-four Grand National races, twenty-seven had been run on dirt, and the Daytona 500 was one of only eight contests waged on tracks one mile or more. By 1969, out of fifty-four races run, only five are on dirt, and nineteen races are on tracks at least one mile in length. The winner's purse at Daytona has doubled in nine years, from $19,000 to nearly $39,000. The fastest qualifier for the 1959 race had driven a little faster than 143 miles per hour; in 1969, two years after Turner's record-shattering run of 180, David Pearson qualifies at better than 190 mph.

Bill France has only gained in prominence and reputation from his sport's expansion. He is the symbol of stock car racing respectability, as always a friendly but iron-fisted pioneer who remains committed to NASCAR's growth away from its grimier roots. The sport is still grappling with its financial difficulties and is only starting to be recognized by larger national corporations as a money-making opportunity, but France is ever vigilant about proving that racing can be more than just a southern sport. Whatever happened between he and Turner in 1961 has only solidified his power, and he is now midway through construction of what will be an even faster, finer racing facility than Daytona, a 2.66-mile track in Talladega, Alabama.

But Turner sneaking into Daytona with some friends, probably after a night of drinking—this is not the way France wants to start his day. He's up to his office at 8 a.m., and in no mood. And Turner's proud little grin makes it seem that much worse.

"Turner, you can't come in here like you own the track," France says with a wave that makes Jennings and Bunny's brothers quickly feel implicated. "That'll count for my insurance. You have to think about that."

Turner glares at France with disgust, the bad blood between them suddenly flowing back. "You son of a bitch," he yells. "I used to feed you bologna sandwiches when you didn't have a pot to piss in. And that's what you have to say?"

The depth of Turner's animosity startles France. It even saddens him. "Now just settle down, Turner, settle down," he says. "It's okay—you can take them around. There's two or three race cars out there already. You can ride your friends in one of those. That way they'll get more of a taste for what it really feels like."

Danny Vance is flabbergasted by the exchange. In the awkward silence, Turner moves off and heads down to the track, finding the cars on pit road.

Jennings sits in the passenger seat; with no other seats in the car, Danny and Jerry Vance must get as comfortable as possible hunched on the floor in back.

Turner starts up the car and takes it out with an angry lurch, and Jennings grabs onto the inside of the door. As the car heads up toward the first high banking, Jennings grows more and more nervous.

"It's gonna turn over, it's gonna turn over!" he shouts above the horsepower. Turner guns it, climbing up, the centrifugal force settling down upon him with a familiar pressure. Danny and Jerry are shouting, holding on to any part of the roll cage and metal piping they can. For lap after lap, Turner works his speed up, hitting each turn a little swifter. After several laps, Jennings is laughing with hysterical joy.

The slower you go at this place, the harder it is, Turner knows. As the RPM's climb, his path is smoother, up toward the guardrail, the force guiding him to the best route around the banking, in what will be his last-ever run in a race car at Daytona International Speedway.

He has no drafting partners; not like years ago, when he could draft with Little Joe or Fireball. But that doesn't mean he can't still move.

For a few moments, for a few laps, Turner does own the place. He keeps it going as fast as he can. It's the only way to fight the inevitable force of each passing second, and ease the pressure.

Chapter Twelve
1969-1970
"I knew Curtis was gone even before Charlie said it."

It is a mid-August night, and Bunny mentions how much she can't wait to see some snow again.

The days have been sweltering and endless, and Turner charges through the house the next morning and says, "Sweet Thing, pack a bag. We're going to see snow. Just take a toothbrush. We'll get what you need when we get there."

They fly across the country to Denver, where a rental car is waiting at the airport. Turner heads to Pike's Peak, so he can show his young wife the route up the Hill Climb, and the caps of snow atop the mountains.

Perhaps it's the air growing thinner, or the switchback routes, but Bunny gets light-headed while Turner takes his swift tour of history, seven years after his triumphant run. Rough roads still make life interesting.

The mountaintops are actually bare. "But we saw four drops of snow on the way back down—I got to see snow!" Bunny remembers. "It was so neat seeing where he had raced, and won."

There are plenty of other times when Turner will say, "Sweet Thing, pack a bag." In the middle of the night, he'll sweep her up out of bed, covers and all, looping her bag around his fingers, and put her gently in the back of the car, or into his plane, and she'll wake up in Kentucky, where her husband is trying to sell coal mines; or Daytona, so they can walk on the beach and watch the sunrise; or Las Vegas, where they're off on a forty-eight-hour gambling spree, with Turner's fortunes rising and falling and rising again. "We had a lot of fun," Bunny says. "And we had a real love affair going."

As large as Turner's life had grown since his days in Floyd, and as much as he is happy to travel anywhere at a moment's notice, there is something much smaller, and more intimate now about life as well. There are two concrete benches beneath the pines in the yard at the Laban Road house, and he and Bunny will sit there in the evenings, drinking wine and looking at the stars and the trees, and watching the planes take off or come back to the airport in Roanoke a couple of miles away. He'll tell her about his wild ideas, about how he'd tried to finance the deal to send satellites up in space, and now with men on the moon, people will be living on other planets one of these days. "My idea don't seem so wild anymore, does it?" he says with a smile.

"I learned a love for nature from him," Bunny remembers. "He saw things, discovered things and said things that would stop you dead in your tracks. He was like a poet when he talked about this. He made you look up! You ask Smokey Yunick about this and he'd think you were absolutely an idiot. But there was this beautiful side of Curtis that saw those kinds of things."

However prevalent this side of Turner had been, it flourishes with Bunny. If he sees their relationship as a second chance, he plans to make the most of it. "She was young and she clearly adored him, but she had an influence on him too," Domer Reeves says. "He seemed to calm down considerably after they got married. He worked a little more than he played."

It is right around the time Turner has completed a lucrative land deal with Georgia-Pacific, when the leaves are out and nature is at its summertime lushest that Bunny begins talking more seriously about wanting a baby. She and Curtis, and Danny and Betty Vance, are in Blowing Rock, a tourist-happy village in the North Carolina mountains a stone's throw from where Bunny grew up. Anything Turner buys for Bunny, he buys for Betty as well. Danny can still see his wife and sister wearing matching sequined dresses with a price tag of several hundred dollars each. "They looked like little high school girls together," he says.

There is a manor in Blowing Rock holding an auction where Hollywood star Tallulah Bankhead's estate jewelry is up for bid. The auction room is full and Turner cranes his neck at the start of the sale, looking at the baubles up front. He begins bidding immediately, and relentlessly.

"I'm buyin' you some jewelry, Sweet Thing," he says, holding up his hand for another bid, as heads turn in his direction. Turner buys the first four items, including an elaborate diamond watch, and a matching three-karat twist ring. "He just went crazy," Bunny remembers. After that, auction officials manage to find some extra seats up front for Turner's party. He spends $24,000 in ten minutes.

"Curtis, *please* don't buy all that stuff," Bunny says later on in their bedroom suite in the Green Acres hotel, with Danny and Betty watching television in the sitting room. "You just got me a beautiful ring."

"It's pretty though; you oughta have it," Curtis says. He's leaning down on the floor, looking up at Bunny sitting on the bed. She's wearing that pretty dress, her hair up in a bun, looking radiant.

"I love you," she says. "I don't need all that."

Turner keeps staring at her, at the little smile curling on her lips. She's right, of course. She doesn't need it; she doesn't want it. What she wants is a baby, Turner says to himself. All she wants is a little boy.

"Sweet Thing, where them ol' pills you take?" he asks.

Bunny reaches over and pulls a packet of birth control pills out of her pocketbook. Turner, still down on one knee, strikes a match and sets the packet on fire. He twists it, letting the flame walk along the label, pulling the wastebasket over from beside the night table, with a grin glowing in his eyes.

"You're gonna get your baby," he says.

Bunny has to laugh. It is quite a sight: her six-foot-two husband, his dark hair wild and curly and tall, wearing a $600 Brooks Brothers suit, down on one knee, burning her birth control pills, and tossing them in the trash.

"Do I smell somethin'?" Danny says from the next room.

"Yep," Bunny says.

The next day, they pick up Bunny's mom for a mini family reunion, and Turner rents a sprawling seven-bedroom cabin in a hotel in nearby Lanville, North Carolina. Bunny jumps from one bedroom to another, a gleeful girl with a throaty laugh in an extraordinary game of hopscotch.

Late that night, she and her husband pool their change: they have just enough to buy some Cokes and snacks from the machine. And they sit by their fireplace, and Bunny lays in her husband's arms, while the rain pours outside.

"Sweet Thing, you're gonna get yourself a little boy," he says again, with assurance and a hint of adventure, the way he might have told her to go pack a bag.

Danny Vance works late at the railroad one night and it's already 10 P.M. when he finally comes home and settles in for supper. He's only had a couple of bites when he hears a grumbling outside the window, a deep, resonant, revving sound: "Uhh! Uhh-uhh!" Vance calmly nods toward his wife.

"Betty look out there and see if that's a bus."

Betty Vance comes back to report that it is, and there are screams and shouts emanating from it. Danny wipes his mouth, smiles and stands up. It promises to be a long night.

Turner hasn't been behind the wheel of a Grand National car in more than a year, not since a mid-September, 1968 race in Hillsborough, North Carolina, where he'd finished thirteenth, blowing an engine in his Plymouth some fifty laps before Richard Petty took the checkered flag. There are no other racing opportunities to truly challenge him, or pay him enough to make the trip worth it. After several hit-or-miss months, the performance school goes bust. But there is always something new and interesting worth driving for the sheer pleasure of it.

Turner buys a city bus from his friend Alan Hill in Chicago, and when Hill heads east to make the delivery, Turner collects Sue and thirty of her college friends for a nightlong joyride. By the time Danny Vance steps aboard, the wine has been flowing for hours, with Hill slinging the bus through curves all the way back to Laban Road so Turner can drive it around his house. "Somebody had bet him he couldn't do it, and you didn't never do that," remembers Danny. "You couldn't hardly get a car around there, and he did knock the gutter off one end but he did make it."

After that, Robert Griffin refurbishes the bus into a stately looking camper, which doesn't stop Turner from steering it across a bridge you can barely squeak a car over, on the way to doing a 180 on the highway.

By then, Turner has also long owned one of President Johnson's old limousines. "It seemed as long as a city block," remembers Ross Turner, and there are two great bullhorns jutting out from the front of the hood. With a friend in the White House transportation department, Turner had discovered that one of Johnson's old stretch Cadillacs was available, and as soon as he had the presidential seal removed, he could ride through Roanoke in style. Driving clients around isn't bad for business either.

Meanwhile, the entire 1969 NASCAR season goes on without Turner, although there are off-track events that Turner monitors with understandable interest. In September, Bill France opens his track in Talladega, Alabama. A month earlier, Richard Petty and ten other drivers had formed the Professional Drivers Association (PDA), an organization meant to bargain with NASCAR for a better retirement plan, fairer insurance payments and higher purses. The plan sounds remarkably like Turner's attempt to unionize eight years earlier. Petty signs up a majority of competitors and star drivers such as Bobby Allison air out the organization's grievances, among them the payment of only $15,000 to a widow of a driver who dies, and no racer input in scheduling. Turner watches the process, waiting for suspensions or bans.

But this situation is different, more contained. There are no Teamsters, no tracks at stake, no pari-mutuel betting and no conflict between two good friends. France, fearing a boycott of his first Talladega race, and being as wily and determined as ever, files an entry blank to drive in the event and tries to join the PDA himself, to infiltrate their meetings. Meanwhile, speeds at Talladega during practice are pushing a blistering 200 mph, but the existing tires are not standing up to the task, and the drivers, fearing for their lives, eventually do stage a walkout. France fills the field with substitutes and puts on the race anyway, and then invites all 62,000 in attendance to use their tickets again, offering everybody a second race at either Talladega or Daytona on the house with each stub. Gaining the public relations upper hand as usual, France eventually busts the PDA.

All the drivers are welcomed back warmly enough, except by some angry fans. For two races, beer bottles and cans are tossed onto the tracks, with one can hitting Petty square in the windshield in the middle of a race; Petty wins the day anyway. By 1970, all is as it was, with factory cars running smoothly and weekly rivalries among beloved, valiant challengers who are more popular than ever. No grand changes are made to purses or pensions, and France doesn't even have to dust off his peace pipe.

For Curtis Turner, a different ban has finally been lifted, and he feels like a free man.

After two years of sneaking out of airports without filing flight plans, landing in cow fields and other nuisances, the two-year FAA penalty for landing his plane in Easley ends, and on February 11, 1970, Turner is once again free to navigate legally in the air at the controls of his own planes.

Two weeks later, Bunny provides the best excuse Turner's heard in a long time for starting a brand new party when he comes home to find two rare sights: his wife cooking dinner, and the candles lit.

"You're pregnant, aren't you," he says.

The next day, he brings home a beautiful snow-white handmade jacket and hat, sized for a child but fit for royalty. It looks as puffy and perfect as a cloud.

"When I got pregnant, he was so funny," says Bunny. "Fans would see us at a table in a restaurant or something and come over—Curtis was never, ever upset when someone did that. And he would introduce me and say 'This is my little pregnant wife, Bunny.' Isn't that sweet? My little pregnant wife Bunny."

Regaining his flying license—and getting a fresh reason to plan for the future—happen not a moment too soon for Turner. Between the loss of some big money racing connections and more economic downturns in the timber business, it's been harder than ever for him to keep his cash flow streaming—not that this stops him from giving cars to friends, sets of tires to acquaintances and golf clubs and old racing trophies to complete strangers who remember seeing him run and come on by for parties. His friend George Mason had once asked how he could spend so much with so little in the bank. "Well hell, if I waited till I made it to spend it, I never *would* have a good time," Turner answered. But waiting for too many major contracts that aren't coming in is taking a toll. For years, as an extra bargaining chip, he's sold or traded again and again one of his favorite possessions, a horseshoe ring with eight large diamonds in it. He's recently bought it back from his friend Ed Martin in Indianapolis, but is ready to sell it again when need be.

"A lot of his business deals at this point in his life were erratic," recalls Brock Yates. "He was always chasing these big payoffs, and I think his financial situation was pretty chaotic."

Of those deals, the one involving Smokey Yunick and South American timber is heating up, but not fast enough.

Yunick had bought a ranch in Ecuador adjoining 150,000 acres of rich jungle land. There are endless tracts filled with teakwood, rosewood, exceptionally high-priced timber; some of the sky-high trees may contain as many as 40,000 board-feet.

Turner visits Yunick's ranch, flying over the majestic forest. The place is a goldmine but it presents a quagmire; anybody who can figure out how to transport the wood through the dense, wet areas will make a killing.

"Curtis was going to be able to buy the timber from me for next to nothing," Yunick recalled years later. "The technology needed to get it out of there at a cost-effective price was going to take a lot of thinking, and I figured he'd be a master at that."

The challenge will take time and resources, and Turner's situation will make this difficult. Yunick suspects that, among Turner's frequent creditors are various Mafia friends he's been indebted to, going back to his days building the speedway.

"I don't think anybody really knew how deeply connected Curtis was," Yunick says. "See, Curtis was on his ass; he'd burned some bridges.

"He was in a real bad place in his life with money. I'd go someplace with him and he'd put up a $10,000 check as a security deposit on a bid on some timber and he was overdrawn at the bank at the time and I said, 'How the hell is *that* gonna work,' and he said, 'Shit, it always works out; don't worry about it.' But we believed in each other, he and I. We always figured we all had some bad days and good days and it balanced out if we kept trying."

When he isn't out flying over tracts or mines, Turner is playing golf. Nothing calms or buoys him like a round or two. "We'd play sometimes thirty-six holes in a day, then play the par three after dinner," remembers Bunny. "We'd been to races where he would blow the car up if it wasn't any good, just to go back, turn around and play golf. He'd literally blow the engine sky-high, and then go play golf."

He plays everywhere he can, frequently at the local Blue Hills Golf Course, where he's made friends with Clarence King, the house pro for the past thirteen years. King has long had a fascination with flying, and Turner happily gives him some tips, which the fifty-one-year-old King exchanges in kind on the course. King and his wife Martha start spending lots of time at Laban Road; there's something warm, unaffected and pragmatic about the pro, and he laughs easily, with a thin-lip smile curling below curious, bemused eyes. Martha calls him Honeybear.

"Clarence was one of the few friends Curtis had who didn't want anything out of him," says Bunny. "He would say 'I'm buying you dinner' and Curtis would say no and Clarence would throw a hundred dollar bill on the tarmac at the airport and say, now you take it, you *take* that money. He was the only man who would ever do that to Curtis."

When not at Blue Hills, Turner tries other courses all over the country, hitting wherever and whenever he can, at any time of day. When he's home, he putts in the house.

Turner loves about golf what he loves about racing: they're each a tug of war between skill and unpredictability, and you're always trying to use the former to battle the latter. Behind the wheel, nobody is more skilled at sizing up a sudden shift in fortune and reacting in a fraction of a second that Turner.

Playing golf in the house, unfortunately, is another matter.

He and Danny, and Charlie Williamson and their friend Gene Newton are drinking shooters one afternoon, trying to make putts into a cup across Turner's lengthy living room. Get the shot closest to the cup and you win the four-dollar pot. Turner wins a round and bends for the money, but Newton, who is a good foot shorter than Turner, and with perhaps a good deal more alcohol swimming in his system, decides to playfully wrestle his friend for the bills. He grabs Turner by the foot and immediately slips, and Turner hits the floor right below him. On the way down, Turner hears a nauseating snapping sound, and as Newton lays there chuckling, he holds Turner's twisted right ankle in his hands.

"Get off me Pop," Turner says calmly. "You broke my leg."

Newton doesn't want to believe it, but twenty minutes later, he's still apologizing when the rescue squad arrives.

Bunny is clearly frustrated, sitting next to her husband in the ambulance. "Curtis, I can't believe you broke your leg playing a stupid game," she says.

"That's all it was, Sweet Thing, just a game," Turner says. But it is galling: he's had thousands of close calls worse than this, all without consequence. He shakes his head and pulls out a Camel, ready to light up.

"You can't smoke in an ambulance, sir," the technician says. "There's oxygen in here."

Turner squints at him. "Then you'd better take the shortest route to the hospital so I can." He looks around at all the hanging equipment in the van's cramped interior and rests his head back. It's not exactly the type of vehicle he's been used to riding in. "Guy like me ain't suppposed to break his leg," he says.

From the moment he arrives at the emergency room, through evaluation, resetting the bone and wrapping the plaster cast from his thigh to his toes, with doctors telling him he'll have to wear it for a few months, Turner wants only to get out of the place. By the following morning, he has wreaked enough havoc to make his point. "He had the place in chaos," says Bunny. "They didn't check him out, they just insisted he leave."

Turner is no happier at home, rolling from room to room in a wheelchair, getting the wheels caught and putting holes in walls. "His leg had to be straight out," says Bunny. "He got so aggravated, he tore the walls to pieces. Then he got crutches. It kept itching him; it drove him crazy."

Having no flying license never kept him out of a plane, and losing a driver's license wouldn't stop him from tooling around town as usual. He might as well be banned from doing either now.

It is summertime, and at this rate, he'll barely be out of the cast before the baby comes. Too much can happen between now and then. There's a timber deal coming up, a big one with Ford Motor Company, involving thousands of acres in Kentucky; if he can sell it, it'll keep him just ahead of his debts for the moment.

Bunny can hear the noise coming from the other side of the door in Turner's office one night. After a few seconds she figures it out: He is working a little hand saw against the plaster as fast as he can.

Days later, he and Bunny are in Kentucky, meeting with reps from Ford.

"I heard you broke your leg," one of them asks, pointing down at his limp.

"It ain't no big deal," he says.

Days later, he is back at the doctor's, getting a new cast put on. "Don't take this one off, Curtis," the doctor tells him. "Don't waste my time or yours."

"It shouldn't be a problem," Turner says, "unless something else happens."

It is the middle of the night when Bunny rolls over lazily to find her husband laying sideways, looking at her with a hand propped under his pillow.

"Curtis, honey, can't you sleep?" she asks, and Turner puts his free hand down on her belly, feeling for a kick in the moonlight a month and a half before he gets to meet his child.

"Sweet Thing," he says, just above a whisper, "If anything happened to me, would you ever get married again?"

Bunny squints. "Curtis it's 3 o'clock in the morning!"

"Would you?"

"Well honey, I don't have any earthly idea what life would have planned for me, if something happened to you—probably *not*."

Turner nods and settles back for a second before rolling her way again.

"I'll tell you one thing. If the sonofabitch ain't good to ya, I'm coming back to kill him." Suddenly content now, he rolls over again. Within seconds, they're both laughing.

"He was so afraid something was going to happen to me and the baby," remembers Bunny. "He would say, 'you're so little, you're so small.'"

Turner has taken out a $20,000 life insurance policy. There's another policy, this one for $250,000, that he has yet to pay all the premiums for. When he climbs out from under this latest rock of debt, that'll be the first thing he does.

Perhaps it's wearing the cast so much, slowing him down, or sensing the full weight of his transition, but Turner has grown more reflective of late. There are still parties in the house, but he continues to drink less than he ever has. He can nurse the same CC and Coke for hours now, content to walk from guest to guest and tell a good tale, cause some mischief or listen to somebody drunker than he is.

And from time to time, he'll tell a friend, or anyone doing an interview, "If I die tomorrow, I guarantee you I've lived every minute of every day to the fullest."

"He'd say, 'If I die, I don't want anybody to be upset,'" says Bob Myers, "'I just want everybody to start another party every fifteen minutes.'"

He says it frequently enough that it seems like a retired driver's epitaph, but it spooks Norris Broadhead when he drops in on Turner unexpectedly on the way home to Mississippi.

"I'd come in with my pilot," he recalls, "stopped by just to see what was going on. And Curtis laid down on the floor there, with his head up on the hearth of his fireplace. He said, 'Pop, if I die tomorrow, I ain't got no regrets 'cause I have enjoyed the hell out of it.' Well, I told the boy flying for me that night, whenever we left there, I said, did you see the death look on that bastard's face? He said, yeah. I said, man, he looks like something's going to happen to him."

Something does happen to Turner.

He can count these moments in his life on one hand, and he knows it. Bill France lifting the ban; getting that car from Glen and Leonard Wood and winning Rockingham, showing everybody he ain't that old. This is a day worth celebrating, and doing something big about. Yes, it's a perfect day to saw off that cast again.

"You saw it off, I'm not putting it back on," his doctor had said the month before. "Three times, that's my limit; after that you're on your own." Turner chuckles as he saws with typical determination.

He is back; there's no doubt. Days later, Smokey Yunick asks him to fly down to South America. Yunick has found a group of investors ready to sign a deal to harvest the timber. "It took them ten days to get to where the timber was," recalls Yunick, but once there, they are ready to negotiate. Turner will fly to Spartanburg so he and Yunick can discuss the details on the flight over to Miami; then they'll catch a 2 A.M. Eastern flight to Ecuador to make the sale.

On Saturday October 3, Turner flies to North Carolina and drives up to the main gate at Charlotte Motor Speedway. He is, as always, a welcome sight, and the guard spreads the gates to let him in. Turner drives around the circuit at about a hundred miles per hour in his rental, taking in the empty stands and the gleaming steel girders. Twice he passes Richard Howard, and Turner can make out the look of satisfaction on his friend's face even at this speed.

He pulls up and the two men start walking through pit road. Howard is in earnest about his proposition: in a week, the place will be filled with Grand National fans, coming to enjoy the National 500. Turner left the sport without a fitting send-off. Howard has a Dodge Daytona ready for him, if he's willing. He can announce his retirement and then give his fans one last bigtime thrill.

The two men climb into Turner's car and take a couple of laps. "That Dodge I have for ya Curtis, it ain't the best car in the world," Howard says with a grin. "Then again, that's right up your alley, isn't it."

"I'll run it now if you want me to," Turner says.

Turner stops back at pit road and climbs from the car. He breathes deep, taking in the familiar smell of oil and gas; in his memory, he hears the grinding sounds of the dirt being sifted.

"What a beautiful place this is," he says.

That night, he and John Griffin head to Griffin's Lake Tillery, North Carolina, cabin, for a meeting with two Turner business partners, Bob Baughman and Ray Austin. After months of preparation, everything is set: the foursome is ready to announce plans to construct a brand new track in nearby Norwood, a 1⅝-mile circuit to be built where the Yadkin and Rocky rivers meet. Financing has been secured, with some investors lured by Turner's name. Perhaps most importantly, the core-drill report for the land looks clean.

Turner has designed a unique, ambitious, state-of-the-art concept for the site, his new dream track. There will be a 7,200-foot jet strip adjoining the place, and a horse track built in the middle. Seats in the stands will be mounted on pivots to turn, making it easier to enjoy all the races. And there'll be betting on the horses, perhaps paving the way for North Carolina to reconsider the para-mutuel question for race cars as well.

Turner shares all his good fortune with John Griffin and the others, and one party starts after another.

"Why would you even think of racing at Charlotte?" Griffin asks.

"Might as well," Turner says, downing another shooter. "It'll be good publicity. And Richard Howard's bein' mighty generous."

"Might not be so generous when he hears you're trying to put him out of business with our new track."

Turner chuckles. "Naah, not Richard Howard. I got plenty of friends,

Pop, and a few enemies, too. I just gotta do what's right for me. Everybody knows that. And I wouldn't change a thing."

"Is that so," Griffin asks, raising a glass.

"Well," Turner says, "not right now, I wouldn't."

When he's conducting business as usual back home in Philadelphia, Bob Baughman is wildly successful, owner of one of the largest coal mines in the United States. When he's busy unwinding at Turner's house in Virginia, Baughman drinks like a man training for an Olympic event. After a typical session, he wakes on Sunday morning, October 4, with a vicious hangover and one thought in mind: it's time to go home. He has a ticket to fly out on Monday on Piedmont Airlines but the way he's feeling, that's one day too long. Baughman knows Turner will happily fly anywhere with any excuse. And Turner knows Baughman, a longtime, cooperative business partner, has always been forthcoming with the cash. Turner isn't about to tell him no, even if he is a little tired.

"I want to come with you," Bunny says. "The doctor says I can, as long as you don't take the plane too high."

"I know, but I want you to stay home, Sweet Thing," Turner says with a smile. His wife could give birth any day now, and he'd rather, for her sake, that it not happen in his Aero Commander, at nine thousand feet.

It is early afternoon by the time Baughman packs up his bag and walks outside, shielding his eyes from the over-generous sunshine. Turner kisses his wife goodbye and puts on his Stetson and his shades, and the two men head down the long driveway to the car. Waiting for them is Hutch, Turner's frequent chauffeur. He is an enormous, hulking, intimidating man with a shaved "Mr. Clean" head but though "he looked like a gorilla, he was as gentle as a spider monkey," Bunny remembers. Turner had found him down on his luck and had practically adopted him.

Turner stops a moment and looks back; Bunny is still at the door, a little woman with a bathrobe covering her growing belly, raising her hand in an enthusiastic wave, the way one might at a parade.

Turner grins as he trudges back up to the house, wincing slightly and limping on that bad leg. And he rubs Bunny's stomach one more time.

"Sweet Thing, I love you more than life," he says. "I'll catch you later."

Turner heads off down the long driveway and stops at Blue Hills to pick up Clarence King, who's looking forward to some flying time. Turner even calls Sue from the car on the way to the airport, asking if she'd like to come along.

"I can't."

"Why not?"

"Dad, I'm in the middle of studying for a test," she says, chuckling. "Remember, I'm trying to go to college?"

"I know it," he says. "I owe you tuition money. I'll bring it by later on—unless you're changing your mind and comin' with me."

"Dad?"

"You're studyin', I know."

At the house on Laban Road, Bunny is sniffing the latest batch of roses when the phone rings.

"Sweet Thing, how 'bout a date tonight?"

"Sure, what do you want to do?"

"Me and Clarence are gonna take you and Martha out for lobsters."

Minutes later, Bunny can hear the faint growl growing louder, and she moves out to the front door. The house is on top of a hill, surrounded by pines, with Roanoke Airport down in the distance, like a stage laying far below Turner and Bunny's upper tier seats. The Aero Commander swoops and hangs perhaps 200 feet in the sky, and Bunny smiles upward. Turner always buzzes the house when he heads home from somewhere, just to let her know he's okay. In a few hours, he'll buzz again and she'll get ready for dinner. She watches the plane move off into the distance. The sky is perfect, like a sea of aquamarine.

Turner, King and Baughman land at DuBois Airport in Pennsylvania at around 3 P.M. and the trio head out for lunch. Turner has hardly eaten all day; in seconds, he dispatches two grilled cheese sandwiches and two glasses of milk, to go along with the couple of shooters he's had on the flight over.

Turner and King are back in the plane a few minutes before 4 P.M., and an attendant, Jack Snyder, tops off the fuel tanks and adds some oil.

"Should I help you run some checks?" Snyder asks, pointing to the nose of the plane.

Turner grins and waves him off. "She's just right," he says.

He starts up the engine, which roars smooth and loud, and he taxis immediately, taking off in seconds. At 3:58 P.M., Turner and King climb into a sky where they can see for miles to a sweet horizon. It is crisp and blue, and Turner rides south toward Punxsatawney, home of the groundhog, and six more weeks of winter.

As always, the sky is about the most relaxing place Turner knows. He and King talk about instruments and settings. Turner had let King fly the plane for a little while on the ride up to Pennsylvania. Turner yawns as he talks. Bunny is right: he is tired, having been up most of the night celebrating his coming stacks of fortune.

The tiredness has sunk into his bones, but nowhere more so than his right leg. It aches no matter what position it's in. Thank goodness for the shooters; they've helped a bit. He has to smile. For a moment he thinks about Little Joe, and he can hear him laughing in his head, after a race, when they'd been beating and banging on each other as usual, treating the day like it was their own personal crusade. And when it was over, they wanted only to do it again. "Hey Pop," Turner would say, "we had some fun out there today, didn't we?" Yeah, they had some fun.

Turner looks at his watch and tries to figure out when they'll be getting home. They've been in the air for only twelve minutes.

And then the whole thing comes apart in seconds.

The left engine of the Aero Commander sputters and halts, like someone has stuck a knife in the propeller about four thousand feet in the air. Turner glances at the gauges: the oil temperature in the left engine is climbing and the oil pressure has bottomed out. Meanwhile, the right engine is running wide open.

Turner starts cranking the left engine, trying to get it restarted.

"What's going on?" King asks but Turner, surprised by the engine failure, answers only by continuing to work the controls again and again. King knows his friend has a tendency to play practical jokes; he has, in the past, asked Turner not to fool with him. Turner pays no attention, his mind intent on the task. The propellor starts and stops, starts and stops again. And it is this that tells King something is terribly wrong, and brings a tightness swelling in his throat and the top of his chest.

The swift force of the right propeller, working hard against a left engine with no airspeed sends the plane jerking fast to the left, heaving it into a sickening arc and a powerful downward spin, and the Aero Commander hurtles into a tight, bullet motion, the G-Force pinning

Turner and King against their seats. Turner instinctively slams his right leg down on the rudder with full force, the only way to control the spin, but pain shoots up his leg into his belly. He stands on the rudder, his hands on the steering yoke, trying to keep it steady. But as he pushes harder with his foot, trying to make up for the loss of strength in his muscles, he can't help but pull on the yoke, yanking the plane back further and keeping the spin tight and true.

And then for a second, he finds that balance, and the plane seems willing to right itself. But out the windshield, the ground races toward him, and the balance is suddenly gone. They're in freefall, with it's G-Force, and the bone shooting something searing through his right leg.

Turner feels again for that balance, looking out at the terrain, trying to spot a landing. There are trees down below him, something soft to land on, a forest to cushion his fall. And then that view is snapped away, and Turner sees something that stops his breath—the bank of a hill just beyond the woods. At this angle, he won't stand a chance.

Twelve minutes after takeoff, and less than a minute after the start of the spin, the Aero Commander slams into the hill. The sudden impact catapults Turner out the side of his plane, forty feet into the distance. He is killed instantly. With the crash, a head rest from the rear of the plane flies right at Clarence King's skull, but King's body is already inert, his life taken by a massive heart attack in the midst of the fall.

The wreckage sits at the bottom of a 150-foot embankment. Beyond the bank, mere feet away, the hill crests and then eases downward, and slopes into a grassy bed.

For the first few seconds, Charlie Williamson has no idea who's on the phone. It takes that long for Bob Baughman to stop crying.

"Bob, what's the matter?"

"Charlie, I have terrible news. Curtis and Clarence, they crashed."

"What are you talking about?"

Bob keeps talking and Charlie keeps denying that it's possible. Nothing about the story registers, not until Bob puts the Pennsylvania state policeman on the phone.

Sue Turner is in the apartment she shares with two girlfriends, feeling terribly agitated. The moment she'd gotten off the phone with her dad, saying she wouldn't fly with him, she'd immediately begun bawling, clutched by some tremendous sadness. A girlfriend tried to console her, with Sue incapable of putting her finger on the source of her emotions.

"I didn't know what happened," she remembered later, "but my spirit knew."

It is 6 P.M., two hours after the crash, and right when her father had promised to come by with her tuition. Sue is laying in her living room reading, and she senses a presence. She looks up and sees nothing, but that doesn't matter: her father is, she believes, in the room with her, somehow. "When I kept looking around and he wasn't there, I knew something was just wrong," she says. "I knew he was gone." Later that night, the call comes from Charlie.

The hours have passed. Martha King is in Turner's house, there with Bunny, who's never changed out of her bathrobe.

First five o'clock came, then six. They'd panicked, had made some calls, but the truth descends on Bunny as day creeps into evening. Turner is nothing if not reliable; if he hadn't buzzed the house, he'd have called by now.

Charlie calls Turner's parents, and his sister Ruby who lives in Floyd. Nobody will believe him. He keeps relaying the phone number of the police department. But all along, he waits for Baughman to call. He won't go to Laban Road until Bob has identified the bodies.

After Baughman calls, Charlie goes first to Danny Vance's house, but Danny isn't home; Charlie's wife Mary isn't around either.

"Here I am, Mary isn't home, and by myself I had to go tell Bunny," he says. "That was the hardest thing in the world I had to do."

Charlie rings the bell and Bunny opens the door. For a moment they stare at each other, unsure of what to say. "I just knew Curtis was gone even before Charlie said it," Bunny remembers.

Bunny's tears begin to well up. And all she can think about is her husband's one great fear.

"Charlie, did it burn up?" she asks, holding herself tight.

Charlie presses his lips, his own lids filling, as he shakes his head. "No," he says.

They stand by the door, embracing, and move into the house.

The radio is on in Ann Turner's apartment; it's been on for hours, like time has been standing still. She sits at the kitchen table, nursing a drink.

Did the phone ring? Did she hear it on the radio? She's heard it before, several times over the years: someone telling her Curtis Turner is dead.

"I just sat there and wondered if it was really true," she later recalled.

But then Sue is at the door, late at night. Ross has come into the kitchen, hearing the noise, unable to sleep and not sure why. He is two days shy of his fifteenth birthday.

The moment Sue delivers the news, Ross tears out of the house. He lets out a cry filled with anguish, and he runs. He doesn't know where he's headed and has only a vague notion he'll end up somewhere. But he runs, the cries pouring out of him.

Sue stands in the kitchen, staring at her mother, who takes a sip of her drink, looks up a moment and then looks out again into the blankness.

The word keeps spreading outward. It comes on the radio when Glen Wood is driving near Danbury, North Carolina, and he pulls over onto the side of the road; he shakes terribly and needs to collect himself. "It was a John F. Kennedy-getting-shot type of a pang in my stomach," he says.

People keep calling people long into the night. The next day, tired of waiting anymore in Spartanburg, Smokey Yunick flies to Miami. When he lands, he walks past a newsstand.

"I saw a headline on the bottom of the paper that read 'Famous Race Driver Killed.' I saw the picture, I knew it was Curtis, and I stopped. I didn't even buy the newspaper; I just read through the part that was important to me. Number one, he was dead. And there wasn't anything that I could do for a dead man."

"It's just—there's a lot of ways Curtis Turner could have died," says Bob Moore. "But the way he died—you never envisioned that being one of them."

Disbelief, however, quickly becomes irrelevant. For years, friends, loved ones, hangers-on, even strangers had tried seeing themselves in Turner. Removing him from the world of the living is like looking in the mirror and seeing somebody else.

On Sunday night, hours after the crash, Wanda Lund comes home to a startling sight—her husband, racer Tiny Lund, is sitting quietly in the living room recliner with tears streaming down his face. The last thing she'd ever expect to see her six-foot-four, 260-pound husband do is cry.

"What is it?" Wanda says, all in a panic.

"Sit down," he says. "He takes his wife's hands, looks her in the eyes and says, "Wanda, I have lost one of the best friends I have ever had, and the racing world has lost the greatest superstar it ever had. And the racing world will never be the same."

And Wanda doesn't have to ask for a name.

"My God, Tiny," she yells, cupping her mouth, "what happened to Curtis?"

The night before the funeral, the house is choking with mourners, so much so that it's nearly impossible to move from one room to the next. Bunny is laying in bed, exhausted by grief and the last stages of pregnancy. Turner's parents are there, as are a roster of friends, competitors, business associates, acquaintances and writers.

Facts fly back and forth from conversation to conversation. Turner and King's bodies had laid out there next to the fusilage by the hill for hours. Witnesses had come by and phoned the police, the airline manufacturers and insurance companies had been called, and the curious came as well. One thing Turner and King had in common was a habit of keeping a thick wad of $100 bills in their pockets. But by the time the bodies were brought back to Virginia, the bills were gone. Turner's gold Darlington watch, a prize for winning the 1956 Southern 500, is also missing. His diamond horseshoe ring, which had long saved him from trouble, is also unfound.

The indignities only make the news seem more unreal. Rumors are tossed out like errant cards from a deck, speculation running rampant about how this could have happened.

"No way he would have let that plane go down like that," someone says.

"The guy with him, he must have been flying it."

"Curtis had to be asleep."

"I bet someone tampered with it; someone he owed money to."

"I'm not even sure it's really him who died in that plane. You know Curtis; wouldn't surprise me if he's even still alive."

Dove Carson, Turner's oldest sister, is in from California. She knows almost nobody in the room, and yet it's abundantly clear that, under these circumstances, she's in charge as she mingles from one group to the next, making sure everybody has what they need. In a time of family crisis, the practical, level-headed, plain-speaking Dove is the ideal person to have around.

"We have to have you here," Minnie Turner had told her daughter on the phone after breaking the news. "You have to handle things for us."

But Dove had just been east to visit with her brother. "We had a nice visit and I'm not coming back," she told her mother. Why spend all the money to fly in again, just to replace a good memory with a bad one?

And yet here she is, knowing there was no choice.

"I didn't go up to my mother and dad's home; I stayed at Curtis' house because they needed somebody," she says. "I'm very independent and a strong woman and they needed somebody like that there who would say yes or no. In an emergency, one is strong, and goes through whatever it is; then it's all over and that is that. You don't even think about it; you just do what has to be done."

To her, every different set of people is another group of strangers, so the two gentlemen who come up to her in the den, with their nondescript faces, dark suits and easy manner, could be any old friends of Curtis'. But they have something important they need to talk to her about, and it's so hard to hear with all the noise. Isn't there someplace else they can go?

Dove ushers the men outside onto the patio. The thick sounds of conversation have grown faint. "What's so important?" she wants to know.

One of the men immediately identifies himself as an aviation official.

"We need to talk to you about your brother's death," he says.

Dove stares from one to the other now, sizing them up. The official can sense her skepticism.

"First of all, you need to understand something, Mrs. Carson. We're not here in any official capacity," he says. "What I'm telling you tonight is entirely off the record."

"What are you telling me?"

"I'm telling you that the wrong type of fuel was put into your brother's plane before he took off from DuBois."

Dove is taken back by the statement; the notion seems ridiculous.

"We've been to the scene and we've been to the airport," he continues. "We've seen proof of this being the case."

"What kind of proof?"

The man smiles. "The kind of proof that everybody will deny."

Dove is silent for several seconds. "Why are you here telling me this?" she says finally.

"Mrs. Carson—"

"Why should I even believe you?" she says loudly.

The man shrugs. "You don't have to; that's your prerogative. We just wanted you to understand. An accident such as this gets classified one way. But there's frequently more to it, as we were able to find."

Dove nods. "So what can be done about it?"

"A few things; that's why we're here."

"They're doing an investigation into the crash," she says.

"Yes, I know," the official says. "Again, this information will be denied by everybody because everybody involved would find themselves in bad trouble. But if somebody were to follow through, and press the point—and I won't lie about it; it would take plenty of time and money—but the truth would come out."

"It can be proven," the other man says.

"Why don't *you* do something about this?"

"We can't," the official says. "Do you have paper and a pen?"

Dove does, and the official dictates the names of several other men.

"You can start by contacting those gentlemen," he says. Dove finishes writing and she and the official stare at each other a moment. He extends his hand finally.

"We just wanted you to know," he says. "And we're very sorry for your loss."

They walk out and Dove looks down at the paper. The names are like a jumble; in a sense she doesn't even want to know them.

"We were living out in California; I had my family, the boys were small, and at that time, we were getting along okay," she remembers. "But I didn't have the money to invest in something like this. And I didn't ask anybody else if they did; I just knew they didn't. And my mother and daddy were too old to be bothered."

Still, she grips the paper in a wad, stuffs it into her pocket and walks back into the house. The noise of conversations hits like a fresh assault, and she weaves through, greeting people numbly and heading for the kitchen.

From the moment of her arrival in Roanoke, she's been looking forward to getting back home. Like her brother, Dove has always seen her existence as being outside her hometown. The piece of paper weighing down her pocket is something that could anchor her right back here. But in a day's time, her brother will be buried, and what good would any of this do?

When she gets back home to California, she'll tell her husband about it; they'll sit up in bed one night and she'll recount the bizarre meeting on the patio.

Dove walks through the house, talking to more guests, cleaning up. She grabs some dishes and garbage and heads back for the kitchen, and when she tosses out the dirty cups and paper napkins, she reaches into her pocket and throws the paper out with it. And then there are more things for her to do as everybody gets ready for the approach of the hard morning.

"I wrote the names down on that paper," she says. "And then I threw the names away, so I wouldn't ever know who they were."

The faithful converge on Oakland Baptist Church in Roanoke the following afternoon for the 2 P.M. service. Three hours earlier, Bunny had been there with Martha for Clarence's service.

There are massive wreaths and flower displays depicting Turner's cars and planes and even a large flowered checkered flag sent by Dan Gurney. The Reverend Ford Philpott, a prominent minister throughout the south and a friend of G.B. Nalley's, delivers the eulogy, during which he remembers once praying with Turner. He recalls Turner being a bit embarrassed, saying, "Lord, I don't know how to do this. I know I'm not worthy but I do pray when I die you will have a stall up there for me."

Richard Howard, Darel Dieringer, Marvin Panch, John Holman, Ralph Moody, Glen Wood, Buck Baker, the list of mourners is a prominent one, even in a sport where most participants usually avoid such an occasion.

"There's this thing among racers about not going to a driver's funeral," says Wanda Lund. "And it's not out of disrespect; it's out of respect. Tiny couldn't bring himself to say goodbye. He said to me, 'I can't go to that man's funeral; it'll be too final. If I never see his casket, then he'll never be dead in my mind.'"

Bill France does not have that luxury. He's lost too many people close to him: Fireball, Marshall Teague, for him the list is especially long. And now Curtis.

He'd gotten the call with the news, and he'd chartered a plane. In a sense, it's not surprising to see him among the mourners that day; it's the very least he can do. And when the pallbearers come up to escort the brass casket, Domer Reeves is there, as is Charlie Williamson and driver Elmo Langley. And Tim Flock and Bill France are together too for this one last task.

It is, understandably, a solemn service, a day where everybody tries their best to hold up well. And yet, recalls Bob Moore, the day didn't seem to fit the man.

"A lot of people have a different view of it," he says, "but from my standpoint—how should I phrase this? It wasn't as 'uplifting' as I thought it could have been, because Curtis was so full of life. And I think the reason might be because it was such a shock. Everyone still couldn't believe that it had happened. Everyone was still saying it: Did he die? Is he really dead?"

Several months will go by before there is any marking on the grave. By then, Bunny has gotten back her husband's wallet and found the poem printed on a folded piece of paper stuck inside one of the pockets, a verse Turner always kept because it was one of his mother's favorites. Ultimately, thousands of dollars are spent on a marker that's truly impressive. When it arrives, it is perhaps the only monument large enough to match the man: Six feet long, three feet wide, gleaming in brass. There is a little model of a plane on the bottom, next to one of Turner's winning cars. The marker reads:

Curtis Morton Turner
"The Babe Ruth of Stock Car Racing"
Born Floyd, VA, April 12, 1924
Lost his life in a plane crash October 4, 1970, in Pennsylvania

A HEAVENLY PARADOX

Love that is hoarded moulds at last
Until we know someday the only thing
we ever have is what we give away

Kindness that is never used but
Hidden all alone will slowly harden
Till it is hard as any stone

It is the things we always hold
That we will lose someday

The only things we ever keep is
what we give away

"They sent that poem back to me from the crash," Bunny says. "That's why I put it on there. That was Curtis—if he had anything, he wanted to share it. That poem was Curtis Turner."

Eighteen days after the death of her husband, Bunny Turner has her baby. He's a boy, just as her husband predicted. Bunny names him Curtis Turner Jr.

She's in the hospital, hugging her boy to her chest when the delivery comes. The baby's father had made arrangements months in advance, and Bunny keeps kissing little Curtis while the men fill the windowsill with roses.

Epilogue
1970-present
"He would have never been happy being old."

Chester Smochek, a mechanic from Mahaffey, Pennsylvania; Arlene Voris, a Mahaffey housewife; and welder Adair McGee each recalled the sounds and sights of an aircraft in trouble. At first, Smochek believed the plane was doing acrobatics, until the spinning craft leveled off and then spun again. All three witnesses to the crash that claimed Curtis Turner's and Clarence King's lives saw the spin, the leveling and the freefall; the action of what appeared to be a pilot attempting to restart one stopped propeller; and smoke pouring from the plane. McGee, standing in a yard below the plane saw blue smoke; Smochek, standing with Mr. McGee, saw black smoke; Mrs. Voris thought it was white. They may have each seen those exact colors, representing different moments in the engine's failure. They each believed the right propeller was stuck, but from the ground looking up, the propeller on the "right side" is actually the left propeller, which is the more logical choice given the facts uncovered by Daniel Sayres, the National Transportation Safety Board air safety investigator assigned to the accident.

Bunny Turner never met Sayres, but there was a time not long after her husband's death where he would call frequently, calls that brought her no small comfort.

"He was so good to me," she says. "He had checked into Curtis' background and the flight and everything. He said Curtis could fly better drunk than most people could sober."

But suppositions of this nature don't make their way into official government documents.

The accident has remained, in the circle of Turner's friends and family, the most vexing mystery of his life, and continues to inspire conjecture some thirty-five years later.

Several months after the accident, the NTSB issued its factual report, detailing conditions of the aircraft, personnel and weather, as well as narrative statements from witnesses at the scene. Finally, the board, having not reached a definite conclusion, issued their statement of probable causes and contributing factors. Probable causes listed were:

Engine failure for undetermined reasons

Pilot in Command—Failed to obtain/Maintain Flying Speed

Pilot in Command—Physical Impairment

Contributing factors listed were:

Partial Power Loss of Power—one engine

Physical condition of passenger

Remarks were also given to support the claims:

Pilot blood alcohol level: 0.17

Evidence shows passenger had a severe heart attack prior to accident.

It is a list meant to do several things: clear up some mystery, bring about a sense of closure, offer a partial explanation and follow regulations to the letter. "Failure to maintain flying speed?" recalls Bunny. "Yeah, I guess if you go into the ground it *is* failure to maintain flying speed."

Clearly, Sayres had his doubts about some of the conclusions, but the team of Federal Aviation Administration, and Pennsylvania Aeronautics Commission personnel assigned to participate—and Sayres himself, in the long run—found it easy to make quick assumptions and ignore glaring inconsistencies.

Yes, it's very strange that the craft's left engine quit suddenly, and the right engine was running wide open . . . but the pilot's blood alcohol level was too high. And there was somebody having a heart attack in the plane with him at the time.

Yet the general consensus among friends and family is that Bunny could have been having a baby in the back of the plane and Turner wouldn't have moved a muscle away from the controls.

Some friends have long insisted that Turner wasn't flying the plane, that he'd been teaching King to fly, and the golf pro had suffered a heart attack while at the controls. Charlie Williamson, who'd gone to the crash site and talked to investigators, believes this isn't possible.

"The guy [at the scene] told me the pilot was still trying to crank the engine when it went into the ground, so I know it was Curtis," he says. "And something hit Clarence behind the head, and I know exactly what it was because I brought it home: it was laying in the woods the day I was up there. It was a head rest that flew from the back and hit him. And Clarence was still in the plane; Curtis I think went out the side of the plane. No, Curtis was flying; all the rest of that stuff was just speculation."

Both Danny Vance and Pee Wee Ellwanger bring up the fact that in the weeks prior to the crash, Turner had repairs performed on one of the Aero Commander's magnetos, which are meant to fire up the spark plugs. If the repairs were not done properly, a bad magneto could lead to a power failure in one engine.

But Ellwanger and Glen Wood are among those who believe that the wrong fuel *was* pumped in just before the crash, and played a big role in the loss of the plane. Certain inconsistencies in the report, along with circumstantial data, appear to at least support the possibility that Dove Carson's visitors the night before the funeral may have been telling the truth.

It's true that a magneto *could* simply stop working at any time. But Turner, King and Baughman had experienced a perfect flight going into DuBois, and the only difference between that journey and the return flight was that Turner had gotten the plane gassed up before leaving.

The Aero Commander could fly only on 100/133 octane fuel, and the report states 133 gallons of 100 octane were pumped into the plane, with one quart of oil put into the left engine and two quarts into the right. But no fuel samples were taken from those engines at the scene; or if they were, that information did not find its way into the factual report. Two years earlier, DuBois Airport had begun offering jet fuel, or kerosene, to jets landing and taking off on its runways. The kerosene could have been inadvertently pumped into one tank or both. With 100 octane still in the carburetors, the plane could conceivably have taken off and flown perfectly until the moment the kerosene worked its way down and into the motor. At that moment, power failure would occur, along with considerable damage.

The report also states that Lycoming, the manufacturer of the engines, picked them up for post-accident evaluation. In many cases, a crash evaluation doesn't even begin until after an engine company representative is present, to make things easier for insurance companies. Both engines were taken to Avco-Lycoming's Pennsylvania factory and placed in test cells, where they each started successfully; afterwards, both engines were also able to operate at full power.

If the wrong kind of fuel was still in those engines, how were they able to do this?

There is no indication whatsoever that the same fuel was in the engines when Lycoming did their tests. A crash of that magnitude could have easily emptied both engines. And regarding the engines, there are glaring inconsistencies in the NTSB report. One section lists the damage to the engines as substantial; in another section the damage is deemed "superficial." In the latter section, officials state that "certain parts were replaced [before testing commenced] but none which altered the operational status of the engines from that prior to impact." That may be so, but one of the magnetos was replaced due to impact damage, making conclusions about magneto involvement in the crash even harder to draw.

Whatever the level of damage to the engines, it's possible that it could have come from the crash, or from the wrong kind of fuel—or both.

There's no way to ever know for sure whether or not fuel played a significant role in the crash; it only appears to be a reasonable conclusion.

In a sense, it reminds one of the death of Dale Earnhardt. When the Intimidator lost his life on the last lap of the Daytona 500, there were cameras, studies, physics analyses and millions of dollars of research that went into seeking medical closure, which both the sport and the Earnhardt family deserved. The ultimate cause of death—basalar skull fracture—was brought about by a long series of horrific angles, turns and speeds, not to mention several other safety-related factors.

And you can throw a long series of reasons into the death of Curtis Turner as well, starting with his desire to keep sawing off his cast before his leg could heal properly. Or perhaps it goes back even further, to the fact that he flew his plane the way he drove: by simply taking off, and not always checking the settings. There's even the odd possibility he had gotten the wrong kind of fuel and *knew* it. If so, it wouldn't have been the first time.

"One time, Curtis flew up to Roanoke from Charlotte and gassed up, and they didn't have anything but regular gas, which you're not supposed to use; you're supposed to use 100 octane or better," remembers Charlie Williamson about another flight. "They put it in one tank and we were taking off and he forgot to switch over to the other tank, the one they hadn't filled up, and we took off and we're going on there and he's trying to get off the ground, and we're going and going and it wasn't picking up speed and I'm looking over and here's this big motor grater sitting right in front of us. I knew what was going on and he finally got it up enough to get the wheels up and that gives you more horsepower to raise you up further. And it went down and then came up, and we went right over the motor grater—a big old steamroller type of thing, the thing you use to put asphalt down. But we just barely cleared it. And I said, you had a hard time getting it off the ground, didn't you? He said, Pop, I didn't know if I was gonna make it or not."

Turner calmly took risks in the air; at a few thousand feet, he felt more invincible than anywhere on earth, weather notwithstanding. But weather may have been one thing, with a series of mechanical failures being quite another. Engine failure, brought about by incorrect fuel, could have led to a physical inability to handle the craft, due to injury, G-Forces or both.

But not enough of this kind of conjecture found its way into the NTSB report. It must have been easy to look at a blood alcohol level of 0.17 and declare Turner dangerously inebriated. Given a person of Turner's size, one would need to consume ten drinks to reach such a level; but given Turner's drinking history, there's every reason to assume his mean level of blood alcohol would be higher than 0.0 to begin with. He'd been drinking the night before—a good half day prior to the crash—and perhaps it only took two shooters to bring the level up to 0.17. For Turner, two shooters might leave him somwhat impaired but certainly not out of control—a condition he frequently flew in. Add his tiredness and you have a contributing factor, not a cause.

The alcohol, the fuel, the magnetos, these are among the factors that will remain part of the speculation, suppositions without concrete answers. Reached now through his former employer, Jack Snyder confirms that sample tests were taken at the fuel pump the morning of Turner's accident and that the fuel was not contaminated, but even this leaves long-ignored questions unanswered. "I hate to say this but when somebody dies and there's really nobody making any noise about it, the NTSB frequently doesn't bother," says Jim Urcinole, Director of Operations for MacDan Aviation, and an expert in the area of accident investigation. "There is a possibility that the airplane *was* fueled with the wrong kind of fuel.

"The first place you go to is why did the engine fail? Well, it's got to be one of three malfunctions: something came apart, or it could be fuel, or it could be ignition. There is a good possibility that he got kerosene in the tanks. Sometimes, depending on the mixture, failure might not happen right away. Did he then shut down the engine, or secure it because it failed? Those are things you have to look at, but they weren't properly looked at because it was deemed 'pilot error.' That conclusion is easy, and it's a shame."

One thing is very certain, despite the years of conjecture and legend: Turner's death had at least something to do with impulsive decisions, simple human error and an air of invincibility. So Turner's death didn't match his legend; it matched his life.

Ross Turner always remembered the moment with great clarity. He was twelve years old, living at his father's house in Charlotte, while his mother was away, being treated for her mental illness. At the house, Ross witnessed firsthand his father's dogged pursuits, his motorized passage through life in a series of races and business deals, triumphs and disappointments.

"He had all these victories under his belt, we had this huge car, when we went on vacation we flew our plane there and that was just the way we lived," Ross later said.

Sometimes Ross travelled with his dad on timber runs, sitting in the back of the Aero Commander, listening to the men talk about lumber and women. He became absorbed in the act of being with his father, flying in a plane, feeling like a man. Turner taught Ross how to play golf, and bought him a set of kid clubs.

But more than anything, Ross saw how the pace wouldn't let his father go.

"And I just asked him one day, I said 'Dad, when do you think you'll have enough?' I don't know what made me ask him this. And he was probably just shocked that I said that. But I saw my dad like a greyhound dog chasing those rabbits around the track and never being satisfied and just running and running and running, but for what? So I asked him that. And he said, 'I don't know.' I've never forgotten that, and from that point on, I kinda realized—I didn't have a premonition but I just kinda had a sense— that the life I was living was not real. It was more surreal and it would be over one day. And when it was over it was completely over and in a hurry."

Upon hearing of his father's death, Ross ran that night and ended up at a friend's house, but in a sense, he didn't stop running for a long time, and he wasn't alone.

Turner died without a will, and whatever insurance policy he took out listed Bunny as sole beneficiary. Turner's first family, after being amply provided for during his life, was left without additional means of support. "My mother went into an institution, I went to an orphanage and within months of my dad's death, it was like our family had never existed."

Quite the opposite was true; for the first time, the surreal nature of living, Ross Turner recognized, had disappeared for everybody.

While Turner's first family aimed their bitterness in Bunny's direction, their financial ruin, after a lifetime without want, came from the shockingly sudden loss of a man many people—starting with Turner himself—believed was destined to live forever. Bob Myers began his tribute to Turner with the words, "I know now that death is very real. If Curtis Turner can die, it is an inescapable inevitability." And yet Ralph Moody more realistically said, "Goddamn, I don't know how Curtis lived as long as he did." The family was, to put it mildly, completely unprepared. Sue, being the oldest of Turner's children, endeavored to represent the first family's financial interest; Jerry Dechow, Ann's brother-in-law, took on the difficult task of legal counsel in their affairs. Both found themselves in way over their heads, Sue from lack of experience, and Dechow perhaps from the reality that too often there wasn't much of a leg to stand on.

"I knew nothing about how to [deal with] an estate," Sue says. "And I should have had better guidance but we didn't get real good advice. They said there were all these debts coming in, all these debts pending, but Dad was owed a lot of money and people just didn't own up to it. He would do deals with people and he would have options on things and have things in his head rather than written down quite often. It's really a toss-up about what his financial standing was. At the time of his death he had a Greyhound bus—nobody knows what happened to it. He had his limousine with these big horns on the front of it. We don't know what happened to that stuff. At the time of his passing, we were told that everything was 'intestate' and not to touch anything."

"I remember stopping with him at banks; we would park at the front door and he would walk into a bank and walk out with enormous checks or amounts of cash and it was all under the table," recalls Ross. "For a person to have to do that instead of the traditional route, you pay a price for that down the road."

Ross felt the loss especially keenly. "When my father died, I was completely aimless," he admits. "I was fifteen years old, I had no idea how to be a man and to be responsible for myelf so for about three years, I had no idea of what to do with my life." Refusing to follow Priscilla and Tyler, who went to live with relatives in Florida, he stayed in a local orphanage. "I'm living in an orphanage thinking, 'Not too long ago, I was driving in a limousine.'"

Ann had taken Priscilla and Tyler to Jacksonville, but the strain of her circumstances only exacerbated her symptoms of schizophrenia. At times together, at times apart, the family bounced back and forth from Florida to Virginia, staying with relatives or in hotels or government-placed housing. Ann's family, raised to believe that one should pull oneself up, intervened only to a small extent.

"We spent ten, fifteen, maybe twenty years just trying to survive," Ann recalled.

Meanwhile, the life they'd known and felt protected by was scattered. All the memories of youth, the kinds of items that more fortunate folk end up taking for granted and storing in a parent's dusty attic, seemed to go the way of dust as Turner's possessions went up for grabs in fire sales.

"When I was younger, when we were struggling, I would be at somebody's house and they would say, 'Oh you're Curtis Turner's daughter? This is his coffee table!'" remembers Priscilla.

But this lowest of ebbs had thrust the family onto a path of necessary self-reliance. There was no way at the time to know where the path might lead, no hint whatsoever that it could all end by making them stronger.

For Ross, the first indication came in his teens, when he found his calling as a minister. "Once I received Christ into my life, I accepted the fact that I now had a father that would not die, would not divorce my mother, was the perfect father—all the things I was starting to realize I needed in a father, I found in my heavenly father," he says.

Ross always had a talent for singing and he began to use his vocal gifts in a choir, travelling all over the country and in time settling in Raleigh, where he married, had a family and started his own church. Priscilla, married and a bank secretary; and Sue, an artist and a married mother of five; each settled around Roanoke, where their mom long lived in a town house she'd gotten at first thanks to government aid. " I came out here, I bought this place, didn't have a stick of furniture," Ann remembered. "I had a few clothes, but just started with a five dollar bill."

The family has grown closer, by necessity at first, but then by choice. What faded, thankfully, was the need to define oneself by a life now long gone, replaced instead by the belief in a steadier future.

"It didn't mean anything, at that time of struggle, to be Curtis Turner's ex-wife, or to be his children. So you had to define yourself," says Priscilla. "And that was a really good thing. That was a really *great* thing. We've come a long way to want to do things together."

For decades, Ann Turner found work where and when she could, struggled with her illness and learned to overcome. Through all her challenges and ills, she became a survivor. Late in her life, growing frail and ill, but with her family around her, she retained more than anything else her pride, and the knowledge of how inspirational she'd been.

"I think Dad had incredible talent and charisma, a lot of great virtues. And I'm really proud of him for those things. And the fact that he won notoriety and all that is great. So I can look at that and appreciate that, in those boundaries. But, you know, my mom never complained," said Ross. "She's not one to be incredibly doting on us or overly dependent on us because she wants to be independent, totally independent. And that says a lot about her, the fire that's in her to go on."

Tyler, staying in the townhouse with her for years, has lived a quiet life, working odd construction jobs and helping out his mom. Some of his dad's rebel streak resides in him, most evident when he attempted to race cars some years back.

"I got my lead foot from him," Tyler says. "One time I went racing, put the pedal to the floor and about gave the guy on the starting line a heart attack. I'd like to get back into it. They announced that I was Curtis Turner's son anytime I went down there. They'd say, 'There's Curtis' boy.' If I had the money to get back into racing, I probably would."

With the least connection to his dad, Tyler revels in the chance to listen to the family tales. His older siblings might carry more baggage about the past; Tyler never fights that bitterness.

"What would I say to my dad now if he were here?" Tyler says, when posed with the question. "I'd say, 'Don't get on that plane.'"

Bunny Turner got a clear indication of what her loss would be almost immediately.

"Clarence's funeral was at 11 A.M. and Curtis' was at 2 P.M. And we went back to the cemetery at 4:30 that evening and there was not one flower on that ground, it was stripped," she remembers. "There wasn't even any styrofoam. People had taken all the flowers as souvenirs. We wanted to go back to see them when nobody was there. And they were all gone."

In a very ideal world, the tragic, sudden removal of Curtis Turner from everybody's life might have become a uniting factor for his two families. Certainly they have always shared one thing in abundance: grief. But the world of each family, especially after Turner's death, became anything but ideal, and poor circumstances, and the timing of the loss drove a wedge that only grew deeper as time passed.

In a sense, the focal point for everybody was the family home. After they married, Turner and Bunny moved into the house on Laban Road where Ann had raised her kids, a turn of events for which Bunny was hardly to blame. In time, the house became a place where she and Curtis could build their own memories.

But three weeks after Turner's death, G.B. Nalley arrived and told Bunny that the house was in his name and that she had to leave.

"It broke my heart completely," she says. "It hurt me terribly—but then I got mad, thinking about all the money Curtis had made that man. I don't think it had been in his name very long. It was like when Curtis would sell that horseshoe ring: at the time, he needed money."

Or perhaps Turner needed less money. Dove Carson remembers her visit east weeks before Turner's death, and her brother telling her about an upcoming lawsuit. To protect his future, he'd signed some assets over to Nalley, just in case the courts came looking. Given the complicated financial partnership Nalley and Turner enjoyed, it's hard to know who owed whom what, and when. But Nalley had the deed to the house with his name on it, and in a court of law, that's all that counts.

Like Ann and her children, Bunny also found herself suddenly without a home, a twenty-two-year-old girl with a brand new baby and a loving future simply ripped away.

To further complicate matters, at the time of his death, Turner was a few final payments shy of fully buying a large life insurance policy. Rumors abounded as to the incredible worth of Curtis Turner, a man who'd made so many fortunes. But those struggles at the time of his death, not to mention the fiscal difficulties Sue Turner found herself dealing with, hardly gave Bunny Turner any kind of head start.

"I got about $20,000," she says of the life insurance policy that had been paid for, "and of that, I spent half on the funeral. My alleged kajillion dollars that he left me—that's a joke."

"Not too long before Curtis got killed, I had a date or something, and we went by Curtis' house beforehand and it was just him and Bunny there," remembers Henry Mason. "We were sitting at the kitchen table, I don't know how we got on this discussion, but it came up: what would you do if someone walked up to you and handed you a million dollars in cash. And you've got to figure this is thirty years ago, a million dollars went a lot farther! Someone said, 'Well, you have a million dollars, you could stock it away and live off the interest.' But then ol' Curtis smiled and said, 'You know, hell, I'd like to have that stuff prorated, and the day I died there would be nothing left.'" Well, when that airplane screwed itself in the ground, he had just about accomplished it."

Finding work and relying on the kindness of her family, Bunny had her own considerable emotional scars to deal with. She'd had the benefit of an ideal married life, but it had lasted less than two years. She was, by her own admission, "still just a child," now suddenly astounded by a rather cruel world, and the notion that she was easy prey.

"I had a guy who actually called me from up in Pennsylvania who offered to sell me the Stetson Curtis was wearing the day that he crashed," she says. "Every kook in the country came out of the woodwork, making offers. Saying this, saying that, promising this, promising that. It was awful."

Perhaps the worst visit came from the son of Gayle Warren, a friend and Performance School associate of Turner's who'd died not long before Curtis, also in a mysterious air crash. Warren's son seemed to imply he had incontrovertible evidence that somebody had buried the wrong bodies.

"I was working at an auto dealership when Gayle's son came in carrying a briefcase full of bones," she recalls. "He said both Curtis and his dad were in South America. *Bones!* He showed them to me and I nearly died! That shook me to the core. Let me tell you something: if Curtis Turner were alive, I don't care if he was in a witness protection program, he would have gotten in touch with me."

All too quickly, Bunny sought to escape. "I just disconnected myself from the racing industry period, for about seven years," she says. "I had no contact whatsoever with anybody, by choice. All I cared about was raising my son."

It wasn't until 1983 when Bunny allowed thirteen-year-old Curtis Turner Jr. to attend his first race, at Darlington. Throughout the running, she kept watching him; he was mesmerized. Looking back now, it almost seems understandable that, regardless of how vigilantly Bunny kept her boy away from auto racing, Curtis Jr. eventually gravitated in this direction. He raced for two-and-a-half years, moving from go-karts to stocks, a long enough period to cultivate a deep love for the sport. For the first time, he came to understand the connection he had with the father he'd never met.

"I wanted to be exactly like him," he says. "I started finding things out about him and that's what I wanted to be. It kind of took over my identity just a little bit."

For a time, Curtis Jr. let it get the better of him. The typical impetuousness of youth requires a different scale when you're the son of Curtis Turner. Recalling those days now, Bunny says, "I'll put it to you this way. I did a lot of praying."

But time brought maturity. "I got out on my own and out in the real world, and I really don't think about that as much anymore," Curtis Jr. says. "I've been successful in what I've done and I hope that my dad would be proud of me. I mean, I hope that he would no matter what I did."

Curtis Jr. is now General Sales Manager for Shelor Automotive, the largest used car dealership in the state of Virginia. Shelor has seven franchises; Curtis Jr. runs the sales end. He's also the married father of three. And his physical resemblance to his father is eerie.

And he managed to make his way in the world thanks to a mother who kept him grounded, despite all the wild tales he'd often heard of his dad.

"My mom was a single parent most of her life and she raised me and we always made it," he says. "She's really my hero. She's just been a great example. Everything that I know, she pretty much taught me."

And that includes whatever she's been able to pass down about the warmer, more inspiring side of his dad. "She taught me that he just really enjoyed life and that he was always happy and positive," Curtis Jr. says. "He lived for every minute, and it sounded like not many things got him down. And my mom talked to me a lot about the things he did for people and kids, and that he had a big heart. That's important."

Also on the staff at Shelor, buying cars for the company, is Tommy Hall. Four years after Turner's death, Bunny married a surgeon, but the union ended after five years. Eventually she married Hall, whom she met at an auto dealership she'd once worked at in Virginia. Tommy is the kind of man Curtis would have been proud to shake hands with.

Turner's first family may have experienced times where they saw no emotional benefit in being relations of Curtis Turner. Bunny has always had the opposite perspective. She remains her first husband's unconditional, unflinching advocate, and the guardian of his legacy and his good name. She'd be the first to admit that he had a wild past, and she's the first to bristle when anyone implies that his "wildness" is the only definition of who he was.

And Bunny is back in auto racing, now doing publicity work for Motor Mile Speedway in Radford, Virginia, where an important annual racing tradition continues to be maintained. Once a year, they hand out the Curtis Turner Hard Charger Award.

While the figures in Turner's ledger book dwindled quickly, what only increased in size as time passed was the legend of the man's name. Stories traded among friends were the only materials that could never lose their value. And as wild as the stories were, the vast majority of the repository *had* to be true. That was Curtis Turner.

And yet, given the truism that "the victors write history," Turner's larger-than-life story has gone virtually ignored. Yes, he's frequently cited when writers want to showcase NASCAR's "rebel past." But the sport has, in the years since Turner's death, made incredible strides in the intentional pursuit of cleaning up an image sullied by its moonshining past. While NASCAR's status as "the fastest-growing sport in America" seems ingrained enough to be trademarked, and heroes such as Jeff Gordon represent a kinder, gentler, all-American age of stock car racing, there's no way the sport could have thrived without its first burst of excitement and popularity, spearheaded in part by Turner. "There were approximately 10 drivers that were the foundation for what NASCAR sits on and it had to be a mighty good foundation because every once in awhile, they've made some decision that could have damn near destroyed NASCAR if that foundation hadn't been so strong, and obviously Curtis was one of them," said Smokey Yunick.

With Turner's death, there remained a remarkable degree of "unfinished business." If he'd lived, chances are he would have eventually either completed another track in North Carolina, or done his best to regain control of his old one, as he'd long sought. The latter plan became the obsession of the only other man who could fully understand the all-consuming bitterness of losing the place: Bruton Smith. After his equally unceremonious removal from the Charlotte Motor Speedway ruling body, Smith moved to another state and remade his fortune through a series of auto dealerships. In time, he relentlessly began to buy stock in the speedway, accruing shares slowly, piece by piece. By the mid-1970s, Smith became majority owner of the track. After hiring Humpy Wheeler to run the place, the two men built the facility—now known as Lowe's Motor Speedway—into one of the crown jewels of the sport, site of the annual Nextel All-Star race, along with the Coca-Cola 600, which still remains the longest contest on the Nextel Cup schedule. In time, Smith purchased and built several other tracks and now stands as one of the wealthiest and most influential voices in the sport, and an outspoken critic of the status quo. He is, of the two visionary partners who originally built the Charlotte Motor Speedway, the surviving success story, and it is an astounding one. If Turner were alive today, he'd visit the place he and Smith founded, and find his one-time partner's contributions a thing of utter amazement.

But as time goes on—further separating the living from the dead—and Smith's influence expands, Turner's original contributions appear to diminish. In a 2003 interview with *Stock Car Racing* magazine, Smith described Turner's role in the building of the track as secondary. No doubt the two men parted with some degree of bile, each blaming the other for not handling things that, at the time, had spiraled way beyond their control. And there's no real reason to doubt that Turner died owing Smith a sum of money he could have very much used. But when you walk through the glorious speedway today, with its grand skyboxes, and even condos that were a revolutionary improvement at the time, you will find various areas named after some of the most famous names in the sport of stock car racing. You won't find Curtis Turner's name on any of them.

Bill France, and the France family, continued to reign over the sport they molded. Not long after Turner's death, Bill France—who turned the reigns over to his son Bill Jr. in 1972—was present at one of the many hall of fame inductions his friend earned posthumously. In an eloquent tribute, he delivered a line meant to wipe away some of the bad feelings that set them at such bitter odds. "Curtis Turner," he told all assembled, "was the greatest race car driver I have ever seen."

France remained active in the sport after his retirement, as a consult-ant to his son and a prominent member of the board. He'd never gotten the kind of closure he might have hoped with Turner, but at least the events that had occurred between them were water under the bridge, now softened by history and the sport's newfound corporate success.

That didn't mean, however, he was always able to escape the past, especially when Smokey Yunick was around. Yunick and France had been at loggerheads their entire careers, with Yunick bitterly chafing against anything the France family monopoly represented in the sport, from strict rule interpretations to the handing out of purses.

As Yunick recalled a few months before his death from cancer, one argument with France, and the perceived bad shake that went along with it, inspired his simmering ire to boil over.

"And I told France, 'I always thought you were chicken shit but I never could figure out how you ever got enough balls to go stick your nose in and be a pallbearer for Curtis, after you spent ten fuckin' years trying to destroy him.' And all France said was, 'You don't know all the facts.'"

Yunick, with all his biterness, would never have considered there were any facts worth noting in a Bill France-Curtis Turner friendship. But until his death in 1992, France would only speak well of the greatest race car driver he had ever seen.

Other tributes continue to survive Turner. The International Motorsports Hall of Fame and the Virginia Athletic Hall of Fame are two of the many other organizations to honor him. In 1998, when NASCAR added a list of the 50 greatest stock car racers to the festivities celebrating the fiftieth anniversary of the sport, Turner made the grade. But one can also see the result of his unique vision by looking at the abundance of satellite commerce and entertainment. And every once in awhile, some new Web company will use the border around the dollar bill for an easy, illegal bit of advertising.

Turner's family is perhaps his best legacy. But it has, in recent times, endured downward swings of fortune.

In April 2003, a documentary of Turner's life, titled *Hey, Pops!*, had its world premiere in Roanoke. Many of Turner's old compatriots, including Glen and Leonard Wood and Junior Johnson showed up to pay tribute. And it was the first time both families found themselves in the same room at the same time.

"They're just super people, and I think we probably wasted a lot of time not getting to know each other sooner," says Curtis Jr. of his half-siblings.

While the families have not reconnected to any great degree, the premiere was a step in the right direction.

It was followed, sadly, by two losses. On November 12, 2003, Ann Ross Turner died after a long illness. Her children were at her bedside; at the moment of her passing, they were calming her spirit by singing her hymns.

The loss of the family matriarch sent everybody reeling, but another cruel blow followed quickly. On January 31, 2004, Ross Turner woke up to find that the tightness he'd felt in his chest the day before had only gotten worse. He jumped into his car and drove as swiftly as possible to Raleigh Community Hospital, but before he could make it from the car to the emergency room, a heart attack claimed his life. Ross was only forty-eight, two years older than his father had been. He left his wife Kathy, their two children and the thriving Freedom River Community Church. Like his father before him, he'd left a memorable legacy.

The family home on Laban Road, which had meant so much to everybody, has changed hands several times in the years since Turner's death. But the ten-acre front yard was sold a number of years ago, and now the one-time Turner home sits at the end of a long cul-de-sac; the pine trees remain but they're peppered here and there between a long block of homes that lead up the hill. The street that now sits on all that land has an appropriate enough name; it's called Past Times Lane.

Ann's and Ross's deaths, the passing of NASCAR legends such as Ralph Moody and Smokey Yunick, and the seemingly boundless success the sport now enjoys—all these things bring Turner's memory rushing right back to those who knew him.

"Everybody respected him, his unreal ability to drive a race car," says Humpy Wheeler. "He may have been literally the best natural race driver that we've seen. Had he been around today, in the last ten years, and he'd gotten into the rhythm of modern day racing, he probably would have won as many races as Jeff Gordon. He was that good."

It's easier for Bunny Hall to think about all her first husband left behind—the potential, the dreams and a lot of missed years.

"Lord he would be heading uphill by now. With NASCAR's corporate deal and all these mega-billions, he'd be right in the middle of it—not racing, on the business end," she believes. "I remember G.B. Nalley would say to me, if Curtis could have ever gotten to the point where he could have financed his own deal, he would have been worth a mint, but he spent money as fast as he made it.

"But I don't think Curtis could have ever gotten old," she adds. "I think if he were alive today, he wouldn't be old. He had a spirit, an inner spring. He never got tired. That was the weirdest thing. It's just like you'd plug him into the wall and rejuvenate his battery. Four hours of sleep and he was ready to rip, ready to go. He was larger than life, gentle—I still feel him there. He used to say, 'Live hard, die fast and die young.' I mean he really believed that. Lord he loved life, but he would have never been happy being old."

Source Materials

SIGNIFICANT INTERVIEWS

Francis Allen—Associate at Holman-Moody in the 1960s

Bobby Allison—NASCAR Winston Cup champion in 1983

Buddy Baker—Former racer; named one of NASCAR's 50 Greatest Drivers of All Time

Eddie Bennington—Virginia businessman, stock car racer from the 1940s-50s

Ron Bost—Executive Director, North Carolina Forest Landowner's Association

Norris Broadhead—Businessman in Mississippi /former associate of Curtis Turner

Dove Carson—Older sister of Curtis Turner

Paul Cawley—Former stock car racer; friend of Curtis Turner

Kim Chapin—Former writer for *Sports Illustrated*

Chris Christopherson—Mayor, Easley, South Carolina

Clyde Conner—Longtime Curtis Turner fan from Yadkinville, N.C.

Jerry Dechow—Onetime attorney for Turner family

Wanda Lund Early—Widow of racing great Tiny Lund

Chris Economaki—Founding Editor, *National Speed Sport News*

Carroll Edwards—Founder, Edwards Wood Products

Pee Wee Ellwanger—Stock car racer, 1950s-'60s, friend/associate of Turner

Greg Fielden—NASCAR historian, author of the *Forty Years of Stock Car Racing* series

Ray Fox—Longtime NASCAR car builder and car owner

James Garner—Actor; former race car driver

Priscilla Gauldin—Younger daughter of Curtis and Ann Turner

Robert Green—Participating driver in the first-ever Mexican Road Race in 1950

Dan Gurney—Star driver on the Indy and NASCAR circuits

Barney Hall—Longtime announcer, Motorsports Racing Network

Bunny Turner Hall—Second wife of Curtis Turner; mother of Curtis Turner Jr.

Hal Hambrick—Track owner, original manager of Bristol Motor Speedway, race broadcaster

Tom Higgins—Reporter, Winston-Salem *Journal*

Jim Hunter—Former reporter/promoter, current NASCAR VP of Corporate Communications

Ned Jarrett—Two-time NASCAR Grand National champion

Junior Johnson—Legendary NASCAR driver

Bob Latford—Journalist, public relations manager for Daytona International Speedway and Charlotte Motor Speedway, inventor of the NASCAR points system in use for 30 years

Fred Lorenzen—Former NASCAR great, winner of 26 races including the 1965 Daytona 500

Henry Mason—President, Mason Distributing Company

Joanne Michaels—Former girlfriend of Joe Weatherly

Bob Moore—Longtime writer for the *Charlotte Observer* and other newspapers and magazines

Bud Moore—Famed car owner for, among other drivers, Joe Weatherly

Little Bud Moore—NASCAR driver during the 1960s

Max Muhleman—Founder of Muhleman Marketing; former writer for the *Charlotte News*

Bob Myers—Famed Charlotte-area sports writer in the 1960s

Don Naiman—Former director, Talladega Superspeedway, and later the International Motorsports Hall of Fame

G.B. Nalley Jr.—South Carolina businessman, son of Curtis Turner's friend/business partner G.B. Nalley

Harmon Nolen Jr.—Son of Curtis Turner's longtime friend Harmon Nolen

Jack Ogorchock—Former manager, Beechwoods Flying Service, Inc. in Pennsylvania

Marvin Panch—Former NASCAR driver; winner of the 1961 Daytona 500

Jacques Passino—Former manager of Ford Motor Company racing division

Charlie Perry—NASCAR fan; producer of proposed outdoor drama on Curtis Turner's career

Tom Pistone—Popular NASCAR driver through the 1950s and 1960s

Dick Ralstin—PR Representative for Goodyear; motorsports journalist and photographer

Domer Reeves—Family friend of Curtis and Bunny Turner

Daniel Sayres—Former investigator, National Transportation Safety Board

Paul Sawyer—Former owner, Richmond International Raceway

Hank Schoolfield—Motorsports journalist, public relations director for Bowman Gray Stadium

Betty Skelton Frankman—Former aviatrix, onetime friend of Curtis Turner

Marshall Spiegel—Longtime racing journalist and author

Gene Stokes—Onetime flagman and pit steward for NASCAR

Bruce Sweeney—Childhood friend of Darnell and Curtis Turner

Billy Triplett—Former aid/employee of Curtis Turner in the 1950s in Roanoke

Ann Ross Turner—First wife of Curtis Turner

Curtis Turner Jr.—Son of Curtis Turner and Bunny Turner Hall

Ross Turner—Oldest son of Curtis and Ann Turner

Tyler Turner—Youngest son of Curtis and Ann Turner

Jim Urcinole—Director of Operations for MacDan Aviation

Danny Vance—Brother-in-law of Curtis Turner

John Wanderer—Former mechanic, USAC

Jean Weatherly—Onetime wife of racer Joe Weatherly

June Wilkinson—Actress, former racing victory lane trophy presenter

Charlie Williamson—Former stock car racer; friend of Curtis Turner

H.A. "Humpy" Wheeler—President and General Manager, Lowe's Motor Speedway

Glen Wood—NASCAR driving great, one-half of famed Wood brothers racing team

Leonard Wood—Engineering half of the seminal Wood brothers racing team

Sue Turner Wright—Oldest child of Curtis and Ann Turner

Brock Yates—Author and one-time editor of *Car & Driver*

Smokey Yunick—Legendary car builder and engineer

BOOKS

Armbruster, Norman W. *Labor Lawyers: Wiley, Craig, Armbruster & Wilburn, The First Fifty Years, 1937-1987.* (Private printer)

Breslauer, Ken. *50 Years of Stock Car Racing: A History of Collectibles and Memorabilia.* Arizona: David Bull Publishing, 1998.

Britt, Bloys and Bill France. *The Racing Flag: NASCAR—The Story of Grand National Racing.* New York: Pocket Books, Inc., 1965.

Chapin, Kim. *Fast as White Lightning: The Story of Stock Car Racing* (Updated Edition). New York: Three Rivers Press, 1998.

Cotter, Tom and Al Pearce. *Holman Moody: The Legendary Race Team.* Minnesota: MBI Publishing Co., 2002.

Craft, Dr. John. *Legends of Stock Car Racing.* Wisconsin: Motorbooks International, 1995.

Craft, Dr. John. *Stock Cars.* Michigan: Lowe & B. Hould Publishers, 2000.

Crider, Curtis. *The Road to Daytona.* Florida: (Private printer), 1987.

DeGeer, Stanley L. *Pikes Peak is Unser Mountain.* New Mexico: Peak Publishing Company, 1990.

Fielden, Greg. *Charlotte Motor Speedway.* Wisconsin: MBI Publishing Co., 2000.

Fielden, Greg. *Forty Years of Stock Car Racing, Volume One: The Beginning 1949-1958.* South Carolina: The Galfield Press, 1992.

Fielden, Greg. *Forty Years of Stock Car Racing, Volume Two: The Superspeedway Boom 1959-1964.* South Carolina: The Galfield Press, 1988.

Fielden, Greg. *Forty Years of Stock Car Racing, Volume Three: Big Bucks and Boycotts 1965-1971.* South Carolina: The Galfield Press, 1989.

Fielden, Greg. *High Speed at Low Tide.* South Carolina: The Galfield Press, 1993.

Fielden, Greg. *Real Racers: Heroes and Record Writers from Stock Car Racing's Forgotten Era.* South Carolina: The Galfield Press, 1998.

Fielden, Greg. *Rumblin' Ragtops: The History of NASCAR's Fabulous Convertible Division and Speedway Division.* North Carolina: The Galfield Press, 1990.

Fielden, Larry. *Tim Flock, Race Driver.* North Carolina: The Galfield Press, 1991.

Fleischman, Bill and Al Pearce. *The Unauthorized NASCAR Fan Guide.* Michigan: Visible Ink Press, 2003.

Golenbock, Peter. *American Zoom: Stock Car Racing from the Dirt Tracks to Daytona.* New York: Macmillan, 1993.

Golenbock, Peter. *The Last Lap.* New York: Macmillan, 1998.

Golenbock, Peter and Greg Fielden, Editors. *The Stock Car Racing Encyclopedia.* New York: Macmillan, 1997.

Hembree, Mike. *NASCAR: The Definitive History of America's Sport.* New York: Harper Entertainment, 2000.

Higgins, Tom and Steve Waid. *Junior Johnson, Brave in Life*. Arizona: David Bull Publishing, 1999.

Hunter, Don and Al Pearce. *The Illustrated History of Stock Car Racing*. Wisconsin: MBI Publishing Co., 1998.

Hunter, Jim. *Stock Car Racing U.S.A.* New York: Dodd, Mead & Co., 1973.

Levine, Leo. *Ford: The Dust and the Glory, A Racing History, Volume I (1901-1967)*. Pennsylvania: Society of Automotive Engineers, Inc., 2000.

Libby, Bill. *Great American Race Drivers*. New York: Cowles Book Co. Inc., 1970.

Libby, Bill. *Heroes of Stock Car Racing*. New York: Random House, 1975.

Menzer, Joe. *The Wildest Ride: A History of NASCAR*. New York: Simon & Schuster, 2001.

Morris, Dr. D.L. *Timber on the Moon: The Curtis Turner Story*. North Carolina: Colonial Press, 1966.

Nault, William H., Editorial Director. *The World Book Year Book: 1967*. Illinois: Field Enterprises Educational Corp., 1967.

Sowers, Richard. *The Complete Statistical History of Stock-Car Racing*. Arizona: David Bull Publishing, 2000.

Stephenson, Morris and Dick Thompson. *From Dust to Glory: The Story of Clay Earles and the NASCAR-Sanctioned Martinsville Speedway*. Virginia: The Bassett Printing Corporation, 1992.

Turner, Ann Ross. *My Life with Curtis Turner*. Virginia: Wright Brothers Publishing, Inc., 1979.

Wilkinson, Sylvia. *Dirt Tracks to Glory: The Early Days of Stock Car Racing as Told by the Participants*. North Carolina: Algonquin Books, 1983.

Yates, Brock. *Sunday Driver*. New York: Farrar, Straus & Giroux, 1972.

Yunick, Smokey. *Best Damn Garage in Town: The World According to Smokey, Vol. I, II and III*. Florida: Carbon Press, 2001.

MAGAZINES

American Racing Classics. January, 1992. "Darlington Raceway" by Godwin Kelly, p. 111.

— April, 1992. "Curtis Turner" by Herman Hickman, p. 28.

— April, 1992. "Bowman Gray Stadium" by Harold Pearson, p. 110.

— October, 1992. "Southern 500 of 1950" by Gene Granger, p. 112.

— January, 1994. "Joe Weatherly" by Gene Granger, p. 18.

Auto Racing. April, 1970. "Curtis Turner's Ten Most Exciting Moments in Auto Racing" by Marshall Spiegel, p. 28.

Car & Driver. March, 1966. "The Editorial Side" by Brock Yates, p. 6.

— April, 1966. "Dan's Own Race" by Brock Yates, p. 86.

— June, 1966. "The Daytona 500: Almost a Runaway for Richard" by Brock Yates, p. 75.

— November, 1966. "Who the Hell Do You Think You Are? Curtis Turner?" by Brock Yates, p. 60.

— June, 1968. "The Graduates: Dick Smothers and Jim Garner Matriculate Under Curtis Turner" by Brock Yates, p. 32.

— May, 1968. "Deadline for Daytona" by Brock Yates, p. 88.

— January, 1971. "Curtis M. Turner, Racing Driver, 46" by Brock Yates, p. 60.

Circle Track. April, 1983. "Smokey Yunick," p. 43.

— August, 1985. "Stock Report" by Bob Myers, p. 6.

— August, 1985. "Pops" by Bob Myers, p. 42.

— October, 1987. "Downsized Racing?" by Smokey Yunick, p. 43.

Hot Rod. December, 1970. "The Roundy-Round Corner" by Steve Kelly.

Motor Guide. April, 1957. "Power Free-For-All in Stock Car Racing" by Stan Walker, p. 20.

Motorsport. March, 1951. "Sportraits: Bill France," p. 3.

— March, 1952. "Mexico Report," p. 6.

— May, 1956, "Callahan and Holland Cover the Speed Spree" by Bill Callahan, p. 6.

NASCAR: The Early Years, 2002. "The Cost of Race-Watching," p. 139.

Popular Mechanics. January, 1968. "The Fastest School in the World" by Bill Kilpatrick, p. 94.

— February, 1968. "Can Ford Halt the Petty Parade? Curtis Turner's Daytona '500' Preview" by Curtis Turner, p. 89.

Racer. June, 2000. "From Rocks to Riches" by Greg Fielden, p. 86.

Road and Track. June, 1950. "Carrera Panamericana Mexico," p. 6.

— September, 1950. "Nash in Mexican Road Race (Correspondence column)," p. 4.

The Roanoker. April, 1984. "Curtis Turner: The Legend Comes Home" by JoAnna Natale, p. 16.

Southern Automotive Journal. December, 1970. "Curtis Turner: 1924-1970" by Bob Myers, p. 41.

Speed Age. August, 1950. "The World's Toughest Road Race" by Jack Cansler, p. 22.

— March, 1956. "Bill France Predicts: The Year Ahead for Stock Cars" by Bill France, p. 26

— January, 1957. "Why Chevy Will Beat Ford in '57!" by Sandy Grady, p. 14.

— January, 1957. "Toughest Driver in the World" by Hank Schoolfield, p. 39.

Sports Illustrated. August 21, 1961. "Scorecard:

Race to Organize," p.4
— November 28, 1966. "A Wild, Wicked Race to the Big Time" by Kim Chapin, p. 84.
— March 6, 1967. "Demolition Run at Daytona" by Kim Chapin, p. 20.
— October 30, 1967. "People," p. 50.
— February 26, 1968. "Letter from the Publisher" by Garry Valk, p. 6.
— February 26, 1968. "Curtis Lives!" by Kim Chapin, p. 48.
— April 29, 1968. "Letter from the Publisher" p. 4.
— October 19, 1970. (Obituary)
— October 19, 1970. "A Fading Hero Strikes Back" by Kim Chapin, p. 62.
Stock Car Racing. May, 1966. "C'mon Back Curtis" by Bob Myers, p. 6.
— May, 1966. "Stock Car Racing: 1965," p. 14.
— May, 1966. "Dan Gurney 'Owns' the Riverside 500," p. 20.
— May, 1966. "American 500 North Carolina Motor Speedway Inaugural," p. 32.
— May, 1966. "The Great Stock Car Controversy" by Dick Gerald, p. 46.
— July, 1966. "ARCA 250: Curtis Turner Turned 'em All Back in the World's Richest Modified Stock Car Race," p. 16.
— November, 1966. "Ford Defectors Speak Out!" by Hal Hayes, p. 8.
— November, 1966. "Volunteer 500: Old Jackrabbits Turner and Goldsmith Really Ran on Short Bristol Track" by Jim Hunter, p. 34.
— September, 1967. "The Inside Groove" (Letters column), p. 6.
— September, 1967. "Curtis Turner Tells...The Terrible Turnover!", p. 49.
— June, 1969. "A Race to Remember—or 'How much do I owe you, Mr. Turner?'" by Bob Carey, p. 9.
— January, 1971. "Southern Strategy" (column), by Bob Myers, p. 7
True. February, 1971. "Death of a Race-Car Driver" by Bill Kilpatrick, p. 78.

NEWSPAPERS
Atlanta *Journal.* 1967 (7/3).
Charlotte News. 1959 (4/24, 4/24, 4/30, 5/8, 11/3, 12/1, 12/1), 1961 (6/14, 8/10, 9/8, 9/8, 9/8, 9/12, 11/7), 1962 (7/5), 1963 (2/11), 1965 (8/2), 1966 (5/14, 8/4, 9/10), 1967 (2/13, 4/27, 10/9, 10/14, 10/31, 12/29), 1968 (8/22, 8/29, 10/12, 10/19) 1970 (10/5, 10/5, 10/6, 10/6, 10/9), 1983 (5/27).
Charlotte Observer. 1958 (6/29, 12/20), 1959 (1/18, 4/12, 4/23, 4/23, 4/23, 4/24, 5/1, 11/4, 11/20, 12/1) 1960 (1/24, 2/21, 3/18, 7/1), 1961 (5/16, 6/9, 7/13, 8/10, 8/10, 8/10, 8/13, 8/22, 8/31, 9/6, 9/9, 9/9, 9/12, 10/18, 11/8, 11/29), 1962 (2/1), 1963 (1/24, 2/14, 8/9), 1964 (10/26, 10/26), 1965 (1/20, 8/1,

8/1, 8/2, 8/3, 8/29, 10/15, 11/1, 11/1, 11/1), 1966 (3/19, 10/12), 1967 (2/21, 4/28, 9/15, 9/29, 10/10, 10/19, 10/20), 1968 (2/23, 4/23, 8/22, 10/20, 12/1), 1970 (10/5, 10/6, 10/6), 1971 (8/29), 1984 (5/20).
Columbia (S.C.) *State.* 1956 (9/4).
Danville Commercial Appeal. 1954 (5/10, 5/17, 7/12, 8/9, 8/30, 9/6, 9/13), 1961 (5/21, 8/14).
Daytona Beach *Journal.* 1961 (8/10, 8/11, 8/12, 8/13, 8/22, 8/23, 9/6, 9/9, 9/10, 9/12, 9/22, 9/28, 10/19, 10/20, 10/21, 10/27, 10/31, 11/28, 11/29), 1962 (1/4, 1/5, 1/20, 1/31, 2/1).
Detroit *News.* 1967 (2/24), 1970 (10/5).
Easley (S.C.) *Progress.* 1967 (7/26).
Greenboro (S.C.) *Daily News.* 1969 (8/21).
Indianapolis *Star.* 1967 (2/25).
NASCAR Newsletter. 1971 (9/15).
NASCAR Winston Cup Scene. 1991 (10/17: "Curtis Turner Jr.—Following in his Father's Footsteps"), 1998 (5/14: "Big Bill vs. The Teamsters").
National Speed Sport News. Various dates through the following years: 1951, 1952, 1953, 1954, 1956, 1957, 1959, 1960, 1961, 1962, 1970.
New York *Times.* 1956 (3/23), 1957 (2/17, 5/1, 5/4), 1958 (2/23, 2/24, 5/11, 9/4), 1964 (10/26), 1965 (11/1), 1966 (2/13, 2/27), 1967 (2/18, 2/22), 1970 (10/6).
Roanoke *Times.* 1970 (10/6), 1998 (9/27), 2003 (11/22, 11/26).
Roanoke *World News.* 1950 (6/7), 1961 (8/11, 8/12, 8/14).
Southern Motorsports Journal. 1970 (10/9, 10/16).
Spartanburg *Herald.* 1965 (8/14).
Winston-Salem *Journal.* 1952 (5/21, 5/24, 5/29, 5/30), 1953 (6/6, 6/7, 6/10, 6/13, 6/17, 6/21, 6/27, 7/11, 7/12, 7/19, 7/26, 8/2, 8/8, 8/9, 8/16, 8/22, 8/23, 8/30, 10/11), 1954 (3/21, 5/7, 6/6, 6/7, 6/12, 7/8, 7/11, 7/15, 7/16, 7/18, 7/31, 8/14, 8/15, 8/19, 8/20, 8/22, 8/26, 8/28, 8/29), 1968 (5/11, 7/16), 1970 (10/9, 12/23).
Various, uncredited. 1948 (7/26, 9/8), 1949 (4/11, 7/30)

PROGRAMS
Langhorne Speedway, Langhorne, Pa. April 16, 1950.

GOVERNMENT AND LEGAL PAPERS
FLORIDA
Volusia County, Seventh Judicial Court, in Chancery
Curtis Turner and Tim Flock (Plaintiffs) vs. National Association for Stock Car Auto Racing, Inc., a corporation, and Bill France (Defendants), Complaint for Injunction and Other Relief (Complete file).

NORTH CAROLINA

State of North Carolina, Department of the Secretary of State: Articles of Incorporation of Charlotte Motor Speedway, Inc., August 6, 1959.

State of North Carolina, Department of the Secretary of State: Articles of Amendment of Charlotte Motor Speedway, Inc., November 30, 1960.

SOUTH CAROLINA

Chester, S.C. Marriage Certificate: Curtis Turner, Carolyn Vance (Turner)

UNITED STATES GOVERNMENT

Federal Aviation Administration: Complete file for airman Curtis Morton Turner (Pilot certificate applications, written test reports, health report, Airman stop order—incident and appeal information, license revocation and reinstatement), 1954-1970.

Federal Aviation Administration: Aerospace medical record for Curtis Morton Turner.

National Transportation Safety Board: Factual Aircraft Accident Report—General Aviation for accident in Mahaffey, Pa., October 4, 1970. Daniel C. Sayres, Air Safety Investigator. Includes eight separate witness statements.

National Transportation Safety Board: NTSB file summary, accident ID#NYC71AN043.

VIRGINIA

Floyd County: Birth Records: Certificate for Curtis Morton Turner.

Floyd County: General Index Chancery Cases, Defendants, Judgment Lien Docket and Execution Records (Various)

Floyd County: Military Records, Honorable Discharge: Curtis Morton Turner.

Floyd County: Marriage Licenses: Certificate for Morton and Minnie Turner.

Floyd County: Last Will and Testament for Darnell Lloyd Turner.

Floyd County: Last Will and Testament for Morton Tyler Turner.

Floyd County: Last Will and Testament for Minnie Thomas Turner (AKA Minnie O. Turner).

FILMS

Hey Pops!, The Curtis Turner Story, Stonebridge Productions Inc., 2003.

1951 Modified-Sportsman Race (Langhorne Speedway) and 1960 Modified-Sportsman Race (Daytona International Speedway), Rare Sportsfilms, Inc.

1952 Modified-Sportsman Race (Daytona Beach), Rare Sportsfilms, Inc.

1956 Ford Racing season highlights

PREVIOUSLY RECORDED INTERVIEWS AND TRANSCRIPTS

Tim Flock (interview conducted by Charlie Perry)

Paul Sawyer and Kenneth Campbell (interview conducted by Kim Chapin)

Ann Turner (interview conducted by Charlie Perry)

Curtis Turner (interviews conducted by Kim Chapin, November 15-17, December 10, 1967)

Fred Lorenzen, Lee Petty, Glen Wood, Cotton Owens, Junior Johnson (obituary comments; from pooled motorsports sources)

PRIVATE PAPERS

Collection of Bunny Turner Hall (Newspapers clippings, photographs)

WEB SITE MATERIAL

martinsvillespeedway.com

motorsportshalloffame.com

racefanguide.com

questia.com (Virginian History Resources at Questia)

easleychamber.org (Easley Chamber of Commerce)

dujairport.com (DuBois-Jefferson County Airport)

ncforestry.org (North Carolina Forestry Association)

raresportsfilms.com (Vintage Videos)

sports.groups.yahoo.com/group/racinghistory/

http://lwf.ncdc.noaa.gov/oa/ncdc.html (National Climatic Data Center)

thevintageracer.com

http://members.aol.com/jalan5000a/comment .html (NASCAR Racing Commentary with Jeff Alan)

lowesmotorspeedway.com

http://www.a-1video.com/vintage.htm (Vintage videos)

http://www.ntsb.gov/Info/gils/gils_index.htm (NTSB information records)

http://ppihc.com/media/(Pikes Peak International Hill Climb)

MISCELLANEOUS

Atlanta International Raceway, Driver Information application: Joe Weatherly.

Automobile Manufacturers Association, Inc.: United States Passenger Car Sales by Manufacturing Groups, 1940-1950 (data: Wards Automotive Yearbook).

Automobile Manufacturers Association, Inc.: World Motor Vehicle Data, 1967/1968, U.S. Passenger Car Production.

History of Faith Baptist Church, Easley, S.C.

Acknowledgments

Marshall Spiegel has spent his life writing about motorsports; among hundreds of credits, he's author of the bestseller *Evel Knievel: Cycle Jumper*. Like many people I interviewed, Spiegel loved Curtis Turner and has yet to find anybody else quite like him. In our conversation, bopping from one outrageous tale to another, Spiegel summed up my particular challenge. "You have selected one of the most difficult subjects to write about," he told me, sounding almost exasperated. "Evel Knievel had parameters. Curtis Turner had *no* parameters."

Writing about "A life without parameters" meant doing more than a hundred interviews, reading hundreds of articles, watching old racing videos, Googling for hours and buying treasures off eBay. It allowed me to continue my reverent study of the rich, incredible history of stock car racing. And best of all, it gave me the chance to talk to the drivers, car owners, family members, executives and fans of stock car racing. A more welcoming collection of people in the sports world do not exist.

Completing this task would have been impossible without the aid of the folks listed below, beginning with this vital ten. I found out early that you don't write about Curtis Turner without going through Bunny Hall, because nobody cares for his great good name more than she does. "Just tell the truth," she once told me, and though she admitted some of that truth might be unpleasant, she was happy to cooperate. For four days, Bunny and her husband Tommy opened their doors and gave me a bedroom, and Bunny plopped her Curtis scrapbooks down and let me work my way through them. Good luck finding kinder, more caring or nicer people. Bunny, thank you for everything. I now understand why writers are so grateful to agents. John Silbersack is a friend foremost, and a mentor, an editor, sounding board and the giver of great advice. Thank you, John, for investing your confidence. To Peter Mayer, the publisher who believed in this book in a way nobody else could, I thank you for the great opportunity. I'm not the first and won't be the last person to offer eternal gratitude to Betty Carlin, the caretaker of NASCAR's legacies, the curator at the International Motorsports Hall of Fame library at Talladega Motor Speedway. Thank you, Betty, for leaving me speechless. Kim Chapin wrote one of the definitive profiles of Curtis, the *Sports Illustrated* cover story, and when he generously sent me the originals of all his notes, it made this job much easier. Charlie Perry's dream is to produce an outdoor drama on Curtis' life. He drove me to all the important stops in Curtis' youth, which cultivated my love for the Blue Ridge Mountains. Larry Rosen was a great friend when I needed one, and the best guide I could have hoped for. He made me understand how to complete this book. Spending seven hours with Charlie Williamson means taking a guided tour of an amazing period in racing history. Charlie was my friend from beginning to end. I refer to Joanne Michael using her maiden name here to protect the woman who, forty years ago, was affectionately called Short Track. Joanne made it clear to me that she was not comfortable speaking at length about two men she loved dearly: Joe Weatherly and Curtis Turner. In fact, her reticence and protectiveness inspired me to take greater care writing about that memorable friendship. And Ross Turner became an understanding, practical, helpful friend. I hardly got to know him enough for my satisfaction but I admired him and I miss him.

I spent an incredible day with Curtis Turner's first family, and I must thank Priscilla Gauldin, Sue Wright and Tyler Turner for their warmth and candor.

I am also immensely grateful to Jim Urcinole, Director of Operations for MacDan Aviation, who spent countless hours with me on the phone, as we considered possible theories about Curtis Turner and Clarence King's final flight. Jim patiently explained the same concepts again and again until I could grasp them. Caroline Trefler, my editor at the Overlook Press, became this book's midwife, not only coaxing it from me (no small task, believe me) but also pointing out necessary questions and vital inconsistencies. Marion Paynter, librarian at the *Charlotte Observer*, supervised the copying of the paper's entire Curtis Turner file, which contained unimaginable treasures. Every once in awhile Suzanne Wise, the librarian of the Appalachian State University Stock Car Racing Collection would send me yet another helpful package of information. I was overwhelmed that Brian Donovan took time from his own project, a biography of Wendell Scott, in order to Xerox reams of newspaper clippings that helped me tremendously. And my thanks and wishes for good health go to Clyde Conner, the ultimate Curtis Turner fan, who sent me an amazing letter that conveyed the wonder of watching his favorite driver run.

Other newspaper and research curators were kind enough to help me. Angie Campbell keyed in the entire *Easley (S.C.) Progress* article on Curtis' plane landing so that it would be easier for me to read. Julie Harris (*Winston-Salem Journal*), Megan Gallup (*Daytona Beach News-Journal*) and Brenda Thompson of the Detroit Public Library were also happy to help and Joy Birdsong and Linda Wachtel opened the doors to the *Sports Illustrated* library for me. My thanks also go to Diane Matousek, Clerk of the Circuit Court, Volusia County, Florida, and to Brooke Palmer in the Circuit Court office.

I have to give a special thank you to Frances Causey. While working on her excellent documentary *Hey Pops!: The Curtis Turner Story*, she practically handed me her contact list and gave me the advice only a fellow traveler could.

It's hard to trust somebody with the lifeblood of your research but Stefanie Sandello, Martha Cooke, Lauren Kanter and Eva Sandoval, all transcribers extraordinaire (when they weren't busy doing much more important things), made it easy.

My bosses at *TV Guide*, Steve Sonsky and Vince Cosgrove, were encouraging and understanding of my need to take extra time for this. Among the vastly talented writers on the NASCAR circuit, David Poole, Monte Dutton, Jim McLaurin and Mike Hembree each offered names and contacts to help ease my way. Jay Gissen's advice and friendship were an immeasurable asset as always. Russ Rieger is unwavering in his support and unceasing in his sage council. As a writer in need of a great editor, I'd be lost

Photo Credits

All photos are from the collection of Bunny "Turner" Hall except as indicated:

4: Collection of Priscilla Gauldin
7. Collection of Pee Wee Ellwanger
8. International Motorsports Hall of Fame Library and Museum
9. Don Hunter
10. Don Hunter
11. Charlie Williamson
14. Collection of Pee Wee Ellwanger
17. Don Hunter
18. Don Hunter
23. Dick Ralstin
24. Dick Ralstin
27. Charlie Williamson
28. Charlie Williamson
30. Charlie Williamson
31. Charlie Williamson
32. Robert Edelstein